THE SMALL-BUSINESS CONTRACTS HANDBOOK

THE SMALL-BUSINESS CONTRACTS HANDBOOK

Lawrence Hsieh, Attorney at Law

Self-Counsel Press
(a division of)
International Self-Counsel Press Ltd.
USA   Canada

Self-Counsel Press acknowledges the financial support of the Government of Canada through the Book Publishing Industry Development Program (BPIDP) for our publishing activities.

Printed in Canada.

First edition: 2010

Library and Archives Canada Cataloguing in Publication

Hsieh, Lawrence, 1962-
          Business contracts handbook / Lawrence Hsieh.

ISBN 978-1-55180-856-7

          1. Contracts — United States. 2. Small business — Law and legislation — United States. 3. Business law — United States. I. Title.

KF889.H84 2010   346.7302   C2009-905078-1

Inside Image
Copyright©iStockphoto/businessman writing on a form/denisenko

Self-Counsel Press
(a division of)
International Self-Counsel Press Ltd.

1704 North State Street   1481 Charlotte Road
Bellingham, WA 98225   North Vancouver, BC V7J 1H1
          USA   Canada

CONTENTS

Part II — BASIC CORPORATE TRANSACTIONS   31

4 Sale of Goods   33

5 Sale of Services   72

NOTICE TO READERS

Laws are constantly changing. Every effort is made to keep this publication as current as possible. However, the author, the publisher, and the vendor of this book make no representations or warranties regarding the outcome or the use to which the information in this book is put and are not assuming any liability for any claims, losses, or damages arising out of the use of this book. The reader should not rely on the author or publisher of this book for any professional advice. Please be sure that you have the most recent edition.

ACKNOWLEDGMENTS

I would like to express my deepest appreciation to Richard Day, publisher at Self-Counsel Press, for sharing my vision on this project, and to Managing Editor Eileen Velthuis and her team for their expert guidance. It's been a pleasure to work with all of you.

About the Author: Lawrence Hsieh is a corporate attorney in Connecticut. He graduated from the University of Chicago Law School and Cornell University. Please visit Lawrence's law blog at http://contractadvisor.com/blog.

To my all-star team; wife Janice, and children Jennifer and Jason,
who amaze and inspire me every day.
Thank you to Janice, and to my mom and dad,
for believing in me.

INTRODUCTION

The Small-Business Contracts Handbook is a resource of first resort to help you, the small-business person and entrepreneur, understand and negotiate a wide variety of legal provisions found in common business contracts. The marketplace is filled with a dizzying array of legal resources, including good books and websites that offer do-it-yourself contract forms for non-lawyers, as well as highly technical treatises and books on the finer points of contract drafting for practicing attorneys and law students. But it occurred to me a few years ago that there are very few resources that actually break down and explain the meaning of common contract provisions (both deal-point and boilerplate) in a way that savvy businesspeople without formal legal training would find useful in their contract negotiations. Enter *The Small-Business Contracts Handbook*.

Non-lawyers are often bewildered by the legal jargon contained in business contracts. I add value by presenting ideas, concepts, and facts that are common knowledge to and used every day by experienced practicing attorneys, but in plain English, in a way that is easy for non-lawyers to understand. This book will arm you with the know-how to enable you to effectively negotiate your transactions, as well as work and communicate more efficiently with your attorney.

While I explain the meaning of many individual contract provisions, I've chosen not to include any complete contract "forms" in the book. Many small businesses purchase or download complete contract forms and use them without careful consideration of all the issues. This one-size-fits-all approach can be dangerous because there are at least two parties with different interests in every business transaction. Furthermore, forms are often passed down from deal to deal and from attorney to attorney. So you may think you're starting off with a bulletproof form (advantageous to you) when in fact, the form may contain provisions that are very much against your best interests, or in some other way significantly watered down or ambiguous in a way that can harm you.

I will present individual contract provisions (organized by topic), explain their meaning, and offer commonly accepted ways that attorneys leverage the provisions to their advantage.

Chapters include sections on corporate infrastructure (including contract provisions found in shareholder agreements and LLC operating agreements), business transactions (including contract provisions found in agreements for the sale of goods and services, asset purchase and stock purchase agreements for the sale of a business, non-disclosure agreements to protect confidential information, loan agreements, etc.), and contract boilerplate (including contracts provisions found at the end of just about every business contract).

If you have any questions or comments, I invite you to visit my blog, the Contract Adviser, located at http://contractadviser.com/blog.

Part I
CORPORATE STRUCTURES

1

BUSINESS ENTITY SELECTION

OVERVIEW

Most readers will already be familiar with the different types of business entities, as well as basic formation documents like a corporation's certificate of incorporation and bylaws. There are plenty of good resources, including free resources on the Internet, comparing the pros and cons of forming one type of entity versus another; for example, a corporation versus a Limited Liability Company (LLC), as well as companies and websites offering the basic formation documents and forms for sale or for free.

While I include a summary of these basic issues in this chapter, I devote the bulk of this section to explaining contract provisions found in the agreements governing the legal relationship between the owners of business entities — the LLC Operating Agreement, and its corporate cousin, the Shareholder Agreement (a.k.a., Stockholder Agreement).

ENTITY SELECTION

The Entity Selection Chart (Table 1) contains basic information comparing the five principal forms of small-business ownership with respect to formation and ownership, liability of owners for business obligations, availability of pass-through taxation, and management/authority to sign contracts. Consult with your attorney and tax advisor on your particular situation, including the availability of methods to convert from one form of business ownership to another.

TABLE 1: Entity Selection Chart

Form of business ownership	C Corporation	S Corporation	Limited Liability Company (LLC)	Limited Partnership	Sole Proprietorship/ General Partnership
Formation/ Ownership	A **corporation** is a business entity formed by filing a certificate of incorporation (or equivalent document) with the state's secretary of state. For federal income tax purposes, corporations are "C corporations" by default (pass-through tax not available – see discussion below). The owners are referred to as **shareholders or stockholders.**	A **Subchapter S** corporation is a corporation that elects pass-through income tax treatment by filing IRS Form 2553 (Election by a Small Business Corporation).	A **limited liability company** (LLC) is a business entity formed by filing a certificate of organization (or equivalent document) with the state's secretary of state. An LLC is a hybrid entity that offers limited liability to its owners (referred to as **members**), like a corporation, and pass-through income taxation, like a partnership or proprietorship.	A **limited partnership** is a pass-through business entity with two classes of owners. The owners consist of at least one **general partner,** and at least one **limited partner.**	A **sole proprietorship** is a business owned and operated directly by one person, but not through a business entity. A **general partnership** is a business owned and operated by at least two people, but not through a business entity.
Minimum (or maximum, if applicable) number of owners	At least one shareholder.	At least one shareholder, but an S corporation cannot have more than 100 shareholders. They must be natural person U.S. citizens or residents.	At least one member. Members can be U.S. or foreign natural persons or business entities.	At least one general partner and one limited partner.	A sole proprietorship by definition has one owner. A general partnership must have at least two owners.
Liability of owners	The owners (shareholders) have **limited liability** for the obligations of the business. This means that the shareholders are liable for the debts of the business only up to the amount of their capital contributions. Once that money is gone from the corporation and if there are no other corporate assets, then the creditors cannot go after the shareholders' personal assets. Creditors, however, can hold shareholders personally liable for business obligations if the shareholders run the business "personally" and not through the corporation, for example, by not keeping separate corporate records, comingling corporate and personal funds or assets, or chronically and severely undercapitalizing the company. Basically, if the shareholders disregard the corporation, so too will a court when creditors seek compensation when the company is insolvent.	An S corporation election does not impact the limited liability of the shareholders. S corporation shareholders have the same limited liability enjoyed by C corporation shareholders, subject to the same exceptions.	The owners (members) have the same limited liability as that enjoyed by corporate shareholders, subject to the same exceptions.	The general partners are jointly and severally liable for the obligations of the business. Provided the limited partners do not participate in management, they have the same limited liability as that enjoyed by corporate shareholders.	A sole proprietor is personally liable for the obligations of the business. The general partners are jointly and severally liable for the obligations of the business.

	C Corporation	S Corporation	LLC	Partnership	Sole Proprietorship
Liability of owners *continued*	A shareholder is also personally liable if, among other acts, he or she **commits fraud** on behalf of the corporation, **injures somebody** (a tort) while acting on behalf of the corporation, or **affirmatively guarantees the corporation's obligations**. The last act, of signing a guarantee, is a way of signing away a shareholder's limited liability by contract.				
Availability of pass-through taxation	**The default rule for corporations is two-tiered taxation.** C corporations must pay income tax on their profits. If the corporation makes a dividend distribution of its profits, then that profit is taxed again to the shareholders. Small business C corporations typically avoid this "double tax" impact by paying its shareholders salary and bonus (which are deductible expenses), rather than dividends (which are not).	**The shareholders must affirmatively elect pass-through tax treatment** (i.e., Subchapter S status) by filing IRS Form 2553 (Election by a Small Business Corporation). This will enable each shareholder to report his or her share of the business' profits (and losses) on his or her personal income tax return, even if the shareholder doesn't take any profits out of the business.	**The default rule for LLCs is pass-through taxation** (see next paragraph) – each member reports his or her share of the business' profits (and losses) on his or her personal income tax return, even if the member doesn't take any profits out of the business. "Check the Box" Rules – The Internal Revenue Service classifies LLCs for tax purposes as a corporation, partnership or sole proprietorship. A multi-member LLC is treated by default as a partnership for income tax purposes (pass-through taxation) unless it elects to be treated as a corporation for income tax purposes by filing IRS Form 8832, Entity Classification Election.. A single-member LLC is treated by default as a sole proprietorship ("disregarded entity" with pass-through taxation) unless the owner elects corporate income tax treatment by filing Form 8832.	**The default rule for partnerships is pass-through taxation.** Each partner reports his or her share of the business' profits (and losses) on his or her personal income tax return, even if the partner doesn't take any profits out of the business.	**The default rule for sole proprietorships and partnerships is pass-through taxation.** Each owner reports his or her share of the business' profits (and losses) on his or her personal income tax return, even if the owner doesn't take any profits out of the business.
Management/ Authority to Sign Contracts	Corporations are managed under the direction of the board of directors. Officers, who are elected by the directors, have day-to-day management authority, and can sign contracts on behalf of the corporation.	Same as C corporation.	LLCs can be **member managed** (managed equally by the owners) or **manager managed** (managed by the designated owners or third party, similar to the way a corporation would be managed). The managers can sign contracts on behalf of the corporation.	Limited Partnerships are managed by the general partner. General partners can sign contracts on behalf of the business. Limited partners enjoy limited liability if they do not participate in management.	The owners manage the business, and can sign (or designate officers who can sign) contracts on behalf of the business.

DBA stands for "Doing Business As." If a sole proprietor, corporation, or any other business entity wishes to conduct business under any name other than his, her, or the business's legal name, then he, she, or it must register its fictitious or assumed name with the respective state's secretary of state.

Keep in mind that only legal persons (individuals or business entities like corporations, LLCs, etc.), may enter into business contracts. A DBA is not a legal entity. So when a business with a DBA enters into a contract, it should sign the contract as "[Legal Name] DBA [Ficticious Name]."

2

ORGANIZATIONAL DOCUMENTS

OVERVIEW

This chapter will discuss selected provisions contained in a corporation or Limited Liability Company's (LLC) formation documents. These include a corporation's certificate of incorporation (or equivalent document), and an LLC's certificate of organization (or equivalent document). These certificates are filed with the secretary of state in the state in which the corporation or LLC is formed.

For small corporations, the **certificate of incorporation** is a relatively short document, typically one to two pages long, because small businesses usually only need to issue one class of common stock. If the corporation plans to issue more than one class of stock, then the certificate will be quite a bit longer because it needs to set forth in some detail the relative rights and preferences of the different classes of stock (see the **Capital Stock Quick Primer** later in this chapter). The certificate of incorporation will contain provisions listing the name and address of the corporation, as well as the name and address of the registered agent who is authorized to receive service of process on behalf of the corporation in a lawsuit.

A corporation's **bylaws** is a private document that is not filed with the secretary of state. While the bylaws establish ground rules for corporate governance (e.g., conduct of shareholder and board meetings, voting, etc.), the bylaws are not a substitute for a well-drafted shareholder agreement. For example, "buy-sell" provisions, which establish the rights and obligations of the shareholders when one of them dies, becomes disabled, or wants to transfer shares, are beyond the scope of the bylaws, and typically are found in shareholder agreements (see Chapter 3 for more about shareholder agreements).

An LLC is formed by filing a short **certificate of organization**, but does not have bylaws. Rather, LLC members may enter into a contract called an **operating agreement** (state law sometimes makes this optional) that contains not only basic bylaw-type provisions dealing with general governance, but also buy-sell and other shareholder agreement provisions. Shareholder agreements and operating agreements are discussed in more detail in Chapter 3.

SAMPLE CONTRACT EXCERPTS

Certificate of Incorporation/LLC Certificate of Formation — Business Purpose

The purpose of the Company is to engage in any lawful act or activity for which corporations [limited liability companies] may be organized under the [insert name of applicable law, for example, General Corporation Law of State of Delaware], as amended from time to time, or any successor thereto.

For most small businesses, it's enough to include something similar to this general purpose provision. In fact, a more detailed purpose provision could hamstring your expansion efforts down the road. Consult with your attorney if you are forming a corporation (typically a Professional Corporation or PC) to engage in professional practice, like law, in which case the certificate of incorporation will need to include a more detailed description of the business purpose. Note that I use the term "Company" thoughout the book for consistency. The term "corporation" is typically used to describe the Company in the certificate of incorporation and bylaws.

Certificate of Incorporation — Authorized Number of Shares

The total number of shares of capital stock that the Company is authorized to issue is [insert number] shares of common stock, without par value.

The authorized number of shares is the maximum number of shares the corporation can issue. See the Capital Stock Quick Primer later in this chapter for a discussion of frequently used terminology such as authorized, issued, outstanding and treasury shares. Consult with your attorney on the optimal number of authorized shares in your state — the optimal number of authorized shares is often the maximum number of shares you can authorize while paying the minimum incorporation fees, which will vary by state.

What Is Par Value?

Par value is the nominal dollar amount assigned by the corporation to a class of stock. Consult with your attorney as to whether your state mandates or gives a choice of designating par or no par stock. For small businesses issuing only common stock, the notion of par is somewhat dated — shares typically are issued for an amount necessary to adequately capitalize the company, which is usually much greater than the nominal par amount.

Preemptive Rights

No preemptive rights exist with respect to shares of capital stock or securities convertible into or exchangable for shares of capital stock of the Company, whether now or hereafter authorized or issued.

If the Company is free to issue shares to whomever it wants, it will dilute the ownership of the existing shareholders. Preemptive rights help the existing shareholders maintain their proportionate ownership (and therefore voting power, right to profits, etc.) by entitling the existing shareholders (typically common shareholders) the right to purchase newly issued shares of stock (or securities convertible into shares of stock) before they are offered to third parties. However, such provisions may place the Company at a disadvantage when seeking third party equity financing to grow the Company. Consult with your attorney and financial advisor on whether preemptive rights are appropriate for your situation. State law varies, so consult with your attorney on whether preemptive rights are automatically granted or denied, or must be affirmatively provided for or denied in the company's certificate of incorporation. Note that preemptive rights can also be granted by contract, and may be provided for in the company's shareholder agreement or operating agreement.

Bylaws
Shareholder Vote — Majority versus Plurality

The election of directors is determined by a plurality of the votes cast at a meeting of Shareholders at which the number of Shareholders representing a quorum is present in person or by proxy.

A majority is a situation where over half of the votes are cast for one of usually two choices, whether regarding a vote on a specific issue or the election of directors. A plurality is useful in situations when there are at least three choices (like the provision presented here for the election of directors), and is defined as a situation where one choice receives more votes than any of the other choices.

Shareholder Vote — Cumulative Voting

At all elections of directors duly called and held, each Shareholder entitled to vote has the right to cast as many votes as are equal to the product of the number of

(i) directors to be elected and

(ii) shares owned by such Shareholder. Such Shareholder may cast all such votes for a single director or may distribute them among any two or more of them in any manner as he or she may see fit, and the directors receiving a plurality of the votes cast shall be elected.

There are two main voting systems for the election of board members. Let's look at an example — a hair salon business owned by Harry Cutter, Manny Cure, Buzz Barbur, and Aldo Stiles. If they form a corporation with each person owning 25 shares of common stock and a board of four directors, then the outcome of the board elections could differ depending on whether the corporation's bylaws call for statutory or cumulative voting.

In either statutory or cumulative voting, each shareholder would be entitled to one vote per share for each vacant board seat. So in this example, each shareholder would have 100 votes (25 shares multiplied by the four vacant board seats). The difference between statutory and cumulative voting is how each shareholder is able to allocate his or her total number of votes.

In **statutory voting**, which typically controls if the bylaws are silent, each shareholder in the example can only vote up to 25 shares for any one candidate. The likely outcome in a non-dysfunctional business would be that the four shareholders would end up filling the four board seats. Statutory voting favors large shareholders — if Harry owned 51 out of the 100 issued and outstanding shares, he would control who fills each board position, including the ability to bring in an outside director of his choosing.

In **cumulative voting** (see sample contract provision above), however, each shareholder would be entitled to vote his 100 shares any way he or she liked. The shareholder could allocate 25 votes to each of the four candidates, all 100 shares to just one candidate (and not vote for anybody else), or any allocation in between. Cumulative voting helps minority shareholders with fewer votes be able to combine votes to vote for their most favored candidates.

Certificate of Incorporation and/or Bylaws

Exculpation of Personal Liability of Directors

A director or officer of the Company shall not be liable to the Company or its Shareholders for breach of fiduciary duty, except to the extent that exculpation from liability is not permitted under applicable law in effect at the time such liability is determined. No amendment or repeal of this paragraph applies to or has any effect on the liability or alleged liability of any director or officer of the Company with respect to any acts or omissions of such director or officer occurring prior to such amendment or repeal.

Consult with your attorney about the extent to which your state corporate law allows the Company to include exculpatory provisions in the certificate of incorporation that limit or eliminate the personal liability of directors (or even officers, employees, and agents) to the Company or shareholders for damages arising from acts undertaken by such persons on behalf of the Company. Companies often include exculpation (and indemnification provisions, discussed below) in their charter documents to enable them to recruit and retain management. For smaller companies whose shareholders also run the business, these provisions provide yet another layer of personal asset protection.

The sample provision works to insulate the directors from personal liability for acts undertaken on behalf of the Company. Keep in mind, however, that these provisions don't work to protect the directors from personal liability for a director's intentional misconduct, illegal behavior, reckless acts, or omissions, as well as a director's involvement or approval of any deal in which the director gained an improper personal benefit (called Improper Behavior).

Indemnification of Directors

(a) To the fullest extent permitted by law, the Company shall indemnify, hold harmless, and defend ("indemnification") any person (an "Indemnified Party") who is or was a party or is threatened to be made a party to any threatened, pending or completed claim, demand, action, suit, or proceeding, whether formal or informal, civil, criminal, administrative, or investigative (the "Action(s)"), by reason of the fact that such person is or was or has agreed to be a director or officer of the Company, from and against any and all damages, losses, and liabilities incurred by such person, including, but not limited to, [reasonable] attorney fees and expenses, judgments, fines, penalties, and amounts paid in settlement incurred in connection with any such Action.

Indemnification provisions work hand-in-hand with exculpation provisions (discussed above) to limit or eliminate the personal liability of the directors for acts undertaken on behalf of the Company. Subsection (a) provides the basic framework for the Company's indemnification of past and present directors in the widest range of proceedings.

The provision can also be drafted to include the provisional advancement of litigation expenses such as attorney fees to a director pending the resolution of the Action. Since the advance is provisional, the Company advances the funds regardless of the director's behavior. If it's later determined that indemnification is appropriate, the advance merely becomes part of what would have had to be indemnified anyway. If it's later determined that indemnification is not appropriate (for example, because of improper behavior), then the director has to return the advance.

(b) Notwithstanding anything herein to the contrary, no indemnification shall be made under subsection (a) above to the extent a judgment or other final adjudication establishes that the Indemnified Party

    (i) engaged in fraudulent or intentional misconduct or a knowing violation of law, that was material to the Action, or

    (ii) personally gained a financial profit or other advantage to which he or she was not legally entitled.

(c) Notwithstanding anything herein to the contrary, no indemnification shall be made under subsection (a) above for any Action initiated by an Indemnified Party unless such Action (or part thereof) was brought to enforce the Indemnified Party's rights to indemnification hereunder.

Subsection (b) works to disqualify Improper Behavior from the right to indemnification. In the sample contract provision, indemnification is limited to the defense of Actions; Subsection (c) excludes an Indemnified Party's counterclaims from indemnification.

(d) Such indemnification is not exclusive of other indemnification rights arising under any agreement, Director or Shareholder consent, or otherwise. No amendment or repeal of this paragraph shall affect any indemnification of any director or officer of the Company with respect to any acts or omissions of such director or officer occurring prior to such amendment or repeal.

Despite the general statutory authority to include indemnification provisions, the enforceability of these provisions is the subject of much litigation. Hence, the case law in this area is constantly shifting, for example, relating to the indemnification of past directors for acts or omissions that took place before the Company amended its certificate of incorporation or bylaws to eliminate the indemnification provision. Subsection (d) is meant to address this issue, but it may be better for the director to also enter into an indemnification contract with the Company; contracts generally cannot be "amended or repealed" without each party's (including the director's) consent.

Capital Stock Quick Primer

Ownership in a corporation is represented by shares of capital stock. Capital stock consists of common stock and preferred stock. Most small businesses issue only common stock, which typically conveys full voting rights. Preferred stockholders have a prior claim (before common stockholders) on dividends and the assets upon dissolution. Preferred stockholders may have limited voting rights. Then there are the various calls, options, puts, rights, warrants, or other "securities" that entitle the holder to obtain shares of capital stock convertible at some future date or based on some other triggering (financial or other) event.

The certificate of incorporation will list the types, as well as the number, of shares (and other "securities") the corporation is authorized to issue. The authorized number of shares is the maximum number of shares the corporation can issue. It's a good idea to issue just a portion of the shares. If a corporation has 1,000 authorized shares, and issues 250 shares to Tom and 250 shares to Josie, then the company has issued 500 shares, with the balance of the shares deemed "unissued shares." Unissued shares have no impact on percentage ownership. In other words, Tom and Josie each own 50 percent of the company. Think of unissued shares as shares that are held in reserve until the corporation needs to issue more shares. If a corporation issues all of its shares, then if it needs to issue more shares at a later date, it'll have to engage in the time-consuming and relatively expensive task of amending the certificate of incorporation to authorize the additional shares.

Once Tom and Josie pay the company for the shares, then the shares are deemed to be fully paid and non-assessable. If at a later date, the company repurchases some of Tom's or Josie's shares, and then the company holds such shares, it is deemed to hold on to them in the form of treasury stock. Tom and Josie own issued and outstanding shares. Treasury Stock is deemed to be issued shares, but not outstanding shares. If the company decides to repurchase and then retire the shares, then the shares revert back to being authorized but unissued shares.

It's a little confusing, so remember these formulas:

Authorized Shares = Issued Shares + Unissued Shares

Issued Shares = Outstanding Shares + Treasury Shares

Therefore: Authorized Shares = Outstanding Shares + Treasury Shares + Unissued Shares

3

SHAREHOLDER AGREEMENTS AND LLC OPERATING AGREEMENTS

Harry Cutter and his friend, Manny Cure, are expert cosmetologists and decide to open a salon in a swanky uptown location. Neither has capital so they recruit their deep-pocketed patrons, Buzz Barbur and Aldo Stiles, as investors. The four friends decide that they'll form a limited liability company, Cut and Cure, LLC, and become equal owners of the business. So far so good. But they neglect to enter into an LLC Operating Agreement, which isn't required by their state law, but helps to establish the rights and obligations of the owners to each other and to the company in case one of them dies; becomes disabled; gets divorced; becomes bankrupt; decides to leave the business; is forced out of the business; doesn't pull his weight; or disagrees with the others; etc. The salon is an instant success, but without an operating agreement, business dysfunction is just one unexpected event away.

OVERVIEW

In this chapter, I will discuss contract provisions typically found in shareholder agreements (used by corporations) and operating agreements (used by LLCs). Where I've included only the shareholder agreement version of the provisions, you can imagine the LLC operating agreement version of such provisions simply replacing the word "Shareholder" with "Member," and the word "Shares" with the word "Membership Interest" or "Interest." To the extent possible, I use the word "Owner" to describe a shareholder or member.

Shareholder agreements and operating agreements typically contain a suite of buy-sell provisions that establish the rights and obligations of the owners and the Company in case any owner is no longer able or willing to continue in the business (for example, receipt of a bona fide third-party offer to purchase its shares, death, disability, incapacity, bankruptcy, retirement, divorce, dissolution, etc.). By including a framework for the optional or mandatory buy-out by the Company or the other owners (of the affected owner's Shares or Membership Interests), buy-sell provisions seek to infuse a certain level of stability so that the Company can continue its operations with minimal disruption, while at the same time provide a pricing mechanism that gives the affected owner (or its estate/successor in interest) a reasonable opportunity to realize its investment (especially considering that investments in small companies tend to be illiquid).

Buy-sell provisions include the right of first refusal, drag-along, tag-along and more provisions below dealing with the disposition of the owner's interest upon death, disability, etc. It's very important to consult with your attorney and tax advisers (including experts in estate taxation) when structuring these provisions, because while choosing one structure over another may lead to the desired or a convenient result from a contract perspective, it may not yield the desired tax result. In fact, an improperly drafted buy-sell provision may work to jeopardize a corporation's Subchapter S election, or induce the IRS to reclassify certain transactions as taxable dividends.

I'll also discuss several provisions dealing with capital contributions, owner loans to the Company, and voting rights. However, I will not discuss the various and sundry tax-related provisions often found in these types of agreements, which are beyond the scope of this book. Consult with your tax adviser on the impact of any such tax provisions.

SAMPLE CONTRACT EXCERPTS
Shareholder Agreement/LLC Operating Agreement
Transfer Restriction

Other than a Permitted Transfer, each Shareholder [Member] shall not, directly or indirectly, sell, convey, give, assign, encumber, pledge, hypothecate, grant a security interest in, grant any option or other security for the sale of, enter into a contract or understanding to do any of the foregoing, or otherwise transfer (each, a "Transfer") any or all of its Shares [Membership Interests].

This sample provision contains a general restriction against the sale, gifting, encumbrance, or any transfer by any owner of any of its shares or membership interests. The protagonists in the example at the beginning of this chapter, Harry Cutter, Manny Cure, Buzz Barbur, and Aldo Stiles have gone to great lengths to negotiate a framework for the joint investment in, and operation of, their business. But because entrepreneurs are such an optimistic bunch, they sometimes take a static view about corporate infrastructure — including the future business relationship among the owners. But in business as in real life, change (for better or worse) is always just around the corner. An owner could retire, die, become disabled, get married, get divorced, have children, find a better business opportunity, or receive an offer to sell shares or even the company.

All of these events impact not only the subject owner or his or her estate, but also all of the other owners. A good shareholder agreement or operating agreement will anticipate these and other changes, and contain the framework to deal with such change, including clearly providing for the rights and obligations of the owners to each other and to the company.

Permitted transfers

Permitted transfers are exceptions to the general transfer restriction, and may be negotiated and included in the agreement. For example, the shareholders or members might permit transfers that take place pursuant to the exercise of rights of first refusal, drag-along rights, and tag-along rights (each discussed below). The owners might also allow other transfers that are tailored to specifically meet the requirements of the parties. For example, a corporate shareholder might negotiate to have the right to freely transfer its ownership interest to an affiliate. An individual (natural person) shareholder might negotiate to have the right to freely transfer his or her shares to a trust established for the benefit of a spouse, child, or other relative in which the shareholder is the controlling trustee. These specially negotiated "permitted transfers" would then be allowed to take place without triggering the drag-along, take-along, or first refusal rights, if any, provided elsewhere in the agreement.

Permitted Transfers Include Sale Events Only

Note that "Transfer" includes not only sales (meaning a disposition of title for value), but also gifts, liens, pledges, encumbrances, and the granting of security interests. As you read on, you'll see that the Permitted Transfer provisions discussed below (for example, rights of first refusal, drag-along rights, and tag-along rights) offer a framework for only the sale of shares or membership interests. Therefore everything else (i.e., liens, pledges, security interests, etc.), is outright prohibited. This means that a shareholder cannot pledge its shares to a bank as security for a personal loan (unless of course it obtains the consent of all the other shareholders and the Company before doing so).

Can you draft the Agreement to give first refusal rights for things like security interests? Yes, but it becomes extremely unwieldy.

Right of First Refusal — to the Company Only

First refusal provisions are designed to address the legitimate desire of the owners to approve who they become business partners with, while at the same time, allowing an owner with a bona fide offer to sell its shares or membership interests to do so utilizing a pre-negotiated transaction framework. A first refusal provision gives the Company and/or other shareholders/members first dibs to purchase (pro rata portion in case of the other shareholders/members) the shares/membership interests from a shareholder/member that receives a bona fide third party offer to purchase such shares/membership interests, pursuant to the same terms and conditions as the bona fide offer. Of course, first refusal rights (as well as the drag-along and tag-along rights discussed below) should terminate upon a public offering.

Depending on your business and financial situation, there are three main ways to structure this provision — to give the first refusal right (i) to just the Company, (ii) to just the other shareholders/members, or (iii) to Company first, and then to the other shareholders/members. The sample provision provides the first refusal right to the Company only. The alternative provision provides the first refusal right to the Company, and the balance of the shares/interests to the other shareholders/members on a *pro rata* basis. If the Company and/or other owners don't purchase all the offered interests, then the selling shareholder/member is permitted to sell to the third party, but only upon terms and conditions no less favorable to the selling shareholder/member than the original third party offer.

(a) If any Shareholder [or Member] (a "Selling Owner") receives a bona fide offer (the "Offer") to purchase any of its Shares from a party other than an affiliate (the "Third Party Offeror"), which the Selling Owner desires to accept, then it shall provide notice to the Company (the "Offer Notice") setting forth the identity of the Third Party Offeror, the number of Shares proposed to be purchased (the "Subject Shares"), the proposed purchase price, and all material terms and conditions of the Offer.

Subsection (a) sets forth what happens when a shareholder or member (Selling Owner) receives an offer from a third party (Third Party Offeror) to purchase its shares or membership interest (Subject Shares). The first thing the Selling Owner has to do is to send an Offer Notice to the Company that describes the offer from the third party. The Offer Notice puts the Company on notice that its first refusal right has been triggered. Keep in mind that all notices are also governed by the Notices provision (discussed on the CD-ROM), including the manner of dispatch and effectiveness. It's best to use redundant notice methods to ensure proper receipt.

(b) The Company has the right (the "First Refusal Right") to purchase all, but not less than all, of the Subject Shares at the same price and upon the same terms and conditions as contained in the Offer, exercisable by the Company's written notice to the Selling Owner no later than [20] days after the Offer Notice (the "Exercise Expiration Date"). If the Company timely exercises its First Refusal Right, then the Selling Owner and Company shall close the Company's purchase of the Subject Shares at the principal office of the Company within [30] days after the Exercise Expiration Date.

Subsection (b) sets forth the Company's right of first refusal to purchase the shares or membership interests. This provision should set forth the time period during which the Company has to exercise its First Refusal Right. I wrote 20 days after the offer notice, but it can be more or less. If the Company exercises its right, then the provision requires the closing to take place within the specified time limit. I wrote 30 days (which is only 10 days after the latest date the Company can exercise its First Refusal Right). Again, it can be more or less, depending among other things, on how long the parties think they need to get their act together for a closing.

(c) If the Company does not timely exercise the First Refusal Right, then the Selling Owner has until [10] days after the Exercise Expiration Date to provide notice (the "Verification Notice") to the Company to confirm whether it will proceed with the sale to the Third Party Offeror. If the Selling Owner timely sends the Verification Notice, it may sell all, but not less than all, of the Subject Shares to the Third Party Offeror, but (i) only pursuant to terms and conditions that are no less favorable to the Selling Owner than contained in the Offer and (ii) on a closing date that is more than [10] days but not more than [60] days after the Exercise Expiration Date.

Subsection (c) sets forth the Selling Owner's right to sell the Subject Shares to the third party if the Company doesn't exercise its First Refusal Right. First, the provision requires the Selling Owner to indicate whether it will go through with the third party sale. If so, the provision stipulates that the closing for such sale has to take place within the specified time period, and only based on terms and conditions that are no less favorable to the Selling Owner than contained in the Offer. The thinking is that if the third party now wants to pay more than the purchase price set forth in its original offer, then this is "good" for the Company, so they may proceed with the sale.

(d) If the Selling Owner fails to send the Verification Notice, or if the closing of the sale to the Third Party Offeror fails to occur, in either case during the stated time periods, then the Subject Shares continue to be subject to the provisions of this Agreement.

Subsection (d) sets forth the reversion of the shares or membership interest back to the status quo if the Selling Owner doesn't sell its ownership interest after all. So if a few months down the line, the Selling Owner receives another bona fide offer, it has to follow the entire procedure again before it can sell.

Right of First Refusal — to the Company and then the Other Shareholders/Members

(a) If any Shareholder [or Member] (a "Selling Owner") receives a bona fide offer (the "Offer") to purchase any of its Shares from a party other than an affiliate (the "Third Party Offeror"), which the Selling Owner desires to accept, then it shall provide notice (the "Offer Notice") to the Company and each of the other Shareholders (the "Other Owners[s]") setting forth the identity of the Third Party Offeror, the number of Shares proposed to be purchased (the "Subject Shares"), the proposed purchase price and all material terms and conditions of the Offer.

Subsection (a) is the same as Subsection (a) of the First Refusal Right to Company Only discussed above, with one critical difference. The Selling Owner has to notify not just the Company, but also the others shareholders or members (Other Owners) of the Offer.

(b) The Company has the right (the "First Refusal Right") to purchase all, but not less than all, of the Subject Shares at the same price and upon the same terms and conditions as contained in the Offer, exercisable by the Company's written notice to the Selling Owner (with a copy to each of the Other Owners) no later than (20) days after the Offer Notice (the "Company Exercise Expiration Date").

Typically, the Company gets first dibs before the other shareholders or members. For ease of administration, I wrote the provision to give the Company one opportunity to purchase ALL the Subject Shares (i.e., shares or membership interests). You can tweak the subsection to allow a partial purchase by the Company, and to offer the balance to the Other Owners, but this would complicate the drafting process quite a bit.

(c) If the Company does not timely exercise the First Refusal Right, then each of the Other Owners has the right (the "Shareholder Option") to purchase its Pro Rata Portion (defined below) of the Subject Shares at the same price and upon the same terms and conditions as contained in the Offer, exercisable by each such Other Owners' written notice to the Selling Owner, with a copy to each of the Other Owners and the Company, no later than [35] days after the Offer Notice (the "Shareholder Exercise Expiration Date"). Each Other Owner's Pro Rata Portion shall be the number of Shares equal to the product of (i) the aggregate number of Subject Shares and (ii) the fraction with the numerator being the number of Shares owned by such Other Owner and the denominator being the total number of issued and outstanding Shares owned by the Other Owners.

The Other Owners get their chance to purchase their pro rata portion of the Subject Shares if the Company does not exercise its First Refusal Right. I include a definition formula for Pro Rata Portion — you have to be very careful with this definition so as not to leave any shares left over (akin to a division problem with a repeating decimal). I introduce a new definition here, the Shareholder Exercise Expiration Date, because I didn't want to look all the way back to the date of the Offer Notice. Be sure to make sure the dates work since changing one of them has the cascading effect of impacting all the deadlines down the line.

(d) If all the Other Owners do not timely exercise their Shareholder Options, then the remaining Other Owners have an additional 10 days after the Shareholder Exercise Expiration Date to allocate the remaining Subject Shares among themselves based on their proportionate percentage ownership (or other manner mutually agreed among such remaining Other Owners).

Recognizing that the Other Owners might not all want to participate, Subsection (d) gives the Other Owners who have exercised one more chance to allocate the leftover Subject Shares among themselves. Note how I don't use the definition of Pro Rata Portion for this because that would require me to tweak the formula with each successive round (that is, the number of available Subject Shares decreases with each round, and the fraction changes because you have fewer Other Owners with each successive round). Instead of having multiple rounds, I opt to cut right to the chase, and have the remaining Other Owners just work it out based on a proportionate framework. Keep in mind that Subsection (f) below calls for ALL the Subject Shares to be purchased by the Company or the Other Owners; otherwise all bets are off, and the Selling Owner can proceed with the sale to the Third Party.

(e) The Selling Owner, and the Company [Other Owners] shall close the Company's [Other Owners'] purchase of their respective portions of the Subject Shares at the principal office of the Company within [20] days after the Shareholder Exercise Expiration Date.

After all the above takes place, Subsection (e) calls for the closing for the sale to the Company or the Other Owners to take place all at once. This is for ease of administration.

(f) If the Company and Other Owners do not timely exercise their rights under this Section to collectively purchase all, but not less than all, the Subject Shares, then the Selling Owner has until [30] days after the Shareholder Exercise Expiration Date to provide notice (the "Verification Notice") to the Company and Other Owners to confirm whether it will proceed with the sale to the Third Party Offeror. If the Selling Owner timely sends the Verification Notice, it may sell all, but not less than all, of the Subject Shares to the Third Party Offeror, but (i) only pursuant to terms and conditions that are no less favorable to the Selling Owner than contained in the Offer and (ii) on a closing date that is more than [30] days but not more than [40] days after the Shareholder Exercise Expiration Date.

Subsection (f) is similar to Subsection (c) of the First Refusal Right to Company Only discussed above, except that I shortened the time period during which the third party closing has to take place, given that the Selling Owner already has plenty of time to prepare just in case nobody exercises their rights. Note that in my version, the Selling Owner has the right to proceed with the sale of all the subject shares to the third party if any of the Subject Shares are still available. You can modify it to allow the sale by the Selling Owner of just the balance of any Subject Shares still available after all the insiders take their share, but it's not likely that the third party will want to proceed with a partial purchase.

(g) If the Selling Owner fails to send the Verification Notice, or if the closing of the sale to the Third Party Offeror fails to occur, in either case during the stated time periods, then the Subject Shares continue to be subject to the provisions of this Agreement.

Subsection (g) is the same as Subsection (d) of the First Refusal Right to Company Only discussed earlier.

Bona Fide Offer versus Purchase Price Formula

The sample First Refusal contract provision above calls for the Selling Owner to offer the Shares or Membership Interests to the Company and/or the Other Owners based on the purchase price established in the bona fide third party offer (**Bona Fide Third Party Price**). There's another way to do it. You can base the purchase price on the lower of the Bona Fide Third Party Price and a price based on a fair market value formula the parties establish directly in the Shareholder Agreement or Operating Agreement (**Formula Purchase Price**). Note that this Formula Purchase Price can also be used to establish the price the Company pays to purchase the Shares of a deceased, bankrupt, divorced, etc., Shareholder.

The parties can even agree to establish the purchase price in advance on an annual basis, but the question then arises as what to do if the parties butt heads and can't agree on the price. In this case, the agreement can call for an appraisal process (expensive) or come up with some kind of default price.

One advantage of coming up with a Formula Purchase Price is that you can also come up with a payment plan (installments, etc.), and plan your financing and insurance requirements in advance, rather than attempting to match the bona fide offer term for term (remember that if the bona fide offer includes 100 percent cash payment, then technically, the Company and/or Other Owners also have to pay cash if they want to exercise their first refusal rights).

Drag-Along Rights

(a) If [name of shareholder or member or group of shareholders/members] (the "Dragging Owners") agrees to sell, in a transaction or a series of related transactions, a number of Shares equal to [50 percent] or more of the issued and outstanding Shares to a party other than an affiliate, the Dragging Owner(s) have the right, upon written notice to the other shareholders (the "Other Owner(s)"), to require that each Other Owner join in such sale on a pro rata basis on the same terms and conditions as the Dragging Owner(s).

This is a basic drag-along provision (a.k.a., bring-along provision). Financial investors (e.g., venture capital firms) sometimes demand these provisions as part of their "exit strategies," which give them (Dragging Owners) the right to "drag along" some or all of the other shareholders/members (Dragged Owners or "Other Owners") in the event the Dragging Owners desire to sell their shares/membership interests to a third party. By requiring the Other Owners to also sell their shares to a third party seeking to purchase the entire company, drag-along provisions force the intransigent or uncommitted owner to participate in the proposed sale. Note that typically, the parties will come up with a name for the Dragging Owner based on the name of the financial investor that invokes the provision, for example, the "XYZ Shareholders," if the name of the financial investor is XYZ Financial Group, Inc.

(b) Notwithstanding the above, such terms and conditions of sale shall (i) require the Other Owner(s) to make its representations and warranties, covenants, indemnities, and other agreements severally and not jointly, (ii) otherwise limit the liability of any Other Owner to the purchase price or other consideration received by it in the proposed sale. Each of the Other Owners waives any appraisal, dissenter or similar rights in connection with such sale.

While drag-along provisions can be drafted to be invoked by the sale of a particular owner's (like a financial investor's) interest, they can also be tailored to be triggered by the attempted sale of a specified percentage of shares of the company, for example, a majority or two-thirds of the shares. These provisions require sales by the Dragged Owners and Dragging Owners to be made upon the same terms and conditions; but otherwise drag-along provisions typically are pretty lopsided in favor of the Dragging Owners — they control the negotiations with the third party purchaser, including the terms and conditions of sale.

Therefore, it's best for entrepreneurs to avoid these provisions; if you have no choice but to agree, then make sure your attorney reviews the drag-along provision with an eye to minimizing your exposure. For example, you can include a purchase price floor so the Dragging Owner doesn't agree to a fire sale without your consent. You should also make sure to include the condition that any representations made by you in the sale agreement be made severally (not jointly) (see Chapter 26 for a more detailed discussion of joint and several liability), and to cap your indemnity (see Chapter 25 for a more detailed discussion of indemnities, including how to limit your liability under an indemnity).

You can also negotiate to make drag-along rights non-transferable, and to delay the right of the Dragging Shareholders to exercise such rights for some time period (for example, not to exercise drag-along rights until two years after the execution date). Drag-along provisions can be quite lengthy, as they usually include various and sundry provisions on mechanical issues, such as notices and paperwork.

Tag-Along Rights

(a) Except in connection with a sale executed pursuant to Section [Drag-along provision section number], if any shareholder agrees to sell, in a transaction or a series of related transactions, any of its Shares to a party other than an affiliate (the "Tag-along Purchaser"), then each of the other shareholders (the "Other Owners") has the right to Transfer to the Tag-along Purchaser (based on the same terms and conditions of sale) up to the number of Shares equal to the product of (i) the aggregate number of Shares to be purchased by the Tag-along Purchaser and (ii) the fraction with the numerator being the number of Shares owned by such Other Owner and the denominator being the total number of issued and outstanding Shares of the Company.

This is a basic tag-along provision. Financial investors sometimes try to negotiate these provisions when they become shareholders/members, as a way to keep the entrepreneurial owners from selling the company from under them. Tag-along provisions give these investors the right, but not the obligation, to "tag along" in any transaction entered into by the entrepreneurial shareholders/members to sell their ownership interests. Keep in mind that tag-along provisions can be drafted to also allow you to sell your *pro rata* portion of shares if the financial investor finds a buyer. Tag-along provisions don't force the third party purchaser to increase the number of shares it needs to purchase. Instead, it gives each shareholder/member the option to sell its pro rata portion so that the third party purchaser purchases the originally agreed-to number of shares.

(b) Notwithstanding the above, such terms and conditions of sale shall (i) require the Other Owner(s) to make its representations and warranties, covenants, indemnities, and other agreements severally and not jointly, (ii) otherwise limit the liability of any Other Owner to the purchase price or other consideration received by it in the proposed sale. Each of the Other Owners waives any appraisal, dissenter, or similar rights in connection with such sale.

Tag-along provisions can be quite lengthy, and usually contain various and sundry provisions on mechanical issues, such as notices and paperwork. As usual, there are ways to try to mitigate your exposure under these provisions. For example, in addition to the ways discussed in the section on drag-along provisions earlier, you can try to get your financial investor to agree to bear all or a portion of the cost of the transaction if it chooses to participate.

Status of Ownership upon Death — No Sale

(a) The death or dissolution (each a "Triggering Event") of a Shareholder [Member] (the "Impacted Owner") does not dissolve the Company. Upon the occurrence of a Triggering Event, the estate or successor in interest of the Impacted Owner becomes the assignee to the Impacted Owner's interest in the Company, subject to this Agreement but succeeding only to the rights of the Impacted Owner to receive distributions hereunder (but not any other rights under this Agreement).

(b) The estate or successor in interest of the Impacted Owner will not be admitted as a substitute Shareholder [or Member] in the place of the Impacted Owner unless (i) [75 percent] of the remaining Shareholders [Members] consent and (ii) it complies with the provisions of Section [list section number of "Transferee Subject to Agreement," discussed below].

There are at least two ways to deal with the death (for natural persons) or dissolution (for legal entities) of a Shareholder or Member (Impacted Owner). This No Sale version of the provision calls for the estate or successor in interest of the Impacted Owner to take over only the economic benefits of ownership (can't sell, can't vote, etc.).

Per Subsection (b), the assignee can become a "substitute" Shareholder or Member replacing the Impacted Owner, but only with the approval of the other Shareholders/Members and if it agrees to become bound to the Agreement.

The alternative Mandatory Sale version (discussed below) requires the Company the right to purchase the Shares or Membership Interests from the estate or successor in interest based on a some kind of fair market formula. Yet another alternative can have the other owners purchasing their *pro rata* portions, or some combination of any of the above.

Status of Ownership upon Death — Mandatory Sale

(a) The death or dissolution (each a "Triggering Event") of a Shareholder [Member] (the "Impacted Owner") does not dissolve the Company. Upon the occurrence of a Triggering Event, the Company shall purchase all, but not less than all, of the Shares owned by such Impacted Owner at a purchase price determined pursuant to Subsection (b) below.

This is the alternative Mandatory Sale version. The Shareholder or Member's death or dissolution triggers the mandatory sale of the estate's or successor in interest's stake to the Company for a purchase price (and upon payment terms and other terms and conditions) that are predetermined (whether based on some kind of fair market value formula or annual mutual agreement).

(b) The purchase price per Share is equal to the book value of the Company divided by the number of Shares issued and outstanding on [the last day of the most recently ended financial reporting period for the Company], as determined by the Company's regular accounting firm using the method of accounting regularly employed by it to maintain the Company's financial records.

If the Company projects that it will not be able to fund any Mandatory Sale with its cash flow, then it will need to find some other way to finance its purchase, typically using the proceeds of life insurance policies on the lives of the owners. While it's possible to structure the provision to mandate the purchase of the shares by the other owners (instead of by the Company), this can get quite messy when there are many owners — in fact, in that case, each owner is going to have to consider how he or she will finance the purchase.

Subsection (b) is a very basic provision (basing price on book value) establishing the formula to determine the purchase price of the Shares or Membership Interests. Work with your attorney and accountant to make sure the formula is a fair representation of the value of the Shares or Membership Interests. For example, a formula based on the adjusted book value might work better if the Company has contingent liabilities (e.g., corporate guarantees, etc.), and incoming life insurance or disability insurance proceeds. If the Company doesn't employ an accountant on a regular basis, it may need to provide a mechanism for appointing a mutually acceptable accountant or appraiser to determine the purchase price. Or the parties can provide in the contract that they will meet annually to mutually agree to the purchase price. If the parties don't or can't agree, then they can fall back to the book value formula.

OTHER SALE OR NO-SALE TRIGGERING EVENTS

Other triggering events are possible. In the above sample contract provisions, the death (natural person) or dissolution (legal entity) of a Shareholder or Member triggers either the No Sale or Mandatory Sale outcome. The No Sale version allows the estate or successor in interest to succeed to the economic rights of ownership — the estate or successor in interest is not forced to sell; it can remain an owner, at least as far as the right to receive distributions is concerned. On the other hand, the Mandatory Sale version requires the Company to purchase the Shares or Membership Interests from the estate or successor in interest.

You can tailor the Triggering Events to include any or all of the additional categories below. You'll also have to negotiate whether you want a particular Triggering Event to trigger the No Sale or Mandated Sale outcome. This may depend on a number of factors including the financial and tax situation of the Company and individual owners.

For example, does the Company have the cash flow cushion to be able to pay the purchase price of a Mandatory Sale and still be able to run its business, or will it need to allocate resources to obtain the requisite financing and/or life or disability insurance (on each owner)? Individual owners should keep in mind that the estate or family of a deceased, disabled, or incapacitated owner typically finds itself dealing with the Company (and the other owners) from a weaker bargaining position, and therefore may be more prone to make rash, emotional decisions that short-change the estate or family. First, there usually isn't a liquid market for the shares or membership interests of a small company. And second, the estate or family may need immediate funds to pay for estate taxes, funeral expenses, hospital care, etc. The pre-determined pricing mechanism of a Mandatory Sale may be the best protection the family has to liquidate its interest at a fair price.

Triggering Event categories may include (but are not limited to):

- **Death, Disability, or Incapacity:** The death, disability, or incapacity (or bankruptcy or retirement) of a natural person Shareholder or Member may mean that one of the Company's principal managers, thought leaders, and financial backers is no longer available.

- **Divorce:** Depending on the divorce laws of your state and the enforceability of any prenuptial agreement, the divorce of a Shareholder or Member may result in a potentially disruptive spouse (especially in an acrimonious divorce) having an ownership claim in the Company.

- **Termination of Employment:** This category would include Shareholders or Members who also work for the Company in some capacity. If someone is terminated for cause (which you can define to include any number of offenses — poor performance, non-performance, committing a felony, etc.), then you may not want this person to be an owner either.

- **Bankruptcy, Insolvency, Dissolution, or Change in Control or Ownership:** These events jeopardize (or in the case of dissolution, terminate) the legal status of legal entity shareholders or members. Some shareholder agreements and operating agreements call for a mandatory sale in these cases. Keep in mind, however, that provisions that impact the debtor are closely scrutinized by the courts; consult with your attorney on whether it may be more prudent to opt for the No Sale option in case of bankruptcy. Another possible Triggering Event is a change of control or ownership of a corporate Shareholder or Member.

- **Other Involuntary Transfers:** These include foreclosure, levy of execution, garnishment, attachment, or any other involuntary seizure of an owner's Shares or Membership Interests. Shareholder agreements and operating agreements sometimes treat these as No Sale events where the creditor becomes an assignee of the economic rights pending supermajority approval of its conversion to substitute Shareholder or Member status. The creditor, however, may take issue with this because it probably bargained for a full-fledged security interest, which entails full ownership rights in the seized property.

Transferees Subject to Agreement

(a) All Shares, including, but not limited to, Shares acquired after the date of this Agreement, are subject to this Agreement.

(b) Any person who becomes a Shareholder [Member] of the Company through the issuance or Transfer [defined in Transfer Restrictions section above] or a substitute Shareholder [Member] of an Impacted Owner shall (i) be subject to this Agreement, and (ii) prior to any such issuance or Transfer, consent to be bound (if it is not already a party to this Agreement) by the terms and conditions of this Agreement by executing and delivering to the Company a Joinder Agreement in the form attached hereto.

(c) Any purported Transfer (including, but not limited to, any attempted conversion of an assignee — of an Impacted Owner's interest — to a Substitute Shareholder) without compliance with the provisions of this Agreement is null and void and of no effect.

This is a provision that seeks to make sure that all future Shareholders or Members (including assignees of deceased owners' interests) agree to become bound to the Agreement before they can become Shareholders or Members.

Preemptive Rights

(a) If the Company desires to issue any securities (the "Offered Securities"), it shall send written notice (the "Preemptive Offer Notice") to each Shareholder [Member] first offering such Shareholder [Member] the right to purchase its Pro Rata Portion of the Offered Securities at the same price and other terms and conditions offered by the Company for the Offered Securities.

(i) For purposes of this provision, "securities" include shares of stock in the Company, or any securities directly or indirectly convertible into, or exercisable or exchangeable for, shares of stock in the Company.

Preemptive rights enable the existing shareholders or members to maintain their proportionate ownership (and therefore voting power, right to profits, etc.), when the company decides to issue new shares/membership interests by giving the existing owners the right to purchase the new shares of stock or membership interests before they are offered to third parties. See Chapter 2 for a discussion of preemptive rights clauses in corporate certificates of incorporation.

(ii) Each Shareholder's Pro Rata Portion shall be the number of Offered Securities equal to the product of (i) the aggregate number of Offered Securities and (ii) the fraction with the numerator being the number of Shares owned by such Shareholder and the denominator being the total number of issued and outstanding Shares, in each case on the date of the Preemptive Offer.

As with all the provisions in this chapter, this provision can be tailored for either a shareholder agreement or an LLC operating agreement. To imagine the LLC operating agreement version of this provision, simply replace the word "Shareholder" with "Member," and the word(s) "Shares" or "shares of stock" with the word "Membership Interest" or "Interest."

(b) Each Shareholder has the right (the "Preemptive Right") to purchase its Pro Rata Portion of the Offered Securities, exercisable by its written notice to the Company no later than [10] days after the Preemptive Offer Notice. The Shareholders that have timely exercised their respective Preemptive Rights, and the Company, shall close such Shareholders' purchase of the Offered Securities at the principal office of the Company within [30] days after the Preemptive Offer Notice.

Non-competition

It's perfectly reasonable to restrict the Shareholders or Members from either owning or working for the Company's competitors, certainly while they are Shareholders or Members, but also for some period of time thereafter. Small companies and large public companies sometimes engage in similar businesses, so an exception can be made for a Shareholder or Member owning shares in a publicly traded company as part of his or her personal portfolio, especially if the portfolio is "managed" by a stockbroker.

See Chapters 4 and 5 for a discussion of non-compete provisions.

Additional Capital Contributions

(a) In the event from time to time that the Shareholders [Members] who hold the power to vote [a majority] of the Shares then outstanding determine that additional capital contributions are necessary for the conduct of the Company's activities, each Shareholder shall promptly make a cash contribution to the capital of the Company equal to its proportionate share of the required funds.

(b) In the event that any Shareholder does not contribute its share of such funds to the Company, the funds advanced by the other Shareholders will be regarded as Owner Loans (defined below).

Subsection (a) provides a framework for the Company to obtain additional capital contributions from the owners. If all the owners participate, then the Company will receive the required funds without any owner being diluted.

Subsection (b) is an anti-dilution provision that allows the Company to receive the required funds without diluting an owner that may not have the wherewithal or inclination to make additional contributions. Funds advanced by the participating owners will be treated as Owner Loans.

Owner Loans

The Shareholders [Members] may from time to time make loans (the "Owner Loans") to the Company as authorized by the Board of Directors [Managers], with an interest rate and terms and conditions to be mutually agreed between the Shareholder making the Owner Loan and the Board of Directors. Owner Loans are not capital contributions and do not entitle the Shareholders to any increase in their respective shares of the allocation of profits or losses or distributions of the Company. The Company shall make principal and interest payments on Owner Loans prior to making any distributions to the Shareholders.

This provision provides a very basic framework for Owner Loans to the Company. It restates the proposition that Owner Loans are not capital contributions and do not determine the allocation of profits and losses of the Company. Shareholders or Members that make Owner Loans are creditors, and this provision confirms that they will be repaid before any distributions are made to the Shareholders or Members. However, as unsecured creditors, they will line up behind the secured creditors. Most financial lenders will require that the inside creditors subordinate their rights behind the financial lenders.

Owner Voting

The following actions require the approval of the Shareholders holding at least [a majority] [two-thirds] of the Shares then outstanding and entitled to vote:

While most management decisions are made either under the direction of the board of directors or by the officers of a corporation or by the Managers of an LLC, the owners may wish to carve out certain important Company actions that require Shareholder or Membership approval. Depending on the voting dynamics of your company, you can require a simple majority or a super-majority, for example, a two-thirds vote. Check with your attorney, because certain actions may by law already require shareholder approval.

(a) any material change in the Company's business;

(b) the sale or other transfer to another person of all or substantially all the Company's assets or business;

(c) the borrowing of any money or the granting of a material lien or security interest upon any of the Company's assets;

(d) any acquisition, merger, consolidation of other business combination to which the Company or any affiliate is a party;

(e) the decision to consent to or commence a voluntary proceeding under U.S. bankruptcy laws; or

(f) an initial public offering of the Company.

The parties might consider requiring Shareholder or Membership approval of the following additional actions:

- **Insider Transactions:** Contracts between the Company and any Insider (e.g., any Shareholder, Member, director, officer, or Manager of the Company, or their family members).

- **Distributions to Shareholders or Members:** The transfer of any Company assets or the payment of any compensation, stock options, or other consideration to any Insider.

- **Decisions Relating to Capital:** Including, for example, the purchase or redemption by the Company of any Shares or Membership Interests, the admission of any new Shareholders or Members, or the issuance by the Company of additional Shares or Membership Interests.

- **Major Contracts:** For example, contracts for the purchase or lease of equipment or other items over a preset dollar threshold.

- **Major Personnel Decisions:** The Company's decision to hire or fire key officers and employees, as well as outside advisors such as attorneys, auditors, and the like.

Part II
BASIC CORPORATE TRANSACTIONS

4

SALE OF GOODS

This chapter will focus on provisions typically found in contracts for the **sale of goods.** "Goods" include tangible personal property like the office supplies you consume in your business, raw materials and components you incorporate in finished goods you manufacture, and finished goods you purchase for resale. Goods do not include real estate, company stock, or other securities or intangibles.

As you can imagine, there is great variety in **service agreements** (and contract provisions), given the size and breadth of the service sector. "Services" run the gamut, and include everything from equipment maintenance, to outsourced data entry, legal work and accounting, to sales and marketing services. In Chapter 5, I discuss contract provisions typically found in sales representative agreements, which are commonly used by large and small businesses to retain the sales solicitation services of independent (non-employee) salespeople.

Contracts for the sale of an entire business (assets or company stock) are covered in Part III.

OVERVIEW

Companies buy and sell Goods by entering into a variety of contract documentation. Some buy by issuing short-form purchase orders, and sell by issuing short-form sales confirmations. Others buy and sell by entering into mutually signed longer forms of sales contracts. Yet others will establish the overall relationship by entering into a longer form contract, but then dispatch short-form purchase orders and sales confirmations for individual transactions. No matter how you proceed, your contact documentation will need to address the following key areas:

- **Front matter:** Every contract typically has the front matter portion, which lists the names and addresses of the parties plus perhaps some recitals (introductory paragraphs). Please refer to the CD-ROM included with this book for a detailed discussion of Front Matter.

- **Principal Obligations:** There must be an undertaking to sell and to buy the Goods in question.

- **Price and Quantity:** The price and quantity of the Goods to be purchased should be listed in the contract or in an exhibit to be attached to the contract.

- **Payment Terms:** The manner and timing of payment for the Goods should be tailored to meet the needs of the Seller and the Buyer. Many sales contracts are back-to-back, meaning that the Seller needs to pay for the goods (or materials to make the goods) to its supplier. So the parties negotiate payment terms based a number of factors — the size of the transaction, the creditworthiness of the Buyer, the back-to-back obligations of the Seller to its suppliers, not to mention of course, the bargaining leverage of the parties.

- **Delivery Terms:** The contract should also dictate the Delivery Point, meaning when and where the Seller is deemed to have fulfilled its obligation to "deliver" the Goods. The Buyer takes control of and responsibility for the Goods at the Delivery Point — the Buyer assumes risk of loss of and damage to the goods, and bears some or all costs (e.g., transportation, insurance, etc.), associated with moving the goods beyond the Delivery Point.

- **Warranty Terms:** The contract should dictate to what extent the Seller will "back up" the Goods (title, fitness for the intended purpose, quality, etc.), including any disclaimers of warranties.

- **Boilerplate Section:** Most contracts usually have (toward the end) a section of boilerplate (standard clauses) covering a laundry list of matters such as assignability, governing law, notices, severability, etc. Please refer to Part V and the CD-ROM for a detailed discussion of these and the provisions listed below. Of special importance to sales contracts are provisions covering the following matters:

  - **Term:** This type of provision has little practical impact on spot sales except to the extent that any indemnity or other provisions survive. However, distribution agreements and long-term supply agreements should dictate the term (length of time the agreement will remain in force).

  - **Termination:** Sales contracts should contain provisions addressing termination for cause, bankruptcy, etc. You should consult with your attorney because state law may make it difficult to terminate distribution agreements, for example, may require the supplier to repurchase unsold inventory.

- **Remedies:** Uniform Commercial Code (UCC) Article 2 contains default provisions covering remedies for the breach of sales contracts by either the Seller or Buyer, and allow the parties to negotiate limitations of liability. For example, the Seller may want to negotiate a liability cap, limiting its liability under the contract to the Purchase Price of the Goods.

- **Force Majeure:** These provisions dictate the rights and obligations of the parties in case the Seller can't deliver the Goods due to an event beyond its control, like a nationwide transportation strike, severe weather, etc.

- **Indemnity:** The Buyer can negotiate an indemnity from the Seller to indemnify the Buyer for damage, loss, or injury arising from the sale or use of the Goods. The Seller can negotiate an indemnity from the Distributor/Buyer to indemnify the Seller for damage, loss or injury arising from the Distributor's resale activities under the Distribution Agreement. Please refer to Chapter 17 and the CD-ROM for discussions of Indemnities and Indemnification, including ways to customize the provision using "thresholds" and "baskets" to vary the degree of risk retention or risk shifting, or even to share the risk.

- **Other Provisions:** Depending on the nature of the Goods, the parties might consider the following other provisions:

  - **Confidentiality:** The Seller might negotiate to include confidentiality provisions in the sale of goods contract. The Buyer may also wish to include confidentiality provisions if it is furnishing secret information, for example, unique specifications, to the Seller. See Chapter 6 for a detailed discussion of confidentiality provisions.

  - **Representations:** Depending on the size of the transaction, consider adding representations from the Seller and/or Buyer regarding its ability to enter into the transaction. Some of these may include the following representations (some of these apply only to non-natural person entites): Organization; Power and Authority to Run its Business, Authority to Sell or Buy, Enforceability, Consent of Third Parties/Government to Transaction, No Conflict with Corporate Documents, Contracts, or Laws.

Remember that this is not a forms manual, but rather a guide to help you interpret the deal-point provisions of, and spot issues in, a variety of contracts. That's why I've organized the sample contract provisions in this chapter (and in all the chapters of this book) by topic, and without assigning section numbers or letters to the provisions.

Distributor (or Distribution) Agreements

These agreements govern the rights and obligations of companies who buy and sell Goods from each other for the purpose of reselling them to other businesses. Distributor agreements can either be non-exclusive, where the manufacturer or supplier is free to sell to any number of resellers (distributors) in a designated territory, or exclusive, where the manufacturer or supplier contracts with just one distributor to resell the Goods to customers in a designated territory.

While distributor agreements are essentially contracts for the sale of Goods, and therefore typically contain all of the provisions discussed above, they may also contain additional provisions dealing with such antitrust-law sensitive issues as resale price, exclusivity, and minimum purchase requirements, which may impact boilerplate-type clauses like the term of the agreement and termination. These and other distributor-agreement type provisions are also included in this chapter.

Terminology

As is customary in this book, many of the capitalized terms used throughout this chapter — terms like "Goods," "Seller," "Buyer," "Purchase Price," etc. — are defined in the sample contract provisions. I also use such capitalized terms as necessary where the context requires in the detailed discussions and various examples.

The Law Governing the Sale of Goods

This chapter mainly covers domestic transactions (i.e., sales contracts between two American contract parties). The domestic sale of goods (i.e., personal tangible property like this book, furniture, equipment, etc., but not real estate, services, company stock or other securities or intangibles) is governed by each State's version of Article 2 of the Uniform Commercial Code (UCC) — adopted by all states except Louisiana. UCC Article 2 contains default rules governing various and sundry matters relating to contract formation and performance, and was promulgated by the American Law Institute (ALI) and the National Conference of Commissioners on Uniform State Laws (NCCUSL), which are private non-governmental entities that advance the establishment of uniform state laws.

If your State has adopted UCC Article 2, (which at the time of printing was every state but Louisiana), then the state law you negotiate to govern your sales contract automatically will include UCC Article 2. The sample contract provisions in this chapter are based on existing UCC Article 2 concepts.

Keep in mind that in 2003, ALI and NCCUSL promulgated Revised UCC Article 2 (and 2A on personal property leases) to modernize Article 2 (which was promulgated in 1951) by reflecting current sales contract practices. In the face of opposition by many industry sectors, no state has adopted Revised UCC Article 2 (or 2A) as of 2008. If in the future, however, even a fraction of the individual states enact Revised UCC Article 2, then this will impact how sales contracts are drafted and negotiated.

Among other changes, Revised UCC Article 2 would eliminate the statutory framework for shipping terms (such as FOB, etc.), and require contract parties to look elsewhere for guidance — for example, current usage of trade (regularly observed trade practice). There is also a movement to fill the vacuum with domestic versions of Incoterms 2000 (International Commercial Terms), which are shipping and delivery terms established by the International Chamber of Commerce for international (not domestic) sales contracts. Other Revised Article 2 changes would raise the statute of frauds requirement for written contracts from $500 to $5000, make it easier to introduce evidence of contract terms outside the four corners of the written contract, amend the rules regarding warranty disclaimers, and even create a new class of "consumer contracts" not currently covered by UCC Article 2.

What about International Sales Contracts?

While UCC Article 2 governs most purely domestic sales contracts (which may be the vast majority of sales contracts you'll enter into as a small business), the Choice of Law situation (the governing law you negotiate with your counterparty) in an international sales contract scenario is a bit more complicated.

The United States was one of the first countries (in 1986) to ratify the United Nations Convention on Contracts for the International Sale of Goods (CISG), which was developed by United Nations Commission on International Trade Law (UNCITRAL) to codify a uniform set of default rules governing the formation and performance of international sales contracts (primarily for the sale of goods, not services). The default rules offer some degree of certainty even as the parties have the freedom of contract to custom-tailor their contract provisions.

The CISG (for international sales contracts) therefore is akin to UCC Article 2 (for domestic sales contracts) — but some of the key differences will be discussed below. Keep in mind that the CISG (and UCC Article 2) cover just the portion of the contract dealing with the sale of the goods (issues like shipment, warranties, etc.). The CISG does not cover a host of ancillary issues, for example, exclusivity and non-competition provisions found in international distribution agreements.

Because the United States ratified the CISG, an international treaty, the CISG is part and parcel of the law of every state in the union. For example, New York law includes the CISG. While this may not matter in domestic transactions, it has important ramifications for international sales contracts.

If you enter into a sales contract with a company located in any of the 70 other countries that have ratified the CISG (including many of the world's largest economies such as China, Japan, Germany, Canada, and the Russian Federation), this means that the CISG by default will likely govern your contract   even if you agree with your foreign counterparty to have State law, for example New York law, govern the contract. The only way to be sure to have American State law (more specifically, UCC Article 2) apply is to specifically exclude the applicability of the CISG in your Choice of Law provision.

If you enter into an international sales contract, work with your attorney to analyze which format (UCC Article 2 or CISG) actually works better for you, and then draft Choice of Law language that will ensure the applicability of the law you want to govern the contract. Keep in mind some of the general differences (not exhaustive) between UCC Article 2 and the CISG. For example, the CISG does not contain a statute of frauds requirement (meaning that oral contracts are permitted) and allows the introduction of parol evidence (evidence outside the four corners of a written contract) to prove the existence of terms and conditions contradictory to the ones printed in your contract. The CISG and UCC Article 2 contain different rules regarding contract formation — when it takes place (offer and acceptance issues) and which terms and conditions govern if the Buyer presents a purchase order and the Seller presents a sales confirmation with different terms and conditions (battle of the forms), disclaimer of warranty issues, and buyer self-help remedies for product defects.

SAMPLE CONTRACT EXCERPTS

Principal Obligations

(a) The Seller shall sell, and the Buyer shall purchase, the goods described in attached Exhibit [insert Exhibit number] (the "Goods") in accordance with the terms and conditions set forth in this Agreement and in each Individual Contract.

These provisions usually can be found at the beginning of the contract and set forth the very basic obligations of the parties to sell and purchase the Goods, including a description or definition of the goods. These basic obligations are subject to the "terms and conditions" of the agreement, meaning that the parties also have to satisfy all of their other obligations covered by the other sections of the agreement.

[Sometimes found in Distribution Agreements or long-term sales contracts where the parties contemplate multiple orders over the time length of the Agreement]

(b) An Individual Contract for the sale and purchase of Goods is deemed made when an order from the Buyer is accepted by the Seller. The Seller may accept any such order by

  (i) dispatching its then current form of Sales Confirmation (a copy of which is attached as Exhibit [insert Exhibit number]), or

  (ii) shipping the Goods or otherwise substantially beginning performance. Each of the Buyer and Seller may, for administrative convenience, use its form of Purchase Order to place orders or Sales Confirmation to confirm orders, respectively, provided, however, that if any [pre-printed] terms in such Purchase Orders or Sales Confirmations conflict with or supplement the terms of this Agreement, such conflicting or supplemental terms are null and void, and this Agreement shall govern.

Subsection (b) is a typical version of a contract provision sometimes found in distribution agreements or other long-term sales contracts contemplating many individual orders. While the main sales contract governs the overall business relationship, each party may need to dispatch some kind of document to either order or confirm the sale of goods that make up the individual transactions (Individual Contracts). The easiest way for many Buyers to place an order is to submit their standard written form or electronic Purchase Order. The easiest way for many Sellers to confirm orders is to dispatch their standard Sales Confirmation form.

Ideally, since the overall sales contract should cover all of the legal issues, this leaves the Purchase Order and Sales Confirmation to memorialize just the deal points specific to the individual transactions (usually limited to issues like quantity, extension price, shipment or delivery date, etc.). However, standard form Purchase Orders and Sales Confirmations often have pre-printed terms and conditions on the "reverse side," which invariably favor the Buyer and Seller, respectively.

For example, the "reverse side" of a Purchase Order may contain no Seller disclaimers of implied warranties, allow the recovery of consequential damages, and contain extended payment terms with no late payment interest, etc. The "reverse side" of Sales Confirmations may contain airtight Seller disclaimers of warranties, stringent payment terms, and a liability cap, etc. And each form will typically have language stipulating that it is the controlling document in the sales transaction.

Subsection (b) attempts to deal with this battle of the forms by having the parties agree in advance to a pecking order on how the documents control the relationship. The parties can agree to allow the Seller and/or Buyer to dispatch its Sales Confirmation and Purchase Order, respectively, but for administrative purposes only, and subject to the clarification that the Agreement trumps both the Sales Confirmation and the Purchase Order.

(c) Subject to any provisions in this Agreement relating to [annual] Minimum Purchase Quantities, the Buyer shall place orders no less frequently than [once a calendar month] in the minimum amount of $[insert dollar amount].

Subsections (c) and (d) deal with Individual Contract proccessing. Subsection (c) is a basic version of a provision that helps the Seller to manage (e.g., allocate goods, arrange transportation, plan cash flow requirements, etc.) its distribution or long-term supply agreements by requiring the Buyer to place regular orders (e.g., monthly, weekly, etc.) of a specified minimum amount (e.g., by dollar amount, by quantity, etc.). The parties can also include the date (or day of the week) by which orders have to be placed.

(d) All orders are subject to acceptance or rejection by the Seller. The Buyer may not cancel, terminate or amend any order which has been accepted by the Seller.

Subsection (d) provides that while the Seller is bound to the overall sales contract, it reserves the right to accept or reject individual Purchase Orders. Once the Seller accepts an order, the Buyer may not modify or cancel it (no change orders — discussed below).

The Buyer can counter and negotiate the right to submit change orders, which are written proposals to amend an Individual Contract, seeking, for example, to change specifications, quantities, packing requirements, the manner of delivery, delivery dates, etc.

While the right to submit change orders can help the Buyer address its changing needs, it can wreak havoc on the Seller's production schedule, inventory, and cash flow, especially if the Goods are custom-made products or if the Seller doesn't have the corresponding right to change its back-to-back order with its supplier. Therefore, if the Seller relents and allows change orders, it should insist on tight parameters regarding the kinds of changes, including, for example, a time limit on the Buyer's ability to submit changes (i.e., no last minute changes), and a limit on the extent to which the Buyer can change the quantity (i.e., no change orders that are effectively cancellations for convenience).

The parties should also account for any cost increases or cost savings resulting from a change order by making an adjustment to the Purchase Price. Of course, there are myriad ways to structure how the parties agree to a price adjustment, each with unique pitfalls. For example, the parties can agree not to proceed with the change order unless they mutually agree to an equitable price adjustment, which even with a good faith requirement can lead to an impasse. One workaround is to agree in advance that in the absense of mutual agreement, the Seller can ship the Goods per the original order. Query, however, whether a Seller will ship Goods that it knows the Buyer doesn't want and may not pay for.

The Battle of the Forms

UCC Article 2 will impose default terms and conditions if the parties either don't enter into a sale of goods contract or enter into one that is missing key terms and conditions. Therefore, it's very important to carefully negotiate a contract for your sale of goods transaction. If negotiating a contract is not possible for whatever reason, then it's important to consult with your attorney to help you understand how default provisions may impact you as a Buyer or Seller and determine the extent to which you confront the situation and negotiate a solution given a variety of factors, including your negotiating leverage and your exposure.

This chapter assumes the Buyer and Seller will enter into a mutually agreed sale of goods contract, but may dispatch their individual forms of Purchase Order or Sales Confirmation to memorialize individudal orders. Subsection (b) provides that the overall sale of goods contract will trump the conflicting or supplemental terms contained in any Purchase Order or Sales Confirmation.

The "Battle of the Forms" issue may also arise in spot purchase situations with no underlying sales contract. Typically in these cases, the Buyer dispatches its Purchase Order, which the Seller confirms by dispatching its Sales Confirmation, or sometimes merely by shipping the Goods. Neither party signs the other party's document, and in most cases, the Goods are delivered and accepted, and payment is made, without incident. But if a problem does arise, the question is which document controls the transaction? Either party may find that it has inadvertently agreed to terms and conditions contained in the other party's form.

Unfortunately, merely inserting that your document will be the document that controls the transaction may not be enough to "win" the battle of the forms. Depending on a variety of factors, including your negotiating leverage, how one-sided your counterparty's document is, and your exposure, you may decide that the best solution is to go through the time and expense of negotiating a mutually signed document.

Price

The purchase price of the Goods is US$[insert dollar amount] (the "Purchase Price"). The Purchase Price does not include any sales, use, excise or other taxes of any jurisdiction, all of which, if and to the extent applicable, are the responsibility of the Buyer.

This is a variation of standard contract language establishing the purchase price of the Goods. The manner and timing of payment are separate issues covered under the Payment Terms provision of the agreement (see below).

Here are some related issues:

- **Open Price Terms:** While UCC Article 2 allows the Buyer and Seller to enter into a sales contract even if they leave the price open and subject to agreement or other criteria, it's best to settle the price and include it in the sales contract. If the price absolutely cannot be determined on the date the contract is signed, then reserve the right to terminate the contract if the price cannot be quickly mutually agreed in writing (establish a deadline). The Buyer will need to return the goods if they've been delivered already, and the parties will also need to work out how to deal with costs incurred by the Seller to ship the Goods or with goods that have already been used by the Buyer. These are all reasons to make sure that your sales contract does not contain open pricing terms.

- **Unilateral Price Increases:** The Seller has the legitimate need in a multi-year contract to have the flexibility to increase prices to cover its anticipated cost increases over time. However, if you are the Buyer, look out for provisions giving the Seller the unilateral right to increase prices. If the Seller insists on having the right to increase prices, try to negotiate a clear-cut formula for increasing prices (limited to once a year) based on objective criteria (e.g., based on the Consumer Price Index or against documented direct costs). Make sure that any price increases apply only to future orders; for example, negotiate at least 60 days' written notice for price increases. You can also negotiate for the right to terminate the contract in the event you don't agree to any price increase.

Buyers should also beware of any provision that gives the Seller the right to make unilateral changes to other important provisions. It's best to negotiate for the right to consent to such changes or if that is not possible, for the right to as long as possible a time gap before the modification takes effect, or even the right to terminate the contract. Keep in mind that it's difficult to argue against the Seller's right to change the payment terms based on objective criteria such as the Buyer's payment history, but even in the case of credit holds, the Buyer should try to negotiate as long a period of advance notice as possible to give the Buyer a chance to resolve any issues so that the credit hold can be lifted.

- **Dealer Support (Distributor Agreements):** These provisions are sometimes found in Distributor Agreements, and reduce the purchase price in the "hope" that the distributor will pass along the discount to its customers (e.g., temporary wholesale price reductions, promotional allowances, reimbursement for cooperative advertising plans, etc.). These are generally permissible under US antitrust law as long as the distributor retains the right to set its own resale prices. Be wary of dealer support provisions that "require" pass-through or are conditioned on compliance with minimum resale pricing.

- **Most Favored Customer (MFC) Pricing:** This is sometimes called Most Favored Nation or MFN pricing, a misnomer based on the analogy to the free trade concept. Basically, an MFC price clause promises that the Seller will offer the Buyer pricing that is no worse than the pricing offered to its other customers. While this sounds great for the Buyer, the Seller can easily skirt this requirement by adding that MFC treatment will only be afforded to customers that purchase like quanties of like goods based on similar terms and conditions.

Payment Terms

(a) The Buyer shall pay for the Goods as follows:

    (i) [20] percent of the Purchase Price upon execution of this Agreement, and

    (ii) the balance of the Purchase Price net 30 days from the date of delivery of the Goods to the Delivery Point.

Payment terms dictate the manner and timing of payment of the purchase price of the Goods, and are negotiated based a number of factors: the size of the transaction, creditworthiness of the Buyer (i.e., the ability of the Buyer to pay), creditworthiness of the Seller (i.e., the ability of the Seller to deliver, based on its track record and credit history), back-to-back obligations of the Seller to its suppliers, cash flow requirements, and bargaining leverage of the parties.

Subsection (a) stipulates hypothetical payment terms requiring a partial advance payment and the balance due "Net 30 days." Net 30 means that the Buyer has until 30 days after the date of delivery of the Goods to make payment. It's important to remember that if the parties don't explicitly agree to payment terms (i.e., the sales contract is silent on the payment term) that UCC Article 2 will fill in the gaps and require payment to be made upon delivery. Therefore, Buyers should not assume if the contract is silent on the payment term, that it can make payment "whenever."

(b) The Buyer shall pay interest on any amount due to the Seller which is not paid when due at two (2) percent above the prime rate as declared by [insert name of bank] prevailing from time to time, or the maximum rate permitted by law, whichever is less.

Subsection (b) requires the Buyer to pay interest on late payments. It also contains a safety valve to make sure that the interest rate charged does not violate any usury (excessive interest) laws.

(c) The Seller may [may not] set off any amounts due to the Seller against any amounts due to the Buyer hereunder.

(d) The Buyer may [may not] set off any amounts due to the Buyer against any amounts due to the Seller hereunder.

Subsections (c) and (d) explicitly allow either party the right of setoff, that is, the right of either party to deduct amounts owed to it by the other party before it pays what it owes to the other party. Subsection (c) tends to show up in documents (like sales confirmations) that favor Sellers, and subsection (d) tends to show up in documents (like purchase orders) that favor Buyers. If either party wants to restrict the other party's right of setoff, it's best to explicitly provide that such other party does not have any right of setoff (by substituting the bracketed [may not] language).

If the parties are entering into a distribution agreement, another possible clause might provide for the right of the Seller to change, in its discretion, the payment terms, from time to time upon giving the Buyer/Distributor prior written notice. The Buyer/Distributor might counter by negotiating the length of such notice, and by allowing such right only when there is objective proof of its deteriorating credit (e.g., late payment, etc.).

Common payment terms found in contracts for the sale of goods include the following:

Advance Payment

The Seller may want advance payment (prepayment) of part (downpayment) or all of the purchase price if it (i) is worried about the creditworthiness of the Buyer and/or (ii) needs the money because it has to quickly pay its own suppliers. Advance payment (in full) is the most secure form of payment for the Seller, especially if payment is made by wire transfer, which the Seller can confirm immediately. On the other hand, a Buyer that dispatches full advance payment puts itself at the mercy of the Seller; the Seller will have the money and still be holding on to the Goods.

Therefore, before the Buyer agrees to make advance payment, it should investigate the creditworthiness of the Seller, including the Seller's track record of making timely delivery.

Cash on Delivery (COD)

COD is a somewhat unwieldy payment method that requires the cooperation of the delivery company. In other words, the Buyer hands the delivery person a check for the purchase price when the delivery person delivers the Goods. While this method sounds failsafe, it's only as "secure" as the bad check that the Buyer hands to the third-party delivery person. Typically, third-party delivery companies disclaim any responsibility to inspect payment checks for issues like forgery.

Letters of Credit

The Buyer's first instinct is to not pay for the Goods until it receives them. But given the distances involved in international transactions, it's difficult to verify (in person) whether the Seller has complied with its delivery obligations. Letters of credit, or L/Cs, offer a partial solution to this dilemma. A detailed discussion of L/Cs is beyond the scope of this book, but basically, in an L/C transaction, the Buyer's bank acts on behalf of the Buyer (the holder of the L/C) to make sure the Seller doesn't get paid until it receives confirmation (in the form of certain documentation) that the Goods have been shipped.

Here's a slightly more technical explanation: An L/C is an "independent" (more on this later) undertaking by a bank (the "issuer" or "opening bank" in L/C parlance) to make payment on behalf of the Buyer (applicant) to the Seller (beneficiary) upon the presentation by the Seller (or its bank, the "presenting bank") of certain documents, which evidence the shipment of the Goods (e.g., bill of lading, commercial invoice, etc.). Payment under the L/C can be made at sight (immediately upon presentation) or deferred until the designated number of days after presentation.

L/C obligations are independent of the underlying sales transaction. This means that the bank's only obligation is to make payment upon or after the timely presentation of the stipulated documents. It has no obligation to check to see if the Goods match up (quantity or quality) with the documents, or to conduct a full-scale investigation of the authenticity of the documents.

The Seller should make sure a) the issuing bank is "a first-class bank acceptable to the Seller", b) the L/C is irrevocable, meaning that it can't be cancelled or amended without the consent of all the parties, and c) the L/C documents are "in form and substance acceptable to the Seller and its legal counsel."

If you are selling goods to a foreign Buyer, and you are concerned about the risks associated with a foreign issuing bank, you should try to negotiate that the foreign L/C be confirmed by a US bank, which is basically a guarantee by the confirming bank to make payment in case the foreign issuing bank defaults.

Payment on Credit

If the Seller is satisfied with the creditworthiness of the Buyer, it might decide to sell Goods on credit (i.e., deferred payment terms). This is the least secure method of payment for the Seller (meaning the Seller dispatches the Goods before it receives any payment — the Buyer has the Goods and the money).

The sample payment terms contract provision stipulates "net 30 days," meaning 30 days after some triggering event. Depending on the credit risk of the Buyer, the parties can insert payment terms of Net 15, Net 45, or some other amount of time. Some payment term clauses give a prompt payment discount, for example, "2 percent 10, net 30," which means that the Buyer gets a 2 percent discount if it pays within 10 days; otherwise it should pay the full amount within 30 days.

For the sake of clarification, it's best to state what the triggering event is; for example, the date of invoice, shipment, or delivery. Another triggering event for long-term contracts involving lots of individual shipments might be the end of the month for all Goods shipped/delivered during that month. The date of invoice may be negotiated as well, buying some additional time for the Buyer.

Milestone payments

Any homeowner who hires a contractor knows not to front-load payments. Home improvement projects are completed in stages, and savvy homeowners try to negotiate payment terms that bear some relation to the work that's been completed so far. It's no different for B2B sale of goods transactions. Always look to spread out payments fairly, especially for contracts calling for time-sensitive deliverables or performance-based results. If you are the Seller, use objective criteria to judge performance results; avoid giving the Buyer the right to determine satisfactory performance "in its discretion." If you are the Buyer, try not to water down strong warranty or performance-based language by agreeing to front-load your payments; you'll only serve to take away some of the incentive of the Seller to perform.

Purchase Money Security Interest (PMSI)

A Seller who agrees to grant deferred payment terms is financing the sale of the Goods based on the creditworthiness of the Buyer. If the Seller is uneasy about the creditworthiness of the Buyer, it can secure payment of the purchase price by obtaining a security interest in the Goods (or the identifiable proceeds from the Buyer's resale of the Goods or any finished goods made by the Buyer from the Goods). In other words, the Buyer pledges such collateral to secure its payment obligation, much in the same way a homeowner pledges a home to secure payment of the mortgage. If the Buyer defaults on payment, the Seller has the theoretical right to seize the collateral, sell it and apply the proceeds to the purchase price.

Any transaction in which a debtor pledges personal property collateral to a creditor to secure an obligation (e.g., the repayment of a loan, or in this case the deferred payment of the purchase price) is called a secured transaction. In the above transaction, the debtor is the Buyer, and the secured party is the Seller. Secured transactions are governed by the individual state's version of Article 9 of the Uniform Commercial Code (UCC), which governs the formation and enforceability of security interests (a.k.a., liens, encumbrances, hypothecations, pledges, etc.), in personal property (and software, but not real estate).

Companies often need to pledge the same collateral to multiple parties, for example, to a bank that provides a line of credit and takes a security interest in everything, including after-acquired property. UCC Article 9 establishes a pecking order among competing creditors based on the order of "perfection" (discussed in more detail below, but basically the order in which the secured parties put the world on notice of their security interests, whether by filing a document called a UCC-1, taking possession, or some other authorized method). If the bank was in fact the first to perfect, then anybody who perfects after the bank has to line up behind the bank when it comes time to seize the collateral.

Fortunately, UCC Article 9 provides a leg up to sellers who provide financing for the purchase of Goods. Generally, a seller of Goods who takes a security interest in those Goods, in order to secure the payment of the purchase price of those Goods, has a "superpriority" security interest called a Purchase Money Security Interest (PMSI), a kind of security interest on steroids that allows the Seller to cut to the head of the line and trump any previously perfected security interests in those Goods.

Linkage among the collateral, the purchase price obligation, the amount of credit, and the security interest is crucial. For example, a security interest in machinery "A" that secures the payment of the purchase price of machinery "B" is not a PMSI. For inventory, the linkage can be quite broad and current PMSI rules allow for the cross-collateralization of inventory, where the credit extended to allow the Buyer to purchase one piece of a group of inventory in which the Seller has a PMSI can be secured by all the other pieces of inventory of that group of inventory.

Creating a valid and enforceable security interest (including a PMSI) is a highly technical undertaking, with lots of opportunity to make errors. It's best to work with your attorney to craft and file the proper documentation. Here is a basic outline of the required steps.

The two main steps are attachment and perfection.

- **Attachment:** There are three basic requirements to "attach" a security interest, that is, create a security interest that is enforceable against the debtor. First, the secured party has to give value (e.g., lend the money or equivalent action, like granting deferred payment terms to the debtor). Second, the debtor has to have the right to grant the security interest (if the debtor owns the goods, then it probably has the right). Finally, the debtor and secured party have to enter into an agreement (Security Agreement) containing specific language granting the security interest in the collateral.

    Depending on your legal services budget and your exposure as a secured creditor, you can work with your attorney to craft a stand-alone security agreement, which can be quite lengthy and set forth in detail the relative rights of the debtor and secured party with respect to the collateral. Or a bare bones "security agreement" can be as simple as including a one-sentence provision in the sale of goods contract stating that the Buyer grants to the Seller a security interest in the described Goods to secure the Buyer's obligation to pay the purchase price of the Goods. The bare bones approach leaves the relative rights of the debtor and secured party to be decided by the default provisions of UCC Article 9, which in some cases favors the debtor, and in other cases favors the second party.

- **Perfection:** Attachment is just the first piece of the puzzle. As a newly minted secured creditor, you'll also need to perfect your security interest in order to establish priority, or your place in the pecking order among other creditors who may have competing interests in the same collateral. Perfection describes the process where a secured party notifies the world at large of its security interest, in most cases, by filing a short document called a UCC-1 financing statement with the Secretary of State and County Recorder in the appropriate jurisdiction.

    The UCC provides other ways to perfect a security interest, for example, by taking control of certain collateral like deposit accounts and letter of credit rights, or possession of collateral like chattel paper, instruments, negotiable documents, money, and even goods. In most cases, however, it's simply not practical for the secured party to take pre-default possession of the Goods it is selling to the debtor, especially goods the Buyer will resell or incorporate into other goods. The pecking order of priority to the goods is determined by the order in which the multiple secured creditors perfect their liens, with a PMSI trumping all previously perfected security interests.

Quantity

(a) The Seller shall sell, and the Buyer shall purchase, the following quantities of Goods: [insert chart listing SKUs and corresponding quantities].

This is a typical clause providing for the quantity of Goods to be purchased in a one-shot purchase transaction. If the contract covers a wide variety of SKUs, then the provision can refer to an exhibit to be attached to the agreement that contains a more detailed list.

For distribution agreements or long-term supply agreements, the parties may include the quantity in the Individual Contract corresponding to each individual transaction. They can also mandate not only the annual Minimum Purchase Quantity (see below), but also include provisions mandating a minimum frequency of individual transactions, as well as the minimum order for individual transactions (see discussion on Principal Obligations above).

Requirements and Output Contracts

In some cases, Buyers that are genuinely concerned about securing a stable supply of hard-to-find goods enter into what is known as a requirements contract. A requirements contract is just like any other contract for the sale of goods, except that the Buyer undertakes to purchase from the Seller all of its requirements of a particular type of Goods for use in its business. The Seller is free to sell the goods to other purchasers, as long as it has satisfied the Buyer's requirements.

On the flip side, an output contract is a contract where the Seller undertakes to sell (and the Buyer undertakes to purchase) all of the Seller's output of a particular type of Goods. The Buyer is free to purchase from other suppliers as long as it has purchased the Seller's output.

UCC Article 2 imposes a good faith requirement in measuring the quantity. The Buyer must not demand, and the Seller must not force a sale, of such quantities that are "unreasonably disproportionate to any stated estimate or in the absence of a stated estimate to any normal or otherwise comparable prior output or requirements." The Buyer cannot buy whatever it feels like, and the Seller cannot unilaterally downshift or crank up production.

Most disputes arising from requirements and output contracts center around the interpretation of their distinguishing feature — the quantity provision. What if in the context of a requirements contract, the Buyer's business grows and it needs a quantity of Goods beyond the ability of the Seller to supply? Or what if in an output contract, the Seller has a genuine business need to increase its capacity beyond the ability of the Buyer to absorb? What if the Buyer finds a supplier that better suits its needs in terms of price or quality? These are the kinds of business issues that often make requirements and output contracts impractical in the small-business context. Furthermore, it's important to consult with your attorney because the enforceability of requirements or output contracts may also hinge on compliance with complex antitrust laws.

Delivery Terms

Shipping or delivery terms in a contract for the sale of goods dictate the "Delivery Point" when and where the Seller is deemed to have fulfilled its obligation to "deliver" the Goods, and the Buyer assumes control of and responsibility for the Goods. At the Delivery Point, the Buyer "takes over" in that it assumes risk of loss of and damage to the goods ("risk of loss"), as well as bears some or all costs (e.g., transportation, insurance, and export and import if applicable) associated with moving the goods beyond the Delivery Point.

(a) The Seller shall deliver and the Buyer shall take delivery of the Goods at the [insert location, such as the Seller's warehouse] ("Delivery Point"). Upon such delivery, [title and] all risk of loss and damage passes to the Buyer. The Buyer shall bear all charges, fees, and expenses incurred after delivery to the Delivery Point.

The Delivery Term provision specifies the Delivery Point, or the physical location where the Seller promises to deliver the Goods. Typically, the Delivery Point also defines where responsibility for the Goods transfers from the Seller to the Buyer. The Seller is responsible for the Goods up to the Delivery Point, and the Buyer is responsible for the Goods going forward from the Delivery Point.

For example, the Seller is responsible for transporting, insuring and all other costs to get the Goods to the Delivery Point. The Seller also bears all risk of loss and damage to the Goods up to the Delivery Point — the Seller is responsible if the Goods get destroyed, lost, or stolen prior to the Delivery Point. Once the Goods arrive at the Delivery Point, then the Buyer takes over.

The parties might agree to specify the Seller's facility as the Delivery Point; in this case, the Seller doesn't have to ship the Goods, but merely has to prepare the Goods to be picked up by the Buyer or its carrier at the Seller's loading dock. The Buyer is responsible for arranging and paying to transport the Goods to its own facility. If the parties specify the Buyer's facility as the Delivery Point, then the Seller is responsible for arranging and paying to deliver the Goods to the Buyer's warehouse or other designated location.

It's important for the parties to negotiate and then specify the delivery terms in the contract. If the contract is silent on the delivery terms, then UCC Article 2 deems delivery to take place at the Seller's facility, or if the parties know that the Goods are elsewhere (like a third-party warehouse), then at that other location. The Buyer that expects the Goods to be delivered to its doorstep may be in for a rude awakening if the contract is silent, because this means that the Buyer may be responsible for transporting the Goods from the Seller's facility, with the cost of such transportation possibly eviscerating any planned profit margin.

A Word about Title

While many sales contracts address the issue of when responsibility for the Goods shifts, fewer address the issue of when title (ownership) to the Goods passes from the Seller to the Buyer. UCC Article 2 leaves it up to the parties to negotiate this issue, but has a series of default rules that govern if the contract is silent. The sample contract provision above, however, reflects one such default rule in that title will pass upon shipment if the Seller delivers by making the Goods available at its facility, and upon delivery to the destination if the Seller delivers at another place. A host of secondary issues may be impacted by the threshold issue of when title transfers — for example, regulatory obligations triggered by ownership, the timing of sales and other taxes, and the Buyer's standing to sue or collect insurance proceeds. Work with your attorney to negotiate a title provision that makes sense for you.

(b) The Seller shall pack the Goods for delivery to the Buyer in accordance with the customary practices of the Seller.

In Subsection (b), the Seller promises to pack the goods appropriately for shipment. The sample contract provision favors the Seller because it allows the Seller to dictate the packing requirements. If you are the Buyer, you can negotiate to include objective packing standards, such as ones that conform to your industry standard, or perhaps you can dictate your own custom packing requirements.

If you are a small business that sells to large entities like chain stores, you'll likely be subjected to a litany of mostly non-negotiable, one-sided packing requirements that help the large Buyer in its supply chain management — requirements that cover everything from pallet size and configuration to radio-frequency identification (RFID) tags. Large Buyers often impose financial penalties if the Seller fails to comply. Carefully consider whether you can absorb these penalties and their impact on your bottom line. If your sales contract provides for an automatic deduction (basically a reduction in the Purchase Price, taken off at the front end) to cover potential non-compliance, then make sure that such deduction is the exclusive remedy for non-compliance (for a discussion of exclusive versus cumulative remedies, see Chapter 24).

Delivery Terms in International Sales Contracts

Many international sales contracts (i.e., contracts between an American and foreign company for the sale of goods) specify that delivery will be governed by "Incoterms 2000," published by the International Chamber of Commerce ("ICC"), a private organization. Incoterms 2000 is the current version of 13 commonly used shipment and delivery terms, which allocate the costs, responsibilities, and risk of loss of the shipment between the Buyer and the Seller based mainly on a delivery point designated by the parties. For example, the contract can provide that the Goods are to be delivered "EXW Seller's warehouse," meaning that the Seller's only responsibility is to make the Goods available "Ex Works," that is, at its warehouse to be picked up by the Buyer. The Buyer would be responsible for everything from that point onward — inland transportation in the Seller's country, export fees, loading costs, ocean or air freight, unloading, broker fees, customs duties, inland transportation to the Buyer's facility, insurance, etc.

Incoterms 2000 helps to provide uniformity to international sales contracts. But Incoterms 2000 does not cover every aspect of delivery, for example, the crucial issue of when the Buyer actually takes title to the Goods (notwithstanding wherever it takes physical possession of the Goods), but allows the parties the freedom of contract to modify or supplement Delivery Terms. Remember to check the official version of Incoterms 2000 (available at the ICC Incoterms 2000 official website — www.iccwbo.org/incoterms) when drafting or negotiating an international sales contract, even if you are being provided a previously used form.

Acceptance of Goods; Claims for Damage, Shortfall, etc.

(a) The Buyer acknowledges that it will be deemed to have accepted the Goods and to have waived all claims for any defect, damage, and/or shortage of the Goods, unless it notifies the Seller within [seven (7)] days of delivery of the Goods of any damage to, or shortage or other non-conformity of, the Goods [that is apparant from a commercially reasonable visual inspection], accompanied by satisfactory evidence ("Claim"). The Buyer shall make payment in full for all Goods as provided in this Agreement notwithstanding any Claim (subject only to the exclusive remedy set forth in Subsection (b) below), and follow the Seller's instructions regarding the disposal of damaged or non-conforming Goods.

Subsection (a) is a variation of Seller-drafted contract language that gives the Buyer a limited amount of time after delivery of the Goods to make a claim with respect to any defects, damage, or shortage to the Goods. The Buyer can negotiate to lengthen the time period if it needs more time to be able to conduct a sufficient inspection. This provision is not meant to replace the warranty provision (discussed below), and therefore Buyers can negotiate to clarify that the provision does not minimize any rights it might have under the warranty provision. Since it's not reasonable (and in many cases not practical or desirable) for the Buyer (or its warehouse personnel) to conduct a full-scale inspection or test of the Goods upon delivery (the Goods may be packed for resale or incorporated as components), the Buyer can negotiate to add the bracketed or similar language. The provision is really meant just to catch obvious errors such as bashed up or missing boxes, incorrect shipments, etc.

(b) In the event that a Claim is accepted by the Seller, the Seller shall at its option, and in full settlement of such Claim, repair any defective Goods or replace them with conforming Goods, replenish any shortage, or reimburse the Purchase Price corresponding to the defective Goods or shortfall in Goods (by set-off or any manner in the Seller's discretion). The Seller shall make delivery of any repaired, replaced or replenished Goods in the same manner as provided herein.

(c) Subsection (b) states the entire liability of the Seller, and is the Buyer's exclusive remedy with respect to any Claim.

Subsection (b) is a variation of standard language giving the Seller the option to repair, replace, replenish the goods, or reimburse the Purchase Price, depending on the nature of the Claim. Subsection (c) states that the repair, replacement, replenishment and reimbursement remedies are the exclusive remedies for any Claim. See Chapter 24 for a discussion of exclusive versus cumulative remedies.

Appointment of Distributor; Territory/Customer Restrictions — Distribution Agreements Only

(a) Subject to the terms and conditions hereinafter set forth, the Seller appoints the Distributor to be its [exclusive] distributor to sell, distribute and market the products described in the attached Exhibit [insert Exhibit number] and any modified or replacement models of such products (collectively, the "Goods") to customers in

Appointment of Distributor and Territory/Customer provisions are found in distribution agreements, which are sale of goods contracts in which the Seller/Supplier sells Goods to the Buyer/Distributor so that the Distributor can resell the Goods to its customers using the Distributor's own sales force (in-house or independent sales representatives). The sample provision also captures modified or replacement versions; the Supplier can't cut out the Distributor merely by tweaking the Goods or changing the label. Another approach is to add any products that perform substantially the same function as the named Goods. Some Suppliers appoint Distributors for entire product lines or for all of their products across all product lines. Yet others appoint different distributors for the same product in the same Territory, but with each distributor servicing a different sector of the marketplace.

Subsection (a) is a variation of standard language where the Seller appoints the Distributor to be its exclusive distributor (i.e., grants the Distributor the exclusive right to purchase and then resell the Goods) to customers in a defined geographic territory (Territory).

(b) Notwithstanding the above, the Seller expressly reserves the right to sell to the customers in the Territory listed in the attached Exhibit [list Exhibit number] (the "Excluded Customers"). The Distributor shall promptly refer to the Seller any sales leads it receives or becomes aware of relating to an Excluded Customer. The Distributor acknowledges and agrees that it is not entitled to any compensation for any sale made to an Excluded Customer.

Subsection (b) provides an exception to Subsection (a), reserving the right to the Supplier to sell to certain "house accounts." These might include previously established accounts (i.e., accounts that pre-date the distribution agreement), government accounts, Original Equipment Manufacturer (OEM) customers, private label accounts, and the right to sell to national accounts with headquarters located in the Territory.

The distribution right can also be restricted by any of or a combination of the other criteria below:

- **Specifically Listed Customers:** In this case, the Distributor has the exclusive right to sell to customers identified by name (e.g., "to the customers set forth in the attached Exhibit").

- **Market Segmentation:** Another way is to limit distribution to customers identified by market segmentation (e.g., "to club stores," "the specialty food trade," or "to consumers [i.e., retail] only").

- **Industry Category:** In this case, the Distributor can only sell to customers identified by industry category (e.g., "to customers in [SIC Code category]").

- **Customer Use:** This one is hard to enforce — limiting resale to customers defined by the customers' use of the product (e.g., "to customers for use in [list the application]").

- **Area of Primary Responsibility:** Sometimes, rather than restrict a Distributor's geographic Territory, it is assigned an Area of Primary Responsibility or APR. The distributor must meet negotiated sales targets in the APR, but is free to sell in areas outside of its APR, and typically turns over a portion of the profits from such sales to the primary distributor in so-called profit passover arrangements.

Other Provisions Relating to the Appointment of a Distributor

(a) The Distributor shall not:

  (i) solicit orders for or sell the Goods to any person located outside the Territory; or

  (ii) sell the Goods directly or indirectly to any entity which it knows or has reason to know will resell the Goods outside the Territory. The Distributor shall promptly refer to the Seller any inquiries or orders for the Goods it receives from outside the Territory.

(b) The relationship of the Seller and the Distributor hereunder is that of independent contractors, and neither party is the partner, joint venturer, employee, franchisee, agent, or legal representative of the other party. The Distributor has no authority to assume, incur, or create any express or implied warranty, liability, or obligation on behalf of the Seller.

(c) The operations of the Distributor are subject to the sole control of the Distributor. All persons employed (the "Distributor Employees") or retained by the Distributor are deemed employees or representatives of the Distributor, and not of the Seller. The Distributor shall, at its own expense,

  (i) provide such office space and facilities, and hire and train such Distributor Employees or representatives, as may be necessary to carry out its obligations under this Agreement,

  (ii) cover all Distributor Employees under any applicable social benefit laws (including workers' compensation and applicable state disability insurance); and

  (iii) make any and all payroll deductions and contributions that may be required with respect to the Distributor Employees.

Sales Outside of Territory Prohibited

In some cases, the Seller or manufacturer will establish a network of independent distributors, with each distributor responsible for its own geographic territory. The Seller will sometimes include Subsection (a) to prevent its distributors from encroaching into its other distributors' territories.

The Distributor can counter several ways:

- **Profit Share:** If the Distributor knows that it has potential customers outside of its Territory, it can negotiate to carve these customers out for itself. The degree to which the exclusive distributor (in the territory where the customer is located) has already made contact or progress with these customers may be a factor in whether the parties can make a deal to split any profit between the two distributors. Of course, you also have to deal with order procedure (e.g., who ships, who invoices, etc.), not to mention how the parties will allocate any negative impact from these transactions, including the customer's credit risk.

- **Seller Transshipment:** This is the reverse of the sample contract requirement that the Distributor not ship outside of its Territory. Here, the Distributor negotiates a provision requiring the Seller to monitor and try to prevent the indirect unauthorized shipment of the Goods into the Territory, which is no easy task in this seamless world economy.

- **Independent Contractor Status:** Subsection (b) confirms that the Seller and the Distributor are independent contractors, and that the Distributor has no authority to bind the Seller. This means that the Seller is not obligated to back up the Distributor if the Distributor grants any warranty to its customers that goes beyond what the Seller has given to the Distributor. Subsection (c) is a belt and suspenders provision that confirms the independent contractor relationship between the Seller and the Distributor.

For example, large chain retailers often demand that manufacturers provide all manner of support for product placement on store shelves (e.g., free fills, end cap fees, coupon support, etc.). To the extent that this type of support is being provided, this provision allows the parties to "expressly set forth" in an exhibit both the kind and the level of support being provided. The bracketed language requires the Distributor to provide documentation proving that the financial support is being used in the authorized manner. I've drafted so that the proof of performance has to be satisfactory to the Seller, which is subjective. You can also have proof of performance be whatever is customary per industry standard.

(d) Except as expressly set forth in attached Exhibit [insert Exhibit number], the Distributor is solely responsible for all costs and expenses related to the marketing and distribution of the Goods and for performing its obligations hereunder. [The Distributor shall provide proof of performance of all supported marketing efforts in form and substance satisfactory to the Seller].

(e) The Distributor shall engage in the purchase and sale of the Goods for its own account and bear the credit risk of sales to its customers (including approved subdistributors).

Subsection (d) is a variation of standard language confirming that the Distributor is solely responsible for the cost of marketing the Goods in the Territory. To some people, this may seem self evident, but it's common in some industries for the manufacturer to provide its distributors with some level of marketing support (as usual depending on the relative bargaining power of the parties).

Subsection (e) clarifies that in a distribution agreement (versus a sales representative agreement, discussed below), the Distributor buys the Goods for its own account (takes title), then resells the Goods (transfers title) to its customers based on terms and conditions the Distributor negotiates with its customers. Keep in mind that a Distributor can transfer some of its risks (e.g., product quality, etc.), to its supplier via back-to-back obligations, it usually cannot transfer credit risk. The Distributor is the "seller" in its transaction with its customer, and bears the credit risk of the customer. And as the "buyer" of the Goods from the Seller, the Distributor assumes inventory risk — the risk that it won't be able to resell the Goods due to market conditions, etc. (although this can be negotiated, depending on the bargaining leverage of the parties).

Sales representatives and distributors both help the Seller (a supplier or manufacturer) market the Goods. But distributors and sales representatives perform different roles and bear different risks. A Distributor purchases and takes title to the Goods before reselling them to customers based on terms and conditions negotiated between the Distributor and the customers. The Distributor makes its profit based on the price mark-up it charges the customers.

On the other hand, a sales representative is a person or company that solicits orders for the Goods on behalf of the Seller (sales representatives can also work for Distributors). The sales representative never takes title to the Goods; rather the sales transaction takes place directly between the Seller and the customer. The Seller bears the entire risk, including credit risk, of the transaction. The sales representative makes its profit based on a percentage commission (or some combination of flat fee or advance, together with commission) negotiated between the Seller and the sales representative, to be paid by the Seller, typically, from collected sales proceeds. So the sales representative bears some risk, but the risk is that the Seller won't pay the sales commission, usually because the customer has failed to pay the purchase price for the Goods. Sales representative agreements are essentially agreements for the sale of services (i.e., sales and marketing services), and are discussed in more detail in Chapter 5.

(f) The Distributor may appoint subdistributors, provided that:

(i) such subdistributors are approved in writing by the Seller, and

(ii) any subdistribution agreement is coterminous with this Agreement.

The Seller in Subsection (f) is restricting the ability of the Distributor to appoint subdistributors (or independent sales representatives), sometimes for quality control purposes (e.g. marketing, use of trademarks, etc.). If subdistribution is allowed, then the Seller should make sure that the Distributor negotiaties subdistribution agreements that are coterminous (i.e., terminate at the same time) with the main distribution agreement since the existence of the subdistribution right depends on the distribution agreement being in place. If you are a Distributor that is negotiating with a subdistributor, you can also use this chapter to help you review your subdistribution agreement — the only thing is that you would "switch roles" because you are now the Seller *vis-a-vis* the subdistributor (who would negotiate from the perspective of a Distributor).

As the Seller to the subdistributor, you'll set your own terms and conditions, including the price (which will establish your profit). Your supplier can't force you to charge a specified price to your customers (including subdistributors), and neither can you force your subdistributor to charge a specified price to its customers. See Resale Price below for the antitrust implications of doing so.

You'll want to make sure that you don't obligate yourself to giving more than you're getting back-to-back from your supplier (e.g., more warranty, speedier delivery, more intellectual property rights, promise to repurchase inventory, etc.). While its legally okay for you to "give less" than you're getting, you'll need to determine for yourself if this makes sense on a provision-by-provision basis from both a business and ethical point of view.

(g) The Distributor shall furnish the following reports:

(i) no later than the 15th day of each month, a written report on its sales activity in the Territory during the immediately preceding calendar month; and

(ii) no later than July 15th and January 15th of each year, a written report on its sales activity in the Territory during the immediately preceding six (6) month period or calendar year, respectively. The Distributor shall include in each report information relating to sales volume to each customer, inventory levels, marketing efforts in the Territory, changes in the competitive and regulatory environment in the Territory, and such other information reasonably requested by the Seller.

Many suppliers will request detailed periodic sales reports from their distributors (Subsection [g]). The parties can negotiate to reduce or expand the scope of the information that is disclosed. For example, some Distributors are understandably reluctant to part with detailed information about their customers, sometimes treating the identity of their customers as secret. Some small businesses may need to get up to speed on the software that may be needed to generate the kind of statistical information that the Seller may be looking for. The Seller may also use this opportunity to obtain updated information about the Distributor, and ask for periodic financial statements, or at least for whatever information that the Distributor may be furnishing already to its lenders. In addition to historical information, the Seller might expand this provision to request purchase projections for future periods, whether or not the parties have agreed to minimum purchase quantity requirements.

(h) The Distributor shall, at its own expense, provide aggressive sales and marketing of the Goods in the Territory and superior service and training with respect to the Goods, as well as maintain facilites and the number of fully trained staff necessary to enable it to fulfill its obligations under this Agreement.

Aggressive Sales and Superior Service: Subsection (h) sets forth the general obligation of the Distributor to have the infrastructure and to work hard to build the business. The provision may be a little bit too vague or even superfluous from the Distributor's perspective, especially if it's already agreed to a Minimum Purchase Quantity requirement. Service and training are areas where the Distributor might be able to negotiate some support from the Seller, especially if the Seller has a specified program for the Distributor to follow. In that case, it would be reasonable for the Distributor to demand training for itself at the Seller's expense.

Antitrust Law Impact

Exclusivity (such as the right to sell in an exclusive Territory, discussed above) and other vertical non-price restraints not only impact intra-brand competition, they also impact inter-brand competition, and therefore fall under the purview of US antitrust law. The antitrust laws work not only to restrict monopolies, cartels, bid rigging, and price fixing, but also to curb more subtle forms of anti-competitive corporate behavior, such as improperly structured market allocation arrangements (for example, improperly structured territorial restraints).

Territorial restraints are not *per se* (automatically) legal or illegal, but have mostly been upheld if determined to be reasonable under a rule of reason analysis. Therefore, make sure to negotiate Territory provisions that are not overly broad in geographic scope or duration, and that serve a legitimate business purpose. For example, it's probably okay to carve out certain house accounts if the main reason is because the distributor is not equipped to service them.

Furthermore, weigh the pro-competive versus anti-competive effects of the provision. The pro-competitive benefits (e.g., giving the Distributor the incentive to robustly market without having to worry about free-riding by laggard distributors) should outweigh any anti-competitive effects (e.g., barriers to entry). Also, use the market share of the supplier as a touchstone; a Fortune 100 company imposing such restraints will have a bigger anti-competitive impact than a small company. Keep in mind that Areas of Primary Responsibility are also analyzed under the rule of reason analysis to see, among other things, if the amount of any profit passover bears a reasonable relationship to the marketing and servicing efforts of the non-selling distributor.

Minimum Purchase Quantity — Primarily Found in Distribution Agreements

(a) The Distributor shall purchase not less than the Minimum Purchase Quantity of Goods set forth in the attached Exhibit [insert Exhibit number] during the corresponding Relevant Period set forth in such exhibit.

(b) If the Distributor fails to purchase the Minimum Purchase Quantity during any Relevant Period, the Seller has the right in its discretion either to (i) terminate this Agreement (the "Termination Right") or (ii) convert the Distributor's exclusive distribution right to a non-exclusive distribution right (the "Conversion Right"), in either case effective [30] days after the end of said Relevant Period.

It's quite a leap of faith for a manufacturer to turn over to a third party exclusive Distributor the work of marketing and reselling its products in a geographic territory. To prevent the worst-case scenario of the distributor doing nothing to market the goods in the Territory, suppliers sometimes impose minimum purchase requirements (Subsection [a]) on their exclusive distributors, which require the Buyer/Distributor to purchase at least the pre-negotiated quantities during the Relevant Periods (e.g., annual, semi-annual, and/or monthly). The parties can negotiate a number of remedies for the breach of this provision, and these are discussed below.

Subsection (b) limits the Seller's remedies in the event the Distributor fails to satisfy the minimum purchase requirement. Seller-drafted agreements typically contain severe consequences for failure to meet minimum purchase quantities — any failure to purchase such quantities is treated as a material breach of the agreement that entitles the Seller to pursue any and all remedies. Instead of allowing the Seller to pursue any and all remedies, it allows the Seller to select from only one of two exclusive remedies. The Seller can either terminate the agreement or convert the exclusive distribution arrangement to a non-exclusive one. If the Seller is able to line up another exclusive distributor quickly, termination might be the better choice.

(c) All rights and remedies provided in this Agreement are cumulative and not exclusive of any other rights or remedies that may be available to the parties, whether provided by law, equity, statute, in any other agreement between the parties, or otherwise. However, the Termination Right or the Conversion Right is the Seller's exclusive remedy for the Distributor's failure to purchase the Minimum Purchase Quantity during any Relevant Period.

Subsection (c) makes sure that the Termination and Conversion Rights are the Seller's exclusive remedies for breach of the minimum purchase requirement, and prevents the Seller from pursuing damages or other remedies. For a more detailed discussion of exclusive versus cumulative remedies, see Chapter 24.

Of special note regarding distribution agreements: Many state laws make it very difficult to fire distributors and give terminated distributors the right to sell inventory back to the company that appointed it. In those states, this is a statutory remedy that cannot be opted out of by an exclusive remedy provision like Subsection (c).

Resale Price

[Distribution Agreements only] Vertical players in the supply chain (e.g., a Seller and Distributor) should avoid any provision that specifies resale prices to be charged by the Distributor to its customers. These provisions include:

Minimum resale prices

Provisions that establish a minimum resale price is illegal *per se* under US antitrust law.

Maximum resale prices

These provisions are also suspect, especially if they involve suppliers with large market share. Resale price ceilings are analyzed under the fact-driven rule of reason, where the pro-competitive benefits are weighed against the anti-competitive effects. See the "Antitrust Law Impact" box above for a more detailed discussion of this analysis.

The key word is "agreement," including concerted actions to vertically fix resale prices even in the absence of a written contract. Unilateral actions such as a supplier refusing to work with distributors that ignore its suggested minimum resale prices, pre-ticketing of goods before shipment, and monitoring resale prices may be acceptable. Also watch for illegal coercion — unsavory supplier practices like manipulating product allocation to retaliate against uncooperative distributors and outright blacklisting. There are a host of other practices that straddle the line. Look beyond the four corners of the contract, and if you find evidence of downstream price control, flag it and discuss it with your attorney.

Warranties

Sale of goods warranties dictate the extent the Seller will back up the Goods, and include express warranties and implied warranties. **Express warranties** are tangible expressions by the Seller about the quality of the Goods that form the basis of the bargain between the Seller and the Buyer (more on Express Warranties to follow).

Implied warranties

Implied warranties are warranties imposed by law (the State's version of UCC Article 2), even if the sales contract is silent. This means that if you are the Buyer of the Goods, that you are entitled to these warranties unless the Seller successfully negotiates to include disclaimer language in the sales contract. Sellers almost always try to include language in the sales contract disclaiming the implied merchantability and fitness for particular purpose warranties — this is allowed as long as the disclaimer is conspicuous (see the sample contract provision below).

The main UCC Article 2 implied warranties include the following:

- **Merchantability:** Unless conspicuously disclaimed (see discussion below), all contracts for the sale of goods contain an implied warranty of merchantability. Merchantability means that the Goods are, among other things, of such quality to be able to pass without objection in the trade as described in the contract and be fit for the ordinary purposes for which the Goods are used. For example, if you sell pens, you warrant that the pens will work to write or draw things on paper. There is no implied warranty that the pens will work underwater, unless you have reason to know that the Buyer needs to use the pens for that purpose (see Fitness for Particular Purpose below).

- **Fitness for a Particular Purpose:** Unless conspicuously disclaimed, the sales contract contains an implied warranty of fitness for a particular purpose, if the Seller has reason to know that the Goods are to be used for a particular purpose, and that the Buyer is relying on the Seller to furnish suitable goods for that purpose. So if you are a supplier of SCUBA equipment and sell pens to a SCUBA shop that needs pens that will work underwater, then you would be deemed to make an implied warranty that the specialty pens will in fact be fit to be used underwater.

- **Title:** In every sales contract, there is the implied warranty that the Seller is transferring clean title to the Goods — the Seller owns the Goods it is selling, and is transferring title to the Buyer, free of any security interests.

- **Infringement:** UCC Article 2 provides that if you are a Seller (merchant) that "regularly deals" in the kind of products you are selling to the Buyer (e.g., a distributor of a particular type of products), then you make the implied warranty that the Goods you sell do not infringe the patent, trade secret, or other intellectual property rights of third parties. If you are the Buyer, and furnish your own specifications for the Goods, then you have the implied obligation to indemnify the Seller against third party infringement claims arising out of the Seller complying with your specifications.

Express Warranties

(a) The Seller warrants to the Buyer that as of the date of shipment, the Goods conform to the Seller's standard specifications for the Goods or to any specifications agreed to in an Individual Contract.

Subsection (a) contains a standard express warranty that the Goods will conform to the specifications. The warranty provisions are drafted from the Seller's perspective; for example, note how the warranty is limited to the time of shipment. Note also Subsection (b), which contains the Seller's disclaimer of the implied warranties of merchantability and fitness for a particular purpose. For the Seller, it's important never to give any warranty stronger or longer lasting than the back-to-back warranty the Seller has from its supplier or the manufacturer.

(b) THE EXPRESS WARRANTIES, [IF ANY,] CONTAINED IN THIS AGREEMENT ARE EXCLU-
SIVE AND IN LIEU OF ALL OTHER WARRANTIES, EXPRESS OR IMPLIED, INCLUDING
WITHOUT LIMITATION ANY WARRANTY OF MERCHANTABILITY OR FITNESS FOR A
PARTICULAR PURPOSE, RELATING TO THE USE OF OR PERFORMANCE OF THE GOODS.
[THE GOODS ARE BEING SOLD "AS IS" AND "WITH ALL FAULTS".]

UCC Article 2 allows a Seller to disclaim the UCC Article 2 implied warranties, but
only if the sales contract contains conspicuous language (e.g., all capital letters) explicitly disclaiming such implied warranties. Subsection (b) sets forth typical disclaimer language. If the Seller is not making any warranties (express or implied), it
can state that the Goods are being sold "AS IS."

If you are the Buyer of custom-ordered items, or products specially
tailored by the Seller to fit your specific needs, then typically you have the expectation
that the Goods will be fit for your particular purpose. If this is the case, you should
not allow the Seller to disclaim the fitness for particular purpose implied warranty. It
may also be prudent to include a brief statement of the specialized purpose of the
Goods when describing the Goods in the contract (see Principal Obligations above).

(c) The Buyer shall

(i) notify the Seller within [ten] days after the discovery of any Goods that do not
comply with the above warranties, and

(ii) return the defective Goods, shipping and handling charges prepaid by the
Buyer, to a location designated from time to time by the Seller, together with
a statement describing the defect.

If the Seller determines that such Goods do not comply with the above warranty, it
shall, at its option,

(i) repair or replace the defective Goods or

(ii) repay the portion of the Purchase Price corresponding to the defective Goods.
The Seller's option to repair or replace the Goods or repay the portion of the
Purchase Price is the Buyer's exclusive remedy for any cause of action arising
under this Agreement.

Warranty Procedure/Exclusive Remedy

While Subsections (a) and (b) establish the extent of the warranty, Subsection (c) is
a basic provision dealing with warranty procedure. Drafted from the Seller's perspective, the Buyer must follow the warranty procedures and wait for the Seller to
make its determination. Subsection (c) also provides that the repair, replacement or
refund (i.e., repayment of the portion of the Goods that are defective) is the exclusive remedy. See Chapter 24 for a more detailed discussion of exclusive versus cumulative remedies.

There are several things a Buyer can try to negotiate to strengthen the Seller's
warranty.

Defects in Design, Materials, and Workmanship

Add the Seller's express warranty that the Goods will be free from defects in design, materials and workmanship for a specified time, preferably for longer than the four year UCC statute of limitations. Don't shortchange yourself if you are the Buyer; try to find out what kind of warranty the Seller has from its supplier.

Warranty for Repaired or Replaced Goods

Confirm that repaired or replaced Goods are also subject to the warranty. The Seller will probably try to limit the warranty period to the balance of the warranty period for the repaired or replaced Goods.

Shift the Logistical Burden back to the Seller

The sample contract provision requires the Buyer to ship the defective Goods at its expense back to the Seller. The Buyer can try to negotiate to shift the cost back to the Seller, especially for valid warranty claims.

Cumulative Remedies

The Buyer should make sure that the stated remedies (e.g., repair, replace, etc.) are NOT its exclusive remedies, but merely one of any number of cumulative remedies to which the Buyer may be entitled.

More on Express Warranties

Express warranties are tangible expressions by the Seller about the quality of the Goods that form the basis of the bargain between the Seller and the Buyer. Sellers are bound by such tangible expressions that are contained in the sales contract, but also by the ones lurking in their sales literature — e.g., brochures, websites, etc. Sellers should carefully audit their sales documents and communications because there is no requirement that statements explicitly contain the words "express warranty" or "the Seller warrants ... " in order to qualify as an express warranty.

While it's possible for a court to tag a tangible expression in a brochure as an express warranty, it's better from the Buyer's perspective to "cut and paste" the desired warranty language so that it's clear that the Seller is making the express warranty directly in the sales contract.

UCC Article 2 provides the following general ways a Seller can make an express warranty.

Affirmation of Fact/Promise or Description of Goods

The Seller makes an express warranty if it either (i) "affirms a fact" or makes a "promise" relating to the Goods or (ii) "describes" the Goods. For example, the Seller warrants in the sample contract provision that the Goods meet certain "specifications." By doing so, the Seller warrants that the Goods will conform to such specifications. Another example is a warranty that the Goods will be "free from defects in design, materials, and workmanship."

Sellers typically try to limit express warranties by placing a time limit on their effectiveness, for example, some period of time lasting a limited amount of time triggered by an event like the delivery of the Goods to the Delivery Point.

Samples

The Seller makes an express warranty if it provides a sample or model of the products being sold that the Goods will conform to the sample or model.

Sellers typically limit express warranties by specifically listing situations where the express warranty will not apply. The following are common exceptions:

Consumables and Wear and Tear

No warranty for the "consumable" portion of the Goods (e.g., batteries, etc.), or for ordinary "wear and tear," or accidental breakage.

Portions Sold by Others

No warranty for any portion of the Goods "sold by persons other than the Seller."

Altered/Misused Goods

No warranty for Goods "altered or modified" or "abused or neglected, or stored, handled, maintained, or used (i) in any manner inconsistent with the Seller's instructions, or (ii) if not specifically specified by the Seller, in a commercially unreasonable manner."

Goods Repaired by Others

No warranty for Goods "that have been installed/repaired/serviced by persons other than authorized personnel of the Seller or its designee."

Intellectual Property — Seller's Ownership

(a) The Buyer acknowledges that any and all patents, trade secrets, production methods, trademarks, service marks and other intellectual property embodied in, or used in connection with the Goods, including all improvements thereto (the "Seller Intellectual Property"), is the sole property of the Seller. The Buyer shall not, directly or indirectly through any other entity, (i) obtain or attempt to obtain in any country, any right, title, or interest in or to any of the Seller Intellectual Property, or (ii) challenge the Seller's rights, title, and interest in the Seller Intellectual Property.

Subsection (a) is a basic provision where the Buyer acknowledges the Seller's ownership of the intellectual property (IP) rights in the Goods, and promises not to do anything to interfere with or contest the Seller's rights, such as filing a patent or trademark on the Goods in its own name.

Subsection (a) works best in a straightforward sale of off-the-shelf Goods. If the Buyer is providing unique specifications it wants to protect, then the provision may need to be tweaked to allocate the ownership of IP rights. Another possible scenario requiring an attorney-crafted solution is a sale involving a Buyer who is authorized to make improvements to the Goods or that plans to incorporate non-commoditized Goods into its own products.

(b) The Seller does not grant to the Buyer any license or other right to or in respect of any Seller Intellectual Property, except as expressly set forth herein and necessary to carry out the express provisions of this Agreement.

(c) [Distribution Agreements only] The Buyer shall use the trademarks of the Seller only to advertise and promote the sale of the Goods in the Territory, and only in a manner approved by the Seller. The Buyer shall not alter, conceal, move, or remove any trademarks, trade names, or labels attached to the Goods.

Subsection (b) clarifies that there is no special license implied from the sale of the Goods. Any license, for example, to manufacture the Goods, needs to be specifically granted under the agreement, or a separate license agreement. That being said, Subsection (c) gives the Buyer/Distributor in a distribution agreement the limited right to use the trademarks of the Seller to help promote the Goods in its sales Territory. Subsection (c) can be expanded substantially (in the body of the agreement, an exhibit or incorporating some kind of Seller manual by reference) to incorporate a litany of Seller rules and regulations regarding the use of its trademarks.

Intellectual Property — Infringement

(a) In the event of any claim against the Buyer asserting that the Goods infringe any patent, trade secret, trademark, copyright, or other intellectual property right of any third party ("Third Party IP Rights"), the Seller has the option to: (i) procure for the Buyer the right to continue the sale and/or use of the Goods, (ii) replace or modify the Goods so as not to infringe such Third Party IP Rights, while conforming, as closely as possible, to original specifications (iii) remove said Goods and refund the corresponding Purchase Price to the Buyer, less depreciation, or (iv) discontinue the further supply of the Goods without liability.

Subsection (a) is a basic provision in a Seller-drafted contract establishing limited rights for the Buyer in case the Goods violate or infringe the patent, trade secret or other intellectual property rights of third parties. In such case, the Seller can either negotiate with the third party to have the Buyer continue to use the Goods, replace or modify the Goods so that they no longer infringe, remove the Goods and give a refund or simply discontinue the supply of the Goods. Right now the sample contract provision is silent as to who bears the cost of choices (i) through (iii) — for example, the Seller can have the Buyer pay for choice (ii) through a Purchase Price increase that reflects the cost of making the modifications.

An even more aggressive Seller might include an exception for infringement claims arising out of its compliance with the Buyer's design or specifications, or any modification of the Goods by the Buyer or third party, or use by the Buyer in a manner inconsistent with the Seller's instructions or guidelines.

Waiver of Implied Warranty/Exclusive Remedy

(b) SUBSECTION (A) IS IN LIEU OF ALL WARRANTIES, EXPRESS OR IMPLIED, OF NON-INFRINGEMENT. THE SELLER DISCLAIMS ALL SUCH WARRANTIES OF NON-INFRINGEMENT.

(c) SUBSECTION (A) STATES THE ENTIRE LIABILITY OF THE SELLER, AND IS THE BUYER'S EXCLUSIVE REMEDY WITH RESPECT TO ANY ALLEGED OR ACTUAL INFRINGEMENT OF THIRD PARTY IP RIGHTS.

The Seller is clarifying in Subsection (b) that it is disclaiming the implied warranty of non-infringement provided by UCC Article 2. This disclaimer, like the one disclaiming the implied warranties of merchantability and fitness for a particular purpose (discussed above) is displayed in the contract conspicuously (all capital letters). Subsection (c) confirms that the stated remedies in Subsection (a) are the Buyer's exclusive remedies. See Chapter 24 for a more detailed discussion of exclusive versus cumulative remedies.

This kind of exculpatory language, which is commonly found in sales confirmations and sales contracts drafted by Sellers, usually doesn't sit well with most Buyers. Most Buyers want to know that what they are purchasing doesn't violate third party IP rights, and think that the Seller is in a better position to bear this risk. These Buyers can negotiate to eliminate these types of Seller exculpatory provisions and perhaps go beyond the implied warranties of UCC Article 2 by including a more extensive indemnity provision. See Chapter 25 for a more detailed discussion of indemnities.

Liability Cap

The Seller's aggregate cumulative liability to the Buyer or any other person arising out of or relating to this Agreement is US$ [insert dollar amount].

This provision seeks to place a hard monetary cap on the Seller's liability (under any warranty, indemnity, etc.). The parties can negotiate a fixed dollar amount, or an amount based on a multiple of the Purchase Price or other consideration paid under the contract (which can be based on the aggregate consideration or an individual transaction). The Buyer may object to an overall cap because it will not have any recourse with respect to future Individual Contracts once the overall cap has been reached.

No Consequential Damages

The Seller shall not be liable to the Buyer or any other person for any indirect, incidental, consequential or special damages suffered by the Buyer or such other person in connection with or arising from this Agreement, any Individual Contract, the sale or use of the Goods, [any delay in delivery, damage to, defect, shortage, or nonconformity of the Goods, or any third party claim that the Goods infringe Third Party IP Rights [defined above], including but not limited to, lost revenues or lost profits, whether arising in contract, tort, negligence, strict liability, breach of statutory duty, or otherwise, and regardless of any notice of the possibility of such damages.

This is a variation of typical broad contract language that limits the kinds of damages (not the amount, which is covered by the liability cap) the Buyer may seek from the Seller for any cause of action arising from the sale or use of the Goods under any legal theory — e.g., warranty or indemnity or for any breach of contract, arising from any tort claim, etc. The provision takes indirect damages such as consequential damages (e.g., lost profits, etc.) off the table. Note that in addition to lost revenues and lost profits, some contracts will list things like loss of production, opportunity costs, loss of anticipated cost savings, lost business, and lost goodwill. While the wording "arising from this Agreement ... the sale or use of the Goods" is arguably quite encompassing, I put in bracketed language you can add to specifically cover things like delays in delivery, damage to the Goods, third party intellectual property claims, etc.

Insurance

Depending on the type of Goods and the relative bargaining power of the parties, sale of goods contracts sometimes contain provisions that require either or both parties to obtain third-party liability insurance to cover things like personal injury or death and property damage caused by the Goods or the activities under the contact. While the prototypical example is a Buyer who seeks recourse under the Seller's policy if the Buyer is damaged by defective Goods, the sample contract provision below contemplates the reverse situation — an also common scenario where a Seller, which is worried about the consequences of having a third party Distributor market and resell its Goods, requires the Distributor to have insurance to cover its activities under the contract. The decision to include an insurance requirement may also hinge on how secure you may feel about any indemnity you may have negotiated in the contract.

You won't be able to negotiate the insurance contract provision in a vacuum. You'll need to understand the parameters of the coverage and limitations of the applicable insurance policies (documents issued by third parties), and work with your attorney and insurance adviser to craft contract language that will work within the confines of such parameters. Either that, or negotiate with your counterparty to make them change the parameters or find another carrier that offers parameters you can live with. Just an extreme example to make a point ... you won't have recourse if your counterparty's policy doesn't cover the type of claim you are making, no matter how successful you are in negotiating being named an additional insured.

(a) The Distributor shall, at its expense, obtain and maintain a comprehensive general liability insurance policy with respect to the Goods and its activities under this Agreement (the "Policy"), from an insurer (the "Insurer") and with such policy limits and coverage as may be approved in writing by the Seller, including, but not limited to, the requirements that (i) the Insurer be rated "AAA" or better in Best's Insurance Reports, (ii) the Policy names the Seller as an additional insured, and (iii) the Policy require at least 30 days prior written notice to the Seller of any expiration, cancellation, or modification of the Policy. The Distributor shall, upon the Seller's request from time to time, forward to the Seller certificates evidencing the existence of such Policy.

Subsection (a) is a basic provision where one party (in this case, the Distributor) promises to maintain liability insurance (Policy). At a minimum, the provision should do several things. First, it gives the other party (in this case, the Seller) the right to approve the Insurer, as well as the policy limits and coverage. Sometimes, the parties will negotiate the coverage and policy limits in advance and put them right in the contract (e.g., $2 million in the aggregate, $1 million per occurence). Second, it names the other party as either an "additional named insured" or "additional insured" (see "Additional-Named Insured versus Additional Insured" box below). Third, it requires that the other party have certificate holder status, which will allow it to be notified of any premature cancellations or modifications to the Policy. Typically, under most policies only the first named insured (in this case, the Distributor) is notified in this way.

(b) The Distributor shall forward to the Seller, no less than [60] days before each expiration date of such Policy, satisfactory evidence that such Policy has been renewed and that the required insurance premiums have been paid.

Some form of Subsection (b) sometimes appears in sale of goods contracts to assure the other party that the insured party has taken the necessary steps to keep the insurance in place, instead of letting it lapse. The last sentence of Subsection (a) above about the insurance certificates fulfills the same function, but on an *ad hoc* basis.

Insurance certificates typically confirm very basic information such as coverage limits and coverage periods, as well as confirming the holder's status under the Policy (e.g., additional insured, etc.). Keep in mind that these certificates don't convey any rights by themselves, in the way that a contract, or the Policy itself does. For example, if you really want to be sure that you are covered as an additional insured, not to mention see what types of claims are covered or excluded, then you should ask to see the endorsement. Remember that endorsements can vary greatly depending on the insurer (see Additional-Named Insured versus Additional Insured box below).

Keep in mind that general liability insurance won't cover everything. For example, while the policy may (or may not) cover product liability claims, most general liability policies do not cover product recall claims, which can be extinction-level events for unprepared small businesses. If you are a distributor of Goods with high recall risk (e.g., food, consumer products, etc.), find out if your supplier has a dedicated product recall insurance policy, and negotiate to have that policy cover you and the Goods you are dealing. Work with your attorney and insurance advisors because individual policies will vary in terms of coverage, limits, etc.

Policies can vary, among other things, in defining when coverage is triggered (e.g., determined by the named insured or government agency or arising due to a specific event) and dictating what costs are reimbursable (e.g., recall communications, overtime or expert expenses, retrieving and destroying defective product, extraordinary storage costs, shipping restored or replacement product, etc.). You should work with your advisors to come up with a sensible crisis management plan (e.g., a plan of action you can quickly execute to stave off further death or injury, adequate reserves of "self-insurance," etc.) and a effective contract indemnity from your supplier, because the cost of a product recall may be significant and easily eat up the policy limits of a product recall policy.

Additional-Named Insured versus Additional Insured

This is a basic summary of the differences; the ramifications are complex and may greatly impact both your ability to recover and the extent of your recovery, so consult with your attorney and insurance advisers to determine which is best for your situation.

If you are added to the Policy as an additional-named insured, this means that you have the same basic "owner" status as the first-named insured (i.e., the owner of the Policy), except to the extent that the Policy allocates certain rights and obligations to the first-named insured. While this may mean that you are afforded more rights than a mere additional insured, it also means that, depending on the Policy, you may shoulder some of the obligations (e.g., pay premiums if the first-named insured defaults, etc.).

If you are added to the Policy as an additional insured, this means basically that the insurance company will cover you (provided of course the claim is covered and the claim is within the policy limits, etc.) for vicarious liability, that is, if you are sued because of injury or property damage caused by the first-named insured. It's not enough to gloss over the insurance contract provision. If you are an additional insured, know what you are getting, and if you don't like what you're getting (for example, you want to be covered for your own actions, as well as for vicarious liability), then you have to negotiate to get it. If you are the first-named insured, know what you are giving.

Make sure there is enough aggregate coverage for both the named and additional insureds. Another thing for additional insureds to keep in mind is not to automatically assume that a Policy will grant identical coverage for you as for the named insured — some policies may cover certain types of claims for a named insured, but exclude them for an additional insured. Additional insureds should also note that not all additional insureds are created equal — some endorsements may provide coverage not only for vicarious liability but

---

also for injury or damage caused by the additional insured; yet others may exclude coverage for vicarious liability if the additional insured contributed in any way to the injury or damage. Another big issue to investigate is whether the Policy requires an additional insured to exhaust its own insurance before it will pay a claim. Work with your attorney and insurance advisors to analyze and determine the best course of action for you.

Termination

See Chapter 23 for a detailed discussion of provisions covering termination for cause, bankruptcy, etc. You should consult with your attorney because state law may make it difficult to terminate distribution agreements, for example, requiring the supplier to repurchase unsold inventory. The sample provision below deals with the conduct of the parties after termination of a distribution agreement.

Upon the expiration or termination of this Agreement, all of the Distributor's indebtedness to the Seller becomes immediately due and payable without further notice or demand. Furthermore, the Distributor shall immediately:

(a) permanently cease all marketing and sales activity of the Goods, including, but not limited to, permanently cease the use of any of the Seller's trademarks, trade names, and other intellectual property rights; and

This post-termination provision is drafted from the Seller's perspective. It provides that all amounts due from the Distributor to the Seller are due upon termination. The Distributor can negotiate to qualify this provision to clarify that it has no obligation to immediately pay any amounts that are the subject of any dispute regarding the Goods, particularly in the event the Distributor is terminating the Agreement due to the Seller's breach.

Subsection (a) calls for the Distributor to cease all marketing activity for the Goods after termination. The Seller wants to protect its goodwill and trademarks in the Territory. It doesn't want a possibly disgruntled or desperate post-termination distributor to handle or dump the Goods. The Seller also doesn't want the terminated distributor to interfere with the marketing operations of any new distributor that might take over.

The Distributor will counter that it's not fair to require it to maintain inventory (either generally or through a Minimum Purchase Quantiy requirement), and then prevent it from selling it off, even if the contract is being terminated because of the Distributor's breach. Usually, the parties end up negotiating some variation of an arrangement that either allows the Distributor to sell off the balance of the inventory in the "ordinary course of business through its normal sales channels," or the Seller to repurchase any remaining inventory that is "in good, salable condition, previously fully paid by the Distributor, at such prices and other terms to be mutually agreed."

(b) The Distributor shall immediately return to the Seller all originals and copies of all data, drawings, documents, materials, samples and other information obtained or discerned by the Distributor in connection with this Agreement.

(c) Upon the expiration or termination of this Agreement, the Seller may engage in any and all dealings with customers who had previous contact and/or dealings with the Distributor, and the Distributor is not entitled to any compensation with respect thereto.

Subsection (b) is similar to the kind of provision you might find in a non-disclosure agreement where the recipient of secret information is required to return all originals and copies to the owner of the information.

Subsection (c) clarifies that the Seller is free after the expiration or termination of the contract to sell Goods to the customers in the Territory, either directly or through a new distributor, and that the Distributor is not entitled to any profit from those sales. This provision can be a source of significant contention between the parties.

Non-competition — Primarily Found in Distribution Agreements

The negotiation of non-competition clauses is often contentious. The parties will bring various levels (quantity and quality) of pre-established customer relationships and other goodwill to the table; parity is rare. Hopefully, the parties will work hard to build the market and secure new customers. And while the parties can argue about how much a party should take credit for any success, it's human nature to want to prevent the other party from exploiting any success for any purpose other than to further their mutual interests, especially after the end of the business relationship (i.e., expiration or termination of the contract).

(a) In consideration of the [exclusive] engagement of the Distributor under this Agreement, the Distributor agrees that during the term of this Agreement and for [one (1) year] after the expiration or termination of this Agreement, the Distributor shall not (i) market, promote, distribute, act as sales representative for, import, or purchase for resale in the Territory any products that compete with the Goods or (ii) render services to, or become a partner or owner of, any person or entity that engages in or contemplates engaging in the competitive activities described in subsection (i) above. In the event a court determines this non-compete provision unenforceable as to geographic scope or duration, then the court has the power to reduce the geographic scope or duration to the extent necessary to render the provision enforceable. The Distributor acknowledges that the remedies at law for any breach of this provision would be inadequate and agrees that the Seller is entitled to injunctive relief to enforce any of the provisions of this Paragraph.

This is a variation of contract language that seeks to prevent the Distributor from competing with the Seller. Note how the clause imposes the non-compete obligation both during the term and for some time after the term of the contract.

Sellers and Distributors may see eye-to-eye about the obligation not to compete during the term of the contract. The Seller doesn't want competitors to freeload off of its goodwill. And for exclusive distributors, the non-compete is a kind of *quid pro quo* for the right to exclusivity.

The parties usually see less eye-to-eye about the time period after the expiration or termination of the contract. Some of the disagreement may arise from the way the parties define post-contract competition.

One way is to base it on customer relationships — for example, to restrict the Distributor's post-contract contact with certain customers. However, this approach may be unwieldy because the parties may have starkly contrasting views on attribution — for example, if the Distributor is primarily responsible for bringing in a customer, why shouldn't it have the right to continue to deal with that customer? And even if the Distributor didn't bring in a particular customer, why shouldn't it be allowed to deal with it on non-competitive products?

The sample contract provision, however, allows the Distributor to deal with anybody in the Territory (even customers brought in by the Seller/supplier) as long as it doesn't sell or promote (or help somebody else sell or promote) competitive products in the Territory.

Take extra care when negotiating non-competition provisions (particularly with geographic scope and duration). Courts have a tendency to scrutinize these provisions closely, and are likely to determine unenforceable any provision that covers too much territory or time — an extreme example would be a provision that restricts the Distributor from selling competitive products "anywhere in the world for a period of 50 years after the expiration or termination of this Agreement." An unenforceable non-compete provision could jeopardize the enforceability of the entire contract. I've inserted severability language allowing a court to alter the terms of an overreaching non-compete provision to salvage the provision (and the entire agreement). See Chapter 25 for a more detailed discussion of severability.

5

SALE OF SERVICES

OVERVIEW

This chapter will focus on provisions typically found in contracts for the sale of services. As you can imagine, there is great variety in service agreements (and contract provisions), given the size and breadth of the service sector. "Services" run the gamut, and include everything from equipment maintenance, to outsourced data entry, legal work and accounting, to sales and marketing services. In this chapter, I discuss contract provisions typically found in **sales representative agreements**, which are commonly used by large and small businesses to retain the sales solicitation services of independent (non-employee) salespeople.

One way to think about sale of services contracts is to think of them as a variation of a sale of goods contract (discussed in Chapter 4). Instead of selling physical Goods, the seller sells Services — for example, a sales representative sells sales solicitation services to the company that he, she, or it represents, and is typically paid a success-based sales commission. That the Services happen to include the solicitation of customers or clients on behalf of the company for the sale of physical products (or other services) is just part of the sales representative's job description. To avoid any confusion, I refer to the seller of Services as the "Service Provider." While many Service Provider-drafted contracts refer to the buyer as the "Customer" or "Client," for the purposes of this chapter, I refer to the buyer as the "Company" (to avoid confusion with the customers or clients that the rep is soliciting). So again, in this chapter, the seller of Services is the "Service Provider," and the buyer of Services is the "Company."

While the Uniform Commercial Code does not cover the sale of services, many of the issues that arise in the sale of physical goods apply also to the sale of services

— for example, trying to define what is being sold (scope of work or services), quality and payment issues, etc. Given the breadth of the service sector, a one-size-fits-all approach doesn't work, but service agreements (including sales rep agreements) tend to share common characteristics and provisions. Common provisions include:

- **Front Matter:** Every contract typically has the front matter portion, which lists the names and addresses of the parties plus perhaps some recitals (introductory paragraphs). Please refer to the CD-ROM for a detailed discussion of front matter.

- **Principal Obligations:** There must be an undertaking to sell and to buy the Services in question, including a detailed description of the Services.

- **Price and Payment Terms:** The price and quantity of the Services to be purchased should be listed in the contract or in an exhibit to be attached to the contract. Services are typically rendered over a period of time, so the parties will need to negotiate appropriate payment terms.

- **Boilerplate Section:** Most contracts usually have (toward the end) a section of boilerplate (standard clauses) covering a laundry list of matters such as assignability, governing law, notices, severability, etc. Please refer to Part V and the CD-ROM for a detailed discussion of these and the provisions listed below. Of special importance to service agreements are provisions covering the following matters:

  - **Term:** Services tend to be rendered over a period of time, either because the Company requires continuous service or because the services by their nature must be provided in stages. The service agreement should dictate the term (length of time the agreement will remain in force), including any conditions for renewal (e.g., automatic annual renewals unless otherwise notified, or for sales representative agreements, perhaps renewal based on the Representative meeting minimum sales requirements, if any).

  - **Termination:** Service contracts should contain provisions addressing termination for cause, bankruptcy, etc. The sample termination provision in this chapter shows what a termination provision in a sales representative agreement might look like.

    If the Service Provider is an individual, be sure to address the status of the contract in the event of death or disability. Refer to Part V and the CD-ROM for a discussion of termination clauses and other boilerplate-type contract provisions.

  - **Remedies:** The parties should analyze and then negotiate the appropriate remedies for breach of contract. The Service Provider may want to negotiate a liability cap, limiting its liability under the contract to the contract fee amount. If the parties negotiate an exclusive remedy for a particular breach, then special care should be taken when drafting the cumulative remedies provision to carve out an exception for the exclusive remedy.

- **Force Majeure:** These provisions dictate the rights and obligations of the parties in case the Service Provider can't perform the Services due to an event beyond its control, like a nationwide transportation strike, severe weather, etc. See the CD-ROM for a discussion of force majeure provisions.

- **Delegation:** If you enter into a service contract to receive certain Services, then you probably expect or demand that your counterparty, the Service Provider, will be the one providing the Services. If you have any concern that the Service Provider will attempt to subcontract or delegate its obligations, then you should include an anti-delegation provision in the service contract.

- **Other Provisions:** Depending on the nature of the Services, the parties might consider the following other provisions:

  - **Confidentiality:** These provisions protect confidential information that a party to a service contract might gain access to during the term of the agreement. For example, a Service Provider like a consultant might need access to the Company's proprietary information (e.g., financial or business information) in order to perform the Services. Sometimes the Service Provider consultant needs to disclose its own proprietary information in order to complete its Services. For example, the Service Provider will want to protect the confidentiality of any proprietary methodology or process disclosed in its written reports to the Company. See Chapter 6 for a detailed discussion of confidentiality provisions.

  - **Representations:** Consider adding representations from the Company and/or Service Provider regarding its ability to enter into the transaction. These might include the following representations (some of these apply only to non-natural-person entities): Organization; Power and Authority to Run its Business; Enforceability; Consent of Third Parties/Government to Transaction; No Conflict with Corporate Documents, Contracts, or Laws. In you are entering into a service contract with an individual, then consider obtaining a representation about his or her US legal employment status (e.g., "The Service Provider is a United States citizen or currently possesses a visa (obtained from the United States Immigration and Naturalization Service) authorizing him to perform his obligations hereunder.") See Chapter 13 for a general discussion of these representations.

  - **Insurance:** The Company should make sure that the Service Provider has liability insurance adequate to cover its activities under the service contract. See Chapter 4 on the Sale of Goods (Insurance) for a discussion of insurance provision issues, including issues relating to the designation of the Company as an additional insured on the Service Provider's insurance policy.

- **Intellectual Property:** Service contracts, particularly sales representative agreements, should contain an acknowledgment that the Service Provider or Representative will take appropriate measures to protect the Company's intellectual property, including trademarks and service marks. See Intellectual Property — Seller's Ownership and Intellectual Property — Infringement in Chapter 4 for a discussion of these and related issues.

Remember that this is not a forms manual, but rather a guide to help you interpret the deal-point provisions of and spot issues in a variety of contracts. That's why I've organized the sample contract provisions in this chapter (and in all the chapters of this book) by topic, and without attempting to assign section numbers or letters to the provisions.

SAMPLE CONTRACT EXCERPTS
Principal Obligations — Service Agreement

The Service Provider shall provide the services described in the attached Exhibit [insert Exhibit number] (the "Services") in a competent, professional, and faithful manner and in accordance with the terms and conditions set forth in this Agreement.

This provision can usually be found at the beginning of the contract and sets forth the very basic obligations of the Service Provider to provide the Services, including a description or definition of the Services. These basic obligations are subject to the "terms and conditions" of the service contract, meaning that the parties also have to satisfy all of the other obligations covered by the other sections of the contract.

The sample contract provision states that the Services are described in more detail in an attached Exhibit, which can be quite lengthy if the services are highly technical. Or Service Providers sometimes incorporate by reference thick manuals contained in electronic format or in three-ring binders, meaning that they become part and parcel of the service contract. In either case, be sure to work with your attorney to review these lengthy documents to identify and then excise hidden, unfavorable legal language like disclaimers.

At the very least, consider adding language in the contract that the main body of the service contract will prevail in the event of any inconsistency between the main body and the non-technical portion of any Exhibit or manual, although this approach may have shortcomings in terms of dealing with provisions not contemplated by (and therefore perhaps not "conflicting" with) any provision in the main body. Attaching or incorporating such documents by reference without a careful review may work to unwittingly eviscerate warranties, indemnities, and other negotiated protections contained in the main body of the service contract. Also make sure your technical people sign off on the technical aspects of the Exhibit or manual.

Principal Obligations — Sales Representative Agreement

The Representative shall, in a competent, professional, and faithful manner, promote the sale [lease] of, and solicit orders for, the Goods in the Territory, identify and engage in regular contact with potential and existing customers in the Territory, and perform such other tasks related to the sales [lease] and marketing of the Goods. [The Representative shall close transactions for the sale [or lease] of the Goods in the minimum annual amount of [insert dollar amount or unit quantities].

This version describes the "principal obligations" of a sales representative. A sales representative (Representative) is basically a Service Provider that provides sales solicitation services. This sample contract provision describes the Services of a Representative broadly to include the solicitation of customers and orders and other related sales and marketing tasks. While it's not practical to list every task, some parties decide for the avoidance of doubt to include a more detailed list of Services — these might include intangible things like establishing and maintaining goodwill toward customers and potential customers, to more concrete tasks like attending specified trade shows, advising the Company of market/competitive conditions in the Territory, and introducing customer personnel to the Company.

Don't assume that your industry standard will automatically include or exclude certain tasks. Depending on the situation, it may be prudent to explicitly include or exclude certain tasks. For example, while some sales reps may not want to be involved in collections or claims (not the most pleasant topic for somebody whose job it is to stay upbeat and sell!), the Company may want the Representative to liaise with the customers to facilitate payment or settlement of the claim. If this is the case, it's best to explicitly include this service within the Services section.

Service Fee/Compensation — Flat Fee

Many of the same issues that arise with repect to the price and payment terms in the sale of goods also arise in the sale of services. Some of these issues are discussed below, but it's also a good idea to review the discussion on Purchase Price and Payment Terms in Chapter 4.

In full and complete compensation for the performance by the Service Provider of all of its obligations under and subject to the terms and conditions of this Agreement, the Company shall pay the Service Provider the following (against the Service Provider's invoice and, in case of reimbursable expenses, appropriate original receipts):

(a) a fee of [insert US dollar amount] to be paid in installments in the amounts and by the dates set forth in the attached Exhibit [insert Exhibit number];

[alternative] (a) the Company shall pay the Service Provider monthly in advance a fixed fee at the rate of [insert US dollar amount] per month; and

This is a variation of standard contract language providing for the payment to a Service Provider of a fixed fee.

Subsection (a) calls for the fixed fee to be paid in installments as set forth in an attached Exhibit. The parties can customize the installment amounts and due dates to reflect the completion of service milestones (based on objective criteria, or depending on the parties' bargaining leverage, upon the Service Provider's simple verification of completion, or at the other extreme, that the work has been completed to the Company's satisfaction). In addition, the Service Provider frequently asks for some kind of advance payment, and is more likely to negotiate front-loading the payments, while the Company (payor) is more likely to negotiate end-loading the payments.

The alternative Subsection (a), which is often found in service contracts for continuous service with regular work hours, also contemplates the payment of a fixed fee. It's drafted to provide for payment in advance at the beginning of each work period. Depending on industry standard and the bargaining leverage of the parties, it can be drafted to provide for payment in arrear at the end of each work period. You can also pay Service Providers on the clock (e.g., per hour like you would pay corporate attorneys). Keep in mind that salary-like fee structures and nine-to-five hours are hallmarks of employment (versus truly independent contractor status for tax purposes); work with your attorney to make sure you properly classify your workers — see the discussion on Independent Contractors later in this chapter.

If the service contract calls for any advance or up-front payments, then the Company should be sure the contract contains a provision that "claws back" or requires the return to it of any advance payment allocated to any portion of the Services not delivered prior to an early termination.

Sellers of services may need to raise their fees for the same reasons sellers of goods may need to raise prices (e.g., increased costs, etc.). For longer term contracts, it's often a good idea to include some objective criteria for increasing the service fee; for example, an annual increase based on the consumer price or other index.

Longer-term or complicated projects are also more prone to cost overruns, and the parties need to negotiate criteria to determine who should bear these. For example, the Service Provider should bear the increased costs caused by the Service Provider's own delays, and the Company should bear any increased costs arising from, for example, its delay in furnishing anything it is responsible for — specifications, parts, or approvals. No matter how the parties decide to allocate the burden, the Service Provider should provide ample advance notice of increased costs.

(b) The Company shall pay the Service Provider for reasonable and necessary expenses incurred by the Service Provider on behalf of the Company with the Company's prior written approval.

Subsection (b) contemplates the reimbursement of only those expenses incurred by the Service Provider with the Company's prior approval. As drafted, the Company exercises absolute or sole discretion whether to grant approval. The Service Provider can counter by modifying that the Company's approval cannot be "unreasonably withheld," and/or negotiate a list of the types of expenses that are reimbursable, for example, reasonable travel expenses for overnight business trips (e.g., coach air fare, etc.), business trip per diems, etc.

Service Fee/Compensation — Percent Commission (Sales Representative Agreement)

This group of provisions is a variation of standard Sales Representative Contract language regarding the payment of commission plus expenses to a sales representative (Representative) that sells Goods on behalf of the Company. It's not enough to provide just for the commission rate; to avoid ambiguity, the parties also have to consider the scope of the amount on which the commission will be paid, what transactions to exclude, when the commission will be deemed "earned," when "earned" commissions will be paid, as well as a variety of other issues. Consult with your attorney because state law may vary regarding permitted commission structures, and may impact when commissions are deemed "earned" or must be paid.

(a) In full and complete compensation for the performance by the Representative of all of its obligations under and subject to the terms and conditions of this Agreement, the Company shall pay the Representative the following (against the Representative's invoice and, in case of reimbursable expenses, appropriate original receipts):

(i) A commission of [insert percent commission rate] of the net invoice amount of the Goods sold to customers in the Territory pursuant to orders solicited by the Representative and accepted by the Company under this Agreement. The net invoice amount of the Goods is the gross sales price of the Goods after deducting all freight, handling and insurance charges, sales and other taxes, return credits, allowances, discounts, and rebates; and

(ii) Reasonable and necessary expenses incurred by the Representative on behalf of the Company with the Company's prior written approval.

The Representative earns compensation based on the commission structure negotiated between the parties. Keep in mind that the provision is subject to the other terms and conditions of the contract, for example, Subsection (e) below provides that the commission is earned only when the sales price is collected. While it's possible to have a fixed dollar amount commission per unit sold, the sample Subsection (a) establishes compensation based on the negotiated percentage of the net invoice amount of the Goods (i.e., Commission = decimal equivalent of percentage rate x net invoice amount).

The scope of the net invoice amount, which impacts the amount of commission, can be negotiated as well. The sample provision shows how the Company has reduced the scope by deducting things like freight, taxes, and allowances. For example, if the commission rate is 5 percent, and the total invoice amount of the Goods is $120 (consisting of $14 shipping and handling, and $6 sales tax), then the Representative would earn a $5 commission on the transaction (5 percent of the net invoice amount of $100). Keep in mind that some sellers reward prompt payment via a prompt payment provision — e.g., 2 percent 10, net 30 days, which allows the customer to save 2 percent off the sales price if it pays within 10 days, instead of 30. If the customer in our example exercises this option, it will save $2 off the sales price and pay $98. If the Representative expects to earn commission based on the original net invoice amount of $100, then it's best to clarify that no deduction for prompt payment will be taken off the net invoice amount for purposes of calculating the commission.

By the same token, the Company may wish to exclude from the net invoice amount (and therefore not pay commission on) the interest portion of purchase price payments for financed sales, as well as default interest or late payment fees paid by the customer. Another strategy is to negotiate to NOT pay any commission for transactions where the customer is very late in making payment, or to negotiate a reduced commission rate based on how late the customer makes payment. The Company's rationale for this position is that it must recoup some of the expenses incurred in chasing after the deadbeat customers. On the other hand, the Representative should walk away if the Company tries to negotiate to set off the amount of unpaid net invoice amounts (and collection costs) against future commissions — a very bad deal for the Representative since the commission amount is but a fraction of each sale, and the Representative can find itself in servitude for a very long time to work off the uncollected debt of just one bad transaction.

(b) The Representative is not entitled to any compensation with respect to sales to (i) any Excluded Customer; (ii) the Representative; or (iii) any person or entity affiliated with the Representative.

Excluded Transactions

Subsection (b) clarifies that the Representative doesn't earn any commission for Goods sold to Excluded Customers, or for sales made to itself or any affiliate, which can be clarified to include any family member, employee, subsidiary, parent company, etc. The Company can also clarify that no compensation will be paid with respect to orders cancelled or Goods refused, returned, or not shipped, which is consistent with the proposition that the commission is not earned until full payment by the customer (see Subsection (e) below). If the Company is aggressive, then it can also exclude the sale of samples, parts, or promotional items, close-out sales, sales made at less than regular prices, or sales involving terms different from the Company's standard terms and conditions of sale.

(c) The Representative agrees that the commission may be reduced from time to time by mutual agreement in order to facilitate the consummation of any given transaction.

(d) The Company has the discretion to determine, in case the efforts of a representative in a certain territory results in an order for the Goods from another territory, the extent to which any commission should be divided between two or more representatives.

Accommodation Transactions

In Subsection (c), the Representative acknowledges that the Company might have to take a cut (on the sales price) in order to close a transaction; for example, a loss leader transaction. While in most cases, the Representative's commission is automatically reduced (e.g., 5 percent of $90 is less than 5 percent of $100), the Company might consider negotiating to reduce the commission rate so that the Company can recoup some of its foregone profit margin or at least have the Representative "share" some of the pain.

Split Commissions

This provision gives the Company the flexibility to determine whether any commission should be split between two representatives. It can be used to force someone to share commission with a representative in another territory if the other representative is primarily responsible for a sale in the Territory; which is not necessarily a bad thing if the other representative opens up an account in the Territory that the first Representative had no chance by itself of opening. The provision also can be used to reward the Representative with a portion of the commission for sales to customers outside the Territory introduced by the Representative.

The Company can also invoke the provision to allocate the commission if a sale is made to a customer that relocates outside of its original territory, or a sale made in a territory based on an outside-the-territory central office purchasing decision. The sample provision gives the Company sole discretion in each instance, however, the parties can negotiate another structure, for example, a split commission for the first transaction, with one or the other representative to take over the account over time.

(e) The commission for an order is deemed earned only upon the Company's receipt of full and final payment thereof from the customer. In the event any adjustment (including as the result of a refund) or allowance is made with a customer, the Representative is entitled to commission based only on the finally adjusted amount, even if a larger amount was previously credited to the Representative. The Representative shall promptly return to the Company any previously paid commission overpayment.

When Commission Is Earned

Subsection (e) confirms that the commission is earned (i.e., the Representative's right to payment vests) only upon full payment of the corresponding purchase price of the order. The sample provision falls somewhere in the middle of the spectrum.

The Representative would prefer, of course, to have the commission vest upon submission or acceptance of the order, but from the Company's perspective, this may give the Representative the incentive to use high-pressure sales tactics without regard to customers' needs or creditworthiness. At the other end of the spectrum, a Company with a lot of bargaining leverage can impose a kind of waiting period — with the commission deemed earned only 10, 20, 30, etc., days after payment of the corresponding purchase price by the customer. This gives the Company a cushion period during which the Company can work out any quality issues, etc., with the customer, including refunds.

If the Company agrees with the customer to a downward adjustment of the net invoice amount (e.g., a partial refund) after paying the commission, then the sample provision requires the Representative to return to the Company the excess commission corresponding to the reduction in the net invoice amount. While the sample provision calls for the Representative to promptly return the excess commission, another way for the Company to recoup the excess is to "claw it back" by set-off against future commission earnings (it's best to avoid deducting the excess from the non-commission portion, if any, of the Representative's compensation, e.g., salary or wages).

Post-termination Commissions

The parties should consider how commissions will be earned and paid for orders placed around the time of the expiration or termination of the contract. Some of these orders may be delivered and/or paid for after the end of the contract, and it's important for the parties to have a clear understanding of what their rights and obligations are with respect to these "twilight orders." See Termination below for further discussion on this topic.

> (f) The Company shall pay any commission earned by the Representative per Subsection (e) above during each [month] by [the 15th day of the following month] against the presentation of the Representative's invoice.

When Earned Commission Is Paid

Subsection (f) sets forth the date of payment for commissions earned in the previous period (e.g., month, bi-weekly period, etc.). Some contracts add belt-and-suspenders language that no commission is deemed to be earned until the Goods have actually been received, accepted, and paid for by the Customer and that all disputes, if any, have been resolved. However, the additional language is superfluous if the contract has a well-written provision (Subsection [d]), which makes it clear when the commission is earned.

> (g) The Company has made no representation as to any minimum compensation obtainable by the Representative.

No Guaranteed Compensation

Subsection (g) clarifies that the Company has made no guarantee of minimum compensation obtainable by the Representative. If the Representative insists on minimum compensation, then the Company instead can consider paying some fixed level of compensation in addition to commissions. Keep in mind that a large fixed salary or wage in addition to commission may cause problems if the Company wants to classify the Representative as an independent contractor. If the Representative's main concern is consistent cash flow, it can negotiate that the Company pay an advance against commissions. Even if the parties negotiate an advance amount that they are reasonably confident that the Representative will achieve, the parties still have to consider and negotiate what happens if the Representative does not achieve enough sales in any given period to cover the advance.

Late Payments/Set-Off

(a) The Company shall pay interest on any amount due to the Service Provider [Representative] which is not paid when due at two percent (2 percent) above the prime rate as declared by [insert name of bank] prevailing from time to time, or the maximum rate permitted by law, whichever is less.

Subsection (a) requires the Company to pay interest on late payments. It also contains a safety valve to make sure that the interest rate charged does not violate any usury (excessive interest) laws.

(b) The Company may [may not] set off any amounts due to the Company against any amounts due to the Service Provider [Representative] hereunder.

Subsection (b) explicitly allows or disallows [bracketed language] the Company the right of setoff, that is, the right of a party (in this case, the Company) to deduct (and keep) amounts owed to it by the other party (in this case, the Service Provider or Representative) before it pays what it owes to the other party.

Appointment of Sales Representative Territory/ Customer Restrictions

(a) Subject to the terms and conditions hereinafter set forth, the Company appoints the Representative to be its [exclusive] [non-exclusive] sales representative to solicit orders for the sale of the products described in the attached Exhibit [insert Exhibit number] and any modified or replacement models of such products (collectively, the "Goods") to customers in [list geographic territory] (the "Territory"), and the Representative accepts such appointment. As such, the Representative shall perform the Services (described in the Principal Obligations — Sales Representative Agreement section above).

Appointment of Representative and Territory/Customer provisions are found in sales representative agreements, whereby the Company appoints the Representative as its exclusive or non-exclusive sales representative for the Goods in a designated Territory. Subsection (a) also captures modified or replacement versions of the Goods; the Company can't cut out the Representative merely by tweaking the Goods or changing the label. Another approach is to add any products that perform substantially the same function as the named Goods. Some Companies appoint Representatives for entire product lines or for all of their products accross all product lines. Yet others appoint different representatives for the same product in the same Territory, but with each representative servicing a different sector (e.g., perhaps different distributors or groups of distributors) of the marketplace.

(b) Notwithstanding the above, the Representative is not appointed as the sales representative with respect to the customers in the Territory listed in the attached Exhibit [list exhibit number] (the "Excluded Customers"). The Representative shall promptly refer to the Company any sales leads it receives or becomes aware of relating to an Excluded Customer or a customer located outside of the Territory. The Representative acknowledges and agrees that it is not entitled to any compensation for any sale made by the Company to an Excluded Customer or customer located outside of the Territory.

(c) The Representative shall, at its own expense, provide aggressive sales and marketing of the Goods in the Territory and superior service and training with respect to the Goods, as well as maintain facilites and the number of fully trained staff necessary to enable it to fulfill its obligations under this Agreement.

Subsection (b) provides an exception to Subsection (a), reserving the right to the Company to sell directly to certain "house accounts" in the Territory without paying the Representative any compensation. These might include previously established accounts (i.e., accounts that pre-date the sales representative agreement), government accounts, OEM customers, private label accounts and the right to sell to national accounts with headquarters located in the Territory.

Independent Contractor Status

One of the most important issues that arises when entering into a service contract is whether the Company treats the Service Provider as an independent contractor or an employee. Small businesses sometimes prefer independent contractors because of the reduced paperwork, tax burden, and expense (for example, typically only employees get the health insurance). Generally, the Company must withhold and/or pay income, Social Security, Medicare, and unemployment taxes on payments made to employees, but not to independent contractors. An incorrect determination by the parties may result in unexpected tax liability, penalties, and paperwork, not to mention from the Service Provider's perspective, health benefits a true employee could have had if he or she was correctly classified as an employee in the first place. For Service Providers that enjoy the freedom of being an independent contractor, if reclassified as an employee, the right to deduct certain business expenses could be lost.

There is already plenty of free information about this topic on the Internet, including, first and foremost, the IRS website, so I'll try to limit my discussion here to contract language typically found in service contracts designed to help secure independent contractor status. Keep in mind that actions (how the Company and the Service Provider interact) truly speak louder than words — the IRS may rule that the Service Provider is an employee even if the service contract contains the sample contract language below showing the parties' intent to treat the Service Provider as an independent contractor. According to IRS Publication 15-A, available on the IRS website: "The general rule is that an individual is an independent contractor if you, the person for whom the services are performed, have the right to control or direct only the result of the work and not the means and methods of accomplishing the result."

Keep in mind, also, that either the Company or the Service Provider can ask the IRS to make a determination on whether the Service Provider is an independent contractor by filing Form SS-8, Determination of Worker Status for Purposes of Federal Employment Taxes and Income Tax Withholding.

Practically, the classification issue only arises in the borderline cases. It's usually a correct determination to treat a Service Provider as an independent contractor if the Service Provider is a large entity that is retained to perform services for a flat fee (or otherwise bears profit/loss risk), off-site, with agreed-to goals, but no directions about the details of how to reach those goals, with its own staff and equipment. Controversy usually arises when a small (or large) business attempts to shift the tax and paperwork burden and responsibility to procure health care insurance and other benefits to an individual that the business supervises and otherwise treats as an employee. Of special note are full-time salespeople, who may be treated as "statutory employees" for certain withholding purposes even if the Company exercises little control over their work — consult with your tax advisor and IRS Publication 15-A for more information.

(a) The relationship of the Service Provider and the Company hereunder is that of independent contractors, and neither party is the partner, joint venturer, employee, franchisee, agent, or legal representative of the other party.

(b) The operations of the Service Provider are subject to the sole control of the Service Provider. All persons employed or retained by the Service Provider (the "Service Provider Personnel") are deemed employees or representatives of the Service Provider, and not of the Company. Except as expressly set forth in attached Exhibit [insert Exhibit number], the Service Provider is solely responsible for, at its own expense, (i) providing such office space and facilities, and such Service Provider Personnel (including their training), as may be necessary to carry out its obligations under this Agreement, (ii) covering all Service Provider Personnel under any applicable social benefit laws (including workers' compensation and applicable state disability insurance); and (iii) making any and all payroll deductions and contributions that may be required with respect to the Service Provider Personnel.

(c) The Service Provider is not required to work during any specified hours or days and is not entitled to any of the Company's employee or other benefits. The Service Provider confirms that it is the sales representative for numerous products on behalf of third parties. The Company acknowledges that the Service Provider is free to engage in these and other activities, provided such activities do not conflict with the Service Provider's [non-compete and other] obligations under this Agreement.

Subsection (a) starts by confirming the general proposition that the parties are independent contractors. Subsections (b) and (c) set forth a litany of parameters, all designed to support the independent contractor classification of the Service Provider. None of the parameters by itself controls the classification of the Service Provider. Nor is there any bright line separating independent contractors from employees — the determination whether the classification is correct is very fact sensitive.

Subsection (c) states that the Service Provider is not required to keep a particular schedule (i.e., punch a clock like an employee). The Company doesn't care how and when the Service Provider does its work; as long as it leads to a satisfactory result. Unlike a typical employee, the Service Provider in this example is allowed to work for other companies, as long as these other activities do not interfere with its obligations to the Company, including any non-compete provision. Again, remember that the contract language is not dispositive. Actions speak louder than words, and if, notwithstanding this language, the Service Provider works only for the Company and nobody else, this may skew the determination toward the employee side of the scale. Sales representatives are especially scrutinized, and full-time salespeople may be treated as "statutory employees" for certain withholding purposes even if the company exercises little control over their work — consult with IRS Publication 15-A for more information.

Employers typically pay for all the infrastructure an employee needs to do his or her work; all the employee has to do is show up, and of course, work. In contrast, this clause provides that the Service Provider is responsible for all the costs necessary to perform its obligations — office rent, copiers, fax machines, computer networks, any human resources, etc. This is the essense of independent business ownership — an independent contractor runs its own business, and sinks or swims based in part on its ability to keep costs down so that it can generate a profit. Note, however, that I provide an Exhibit for any reimbursable out-of-pocket expenses negotiated between the parties — things like extraordinary overnight travel expenses.

Other Provisions Relating to the Appointment of a Sales Representative

(a) The Representative shall not solicit orders for the Goods:

(i) from any person located outside the Territory; or

(ii) directly or indirectly from any person which it knows or has reason to know will resell the Goods outside the Territory. The Representative shall promptly refer to the Company any inquiries or orders for the Goods it receives from outside the Territory.

(b) The Representative has authority to solicit orders only. The Representative has no authority to accept orders or to assume, incur, or create any express or implied warranty, liability, or obligation on behalf of the Company. As such, the Representative shall submit quotations to customers in accordance with prices, terms, and conditions specified by the Company, and provide a simple acknowledgment of receipt of the customer's order, but in each instance shall clearly disclose that all matters are subject to final acceptance by the Company. The Representative acknowledges and agrees that the Company may in its discretion accept or reject in whole or part any order or any other proposed transaction, and that the Representative is not entitled to any compensation for any transaction or part of any transaction that is rejected by the Company.

Sales Outside of Territory Prohibited

In some cases, the manufacturer (in this instance, the Company) will establish a network of independent sales representatives, with each representative responsible for its own geographic territory (or its own list of customers, distributors, etc.). The Company will sometimes include this provision to prevent its sales representatives from encroaching into its other representatives' territories. See the corresponding provision in Chapter 4 for a more detailed discussion of this provision, including ways the Representative can negotiate to split the commission with other representatives in case it is able to secure a customer outside of the Territory.

Representative Has No Authority to Bind

The Representative's job is to solicit orders; it can't bind the Company, for example, by sending a sales confirmation accepting an order on behalf of the Company without the Company's consent. Assuming that the contract is structured so that the Representative is paid a commission based on only the collected proceeds of actual sales, then the Representative will not earn any compensation for rejected orders. A rejected order has no impact, however, on the straight salary portion, if any, earned by the Representative.

The Company certainly has a legitimate reason for wanting the right to approve or reject orders; it will, after all, bear the credit risk of the sale as the actual seller of the Goods. The Representative has less incentive to screen out bad customers because it's not out of pocket. However, the Representative may want to minimize the risk that the Company might exercise its discretion for more nefarious purposes; for example, to adversely impact the ability of the Representative to reach any Minimum Order requirements so that it can fire the Representative and retain somebody else. With this in mind, the Representative can try to negotiate some objective criteria for acceptance, perhaps linking the decision to the prospective customer's credit history, sales projections, available inventory, etc.

(c) The Company is not liable to the Representative for the Company's failure or delay in the performance of any order obtained by the Representative and accepted by the Company. The Company may, without any liability, discontinue or suspend the production, import or sale of, or modify the prices or designs of the Goods (each a "Change"). The Company will endeavor to give the Representative prior notice of any such Change, but will have no liability for any failure to provide such notice.

Company Not Liable to Representative

The Company owes its obligation to perform the order to the customer, not the Representative. Any delay or other breach will be dealt with in the sale of goods contract (see Chapter 4) between the Company (as the Seller) and the customer (as the Buyer). That's not to say that the Representative doesn't have a stake in the Company's performance; after all, payment of the Representative's commission is jeopardized if the customer decides not to pay for the Goods based on the Company's breach.

(d) The Company will invoice the customers, and all payments for the Goods will be made directly to the Company. The Representative shall direct all customers to make payment directly to the Company. If the Representative receives payment from a customer, it shall promptly forward such payment (with appropriate endorsement) to the Company, and take appropriate action acceptable to the Company to correct the customer payment procedures.

(e) The Representative shall furnish the following reports:

(i) no later than the 15th day of the month, a written report on its sales activity in the Territory during the immediately preceding calendar month; and

(ii) no later than July 15th and January 15th, a written report on its sales activity in the Territory during the immediately preceding six (6) month period or calendar year, respectively. The Representative shall include in each report information relating to sales volume to each customer, marketing efforts in the Territory, changes in the competitive and regulatory environment in the Territory, and such other information reasonably requested by the Company.

Subsection (c) also confirms that the Company is allowed to come up with new pricing and designs (Changes). The Company notifies the Representative so that the Representative can adjust its sales pitch. The Company, however, doesn't want to be liable for any failure to notify, especially if it is reselling products made by third parties because it may have no control over the occurence or timing of Changes made by third parties.

Customers to Pay Purchase Price Directly to the Company

Since the sale of Goods takes place between the Company (as the Seller) and the customer (as the Buyer), payments will be made directly to the Company for the Goods. However, in case any customer makes payment to the Representative (mostly inadvertent because the customer should know that any payment to the Representative does not extinguish its liability to the Company), Subsection (d) requires the Representative to forward these payments to the Company. The Representative will not be permitted to use these funds to offset any obligations of the Company to the Representative.

Sales Reports

The sales and marketing information (Subsection [e]) requested by the Company from a Representative can be similar to the kind of information provided by a Distributor. See the corresponding provision in Other Provisions Relating to the Appointment of a Distributor in Chapter 4.

Termination

See Chapter 23 for a detailed discussion of provisions covering termination for cause, bankruptcy, etc. The sample provision below deals with the conduct of the parties after termination of a sales representative agreement.

Upon the expiration or termination of this Agreement, the Representative shall immediately:

(a) permanently cease all marketing and sales activity of the Goods, including, but not limited to, permanently cease the use of any of the Company's trademarks, trade names and other intellectual property rights; and

(b) return to the Company all originals and copies of all data, drawings, documents, materials, samples and other information obtained or discerned by the Representative in connection with this Agreement.

(c) Upon the expiration or termination of this Agreement, the Company may engage in any and all dealings with customers who had previous contact and/or dealings with the Representative, and the Representative is not entitled to any compensation with respect thereto; provided, however, that that the Company shall pay the Representative all compensation accrued prior to the date of termination, minus any set-offs to which the Company may be entitled.

This post-termination provision is drafted from the Company's perspective. Subsection (a) calls for the Representative to cease all marketing activity for the Goods after termination. The Company wants to protect its goodwill and trademarks in the Territory. It doesn't want a possibly disgruntled or desperate post-termination sales representative to misrepresent the Goods. The Company also doesn't want the terminated representative to interfere with the marketing operations of any new representative that might take over.

Subsection (b) is similar to the kind of provision you might find in a non-disclosure agreement where the recipient of secret information is required to return all originals and copies to the owner of the information.

Subsection (c) clarifies that the Company is free after the expiration or termination of the contract to sell Goods to the customers in the Territory, either directly or through a new representative, and that the Representative is not entitled to any compensation from those sales. The Representative, however, is entitled to all commissions accrued prior to the date of termination.

An issue for negotiaton, however, may be what constitutes "accrural" for purposes of twilight orders (i.e., orders placed near the expiration or termination of the Agreement). Does the Representative's right to compensation vest upon its submission of an order, upon the Company's acceptance of the order, or upon payment of the Purchase Price of the Goods?

"Accrural" takes on special significance when the Agreement is about to end, which can be a very emotional time for the parties. Depending on how the parties define accrural, the Representative may feel that the Company is rejecting orders or delaying delivery for the purpose of denying compensation, while the Company may feel that the Representative is loading up on orders for the purpose of increasing its commissions. However, if the parties have already agreed for compensation to be paid from the collected sales proceeds, then from the Company's perspective, there's really no reason to deviate from this approach for twilight orders, especially if the parties have already agreed to the Company's discretion for acceptance of orders (see Other Provisions Relating to the Appointment of a Sales Representative earlier in this chapter). The only exception might be the Company negotiating to exclude any right to commission for twilight orders if the Agreement is being terminated because of the Representative's breach.

The Representative might want to tweak the clause by providing that its commission for orders that are submitted, say, within two weeks of expiration or termination, accrue upon the Company's acceptance of such orders (either before or within, say two weeks, after expiration or termination) and that payment of such commission must be made within 30 days after the expiration or termination of the Agreement, notwithstanding any delivery issues or payment issues with the customer. This will allow the Representative to tie up loose ends so that it can close the books on the relationship. In response, the Company might condition such payment to an undertaking by the Representative to "stick around" to liaise regarding any issues between the Company and the customer, or to its right to "claw back" paid commissions in extraordinary cases. If the commission amount is very large, then the parties can also consider spending the effort and expending the administrative fees of putting the commission into escrow pending the customer's payment.

Termination Provisions in Other Service Contracts

These contracts should also contain provisions addressing termination for cause, bankruptcy, etc. — for a detailed discussion of termination provisions, see Chapter 23. Consider the additional issues below when negotiating termination provisions for service contracts.

If the service agreement calls for the Services to be provided in stages, the Company should consider negotiating the right to terminate (together with appropriate remedies) or delay payment if the Service Provider fails to satisfy performance milestones or deadlines. By the same token, the Service Provider should negotiate the right to terminate (or withold the deliverables) in the event the Company defaults in the payment of any installment.

From the Company's perspective, be sure the service contract contains a provision that "claws back" or requires the return to it of any advance payment allocated to any portion of the Services not delivered prior to an early termination. Another issue that may arise is the disposition of any work-in-progress upon early termination. For example, the Services may include work the Service Provider is furnishing at its work site on equipment owned by the Company. Upon termination, the Service Provider should promptly return the equipment or allow the Company to retrieve the equipment.

In addition, the parties should consider whether the Company should be permitted to "keep" the partially completed work that has been performed prior to termination. This depends on a variety of factors, including the extent to which (i) the Company is purchasing custom-tailored services or has already made up-front payments (i.e., paid for services already performed or parts already incorporated), and (ii) the Service Provider has already invested in resources (e.g., parts, labor, licenses, etc.), required to perform the Services, especially custom-tailored services, as well as (iii) the parties' relative bargaining leverage. The parties might also consider different outcomes depending on whether the early termination is due to the Company's or the Service Provider's default.

The parties also have to consider the disposition of any prepaid amounts in a way that is consistent with the delivery or "dismantling"/return of any work-in-progress. Another issue to consider is the remedies for default, including indemnity or the imposition of an exclusive remedy (versus cumulative remedies) including liquidated damages. See Part V and the CD-ROM for a detailed discussion of these issues.

Non-Competition

In consideration of the [exclusive] engagement of the Representative under this Agreement, the Representative agrees that during the term of this Agreement and for [one (1) year] after the expiration or termination of this Agreement, the Representative shall not (i) market, promote, distribute, act as sales representative for, import, or purchase for resale in the Territory any products that compete with the Goods or (ii) render services to, or become a partner or owner of, any person or entity that engages in or contemplates engaging in the competitive activities described in subsection (i) above. In the event a court determines this non-compete provision unenforceable as to geographic scope or duration, then the court has the power to reduce the geographic scope or duration to the extent necessary to render the provision enforceable. The Representative acknowledges that the remedies at law for any breach of this provision would be inadequate and agrees that the Seller is entitled to injunctive relief to enforce any of the provisions of this Paragraph.

This sample provision follows the basic format of the non-competition clause found in a distribution agreement (see Chapter 4). The clause imposes the non-compete obligation both during the term and after the term of the contract.

From the Company's perspective, the agreement not to compete during the term is a reasonable requirement if the Representative is the exclusive representative. However, the post-termination non-compete has a far greater impact on the Representative's (especially a natural-person sales representative's) ability to make a living after expiration or termination, and is therefore closely scrutinized by the courts.

Claims of Service Provider — Liability Cap and No Consequential Damages

(a) The Service Provider [Representative] shall submit to the Company any claim it may have against the Company for money damages, compensation, equitable relief or otherwise within [30 days] after the event giving rise to such claim, including detailed documents supporting its claim. If the Service Provider fails to timely submit such claim, then it will be deemed to have waived such claim.

(b) The Company's aggregate cumulative liability to the Service Provider [Representative] or any other person arising out of or relating to this Agreement is US$[insert dollar amount].

(c) THE COMPANY SHALL NOT BE LIABLE TO THE SERVICE PROVIDER [REPRESENTATIVE] OR ANY OTHER PERSON FOR ANY INDIRECT, INCIDENTAL, CONSEQUENTIAL OR SPECIAL DAMAGES SUFFERED BY THE SERVICE PROVIDER OR SUCH OTHER PERSON IN CONNECTION WITH OR ARISING FROM THIS AGREEMENT, THE SALE OR USE OF THE GOODS, [ANY DELAY IN DELIVERY, DAMAGE TO, DEFECT, SHORTAGE OR NONCONFORMITY OF THE GOODS, OR ANY THIRD PARTY CLAIM THAT THE GOODS INFRINGE THIRD-PARTY INTELLECTUAL PROPERTY RIGHTS], INCLUDING, BUT NOT LIMITED TO, LOST REVENUES OR LOST PROFITS, WHETHER ARISING IN CONTRACT, TORT, NEGLIGENCE, STRICT LIABILITY, BREACH OF STATUTORY DUTY OR OTHERWISE, AND REGARDLESS OF ANY NOTICE OF THE POSSIBILITY OF SUCH DAMAGES.

Subsections (a), (b), and (c) are Company-drafted provisions sometimes found in service contracts, especially sales representative agreements where the seller of goods wants to limit its liability to its Representative to just the amount of commissions paid. The provisions limit the (a) amount of time the Service Provider or Representative has to make a claim against the Company, (b) aggregate liability of the Company to the Service Provider or Representative, and (c) the types of damages that the Company can be liable for.

In many cases, a Service Provider with a lot of bargaining leverage will draft these provisions the other way around with the Company (i.e., recipient of the Services) having a limited number of days to make a claim of faulty service by the Service

Provider, and the Service Provider limiting its liability with its own version of Subsection (b) liability cap and Subsection (c) no consequential damage provisions.

Compliance with Laws

(a) The Service Provider [Representative] shall conduct its operations and perform its obligations hereunder at all times in strict compliance with all applicable existing and future laws, rules, and regulations.

(b) The Service Provider [Representative] shall not make any payment or gift, directly or indirectly, which may constitute or may appear to constitute a bribe, kickback, or illegal payment under United States or other applicable laws.

[(c) The Representative shall not attempt to establish the prices at which any customer or prospective customer may resell the Goods. The Representative acknowledges that such customers are free to determine resale prices in their discretion.]

Subsection (a) is a basic example of a compliance with laws provision — the Service Provider undertakes to conduct its operations and perform the contract lawfully. The topic of Subsection (b) is technically covered by Subsection (a), but for safety's sake and especially if the Company is retaining the services of a sales representative in a foreign country, many sales representative agreements will contain an undertaking by the Representative not to offer or make anything that might be interpreted as a bribe or kickback. In Subsection (c), which applies to sales representative agreements, the Representative promises not to dictate resale prices to be charged by any customer — a provision that establishes resale prices may be illegal under US antitrust law.

Indemnity

The Service Provider [Representative] shall indemnify, hold harmless, and defend the Company and its subsidiaries, and their respective stockholders, officers, directors, employees, and agents, in each case past, present, or as they may exist at any time after the date of this Agreement (the "Indemnified Parties"), from and against any and all claims, damages, losses, liabilities, and suits (including, but not limited to, [reasonable] attorney fees and expenses) incurred by the Indemnified Parties (whether actual, contingent, known, or unknown) arising out of:

(a) any failure by the Service Provider (or its agents or employees) to fulfill any of its obligations hereunder;

(b) any unlawful act committed by the Service Provider (or its agents or employees); or

(c) any act, omission, or misrepresentation by the Service Provider (or its agents or employees).

In this Company-drafted provision, the Service Provider undertakes to indemnify the Company for damage, loss, or injury incurred by the Company arising from the Service Provider's activities under the service contract; for example, the defective provision of Services, acts, or omissions of the Service Provider that cause injury or property damage, or unlawful acts committed by the Service Provider. Please refer to Chapter 17 for more on indemnity and the CD-ROM for more on indemnification, including ways to customize this provision using "thresholds" and "baskets" to vary the degree of risk retention or risk shifting. The Service Provider can limit its liability under the indemnity (and the contract in general) by negotiating its own liability cap and no consequential damages clause (see above).

In sales representative agreements, the Representative can negotiate an indemnity from the Company to cover the situation where the Representative is dragged into a customer or third-party lawsuit involving defective Goods, trademark infringement, or other matters relating to the Goods. The Representative's rationale is that the Company (and not the Representative) is the seller of the Goods and should be responsible for these claims.

6

NON-DISCLOSURE AGREEMENTS (NDAS)

OVERVIEW

Joe E. Gasket owns Joe's Farming Supplies, a successful dealer of farm equipment, including tractors made by National Standard Tractor Company. Joe loves to keep his customers happy, and one of his biggest frustrations is that the piston rings of tractors wear out too quickly, causing lower engine performance. Being something of a motorhead, Joe decided to do something about it. Under a veil of secrecy, Joe develops a piston ring using a new blend of composite materials that, he feels, will make existing piston rings obsolete. He is eager to sell National on the idea of using his new technology, but Joe knows that National buys all of its piston rings from another multinational, Allied Piston Technologies Inc. Joe is concerned that National might use his information without compensation or reveal his information to Allied, essentially helping his competitor while gaining nothing for himself.

Joe has good reason to be concerned. Although Joe is a very successful local businessperson, he doesn't have the financial or human resources of National or Allied. Nor does he have the close institutional relationship like the one shared by those two companies. Joe is the classic "outsider."

But it's precisely Joe's outsider status that's enabled him to bring a fresh solution to an age-old problem. Joe has a great idea. But it'll take teamwork to bring his idea to market. For example, he may need outside service providers like subcontractors, consultants, as well as financial backers or partners. Joe will likely need to disclose his proprietary information in order to help these people provide services or to evaluate the feasibility of entering into a business relationship with him.

Let's say that after a preliminary meeting, Joe is able to convince National Standard that his idea may have some merit. While National Standard is keen on Joe's idea, Joe is a smart businessperson, and holds back on disclosing the details of his idea until he is sure that National Standard will keep his idea confidential. Therefore, prior to disclosing the details of his idea, Joe correctly insists that National Standard enter into a Confidentiality Agreement (also known as a Non-Disclosure Agreement or "NDA").

The parties to a Confidentiality Agreement typically include the Disclosing Party and the Receiving Party (also commonly called Recipient). The Disclosing Party furnishes or discloses the confidential information to the Recipient. The Recipient is the party that receives the information and promises to keep the information confidential. In this case, Joe is the owner of the information, and would be the Disclosing Party; National Standard would be the Recipient. By signing a Confidentialty Agreement, the Recipient agrees to keep the disclosed information confidential and not to use such information for its own purposes.

In some cases, information flows both ways. If so, the parties may enter into a mutual NDA, where each party is both the Disclosing Party and the Recipient. In other words, each party is the Disclosing Party with respect to its own information it wants to protect, and the Recipient when it receives protected information from the other party.

In the above example, Joe E. Gasket uses an NDA to protect his invention. But NDAs don't apply just to inventors. You can also use NDAs in these other situations:

- **Outsourcing:** Any situation where you need to reveal information to enable you to outsource a specific task to a third party. Examples include:

  - You're a software developer, and you need to subcontract a portion of the development work to another developer. For example, you want to make sure that the subcontractor doesn't leak your source code or other confidential information.

  - You're a retailer, and you need to hire a firm to create an advertising and marketing plan for your stores. For example, you want to make sure that the firm you hire doesn't disclose your plans to your competitors.

  - You own a business, and you need to hire a consultant to maintain and service your computer network, which may contain your confidential financial information. You want to make sure that the consultant doesn't leak your cost information to your competitors.

  - You're a manufacturer that needs to subcontract the production of certain parts to another company. For example, you want to make sure that the subcontractor doesn't leak your specifications or secret recipe to your competitors, or use it for itself.

- **Sale of Business:** Let's say you are the owner of a successful business that you're putting up for sale. You'll need to make sure that the prospective purchaser enters into a confidentiality agreement to protect the information you disclose about your business to enable the prospective purchaser and its advisors to assess the feasibility of purchasing your business. If you decide to structure the sale of your business so that the purchase price is paid in installments (downpayment plus payments over time), then you are essentially extending credit to the purchaser. In this case, you'll need to review financial information pertaining to the buyer to determine if it is creditworthy. Most likely, the prospective purchaser will require that you also sign a confidentiality agreement to protect its sensitive financial information. In case the negotiations fall through, each party will want to make sure that the counterparty won't leak the information or use it for itself. If the sale of the business does go through, the purchaser will want to protect its new investment, so the purchaser of your business will likely ask you to sign a confidentiality agreement to keep confidential the very information you disclosed to the purchaser at the beginning of the negotiations. In fact, the purchaser might want you to remain with the company as a consultant or employee for a transition period of time, or even indefinitely. Thus, even though you've sold the company and no longer own it, the purchaser (your new boss) may ask you to sign a confidentiality agreement to protect not only the information you disclosed, but also any information belonging to the purchaser you might learn in your new capacity.

- **Employees:** Your employees will routinely have access to sensitive information about your company. While certain laws (see next paragraph) protect sensitive company information from being divulged to third parties or being used for personal gain, this protection may be limited in scope and type of information covered, so many companies take the extra step of requiring its employees to consent to confidentiality provisions found in their company handbooks. Employees in key positions or with access to particularly sensitive information are often required to enter into separate confidentiality agreements, or employment agreements that contain confidentiality provisions.

    Here are just two of many ways in which our laws protect certain company information. The corporate laws of most states include the concept of the **Duty of Loyalty**, which requires directors and officers of corporations and limited liability companies to act in a way that places the interests of the company first. So the Duty of Loyalty would prohibit a director or officer of the company from using anything "belonging to" the company (information, business opportunities, etc.) for his or her own personal use. The **Federal Securities Laws** also protect certain company information from being divulged or used for personal gain. For example, the Federal insider trading provisions generally prohibit a person from buying or selling a security (an ownership interest in a company such as stock) while in possession of material (basically high impact information likely to sway the price of the security if made public), or nonpublic information about the security. The law also prevents circumvention by company insiders, for example, by prohibiting the "tipping" of such information to relatives and friends, securities trading by any person that gets "tipped," as well as securities trading by those who steal such information.

- **Joint Ventures:** Partners in a joint venture usually have to disclose proprietary business information in order to maximize synergy in their business relationship. But even before beginning the venture, the parties will want to do their due diligence about the other party to help them decide whether to enter into the joint venture in the first place, once again requiring the mutual disclosure of information. If you are thinking about entering into a joint venture, you'll want to enter into a confidentiality agreement to protect any information you bring to the table.

- **Settlement to Litigation or Other Dispute:** First, keep in mind that litigation is an area where you should be retaining competent legal counsel; it's never a good idea to represent yourself in court (this is called *pro se* representation), especially in a high-stakes litigation. In any event, with the exception of small claims court, most courts will not allow *pro se* representation.

  There are generally several possible outcomes to civil (that is, noncriminal) litigation (or arbitration or other formal dispute resolution procedure). If the litigation or other procedure plays itself out to completion, the losing party may be required by the court (in addition to providing equitable relief) to pay monetary damages to the winning party. The court might even make the losing party pay the winning party's legal fees. Depending on the perceived strength of its case and its distaste for the negative publicity of a lawsuit or high legal fees, either or both parties to a dispute may be reluctant to take the case "all the way" and allow its fate to be decided by the court or jury.

  Therefore, the parties may in certain instances be willing (or feel compelled) to negotiate a settlement of the case, where one party agrees to pay the other party a negotiated monetary settlement and perhaps take other actions. If so, the parties will enter into a Settlement Agreement, whereby each party "releases" the other party (that is, gives up the lawsuit), and agrees to hold the terms of settlement, including the amount of any monies paid, confidential. Disclosure of the settlement terms, especially generous ones, might trigger a flood of similar lawsuits.

These are just a few examples of situations where you should consider using an NDA to protect your confidential information. Keep in mind that businesspeople often reveal secret, sensitive, and sometimes embarrassing information to their attorneys and accountants. These professionals are already subject to client confidentiality rules mandated by their respective governing bodies, and are subject to sanction or censure in case any confidence is unethically breached.

Business lore contains many a litigation story of small-business people who show their ideas to large companies (with or without the "protection" of a Confidentiality Agreement), get rejected and then end up reading in the newspaper about the launch of "their invention" by the large company. A confidentiality agreement is, in the end, just a contract, a piece of paper. So in addition to spending time on the confidentiality agreement, you should also know your counterparty. You should do some due diligence on the party you are thinking of disclosing information to, and use common sense. Does the prospective recipient have a history of litigation where others have alleged trade secret misappropriation? When you interview them, ask them some questions to test how loose their lips are with sensitive information. Take a look around their offices. If you see piles of disorganized papers all over the place, that's probably not a good sign.

KEY PROVISIONS OF CONFIDENTIALITY AGREEMENTS

Now, let's take a look at the key provisions of a typical confidentiality agreement. Your Non-Disclosure Agreement (NDA) will need to address the following key issues:

- **Principal Obligations:** Recipient's principal obligations are to keep Confidential Information provided by Disclosing Party confidential and not to use it for unauthorized purposes. Once the Recipient is in possession of the information, it typically is allowed to disclose the information only to its employees, subcontractors, attorneys, etc. who "need-to-know" the information to do their jobs. Under certain circumstances, the Recipient may also be allowed to disclose the information if it receives a subpoena or is otherwise ordered by a court or government agency to disclose the information.

- **Definition of Confidential Information:** If you are the Disclosing Party, you'll want to the broadest possible protection for your information. One way you can do this is to negotiate to define Confidential Information as broadly as possible. If you are the Recipient, you'll want to limit your obligations as much as possible. One way you can do this is to define the scope of Confidential Information more narrowly.

- **Exceptions to Definition of Confidential Information:** Disclosing Party will try not to have any exceptions because it wants everything to be covered. However, most standard-form confidentiality agreements contain certain exclusions from the definition of Confidential Information. Examples of such exclusions include information that is already known to the public or Recipient before disclosure, and perhaps information developed by the Recipient not using confidential information of the Disclosing Party. If the information is covered by an exception, then the Recipient is not required to afford confidential treatment to such information.

- **Term:** This provision dictates how long the Recipient's confidentiality and non-use obligations will last. If you are the Disclosing Party, you'll want to make the Term as long as possible; if you are the Recipient, you'll want to make the Term as short as possible.

- **Return of Confidential Information:** This provision requires the Recipient to promptly return Confidential Information to the Disclosing Party either at the end of the term of the NDA or upon the Disclosing Party's request.

- **No Obligation to Enter into Transaction:** Parties often enter into Confidentiality Agreements to enable the parties to freely share information during negotiations so that they can decide whether to enter into a business transaction like the sale of a business, a joint venture, or an outsourcing agreement. But as often happens, the transaction could fall through for any number of reasons. Maybe something unfavorable happens to the Recipient or in the marketplace, or is discovered during due diligence, that gives one or both parties pause about entering into the business transaction. Perhaps the transaction is contingent on outside financing that never materializes. There are many factors that can cause well-intentioned parties to abandon the transaction. Therefore, it's prudent to include a provision in the confidentiality agreement stating that neither party is obligated to enter into the bigger business transaction.

Stand-alone NDA versus Definitive Agreement

In the example at the beginning of the chapter, Joe enters into an NDA with National Standard and then furnishes National with information about, and perhaps a sample of, his new piston ring. National then analyzes and determines if it wants to do business with Joe. If the parties decide to go beyond the "get to know you" phase, then they'll enter into an agreement governing the actual business relationship. Maybe the parties decide that Joe will supply the piston rings to National, or perhaps Joe will license the technology to National so that National can mass produce them for Joe, or maybe National will buy the technology outright from Joe. The terms and conditions of whatever business relationship they negotiate will be incorporated into a longer contract — the Definitive Agreement. The parties may find it useful to incorporate or restate the confidentiality provisions into the larger Definitive Agreement. In some situations, however, the parties will skip the stand-alone NDA, and negotiate and directly enter into their Definitive Agreement. In such case, the party disclosing proprietary information should try to negotiate NDA-type provisions directly into the Definitive Agreement. The sample excerpt provisions that follow in this chapter appear in both stand-alone NDAs as well as in Definitive Agreements.

SAMPLE CONTRACT EXCERPTS

Principal Obligations

The Recipient has two principal obligations. The first is to keep the confidential information confidential, in other words, not disclose it to anybody. The second obligation is not to use it for any unauthorized purpose. These are explained in more detail below.

Confidentiality

Recipient shall keep confidential all Confidential Information and not use Confidential Information for any purpose except to [state business purpose, e.g., evaluate the feasibility of entering into an agreement for the purchase of piston rings from Disclosing Party].

Recipients will sometimes try to negotiate a reduced level of care by requiring only that the Recipient use "reasonable care to keep Confidential Information confidential, using the same degree of care Recipient uses to protect its like [similar] information." In this case, Recipient is only required to use the same level of care to protect Disclosing Party's information as it uses to protect its own information. The minimum level of care is, however, "reasonable" care, so a Recipient who is extremely careless with its own information can't use this provision to justify being careless with Disclosing Party's information.

From Disclosing Party's standpoint, it's still better to have the stricter requirement that Recipient "shall keep confidential all Confidential Information." It's better because it doesn't leave open for a court or a jury to decide the issue of what level of care is "reasonable."

Non-use

Recipient also has to agree to use the Confidential Information only for authorized purposes. One example of an authorized purpose is the evaluation of the information as part of due diligence — that is, to determine the feasibility of entering into a business transaction with Disclosing Party. In the example at the beginning of the chapter, National Standard would be allowed to test the piston rings to see if they work properly in its engines, but would not be allowed to reverse engineer and then sell a knock-off without Joe's consent. That would be an unauthorized use, and therefore a breach of the NDA. In an outsourcing situation, an authorized use might be to allow the subcontractor/Recipient to use the information, for example, specifications or a secret recipe, to manufacture goods for Disclosing Party. An unauthorized use, for example, would be for Recipient to use the information to produce a competing line of goods.

Need-to-Know Exception

Notwithstanding the above, Recipient may disclose Confidential Information to its and its affiliates' employees, officers, directors, and agents ("Recipient Disclosees") on a strict need-to-know basis, provided it (i) causes Recipient Disclosees to be bound by confidentiality, non-use and other obligations no less stringent than those contained herein and (ii) remains liable to Disclosing Party for any breaches of such obligations caused by Recipient Disclosees.

Recipients usually need to involve other people in the organization to be able to analyze or use the information. That's why most NDAs typically allow Recipients to disclose Confidential Information "to its and its affiliates' employees, officers, directors and agents," but only on a "strict need-to-know basis." For example, in an outsource situation, Recipient's accountants have no business knowing Disclosing Party's secret formula, but Recipient's production department may need to know the secret formula in order to make the goods for Disclosing Party.

Sometimes, Disclosing Party will require that any person on the Recipient side that needs to know to sign a separate NDA with Disclosing Party before such person can have access to the information. However, in the above example the paperwork logistics can be a nightmare for Joe E. Gasket if he has to keep track of individual employees of National Standard and get them to sign separate NDAs. And what if some National Standard employees slip under the radar and get access to the information without first signing a separate NDA? Therefore, Joe E. Gasket might be better off only requiring that Recipient "causes such persons [of National Standard who need to know] to be bound by confidentiality obligations no less stringent than those contained" in the NDA. National Standard is free to determine how to ensure that its employees comply with the agreement.

For example, National Standard might enter into its own NDAs with its employees, or maybe National Standard already has secrecy language in its employee manual. But no matter how the Recipient handles it internally, the Recipient is ultimately responsible for breaches of the NDA by its employees and advisors.

Court-Ordered Disclosure Exception

Notwithstanding the above, Recipient may disclose Confidential Information to those persons mandated by court order or otherwise required by law. In this case, Recipient must at its own cost and expense (i) give prompt written notice to Disclosing Party as soon as it receives actual or constructive notice of such requirement, (ii) render assistance to Disclosing Party to enable Disclosing Party to comply with and/or object to any such requirement, and (iii) disclose only that portion of such information, and only to those parties, in each case as necessary to comply with such requirement, provided that receiving parties agree in writing to be bound by confidentiality obligations no less stringent than those contained herein.

Many NDAs allow disclosure of Confidential Information "pursuant to court order or otherwise required by law." For example, the Recipient may receive a subpoena or other request for information in a litigation situation or government investigation. Here, the Recipient is between a rock and a hard place. If it complies with the request for information, then it risks breaching the NDA. If it complies with the NDA and refuses to provide the information, it risks court or government penalty, possibly criminal sanction. NDAs try to get around this by adding four conditions to disclosure. First, the Recipient has to "give prompt notice to Disclosing Party" as soon as it learns of such disclosure requirement. This will give the Disclosing Party time to prepare for disclosure and/or try to fight disclosure. Second, the Recipient has to "render assistance to enable Disclosing Party to comply or object to any such requirement." Third, if the Disclosing Party consents to disclosure, the Recipient may disclose only the minimum amount of information absolutely required — that is, disclose only that part of the Confidential Information, and only to those parties, in each case as necessary to comply with such requirement." Fourth, even after the Recipient jumps through all of these hoops, it can only make the disclosure if the person demanding disclosure (e.g., government agency, etc.), has also agreed to keep such information confidential.

While the Sample Excerpt requires each party to bear its own costs and expenses, keep in mind that the parties can try to negotiate and include in the agreement how they will share the costs and expenses of complying with or fighting disclosure.

Non-competition

If two people decide to do business together on an exclusive basis, it seems reasonable that each party should not be permitted to go off on its own or team up with a third party to compete against the business. The parties would negotiate a non-competition clause to be included in the Definitive Agreement covering the business relationship. However, Recipient should be wary of agreeing to a non-competition clause contained in a "get to know you" type NDA. In this case the parties are just exploring business opportunities, and the Recipient should tell the Disclosing Party that the Recipient's obligations of confidentiality and non-use should be enough to protect the Disclosing Party. If the Recipient agrees to a non-competition clause in a "get to know you" type NDA, it is essentially agreeing not to compete with the Disclosing Party for the agreed upon number of years EVEN IF the parties go their separate ways after the Disclosure Period (time period in which information is disclosed and analyzed). That is quite a price to pay just to be able to take a "look-see" at some information.

Definition of Confidential Information

Confidential Information includes any information disclosed by Disclosing Party to Recipient or discerned by Recipient, whether in written, tangible, or verbal form, including, but not limited to, business, financial, sales, marketing, and technical information, and the terms and conditions of any business transaction entered into between the parties.

Notwithstanding anything herein to the contrary, while Disclosing Party has endeavored to include in any information disclosed hereunder, information it believes is suitable for the uses contemplated hereunder, Disclosing Party does not make any representation or warranty as to the accuracy or suitability of any information disclosed hereunder.

It's very important to pay special attention to how Confidential Information is defined in an NDA. After all, if a piece of information is not covered under the mutually agreed definition of Confidential Information, then Recipient has no obligation to keep it confidential.

There are two main issues to consider when negotiating the definition of Confidential Information. The first is the **Information Types** to be covered (i.e., the kind of information — e.g., financial information, etc.). The second is the **Information Formats** to be covered (i.e., how the information is presented — e.g., written, verbal, etc.).

Information Types

The last sample excerpt describes the Information Types pretty broadly — basically all kinds of business and financial information. These might include technical information, specifications, manufacturing processes, know-how; or sales and marketing information like customer lists, prospects and projections, financial information, employee compensation, and the like.

If you are the Disclosing Party, however, you should tailor the scope of the Information Types to be disclosed to fit the contemplated business transaction. For example, if you plan on outsourcing the manufacture of your products to a subcontractor, you may find that you may only need to disclose product specifications. The subcontractor needs to see the specifications in order to manufacture your products; it doesn't necessarily need to know anything else. Of course, in this example, some subcontractors may in fact want to see your financial information to assure itself that you will be able to meet their credit terms. But the idea is the same; if you are the Disclosing Party, you'll want to try to limit the Information Types to be disclosed. If you are the Recipient, you'll want to try to expand the definition of Confidential Information to cover those Information Types you feel you need to do your job or make your evaluation. So it's going to be a negotiation.

If you want to sell your business to the Recipient, you'll likely need to disclose basically everything to enable the Recipient to do its due diligence. Even in this case, however, you should try to limit the scope of the Information Types to be disclosed. For example, if you are selling your company, you probably don't want to be disclosing your personal financial information, although some purchasers will ask to see your personal financial information, especially if you are in some way personally guaranteeing any obligations.

Finally, the sample excerpt contains language stating that Disclosing Party does not promise that any information disclosed will be accurate or suitable for the intended purposes. Keep in mind that if the parties go beyond the NDA stage and actually enter into a business transaction, then the parties will need to enter into a separate agreement, what is known generically as a Definitive Agreement, which will contain detailed terms and conditions of the underlying transaction. For example, if you are selling your business, then the Definitive Agreement might be the Stock Purchase Agreement or Asset Purchase Agreement (both discussed in more detail in Part III). In most cases, the Disclosing Party will make certain representations and warranties directly in the Definitive Agreement about the business, as reflected in information previously disclosed pursuant to the NDA. The excerpted language allows the Disclosing Party to leave the representations and warranties out of the NDA until the parties are actually ready to enter into a transaction.

Information Formats

Information Format is the area where there is usually a good deal of negotiation between the parties. On the one hand, the Disclosing Party will want Information Formats to be as broadly defined as possible. The Sample Excerpt, for example, defines Confidential Information very broadly to include both information disclosed to and information discerned by the Recipient.

The excerpt covers information disclosed (i) in written form (e.g., documents, specifications, customer lists), (ii) in tangible form (e.g., photos, information in hard drives and other electronic media, samples and prototypes), and (iii) verbally (it's rare for disclosure to be limited to a package of documents; there's also usually verbal discussion of the contents). A Disclosing Party will also want Confidential Information to include any copies of the information, as well as any reports, notes, etc. prepared by the Recipient containing or analyzing the Confidential Information.

A Recipient can learn a lot about a Disclosing Party just by "looking around," for example during a factory tour or other inspection. Therefore, if you are the Disclosing Party, you'll want to include any information "discerned" by the Recipient in the course of the business relationship.

On the other hand, if you are the Recipient, you'll want to limit the Information Formats as much as possible. For example, you might try to negotiate having Confidential Information cover only information disclosed "in written or tangible form and marked as 'Confidential.'" So instead of just handing over a package of documents, the Disclosing Party will need to stamp each document as "CONFIDENTIAL" if it wants to protect the information.

If you are the Recipient, and are unable to exclude verbally disclosed information from the definition of Confidential Information, then you should try to add the condition that any verbal disclosures be "identified as 'Confidential' at the time of verbal disclosure," and maybe even negotiate the requirement that the "Disclosing Party reduce such verbal information to written or tangible form within [a certain number of days] of verbal or visual disclosure and mark such information as 'Confidential.'" In this case, Disclosing Party will need to start confidential conversations with the statement that "What I'm about to say is confidential," and then prepare a written summary of such conversation and mark it "CONFIDENTIAL." This puts the onus (and risk of clerical error) on the Disclosing Party to clearly identify to you which disclosures are confidential.

Exceptions to Definition of Confidential Information

Recipient's obligations hereunder shall not apply to any information disclosed or discerned hereunder that:

(i) is or becomes part of the public domain through no fault of Recipient;

(ii) is already known to Recipient prior to disclosure, as shown by written records of Recipient;

(iii) becomes known to Recipient via disclosure from a third party, provided that the third party has the lawful right to make such disclosure; or

(iv) is independently developed by Recipient, as shown by written records of Recipient.

The sample excerpt above contains common exceptions to the definition of Confidential Information. The basic idea is to exclude any information that is already known or becomes known to the public or Recipient outside of the NDA without fault of the Recipient.

For example, oftentimes the parties to a business transaction will agree to keep the financial terms confidential. If a leak occurs, and the sale price is reported on CNBC, neither party will be liable if (a big "if") it didn't cause the leak. The information became "part of the public domain through no fault of Recipient."

Another common scenario is the Disclosing Party disclosing something to the Recipient that the Recipient has already learned or later learns from a third party. Provided that the third party is authorized to disclose the information to the Recipient, then that tidbit of information is not confidential. In the above example, let's say that Bobby Wankel, a total stranger to Joe E. Gasket, independently develops the same piston ring technology and posts the details of the technology on Wikipedia one month after Joe's preliminary meeting with National Standard. Bobby has made the information public, and Joe E. Gasket would have a hard time arguing that the information is still protected Confidential Information.

The parties should especially be careful about the exception regarding "independently developed" information. In a dispute, at what point does lawful independent research turn into suspect reverse engineering? The problem is that nobody really knows the answer to that question until after a jury looks at all the facts during a long and expensive trial. Recipients (large ones like National Standard) might insist on this exception only because they may not have a central clearinghouse of ideas — the left hand may not know what the right hand is doing. In this case, the Disclosing Party should be sure that it is comfortable that Recipient has institutional mechanisms (typically referred to as "Chinese Walls" or "firewalls") to keep their various businesses separate.

Exceptions to exceptions

Any information disclosed is not deemed to be within the above exceptions merely because such items are embraced by more general knowledge in the public domain or in the possession of Recipient. No combination of features shall be deemed to be within the above exceptions merely because individual features are in the public domain or Recipient's possession unless the combination itself and its principle of operation are in the public domain or Recipient's possession.

These clarify the exceptions — a kind of exceptions to the exceptions. Here's a simple example to illustrate the concept of the first sentence. Let's say you've invented a new way to toast bread. You pitch it as the best thing since sliced bread and are seeking to outsource the manufacture of the toaster to Recipient. The first sentence means that Recipient cannot claim that the new way to toast bread is not confidential just because toasting bread is a concept that everybody already knows about. Now let's say that you invent a new way of toasting bread involving the use of a lever and a laser beam. The second sentence means that Recipient cannot claim that the new way to toast bread is not confidential just because levers and laser beams are well-known devices used for many applications. Recipient may argue that levers have been used since ancient times, and "laser" beams have been used since at least the time of Austin Powers. The sample excerpt provides that as long as the way the lever and laser beam are used in combination is not publicly known, then your information is still confidential.

Patents versus Trade Secrets

While patents and trade secrets are similar in that they are both proprietary, meaning that the owner has all the rights that exclusive ownership conveys, they are not the same in terms of disclosure. When you file a patent, you make the conscious decision to put the world on notice that whatever technology you are patenting belongs to you, and that if anybody wants to use the technology, he or she has to obtain a license from you. By filing a patent, you are broadcasting the patented technology for the whole world to see. So "disclosure" is a foregone conclusion. You really can't keep patents confidential, except to the extent that you are still preparing the paperwork and have not yet filed. Some owners, however, feel that some information is either too valuable to disclose no matter what, or do not file a patent because the information, although valuable and unique, may not be patentable, for example, a "secret" recipe for chocolate. (Whether an invention or formula is patentable is beyond the scope of this book and something about which you should consult a patent attorney.)

These are referred to as trade secrets. Trade secrets stay secret only if the owner takes all necessary precautions to keep the information under "lock and key." So if the owner of the recipe needs to outsource chocolate production to a third-party factory, it will probably need to disclose the secret recipe, and make the factory sign an NDA to keep the recipe confidential.

Term of Confidentiality Agreement

[Disclosure Period] Recipient's obligations of confidentiality and non-use apply to all Confidential Information disclosed or discerned during the [one month] after the execution of this Agreement ("Disclosure Period").

[Obligation Period] Recipient's obligations hereunder shall remain in effect during the Disclosure Period and for a period of [5 years] thereafter.

There are lots of ways to draft this provision. There are two time periods to consider for NDAs. The **Disclosure Period** is the time period during which disclosures are made. The **Obligation Period** is the time period during which the parties must comply with their obligations of confidentiality and non-use. Not all NDAs separately define these time periods, but it's usually prudent to have the Obligation Period last beyond the end of the Disclosure Period.

For example, if the parties first enter into an NDA to determine the feasibility of entering into a business transaction, then they'll probably want to define a relatively short Disclosure Period, for example, one month, in which to disclose information. It's in both parties' interest for the Disclosing Party to quickly prepare the package of information and get it to the Recipient so that the Recipient can quickly decide whether to proceed beyond the "get to know you" phase. In this case, the Disclosing Party will want to include an Obligation Period of several years or more during which the Recipient must keep the information confidential, even if the parties go their separate ways and don't enter into a business relationship.

If the parties decide to enter into a business relationship, they should incorporate or restate the NDA provisions directly in their Definitive Agreement. The Disclosure Period would usually be the life or term of the Definitive Agreement. But it's usually prudent for Disclosing Party to negotiate a kind of "tail coverage," that is, having the Recipient's confidentiality obligations extend for a few years beyond the end of the termination or expiration of the Definitive Agreement.

Take care when negotiating the term of an NDA. Some NDAs contain language requiring that Recipient keep confidential each piece of information for some period of time after disclosure of that piece of information. We'll call this "Approach A." Keep in mind that this is not the same thing as saying that ALL disclosures should be kept confidential for some period of time after the execution of the NDA ("Approach B"). It's also not the same thing as saying that ALL disclosures should be kept confidential during the term of the agreement and for a fixed time afterwards ("Approach C"). Approach A has different "confidentiality expiration dates" for EACH disclosure; and unless the parties have excellent recordkeeping infrastructure and limit disclosure to written and tangible objects, they will be hard pressed to keep things straight. Sometimes, it's clearer to pick Approach B or Approach C, where the expirations dates are not moving targets. In Approach B or Approach C, any information must be kept confidential until the specified date, regardless of when the information is initially disclosed.

Just make sure the date the confidentiality obligation expires is long enough after the last possible day you can make disclosure. The last day of disclosure is usually the last day of the term of the Agreement. On the other hand, some Disclosing Parties may prefer Approach A because the Disclosing Party will, in fact, be making disclosures over a long period of time, especially in the context of long-term business relationships.

Return of Confidential Information

Recipient shall, within [3 days] of Disclosing Party's request, return all Confidential Information to Disclosing Party, including, but not limited to, any and all copies, reproductions, and notes thereof.

This provision requires the Recipient to return all Confidential Information. The sample excerpt requires the return of information within three days of the Disclosing Party's request. Other NDAs require the return of information by a certain date, for example, by the end of the Disclosure Period. The Disclosing Party knows that the Recipient will be analyzing and taking notes on the Confidential Information, perhaps even testing any samples submitted. The Recipient does not necessarily want to return such notes, analyses or test results to the Disclosing Party. In some cases, these notes may even contain proprietary information of the Recipient. Therefore, one way to handle this situation is for the parties to agree that "Recipient shall destroy any analyses, test results or notes discussing or containing the Confidential Information within 3 days of Disclosing Party's request."

An alternative is the destruction of such notes, etc. within several days after the end of some certain date, like the end of the Disclosure Period. The Disclosing Party might try to negotiate obtaining a certificate from Recipient that such notes, etc., have in fact, been destroyed per the NDA.

No Obligation to Enter into Transaction

Nothing in this Agreement obligates either party to enter into any transaction with the other party. No right or license is expressly or implicitly granted to any of Disclosing Party's patent, trademark, or other intellectual property rights by virtue of the parties entering into this Agreement. Any such transaction, including, but not limited to, the licensing of any intellectual property rights, shall be entered into only pursuant to a formal written agreement to be negotiated between and executed by the parties.

This provision is typically found in NDAs that are entered into to enable the parties to evaluate the feasibility of entering into a business transaction. In the above example, it's the early stages of discussions and the Disclosing Party and the Recipient are just evaluating the situation. Neither party knows if some unsavory information about the other party might come up during their due diligence that will cause it to walk away. Or the parties might decide that the transaction just doesn't make sense from a financial point of view (pricing, cost, market potential, etc.). This provision allows either party to walk away from entering into a long-term business relationship. You should keep in mind that the Recipient is bound, no matter what, to the confidentiality and non-use obligations. And, there is no implied right or license to use any Confidential Information except for evaluation purposes. Neither party is bound to go beyond the evaluation phase.

Part III
BUYING OR SELLING A BUSINESS

7

STRUCTURING THE DEAL

OVERVIEW

In 1945, Bob and Bill Kavinski returned to the Lower East Side after serving in World War II. The two brothers cut their teeth working in food retail for a couple of years, and then decided to use some of their savings to start a charcuterie right in their neighborhood. It wasn't the fanciest store, but the business thrived because for New York gourmands, it's always been just about the food. Despite their success, the brothers were reluctant to expand, concerned that it would dilute the quality of the customer experience. Eventually, the brothers retired, selling their ownership interests to their adult children. Bob's children Bitsy and Max, and Bill's children Reba and Jeremiah, each own 25 percent of the company. The children then embarked upon an aggressive expansion program, incorporating under the new name Cavendish Markets, Inc., and growing the enterprise into an upscale chain of 25 specialty food stores located throughout the Tri-State Area. The success of Cavendish has caught the attention of Consolidated Food Co., a privately-held supermarket club-store-type chain seeking to break into the specialty food market. Eager to reap the rewards of their hard work, the relatives decide that it is in their best interests to sell the company to Consolidated.

Before proceeding to the chapters on contract provisions typically found in the two main types of definitive agreements governing the sale of a privately-held business (Asset Purchase Agreement [APA] and Stock Purchase Agreement [SPA]), this chapter discusses several preliminary matters you should engage in prior to entering into the definitive agreement. These areas include due diligence, the letter of intent, and determining the legal structure of the transaction.

This book discusses contract matters related to the basic taxable asset or stock sale of privately-held businesses, which are companies owned by one or a few owners, rather than companies whose shares are publicly traded. Small businesses are typically privately held, but size alone is not a factor (there are many large privately held companies). There is no discussion in this book about either Federal Securities laws or the myriad ways to structure an acquisition as a tax-deferred reorganization.

Purchasers generally fall into two categories. **Strategic buyers** are usually in the same or related business as the company being acquired. For the purposes of this book, strategic buyers also include "entrepreneurial buyers" — individuals or small-to-medium-sized companies that desire to purchase a business, and then run it. Larger strategic buyers may have the industry-related expertise and infrastructure, as well as market position, to be able to take advantage of the synergies and economies of scale resulting from the acquisition of the company. Whether their goal is vertical or horizontal integration, strategic buyers are sometimes willing to pay a premium over fair market value to acquire the company. However, an extremely general characterization of **financial buyers** (like private equity funds and venture capital firms) would be that they have a high degree of financial and investment expertise, but usually only tangential industry-specific expertise (unless they are a portfolio company that makes investments in particular industries). Financial buyers are "professional buyers"; they scour the marketplace for targets that make good investments, and sometimes leverage the transaction with debt, if it is cheaply available. While the legal issues impacting strategic and financial buyers/sellers overlap, this book has been written mostly with the strategic "entrepreneurial" buyer or seller in mind.

This book discusses the two traditional ways to purchase a business; purchasing the assets or purchasing the stock of a company using only two kinds of consideration — cash and/or promissory notes. There will be no discussion of spin-offs, joint ventures, any tax-deferred transaction where the purchaser uses stock in itself to purchase the assets or shares of the target, or any of the myriad other transaction structures used by large companies.

DUE DILIGENCE

Before the parties can enter into the definitive agreement for the sale of a business, they're going to need to do some homework.

Let's say, for example, that you're in the market for a new car. You're never going to want to buy a car without first doing some research: check out reviews in car magazines, visit dealers to get the best price, and take the car out for a test drive. And most car dealers are not going to sell you a car without first doing some research about you — your driving habits, your personal preferences, and especially your credit history.

In the business world, the parties to a proposed transaction also will want to "kick the tires" and conduct research about the other party and the transaction. This is called due diligence. Due diligence helps the parties evaluate the proposed business opportunity. Most due diligence includes some cooperative information sharing, as well as unilateral investigations:

- **Cooperation:** Each party allows the other party access to its facilities, employees, books and records, contracts, and other information. The parties typically enter into a Confidentiality Agreement to protect information disclosed or discerned during due diligence. Please refer to Chapter 6 for a detailed discussion of Confidentiality Agreements.

- **Unilateral:** Of course, some due diligence about your counterparty can be done unilaterally, like obtaining a credit report from a credit agency or ordering a good standing certificate from the state of incorporation.

- **Self-examination:** While we don't typically call it due diligence, an examination of your own situation, for example, contracts that you've entered into, your own tax situation, etc.), should be included in due diligence. Whether you are the seller or purchaser of a business, a thorough self-examination will help to verify information about your own situation so that you can work with your attorneys and financial advisors to best structure and negotiate the transaction, to enable you to maximize your return and minimize your risk and tax liability.

- **Legal Environment:** You should work with your attorneys to identify any facts (lawsuits, claims, legislation, regulations, etc.) that may impact the transaction. In the above example, if the seller Cavendish is the defendant in a lawsuit or investigation stemming from the sale of tainted ground beef, this is the kind of information that purchaser Consolidated will want to know. Consolidated can either negotiate a reduced price, wait to enter into the definitive agreement until after Cavendish has settled all claims, make sure all of the liability stays with Cavendish (not assume any such liability), or just walk away from the deal altogether.

At first, it seems intuitive that the Purchaser (in the sample contract provisions, I refer to the buyer as the "Purchaser"), has more reason to conduct thorough due diligence than the seller (the Seller in an APA or selling Stockholders in a SPA). After all, if you are the Purchaser, you're going to want to know all about what you're buying. But if you are the seller, you're also going to want to conduct thorough due diligence, including verifying the creditworthiness of the Purchaser, and reviewing the Purchaser's organizational documents and contracts. In fact, the Purchaser's contracts may contain language that either restricts, or creates impediments to, the ability of the Purchaser to enter into the transaction or to run the combined entity going forward. For example, the Purchaser may have previously pledged after-acquired property to a third-party creditor. Any assets acquired in an APA would be included in "after-acquired property," and have to be pledged to this creditor. This could create a conflict if the Purchaser needs to borrow "new money" in order to finance the APA, because the lender will likely require a lien in the assets to secure the financing (remember, these assets in this example have already been pledged to somebody else). This is the kind of thing that can jeopardize the APA, and the seller should be aware of the situation so that it can make sure that the Purchaser structures a work-around before the Closing Date.

The **Due Diligence Checklist** below contains a more detailed discussion of the kinds of information you should be looking for during due diligence. It's easy to miss the forest for the trees when looking through boxloads of paperwork, so try to remember that due diligence has the following general goals.

- **Legal Roadblocks:** Your attorney can help you determine whether there are any legal roadblocks to the transaction. You can find roadblocks in corporate governance documents like the certificate of incorporation or bylaws, and in other documents like contracts and labor agreements. For example, if you are purchasing a business, and the selling business has a valuable distribution contract with a third party, then you're going to want to review the distribution contract to make sure that it can be assigned (that is, transferred) to you. Your attorney can help you to sift through these documents, and identify and navigate around roadblocks that may exist in these documents as well as hurdles that may arise because of applicable laws and regulations.

- **Dealbreakers/Deal Changers:** You need to determine whether there is any information that will impact your decision to proceed with the transaction at the price and under the terms and conditions preliminarily agreed to among the parties. For example, if you are the purchaser of a business, you might discover some hidden liabilities of or other unfavorable information about the seller. Or you might find contract provisions that either prohibit or impede the transaction or the ability of the Purchaser to run the combined business after the Closing (see above "after-acquired property" example.) Armed with this information, you can try to negotiate a price concession or a work-around, or to restructure the transaction to minimize your exposure.

DUE DILIGENCE CHECKLIST

Below is a general discussion of the some of the types of things the Purchaser's attorney typically looks for during due diligence in an asset purchase or stock purchase transaction.

Contracts — Full Force and Effect Analysis

Validity: A threshold question is whether the contract is in writing. For example, big-value exclusive distribution agreements almost certainly have to be in writing and signed in order to be valid under a legal concept known as the **statute of frauds**, which requires contracts for the sale of goods to be in writing if their value is beyond a minimum monetary threshold ($500). While your counterparty might argue that it's not standard industry practice to have this or that type of contract in writing, chances are you won't be able enforce a verbal contract in the event of breach.

Other issues include whether the contracts were properly authorized by the company and whether proper consideration was or is being given.

Term and Termination: Another issue is the ease with which the contract can be terminated. Look for provisions that allow for either party to "**terminate without cause**" or "**terminate for convenience**." This means that a contract party can terminate the agreement for any reason or for no reason at all usually by giving some period of notice. Think of it this way: What use is paying a lot of money to acquire an "exclusive" distribution agreement as part of an APA or SPA, if the manufacturer can cancel the agreement at any time for no reason with 30 days' notice? Also, take a look at the renewal provisions of the contract. A short-term contact with annual renewals is less secure than a longer-term contract with longer renewal periods.

Contracts — Restrictions on Transfer/Purchase

In **asset sales**, you'll be looking for several things generally.

Restrictions on Sale/Purchase of Assets: Look for provisions in the the Seller's (and Purchaser's) contracts that restrict the sale (or purchase) of the Acquired Assets (i.e., assets acquired in an APA), or require the consent of the counterparty. A key phrase to look for is "sale of all or substantially all of the assets" or similar language. Be on the lookout also for contract provisions that cause any such sale (or purchase) to induce some kind of negative consequence. Negative consequences could include a breach, default or termination of the contract, acceleration of debt under the contract, or the creation of an unwanted lien under the contract. Some contacts even forbid the Purchaser from entering into new kinds of business, and that could be an indirect restriction on the purchase of the assets.

Restrictions on the Transfer of Contracts: If the Seller's contracts are part of the Acquired Assets, you'll also need to confirm that these contracts are assignable to you. In most cases, the contract will provide that the consent of the counterparty is required.

Entity or Stock Sale: Look for **change in control provisions** in the Acquired Company's contracts that prohibit, or require the counterparty's consent for, a change in ownership, or that cause any such change in ownership to induce some kind of negative consequence (like a breach, termination, or acceleration of debt, etc., discussed above). A change in board composition (which typically happens in the sale of a business) also often triggers the change in control provision. Look for any provisions in the Purchaser's contracts limiting its right to make investments or to purchase shares.

Review the **Shareholder Agreement, LLC Operating Agreement** or similar contracts of the selling Stockholders (LLC members) to make sure that those contracts do not restrict the transfer of the stock, such as would occur under a SPA. For example, Shareholder Agreements typically contain a litany of provisions giving the other shareholders the right of first refusal (or tag-along rights, drag-along rights, etc.), to purchase shares offered for sale to third parties.

Encumbrances

The Purchaser in an asset or stock transaction wants to acquire clean title; it doesn't want to purchase assets or stock that is encumbered (think "tied up") by liens. Furthermore, because lienholders have an interest in the property, they're likely to have the contractural right to impede the transaction. Lienholders might have the right to consent to the transaction or to accelerate the loans that are being secured by the liens.

Asset Sale

There are several ways the assets could be encumbered. The Seller may have already granted somebody else a lien in its assets (Seller Grants Security Interest). Check the Seller's contracts for provisions granting any such security interest. Liens in **personal property** generally aren't fully enforceable unless the lienholder takes the extra step of **"perfecting"** the lien by either obtaining possession of the asset (not always practicable since the debtor needs to use it) or by filing a form called a UCC-1 with the appropriate state authorities. So you can also find liens by conducting a lien search through a reputable search company. Of course, you'll also want to do a search for **mortgages on real property** owned by the Seller. Keep in mind that even **intangible assets** can be pledged as security. For example, the Seller may have used its accounts receivable to secure receivables financing (called factoring).

After-Acquired Property

The Purchaser may have previously pledged after-acquired property to a third-party creditor. Any assets acquired would be included in "after-acquired property," and have to be pledged to this creditor. This could create a conflict if the Purchaser needs to use the assets to secure acquisition financing (where the Purchaser borrows "new money" to finance the APA) Check the Purchaser's contracts and conduct a lien search through a reputable search company.

Leases and Licenses

These are not liens in the strict sense of the word. But if the Seller is leasing its photocopier or office space, and licensing the use of certain patents, this means that it doesn't own them, and therefore doesn't have the right to sell them to you outright. Even so, the Seller may be able to assign you their rights in the leases and license agreements.

Entity or Stock Sale

Look for provisions in the Acquired Company's contracts granting a lien in its assets to a lender or other third party. It's also conceivable that the selling Stockholders, whether one or a group of individuals or a parent company, may have pledged the stock to third parties in a separate transaction.

Issuance of New Shares

Preemptive rights are a kind of encumbrance to the issuance of new shares (new investments) because these rights entitle the existing shareholders the right to purchase new shares of stock before they are offered to third parties. This may have the effect of stifling new third party (e.g., venture capital) investment in the company. Check the certificate of incorporation of the company to see if it contains a preemptive rights provision. Note that state law varies, so consult with your attorney on whether preemptive rights are automatically granted or must be affirmatively provided in the company's certificate of incorporation. Note that preemptive rights can also be granted by contract, so also check the company's shareholders agreement (if it has one) for preemptive rights provisions.

Environmental

If you are buying a business that owns (or even leases) real property, then you have to be concerned about your potential liability under the environmental laws. In a stock purchase transaction, the Purchaser automatically takes over all the known and hidden liabilities of the acquired business, including environmental law liabilities. The Purchaser's environmental exposure in an asset transaction depends on how the parties negotiate the allocation of liabilities, not just in terms of the obligations to be specifically assumed by the Purchaser, but also in terms of the strength of the seller's environmental representations and warranties and indemnity. Environmental insurance (e.g., pollution, casualty, etc.), is another risk allocation tool available to help deal with contaminated properties. These policies can help to cap clean-up costs and build cost certainty into the transaction.

The stakes are very high. For example, the **Federal Superfund law** (Comprehensive Environmental Response, Compensation, and Liability Act, or CERCLA) imposes joint and several liability on current and past owners and operators, as well as companies that arrange transportation from an impacted site. Your attorney should also be familiar with other Federal laws such as the Clean Air and Water Act, Resource Conservation Recovery Act, as well as state environmental laws on the storage of hazardous materials, pollution, oil spills, state superfund site laws, etc. He or she should also be familiar with financial and other programs to help innocent Purchasers of contaminated (or formerly contaminated "brown field") property.

The environmental laws impact not just industrial property, but even plain vanilla office space in terms of lead and asbestos abatement, and other laws and regulations impacting work spaces.

Sellers should keep in mind that Buyers will attempt to cast the least favorable light on environmental problems in order to negotiate Purchase Price or other concessions. So both sides to the transaction (not just the Purchaser) should consult with their attorneys (and environmental consultants if needed) to assess the impact of environmental problems. It might even be a good idea for the seller to remediate before seeking a buyer for the company; this may take the haggling over environmental issues off the table. Conduct due diligence not only on the condition of the properties, but also any notice or filing requirements imposed by environmental laws (including permits and consent orders) as a condition to the transaction.

Depending on the condition and type of the property, the Purchaser often demands a professionally conducted environmental site assessment, followed by the remediation of problems discovered in the assessment. Federal and state law may provide a defense to environmental liability to Purchasers who take appropriate steps to assess existing and potential contamination prior to acquiring property and to remediate or mitigate any violations. An assessment can establish a baseline profile of contamination to help Sellers quantify post-closing contamination caused by the Purchaser.

The environmental assessment is conducted in phases following testing standards and procedures established by the **American Society of Testing Materials** (www.astm.org). The parties can negotiate the other parameters, including who bears the cost, the environmental consultant to be retained, etc. A **Phase I** (or Level 1) assessment is a preliminary or surface level onsite (and documentary/database) investigation of existing or potential site contamination (land plus improvements); no chemical analysis is conducted during a Phase I assessment. If the Phase I report indicates a potential environmental contamination, then typically **Phase II** is conducted to chemically evaluate the type and extent of contamination. Finally, if Phase II confirms the presence of contamination, then the parties may need to enter into **Phase III**, which deals with remediation of the contamination.

Litigation and Government Investigations

Litigation or government proceedings like an IRS audit can divert significant resources away from the acquired business, not to mention impact its future prospects. If you are purchasing the stock of the company in a SPA, then you will be inheriting all the liabilities of the Acquired Company, including any liability that arises from such litigation or government investigations. Even if you are purchasing the assets in an APA, you'll want to know about such litigation and investigations, because they may have a negative impact on the future of the acquired business.

Incentive Compensation/Retirement Plans

The Purchaser's decision to assume, restructure, or terminate the acquired business's plans, and the way it implements its decision may have substantial risks. For example, the Purchaser could inherit a non-compliant plan (e.g., an underfunded defined benefit plan, an excessively funded 401(k) plan, or a putative qualified plan that does not in fact meet the requirements of a tax qualified plan).

Or, the Purchaser could unwittingly trigger joint and several liability for itself and the other companies of its Federal tax/ERISA control group by assuming an otherwise compliant plan (when scrutinized on a stand-alone basis) that is discriminatory when analyzed together with the plans of all the companies of the Purchaser's control group.

If the Purchaser wants to terminate a plan, it's got to worry about a litany of other legal issues; first and foremost, the requirement that it can't terminate a plan unless it's fully funded. If the plan to be terminated is overfunded, then the parties need to negotiate how the parties will allocate the surplus (and any tax for taking the surplus out) or otherwise deal with the surplus within legal guidelines.

If due diligence identifies a defect in the acquired business's plan, the Purchaser can condition the closing on the seller repairing the defect (the IRS has programs to correct plan defects) and/or use the opportunity to extract a concession, or renegotiate the Purchase Price.

During due diligence, the Purchaser should review the formal plan documents (including amendments, proposed amendments, and trust documents), summary plan descriptions (setting forth the rights, benefits, and responsibilities of participants and beneficiaries in ERISA plans in everyday language), summary of material modifications (describing changes made to plans and summary plans), annual reports such as Form 5500 (which, among other information, contains information on the adequecy of pension plan funding), and Form M-1 (for multiple employer welfare arrangements (MEWA) which offer medical benefits to the employees of two or more employers), as well as IRS compliance determination letters and other documents related to the acquired business's current and recently terminated plans.

The Purchaser should obtain these documents from the plan administrator. The Purchaser can also independently obtain some of these documents through the Employee Benefits Security Administration of the US Department of Labor.

Don't forget to look at the employee handbook to determine whether the acquired business has implemented informal plans. The Purchaser should also look at any contract entered into between any plan and third parties, for example, loan documents between a bank and a leveraged ESOP. In addition to plan defects and other non-compliance, look at the plan documents to see whether they throw any wrench into your planned asset or stock purchase transaction. For example, will the transaction trigger a partial termination of, or acceleration of vesting rights under any plans? Can the plan be modified or terminated in the sponsoring employer's discretion?

The Purchaser should also review employment agreements for golden parachute and other severance type payments that may be triggered by a sale of business transaction. It's well known that golden parachutes raise issues of management self-dealing. But fiduciary duty issues are also implicated in all areas of incentive compensation. For example, if the company stock price drops precipitously, do the 401(k) participants have a claim based on the assertion that management bought plan stock at inflated prices? Careful due diligence will help you to root out potential problems, and structure appropriate indemnification or other solutions. After the sale, the Purchaser must act quickly, lest the plan participants have a claim if they miss out on a stock market run-up because it takes too long to transfer an account after the closing.

So work with your attorney and tax and benefits specialists to perform adequate due diligence about the Acquired Company's plans (including, but not limited to, **Qualified Plans** — e.g., **defined benefit plans** such as pension plans, as well as **defined contribution plans** such as 401(k) plans, employee stock ownership plans (ESOP) and profit sharing plans, and **Nonqualified Deferred Compensation Plans** i.e., non-ERISA plans, such as bonus and performance based plans, stock appreciation rights, phantom stock plans and SERPS), and to select and then structure the correct option (or another option not mentioned above) to minimize your liability and take care of your new employees.

Health Benefit Plans

The Purchaser in the sale of a business will also need to conduct due diligence on the status of the acquired business's health insurance and related plans (e.g., cafeteria plans, etc.).

If the acquired business has a fully insured health plan, then the Purchaser needs to confirm that the acquired business is up-to-date on its premium payments to the insurance company. The insurance company pays employee claims directly. The creditworthiness of the insurance company is therefore an issue because it, rather than the employer, bears the insurance risk.

If the employer maintains a self-insured health plan, this means that it pays employee medical claims out of its own pocket typically without the cushion of any reserves. The employer bears the insurance risk and has the obligation to pay even if the company performs poorly, but can mitigate this risk somewhat with the purchase of an umbrella policy. The Purchaser's due diligence will include an analysis of the acquired business's ability to support the plan, including payment history, etc.

Intellectual Property

Due diligence of intellectual property (IP) matters focuses on confirming the ownership and strengths and weaknesses of the IP, as well as the existence of infringement claims (both to enforce and defend against). Intellectual property is a good example of how the Purchaser can conduct due diligence to independently verify seller supplied information. Publicly available information for registered IP includes patents, certain patent applications, trademark registrations, and other documents available from the **US Patent and Trademark Office** database.

Ownership

If you are the Purchaser, one of the first things you'll want to confirm is the ownership of the registered IP. You'll need to verify that the Acquired Company (SPA) or Seller (APA) actually owns the IP it purports to own. For example, US patents are issued to the inventors. Typically, employees are required by their employers to assign any patents on their inventions to the employer. While such assignments are often a condition of employment, it's possible that the paperwork to record such assignments was never prepared or filed. This constitutes a break in the chain of recording. These and other errors in previous recordings could jeopardize the Purchaser's interest in the acquired business's registered IP, including its right to use or enforce the the IP after the Closing. Don't forget also to review any arrangements with third-party vendors and independent contractors regarding ownership of inventions made by these vendors or contractors.

Ownership issues also arise when you're purchasing a division or a subsidiary. The question in these cases is whether the IP is being used by just the division or subsidiary, but also by the part of the business that is not being sold. Yet another issue is licensing — after all, just because the Acquired Company or Seller doesn't own the IP doesn't mean that it doesn't have the right to use it; so carefully review any license or other arrangements giving the acquired business the right to use third party owned IPs, including whether such rights can be transferred to you.

Strength of IP

Regardless of whether it's a stock or asset transaction, the Purchaser will also want to investigate how strong the acquired business' intellectual property rights are. This is an area where the seller does not have the incentive to look for subtle weaknesses in its portfolio; its focus will be to look like it's got its act together because it wants to maximize the purchase price of the transaction.

Patents

Patents give the owner the right to prevent others to use the invention for a specified period of time. If you find during due diligence that some part of the acquired business's patents are covered by a prior third-party patent, this means that the third party may have the right to prevent you from using the very patent you've shelled out good money for. It's best to identify this reduction in value early in the negotiations, when you still have the ability to lower the Purchase Price or extract some other concession from the Seller.

Trademarks

Trademarks give the owner the exclusive right to use the mark, but the owner has to be able to show not only that it's been using the mark, but also that it's enforced its rights against infringers. If the seller hasn't done a good job enforcing its rights against infringers, for example, allowing similar unregistered common law marks to crop up without protest, then the Purchaser should wonder whether it's paying too much for the trademark. The Purchaser should enlist a reputable trademark search company to conduct a thorough search of similar marks, including unregistered common law marks, brand names, etc., that are not part of the USPTO database.

A common misconception is that if you've been able to form a corporation or LLC under a particular name, that you also own the trademark on the name. The name of the legal entity is a matter of state corporate law, not trademark law. The Secretary of State of a particular state will not cross-check against the USPTO database (much less clear the name against common law trademarks), or even cross-check against out-of-state corporate name databases. In other words, if the name has not been taken by somebody else in your state, then the Secretary of State will allow you to use it for your entity's name. This is not the same thing as having the right to use (and enforce against others) the name as a brand name — that right can only be conferred by trademark law.

Trade secrets

Trade secrets are a more sensitive issue to tackle in due diligence. Trade secrets have value precisely because they are secret; there is no patent for the Kentucky Fried Chicken recipe. The secret recipe is held under lock and key someplace, or maybe safe and secure in the memories of a few key personnel. The seller in a case where there are trade secrets is reluctant to disclose the secret until it is absolutely sure that the Purchaser will close, yet the Purchaser needs to analyze the secret for due diligence purposes. The parties will need to work with their attornies to overcome this chicken and egg situation — negotiate timing the disclosure just right, plus confidential treatment for this information, including practical ways to draft the sale of business agreement in a way that clearly identifies what the information is, without disclosing the details in an exhibit.

Claims

The basic principles for uncovering existing and potential claims is the same as for any kind of litigation. Existing lawsuits are a matter of public record. You can assess the threat of an infringement claim as you analyze the relative strength of the IP portfolio, plus the existence of warning letters or other paper trail in the seller's files.

Due Diligence versus Representations and Warranties

To some people, it seems superfluous to spend lots of time and money conducting due diligence when the counterparty will be making representations and warranties in the Asset Purchase or Stock Purchase Agreement. After all, goes the thinking, if the seller is making a representation in the agreement that it hasn't violated any environmental laws, then why does the purchaser need to separately investigate?

Keep in mind that it is very important to conduct thorough due diligence AND obtain the most coverage in terms of representations and warranties. You never want to rely solely on your counterparty's representations and warranties. If your counterparty breaches the agreement by making a misrepresentation, the only way you can recover is to sue for damages, which can be an expensive (good money chasing after bad) and time-consuming process without any guarantee of a favorable outcome. Also, by that time, the seller may have taken your purchase price money and disappeared, not necessarily maliciously, but just by virtue of the fact that there's really no practical reason to stick around after selling its business. There are certainly ways to reduce your exposure; for example, spreading out payments to the seller over time, or obtaining a personal guarantee or other security. But due diligence will enable you to verify (or at least give you some degree of comfort) that your counterparty is being truthful in making its representations and warranties. And the party making the representation will be forced to take a good, hard look at its own situation (through self-examination due diligence discussed above), and have a good idea of whether, and to what extent, it can make certain representations in the agreement.

LETTER OF INTENT

In the above example, let's say that the seller, Cavendish, and the purchaser, Consolidated, have come to a preliminary agreement on the key points of the transaction, such as the legal structure of the transaction (more on that in the next section of this chapter), the purchase price, and payment terms. However, at this formative stage of the negotiations, the parties might need more time to think about the details of the transaction. And even the key deal points may need to change based upon what the parties find during their due diligence. Furthermore, once the attorneys are able to complete the final draft of the definitive agreement (Asset Purchase Agreement or Stock Purchase Agreement) incorporating all the agreed-upon terms and conditions, the parties may still need some additional time before the closing (when title to the assets or stock is transferred, and the purchase price is paid) can take place. Depending on the transaction, the closing may take place at the same time the definitive agreement is signed (execution date), or a set amount of time after the execution date, in order to allow the parties time to gather all the ancillary paperwork, obtain all the third-party consents, obtain any financing and perform the other closing conditions required by the definitive agreement. The reality is that even in cases where the negotiations are going smoothly, it takes time for the parties to put together and close the transaction.

You should also keep in mind that any company (like Cavendish) that is attractive as a potential acquisition target is likely to be attractive to any number of suitors besides Consolidated. And companies (like Consolidated) on the lookout to acquire will likely be looking at several companies at the same time — Cavendish is likely just one of several companies on its hit list.

Given these realities, oftentimes the parties will buy some time to complete the transaction by entering into a short Letter of Intent (or a Memorandum of Understanding, Agreement in Principal, or Term Sheet), which sets forth the basic terms and conditions of the transaction, while perhaps carving out a specified time period for exclusive negotiations. In some cases, the Letter of Intent will provide for the payment of "earnest money" to be applied to the purchase price, as further consideration for such exclusivity. Provided the Letter of Intent is drafted in a way that creates an obligation only to negotiate in good faith (and does not create the obligation to actually enter into a definitive agreement), then the Letter of Intent is a useful starting point to help the parties negotiate the definitive agreement while keeping other suitors or candidates at bay.

LEGAL STRUCTURE OF SALE OF BUSINESS

One of the threshold issues for the parties is how to structure the transaction. There are two principal ways to structure the sale of a business. The seller can sell just the assets of the business (contracts, real property, fixtures, furniture, inventory, intellectual property, accounts receivable, etc.). In this case, the purchaser is just buying the assets of the business, and is not assuming any liabilities of the business (except those specifically agreed to, and those liabilities such as successor liability imposed by law). In an asset sale, the parties would enter into a definitive agreement called an **Asset Purchase Agreement**. Or, the seller can sell its ownership interest (stock, membership or other ownership interest) in the legal entity (corporation, limited liability company, etc.) that owns the assets. In this case, the purchaser is buying an ownership interest in the selling entity itself, and through such ownership, all the assets of the selling entity, as well as assuming all the liabilities (known and unknown) of the selling entity — basically everything, including the kitchen sink. In an entity sale, the parties would enter into a definitive agreement called an Entity Purchase Agreement. Entity purchases typically involve the sale of stock in a corporation, so I will use the term **Stock Purchase Agreement** interchangeably with Entity Purchase Agreement.

If you are purchasing a business from an individual (sole proprietor) or a group of individuals, rather than from a corporation, multi-member limited liability company, or other "non-natural" legal entity, then you'll have little choice but to structure the transaction as an asset sale. After all, since there is no entity that can be purchased, it's not possible to structure the transaction as an entity purchase.

If, however, you are purchasing a business that is being run as a corporation or other legal entity, then you'll have the choice of whether to structure the transaction as an asset or entity sale. You'll need to consider the pros and cons, including the liability and tax issues discussed in this section, to determine how you want to structure the transaction.

100 Percent Ownership versus Partial Ownership

This book addresses the situation where a purchaser desires full control, that is, to purchase 100 percent ownership so that it can "run the business." That being said, there may be situations where you might want to "buy into" a business and partner up with the existing owner. In this case, you would own the corporation together with the existing shareholders. There are two basic ways to structurally achieve this — first, the corporation can issue you shares, essentially issuing you the number of shares so that you end up owning the agreed-upon percentage of shares in the corporation. Or, the existing shareholders can sell a portion of their shares directly to you. In either case, you would end up owning a certain percentage of the corporation, while automatically diluting the percentage ownership of the existing shareholders.

Oftentimes, corporate governance documents (certificates of incorporation, bylaws, shareholders' agreements, etc.) place first refusal rights or other restrictions on the extent to which, and the manner in which, these transactions can take place. If you are contemplating the purchase of partial ownership in a corporation (or limited liability company or partnership), in most instances you'll be asked to sign their form of Shareholder Agreement (or Limited Liability Company Operating Agreement or Partnership Agreement), which contains various and sundry provisions governing the rights and obligations of the owners, including the right to resell your interests. Since these documents protect all owners, not just the existing ones, you should consult with your attorney about drafting one for the corporation or other entity you plan on becoming a part owner in, in case it does not already have one. Please refer to Part I for a detailed discussion of corporate governance documents.

ASSET VERSUS STOCK SALE

Asset Sale

In an **asset purchase**, the Purchaser will purchase only the assets listed in the Asset Purchase Agreement (APA). These assets are described in the body of the APA and/or in further detail in exhibits that are attached to, and made part and parcel of, the APA. For example, if the assets include motor vehicles, the APA will likely contain an exhibit that lists the make, model, year, and VIN of each vehicle being sold. The parties can negotiate which assets will be purchased, and which assets will be left behind with the Seller.

A non-exhaustive list of asset categories includes: equipment, real estate, furniture, fixtures, motor vehicles, contracts, intellectual property (patents, trade secrets, trademarks, servicemarks, copyrights, etc.), the continued right to employ existing employees, inventory, accounts receivable, and goodwill.

Liabilities of the Business Assumed by the Purchaser in an Asset Transaction

From a contract drafting perspective, the parties will negotiate and set forth in the APA the extent to which the Purchaser is assuming any specific liabilities of the Seller. For example, if you are the Seller in an asset transaction, and you want the Purchaser to assume your obligation to repay loans for money that you've borrowed for the business, or you want the purchaser to assume outstanding warranty obligations on products previously sold, then you must include language in the APA specifically requiring the Purchaser to assume these obligations. If you're the Purchaser in an asset transaction, it's always better to take a "clean slate approach" and not assume any of the Seller's liabilities. You'll want to have language in the APA that unequivocally limits the extent to which you assume any of the Seller's liabilities. In the sample excerpts in the following chapters, I'll show you ways in which you can try do that.

If the owner of the assets to be sold is one or more individual(s), then the transaction would take place between the Purchaser and the selling individual(s). If the owner of the assets to be sold is a corporation (or other legal entity), then the transaction would take place between the Purchaser and the selling corporation, rather than the selling corporation's shareholders. After the closing, the selling corporation will remain in existence as a shell with little or no assets, except of course the purchase price paid to it or to be paid to it if payments are to be made in installments. The shell will also have its remaining liabilities intact. The selling corporation then can use the purchase price paid to it by the Purchaser to pay off its liabilities. It can then make a distribution of any remaining balance to its shareholders, and dissolve. Note that in an asset transaction, the selling entity (if a "C" corporation) is taxed on the payment to it of the purchase price, and the shareholders are taxed when the money is distributed to them as a liquidating distribution. This double-tax is a major pitfall of asset transactions.

Stock Sale

In an entity purchase, the Purchaser will purchase the ownership interest in the Acquired Company, the legal entity that owns the assets. The most common example of an entity transaction is the purchase of stock in an Acquired Company that is a corporation. In this case, the Purchaser would become the new shareholder of the corporation, and would by virtue of such share ownership, become indirect owner of all the assets of the Acquired Company. Since the transaction takes place between the Purchaser and the owners (selling Stockholders) of the Acquired Company, the purchase price would be paid directly to the selling Stockholders, who would no longer own any stake in the corporation.

The Purchaser would also become, through its new stock ownership, the indirect "owner" of all the known and hidden (undisclosed or even unknown to both parties) obligations or liabilities of the Acquired Company — including any future claims arising from acts or failures to act of the previous owner (unknown personal injury claims, unpaid taxes, you name it), extending even to statutorily imposed strict liability where the selling Stockholders may not even have been at fault.

As a shareholder of the corporation, you would in most instances have the statutory protection of the "corporate shield" (see sidebar for discussion), and thus you would not be personally liable. However, the corporation you just spent good money on would be liable. The assumption of these obligations is one of the biggest pitfalls of purchasing stock in a corporation. This risk can be mitigated by the Purchaser thorough, for example, due diligence; obtaining good representations and warranties; negotiating installment payment terms; as well as obtaining a solid indemnity; security from the selling shareholders; and adequate insurance (to cover product liability and personal injury claims). These issues are addressed in the sample excerpts contained in the following chapters.

Tax Impact

The tax requirements of sellers and buyers will vary depending on their own tax priorities. However, the parties generally will want to structure the transaction to minimize any negative tax consequences. The seller will want to pay as little tax as possible on the consideration (cash, notes, etc.) it receives for the sale. It also wants to pay the tax as late as possible. The Purchaser will generally want a step-up tax basis in the assets of the acquired company so that it can maximize its deductions, for example, through the depreciation or amortization of the assets. The parties should work with their attorneys and tax advisors to come up with the best solution to overcome these sometimes conflicting priorities.

Some of the tax issues that may impact the parties' decision whether to structure the transaction as an asset or stock transaction include:

- **Taxable versus Tax-Deferred Transactions:** Given space constraints, this book only discusses the two basic ways to acquire a business: purchasing the assets and purchasing the stock of the target company by paying a Purchase Price consisting only of cash or notes (the promise to pay cash over a period of time). These transactions are **taxable transactions**, meaning that the seller (either the Seller in an APA or the selling Stockholders in a SPA) recognizes immediate taxable gain to the extent that the Purchase Price exceeds the seller's tax basis (generally its cost) in the sold property. The Purchaser in a taxable transaction obtains a **step-up basis** in the property acquired equal to the Purchase Price (allocated as necessary), which enables the Purchaser to take tax-saving depreciation and amortization deductions going forward and works to lower the potential gain in the eventual resale of the property.

This book will not discuss (given space constraints) the numerous other ways to structure a taxable acquisition (e.g., statutory mergers with either the Purchaser or the target company as the survivor, forward or reverse subsidiary mergers for cash, etc.). Nor is there room in this book to discuss the myriad ways in which the parties can structure the deal to be **tax-deferred** (where the seller does not recognize gain on the transaction). While the requirements for tax-deferred acquisitions are beyond the scope of this book, there are several basic common denominators in tax-deferred transactions. First, the Purchaser and the target company generally must be corporations. Second, the Purchaser must pay consideration principally (or sometimes solely) in the form of stock in the Purchaser, rather than cash. Stock, rather than cash, consideration forms the very generalized justification for tax-free treatment that goes something like this: "There is no tax because the seller is not cashing out, but is deemed to be continuing its investment in the combined business by swapping its stock or assets for the stock of the Purchaser." Third, and this is the *quid pro quo* for tax-free treatment, the Purchaser obtains a **carryover basis** in the acquired property, which tends to hamper the ability of the Purchaser to maximize its deductions going forward and works to increase the potential gain in the eventual resale of the property.

Tax-deferred transactions include Internal Revenue Code **Section 368 Reorganizations, Section 355 Spin-offs, Split-offs** and **Split-ups**, as well as acquisitions utilizing **Section 351 incorporations** and a host of other transaction structures too numerous to fit here. Consult with your attorney and tax advisors on whether a tax-deferred structure might work well for you.

Keep in mind that many of the same legal issues apply to a broad spectrum of transactions, so you're likely to find in a tax-deferred transaction many of the representations and warranties, covenants, closing conditions and other provisions discussed in this book (adjusted as necessary to fit the particular legal structure and factual situation).

- **Step-up Basis versus Carryover Basis in Taxable Transactions:** All other things being equal, the Purchaser may prefer the asset purchase structure because the Purchaser can obtain a step-up basis in the acquired assets. The step-up in tax basis allows the Purchaser to take tax-saving depreciation and amortization deductions going forward and works to lower the potential gain in the eventual resale of the property. In a stock transaction, the Purchaser obtains a step-up basis in the acquired stock, but inherits a carry-over basis in the target company's assets. A discussion of **Internal Revenue Code Section 338** and **338(h)(10)** is beyond the scope of this book. These provisions allow an election to treat a sale of stock as a sale of assets for tax purposes, thus enabling the Purchaser to obtain a step-up basis in the assets of the target.

- **Double-tax Impact:** Of course, "all other things" are never equal in real life, and the parties have to consider the double-tax impact of typical asset transactions, and whatever effect it might have on the negotiated Purchase Price of the transaction. In a plain-vanilla asset transaction involving a C corporation, the Seller (i.e., the company selling its assets) recognizes taxable gain on the sale of each asset to the extent the allocated Purchase Price exceeds its tax basis in the asset. Then, each shareholder of the selling corporation recognizes taxable gain on any distribution made by the selling corporation to the shareholder. If the selling corporation has profit and stays in existence, then the distribution is treated as a dividend and if the corporation liquidates, then the distribution is treated as capital gain to the extent the distribution exceeds the shareholder's tax basis in its stock. By contrast, there is one layer of tax in a plain vanilla stock (for cash) transaction — each selling Stockholder recognizes taxable gain to the extent its portion of the Purchase Price exceeds its tax basis in the stock.

  Consult with your attorney and tax advisor because the double-tax impact of an asset transaction might be eliminated or reduced to the extent that the selling company is a pass-through entity like an S corporation, or the selling company has net operating losses it can use to absorb any gain prior to making its liquidating distribution. Also keep in mind that there are strict limitations on the extent to which the Purchaser can continue to use any net operating losses of the target company going forward.

- **State Tax Laws:** Don't forget to consider the impact of state and local tax laws on your transaction. The state and local tax law ramifications vary from jurisdiction to jurisdiction and are beyond the scope of this book. Work with your attorney and tax advisor because even if you have a handle on the Federal tax law ramifications, you assume at your own risk that state and local tax laws mirror Federal tax law. For example, some states do not even recognize a Federal Subchapter S election and require the taxpayer to file separately in the state. Even a slight difference in the way the Federal and state tax authorities treat a transaction could eviscerate your profit margin in your transaction.

Allocation of Purchase Price

One of the main advantages of an asset transaction is the flexibility to negotiate an allocation of a portion of the purchase price to each asset purchased. Each party will negotiate an allocation that will give it the best tax-saving advantage. The Seller will negotiate to minimize the gain on the sale of particular assets, and the Purchaser will negotiate to minimize potential gain on resale plus maximize the ability to take tax-saving deductions on the purchased assets. The IRS will likely recognize any reasonable allocation of the purchase price that is negotiated between the Seller and the Purchaser on an arm's-length basis. It's crucial that you work with your attorney and tax advisor to negotiate an allocation that best suits your needs. See Purchase Price and Payment Terms (Chapter 11) for a more detailed discussion of allocation.

Incentive Compensation/Retirement Plans

Incentive compensation/retirement plans include **qualified plans** (including defined benefit pension and defined contribution 401(k), profit sharing, ESOP, and other plans) and **nonqualified deferred compensation plans** (typically used as a way to defer income tax for highly compensated executives). In an asset purchase transaction, the parties will negotiate to determine which plans the Purchaser will assume, and which plans will be left for the Seller to terminate or otherwise deal with.

Due diligence will be very important. If the Purchaser decides to assume some of the Seller's plans, then it needs to confirm that it is not inheriting any non-compliant plans (e.g., an underfunded defined benefit plan or a putative qualified plan that does not in fact meet the requirements of a tax qualified plan).

Even the assumption of an otherwise compliant plan (when scrutinized on a stand-alone basis) could run afoul of Federal tax and ERISA requirements of non-discriminatory coverage (when analyzed together with the plans of all the companies of the Purchaser's "control group" — at a minimum the Purchaser parent company, but also affiliates). This could trigger something much more than the Purchaser bargained for — joint and several liability for every company in the control group.

In a stock purchase transaction, the Purchaser automatically assumes all employee benefit plans not terminated by the Acquired Company before the Closing. Alternatively, the Purchaser can negotiate to make the termination of the Acquired Company's plans a condition to closing the transaction if it wants to cover the Acquired Company's employees under its own plans. Or it can close the transaction, and then either terminate the Acquired Company's plans and distribute the funds to the participants, or freeze the plans (i.e., no more contributions or accruals) and pay the participants as and when due (e.g., retirement, etc.).

Another option is for the Purchaser to merge the Acquired Company's plans into its own. Yet another scenario is where the Acquired Company's employees are covered under plans maintained by its parent company; in this case, the Purchaser in an SPA won't automatically be assuming the plan, so it needs to structure its own plan to accommodate the new employees post-closing. You'll need to work with your attorney, tax advisor, and human resources expert to negotiate the best solution for the disposition of employee benefit plans.

Collective Bargaining Obligations

One of the most important labor law issues in a sale of business transaction is to determine the extent to which the Purchaser has the obligation to recognize and bargain (to agreement or impasse) with any unions representing the acquired business's employees, including the status of any **collective bargaining agreement** (CBA) in place.

As discussed, the Purchaser in a stock purchase transaction generally automatically assumes all the obligations of the Acquired Company. It follows that the Purchaser must recognize and bargain with the existing unions. Any CBA in place will remain in effect until its natural expiration date or earlier termination date as provided in the CBA.

This issue is more complex in an asset purchase transaction. In an asset transaction, the Purchaser generally can negotiate which obligations it wants to assume but the rules are more rigid for collective bargaining obligations. The Purchaser cannot simply walk away. The case law standard to determine whether the Purchaser is a successor to the Seller's obligation to recognize and bargain with existing unions is whether there is **"substantial continuity"** in the acquired business (especially its work force) after the closing.

This is not an easy determination because Purchasers often make changes to the work force to take advantage of economies of scale, etc. A Purchaser has the general freedom to make changes (e.g., hire who it wants to, establish initial employment terms, and even negotiate a new CBA), as long as it doesn't discriminate against union workers, especially in an attempt to avoid becoming a successor.

Substantial continuity is determined around the closing of the transaction but usually when the Purchaser has hired its **representative complement** of workers, that is, generally speaking, hired most of its workers for most of its job categories. The hash mark for substantial continuity is set around the majority; if over half of the post-closing representative complement is made up of former Seller union workers, then a good case can be made for "substantial continuity" (even if they form less than a majority of the eventual full complement of workers). In that case, the Purchaser would generally be obligated to recognize and bargain with the union, as well as honor the CBA.

But there are other factors to consider. Is there continuity of operations, supervisory staff and product lineup? Is there a plan to shut down the plant for renovations for awhile after the closing?

Work with your attorney and labor specialist to conduct your due diligence. If you are the Purchaser, work with your experts to determine your obligations to the acquired business's workers in either an asset purchase or stock purchase transaction. Consult with them when you write your employee communications because the outcome of any claim in a dispute could hinge on what and how you communicate to the Seller's former employees. Work with them to structure your post-closing collective bargaining obligations, including anticipating and dealing with potential union claims that it should represent all the workers (not just the Seller's former employees but also your new hires) based on the community of interest principals of accretion. National Labor Relations Board factors for accretion include how integrated the two groups of employees are in terms of physical contact, supervision, and operations, among other factors.

Intellectual Property

As discussed, in a stock purchase transaction, the Purchaser takes over the ownership interest in the legal entity that owns the assets, including all of the intellectual property assets of the Acquired Company. In an asset purchase transaction, each piece of intellectual property is an asset of the Seller (the legal entity that is selling its assets) that would need to be assigned to the Purchaser. And in an asset deal, if patents, registered trademarks, or other registered intellectual property rights are part of the Seller's portfolio, then the parties would need to take all steps to prepare and record the transfer of ownership with the US Patent and Trademark Office (USPTO), as well as in foreign jurisdictions, if applicable. This is a time-consuming and expensive process and it's best to research these issues well in advance of the closing. Due diligence is crucial; any break in the chain of recording or errors in previous recordings could jeopardize the Purchaser's interest in registered intellectual property.

KEY PROVISIONS OF SALE OF BUSINESS AGREEMENTS

Now, let's take a quick look at the key provisions of a typical agreement for the sale of a business. In many cases, these types of key provisions are common to both Asset Purchase Agreements and Stock Purchase Agreements, with the obvious caveat that the individual provisions may need to be adjusted depending on whether the transaction is an asset or stock sale.

Summary of Key Provisions

Sample contract excerpts of these key provisions, together with detailed discussions of the excerpts, are contained in the following chapters and on the CD-ROM. I'll also indicate to what extent the sample provisions apply to asset sales, stock sales, or both.

- **Front Matter:** Every contract, including Asset Purchase and Stock Purchase Agreements, have the front matter portion, which lists the names and addresses of the parties plus perhaps some preambles (introductory paragraphs). Please refer to the CD-ROM for a detailed discussion of front matter.

- **Obligation to Sell and Purchase:** The Seller will have the obligation to sell, and the Purchaser will have the obligation to purchase, either the listed assets of the business, or the stock or other ownership interest of the selling owners. If the transaction is structured as an asset sale, then the parties will also need to clarify, which, if any, of the liabilities of the acquired business will be assumed by the Purchaser. The sale and purchase is contingent on the representations and warranties, negative and affirmative covenants, and closing conditions set forth in the agreement.

- **Purchase Price and Payment Terms:** The Purchaser will have the obligation to pay the Purchase Price set forth in the agreement. The purchase price may be subject to adjustment depending on events that occur either before or after the closing. For example, if you are the purchaser of the assets of a business, and you negotiate a purchase price based, in part, on the successful collection of most of the acquired business's accounts receivable, then you can negotiate some kind of formula in the agreement that adjusts the purchase price downward in case you cannot collect a certain percentage of the receivables. The purchaser will have the obligation to pay the purchase price according to the **payment terms** set forth in the agreement. For example, payment may be made entirely at closing, or in **installments** over a period of time. In case payment is made in installments, then the purchaser will also need to provide a **promissory note**, and perhaps other security. And if the parties can't come to terms about what the company is actually worth, they might consider structuring an **earnout**, where the Purchaser agrees to pay additional consideration after the Closing if the company's performance exceeds agreed-to targets. Another scenario might be that the Purchaser is very worried about the company's risk profile. For example, maybe the company has a history of environmental problems. In this case, the Purchaser might negotiate that some portion of the Purchase Price (for example, up to 15 percent) be put into **escrow** to help cover any future indemnification claims the Purchaser might have against the Seller (either the Seller in an APA or selling stockholders in an SPA). The escrowed funds might also be used to pay any purchase price adjustment, if needed.

- **The Closing:** This section sets forth the logistics of the Closing of the transaction, including the location, date, and time of the Closing, as well as details about the exchange to take place at Closing between the parties (for example, the Purchase Price, title documents, and other documents).

- **Representations and Warranties:** Both the Purchaser and the Seller (either the Seller in an APA or selling Stockholders in an SPA) make a litany of representations and warranties (from a practical point of view, these terms are interchangeable) to induce the other party to enter into the transaction. These mainly relate to their ability to enter into and perform their respective obligations under the agreement. Just one example is the Seller's representation that it, in fact, owns whatever it is selling to the Purchaser. Many of the facts being represented in the agreement can also be verified through due diligence. The seller of a business typically makes the lion's share of representations and warranties in a sale of business transaction, but no matter whether you are selling or buying a business, you'll want to negotiate limiting the scope of your representations if you are making them, and to negotiate expanding the scope of your counterparty's representations if you are the beneficiary of them.

- **Affirmative and Negative Covenants:** While representations and warranties are statements made affirming facts about the seller, purchaser, or business being sold, covenants are promises each party makes to act or not act in a certain way. For example, the Seller (either the Seller in an APA or the selling

Stockholders in an SPA) will make a litany of covenants to ensure that whatever is being sold doesn't lose value before closing. **Affirmative covenants** are promises to take action, such as the covenant to grant the Purchaser and its personnel adequate access to conduct due diligence. **Negative covenants** are promises not to do anything that may harm whatever is being sold, such as the negative covenant that the Seller will not do anything to jeopardize the customer relationships that are being sold. The seller of a business typically makes the lion's share of covenants in a sale of business transaction, but no matter whether you are selling or buying a business, you'll want to negotiate limiting the scope of your covenants if you are making them, and to negotiate expanding the scope of your counterparty's covenants if you are the beneficiary of them.

- **Closing Conditions:** These are all of the things that have to happen before the exchange (transfer of title and payment of the Purchase Price) can occur on the Closing Date. Think of the Closing Conditions for the sale of a business in the context of hosting a big dinner party (the "transaction"). If you are planning an elaborate party, you'll want to make sure that all of the pieces (the "Closing Conditions") fall into place before the first guest arrives for the big event (the "Closing"). Some of these pieces might include preparing the menu or making sure the caterer shows up on time, cleaning the house, and sprucing up the backyard.

- **Indemnity:** This section sets forth the conditions under which either party can seek from the other party a remedy for its losses. Although mutual indemnities can be found in other type agreements, most indemnities in APA and SPA flow one way — from the seller in favor of the Purchaser. Most indemnities are negotiated to allow indemnification where the seller has breached the APA or SPA (for example, the seller makes a misrepresentation). In many cases, however, indemnification is also used as a risk allocation strategy, even in the absence of a breach. For example, there is no misrepresentation if the seller makes full disclosure about an environmental problem at one of its sites. Despite the lack of breach, the Purchaser will usually try to negotiate indemnification from the seller for any losses it incurs as a result of high risk matters impacting the Purchaser when purchasing a business — things like disclosed environmental problems, litigation and product liability matters.

- **Boilerplate section:** Most contracts usually have (toward the end) a section of boilerplate (standard clauses) covering a laundry list of matters such as assignability, governing law, notices, severability, etc. You and your attorney should pay special attention because if improperly drafted, these ostensibly routine and mundane provisions can come back to haunt you. Please refer to Part V and the CD-ROM for a detailed discussion of standard boilerplate provisions.

8

PRINCIPAL OBLIGATIONS OF THE BUYER AND SELLER

OVERVIEW

Principal obligation provisions can usually be found at the beginning of the **Asset Purchase Agreement (APA)** or **Stock Purchase Agreement (SPA)** and set forth the very basic obligations of the parties to sell and purchase the assets or stock. These basic obligations are "subject to the terms and conditions of the Agreement," meaning that the parties also have to satisfy all of their other obligations covered by the other sections of the Agreement.

Terminology

In the sample contract provisions, I refer to the seller in an asset transaction (the individual, corporation, or other entity selling his, her, or its assets) as the "Seller" (capitalized). I refer to the sellers in an entity or stock transaction as the "selling Stockholders" (the term stockholder and shareholder can be used interchangeably). I refer to the corporation or other entity whose stock or ownership interests are being acquired in an entity or stock transaction as the "Acquired Company."

In the detailed discussion of the contract provisions, I sometimes use the shorthand "seller" (not capitalized) when referring to either the Seller (APA) or the selling Stockholders (SPA). Sometimes I use the term "acquired business" when referring to either the Seller (APA) or the Acquired Company (SPA). Finally, sometimes I use the term "Stockholders" to refer to either the selling Stockholders (SPA) or the owners of a corporate Seller (APA).

136

To the extent that a sample contract provision is used to show both the APA and SPA versions, I usually only use the APA "Seller" in order to reduce clutter, with the SPA "[Acquired Company]" appearing in brackets just the first time it is used in the provision.

SAMPLE CONTRACT EXCERPTS

[APA version] Subject to the terms and conditions of this Agreement, on the Closing Date,

(a) the Seller shall sell, assign, transfer, and deliver to the Purchaser, and the Purchaser shall purchase and acquire from the Seller, the Assets (defined below), and

(b) the Purchaser shall assume and agree to satisfy and discharge the Obligations (defined below).

The Seller's principal obligation in an Asset Purchase Agreement (APA) is to sell to the Purchaser all of its rights in the listed assets (Assets). The conveyed rights include whatever ownership or leasehold rights that are held by the Seller in the various Assets. The Seller will confirm these rights in the Seller's representations and warranties. The Purchaser's principal obligations in an APA are to make payment of the Purchase Price (see Chapter 11) and acquire all such rights. Provided that all the "terms and conditions of the Agreement" are satisfied, then on the Closing Date, the Purchaser will become the new owner of the Assets. The parties have the flexibility to tailor the scope of the Assets to include only certain assets of the Seller (see Chapter 9). The parties can also include in the APA a list of unwanted or Excluded Assets that will remain with the Seller.

If you are the Purchaser, it's not a good idea to voluntarily assume the obligations of the Seller. However, I've included the bracketed language in case you've agreed to assume some of these obligations (Obligations), in which case you'll want to refer to Chapter 10 for language you can add to limit the extent to which you assume such Obligations. You can also refer to Chapter 10 for sample contract language to affirmatively declare that you will not be assuming any obligations of the Seller. Consult with your attorney because fraudulent conveyance and other laws may impose successor liability on an APA Purchaser regardless of any explicit non-assumption of liabilities by the Purchaser.

[SPA version] Subject to the terms and conditions of this Agreement, on the Closing Date, the selling Stockholders shall sell, assign, transfer, and deliver to the Purchaser, and the Purchaser shall purchase and acquire from the selling Stockholders, all of their shares of stock in the Acquired Company.

The selling Stockholders' principal obligation in a Stock Purchase Agreement (SPA) is to sell to the Purchaser their ownership interest in the stock of the Acquired Company. Rather than directly purchasing the assets of the Acquired Company, the Purchaser purchases an ownership interest in the legal entity (the Acquired Company) that owns the assets. The Purchaser in a stock transaction cannot "disown" the Acquired Company's liabilities; those liabilities automatically stay with the Acquired Company. If the Acquired Company is a corporation, however, the Purchaser will enjoy a qualified limited liability for the debts and obligations of the Acquired Company.

9

CORPORATE ASSETS PURCHASED

OVERVIEW

This chapter is about contract provisions that define the scope of the assets to be transferred in an Asset Purchase Agreement (APA).

One of the advantages of structuring the transaction as an asset purchase is the ability to pick and choose (that is, negotiate) which assets will be transferred to the Purchaser, and which assets will remain with the APA Seller. You need to make sure that all parts of the Agreement work to get you what you are paying for. For example, you might decide that you want to purchase only some of, rather than all, the inventory of the Seller. But ideally you're still going to want the Seller to make representations and warranties about all its inventory. Adding to this confusion is the fact that inventory levels will change between the date the APA is signed and the Closing Date. As a Purchaser, you certainly want the Seller to keep selling product (and keep the business running) until the Closing Date when you formally take over. Yet the Seller's inventory representations confirm facts about the inventory only as of the date the APA is signed. What about the inventory after the signing date but before the Closing Date?

Attorneys spend a lot of time on Bring Down clauses, covenants, indemnity provisions, and survival language in an attempt to patch any gaps in coverage (in terms of definition or time). You can help by working with your attorney to make sure that the definitions in the APA are internally consistent. For example, I've defined the assets to be acquired under the APA as "Acquired Assets" (rather than just "Assets"), and the asset categories to be acquired under the APA as "Acquired Inventory," "Acquired Equipment," etc., (rather than just "Inventory," "Equipment," etc.). This will help you to distinguish between the assets that are actually being purchased, and the assets of the Seller in general. While your attorney may have his or her own approach to defining the terms, be sure that he or she is careful to keep all the provisions of the agreement internally consistent.

SAMPLE CONTRACT EXCERPTS

Assets (to Be Sold)
Alternative 1

Acquired Assets mean all of the Seller's rights to and interests in the following assets and properties, which are owned or leased by the Seller and used in the conduct of the Business: [list Asset Categories below]

This provision describes the assets to be sold. While there are as many ways to draft this provision as there are attorneys out there, I've included three basic alternatives that show different approaches to drafting this provision. Alternative 1 lists only the assets to be sold. Anything not listed in the Agreement will stay with the Seller. Alternative 2 casts quite a wide net with its language "all the assets … including, but not limited to," but then carves out an exception by listing the Excluded Assets, which are defined later in this section. In either case, if both parties are careful with the lists, they'll have a clear understanding of what is being sold, and what is being excluded. Like Alternative 1, Alternative 3 also lists only the assets to be sold, but (somewhat superfluously) for good measure, also lists the assets that will remain with the seller.

Alternative 2

Acquired Assets mean all of the Seller's rights to and interests in all of the assets and properties, of every character and whether real, personal, tangible, intangible, or otherwise, as the same exists on the Closing Date, which are owned or leased by the Seller and used in the conduct of the Business (other than Excluded Assets) including, but not limited to: [list Asset Categories below]

In all of the Alternatives, you must list the specific assets to be sold. For ease of drafting, these assets are grouped into categories like equipment, contracts, etc. I've not included a fourth basic alternative, one in which the APA Seller conveys "all the assets of the Seller used in its business" without any description or qualification. While it's tempting to draft a one-sentence provision to convey "all the assets," I don't recommend using this approach because you will be sacrificing clarity just for the sake of shortening the document. For example, if in the above example, Cavendish has certain assets (perhaps a cookbook deal or a television show on the Food Network) it wants to exclude from the assets being sold to Consolidated, then it should specifically exclude them.

Alternative 3

Acquired Assets mean all of the Seller's rights to and interests in the following assets and properties, which are owned or leased by the Seller and used in the conduct of the Business: [list Asset Categories below]

For purposes of clarification, the Assets shall not include the Excluded Assets (defined below).

Another benefit to specifically listing the assets is that it will force you (whether you are the Seller or the Purchaser) to really dig in and analyze the transaction and determine exactly what you are selling or buying so that you will be able to set the right price, etc.

Asset Categories

These provisions describe in more detail the categories of property typically transferred in an asset transaction: equipment, inventory, accounts receivable, real estate, contracts, intangibles like intellectual property, etc. There are many approaches to APA contract drafting — some resulting in very short, and some resulting in very long contracts. Verbiage will vary significantly from APA to APA. Some of the provisions below ultimately may not apply to your situation. Nevertheless, you should becoming familiar with the sample contract provisions below because they will help you to spot issues, and to really think about what it is you are buying or selling.

Exhibits or Schedules

APAs (and SPAs) make heavy use of Exhibits or Schedules, which are attachments to the agreement, identified by number or letter (e.g., "Exhibit 1" or "Exhibit A"). They are part and parcel of the agreement, and disclose factual information too numerous or unwieldy to put directly into the body of the agreement.

For example, an APA exhibit might list all the personal property leases being transferred to the Purchaser. The exhibit would list for each lease: the name of the counterparty, date of the lease and other information, the equipment being leased, lease amount, and perhaps the expiration date of the lease. Other Exhibits go beyond just listing facts and contain a more detailed description. For example, the exhibit showing the real estate to be transferred in an APA probably will contain the legal description of the property, and not just the street address. Or maybe the parties decide that they actually want to attach the financial statements of the Seller as an exhibit, instead of just saying in the representations that the Seller has previously furnished copies to the Purchaser.

The general practice is for the Purchaser's counsel to prepare the first draft of the APA (or SPA). This makes sense since the Purchaser has an interest in making sure the agreement contains the kinds of expansive representations, covenants, and conditions that give it the comfort level it needs that it will be getting what it's paying for. The only exception (beyond the scope of this book) is an auction situation, where the seller prepares the sale document and furnishes it to the bidders.

Since the bulk of the exhibits contain information pertinent to the Seller (its equipment, its inventory, etc.), the exhibits are typically prepared by the Seller or Seller's counsel, and kept in a word-processing document separate from the body of the agreement. While agreements often use the phrase, "as [set forth] [listed] [described] in the attached Exhibit," I have decided throughout this book to use the phrase "as disclosed in the attached Exhibit," because I'd like to reinforce the concept that the Seller should use exhibits only to disclose or reveal factual information. It's dangerous for a Seller to voluntarily or inadvertently add language to an exhibit that could be interpreted as additional representations or covenants (promises to do or not do something).

To illustrate this point, let's talk about the standard litigation representation. Some Sellers may understandably be embarrassed by litigation or want to assure the Purchaser that the litigation will soon be resolved in the Seller's favor. But it's a really bad idea for the Seller to put in the litigation exhibit language to the effect that "the Seller believes that [said litigation] will be resolved in favor of the Seller." This turns a relatively innocuous disclosure exhibit into a new representation that the Purchaser can use as the basis of a claim in the event the Seller loses the litigation. Even if the Seller only represented that it "believes" a certain result, it's given a litigious Purchaser just enough ammunition to threaten a claim, or maybe to extract a concession.

Equipment (and Other Personal Property)

All equipment, machinery, parts, furniture, computers, trade fixtures, leasehold improvements, and other tangible personal property owned by the Seller, and more specifically disclosed in the attached Exhibit [list Exhibit number] (the "Acquired Equipment").

There are several basic categories of property: **real property** (which includes land and buildings), **fixtures** (which are more or less physically attached to real property — think of a nice chandelier or other light "fixture"), and **personal property** (everything else). In this context, "personal" doesn't mean "belonging to you personally"; try to think of "personal property" as something (either tangible or intangible) not attached to real estate. Equipment includes tangible personal property, like machinery and office equipment. Things such as office supplies, furniture, packing supplies, and marketing literature are often also lumped together under equipment. While some APAs separately list motor vehicles, you can include them in this category if you want to. Just be sure to include the make, model, year, and vehicle identification number (VIN) in the Exhibit.

Intangible property like trademarks and goodwill are dealt with below. If you want to rein in the length of the Exhibit, you can indicate in the provision that you are just listing Equipment having a value in excess of, for example, $500. This will help you from going crazy listing every paper clip in the office supply room.

Inventory

All inventory of the Seller as of the Closing Date, which is in [salable condition], [except the excluded Inventory more specifically disclosed in the attached Exhibit [list Exhibit number] (the "Acquired Inventory").

In the example at the beginning of Part III, if the parties structure the transaction as an asset purchase, then the seller Cavendish will likely transfer its inventory to Consolidated. Inventory is any product (finished goods or commodoties) that is available for resale by the Seller in the ordinary course of business, the raw materials and parts used to make the finished goods, as well as works-in-progress (almost finished goods).

Since the amount of inventory will constantly change until the Closing Date, The Purchaser, Consolidated will want to obtain a covenant (see Chapter 15) from Cavendish that it will act in the ordinary course of business (meaning act in a reasonable "business as usual" manner) until the Closing Date, including with respect to the purchase and sale of inventory. This will help to minimize the number of surprises on the Closing Date, including finding a warehouse full of perishable truffles that the new owner, Consolidated, can't sell through. The parties can also negotiate an adjustment to the purchase price based on a variety of factors, including inventory levels as of the Closing Date.

If you are the Purchaser, then you'll want to be sure to include the caveat that whatever inventory that is being transferred to you must be in **salable** condition. For a Purchaser like Consolidated in the food industry, this means food that hasn't gone past the expiration date, is properly packed, and can be sold. Remember that most inventory has some kind of perishable component — for example, if you are purchasing a clothing manufacturer, you're not going to want to purchase inventory of last year's fashions at full price.

Another Word about Exhibits

There are two ways to use exhibits. The first way is to use the exhibit to **list all information**. The second way is to use the exhibit to **list only the exceptions**. Since the amount of inventory will constantly change until the Closing Date, I've decided to take the second approach in defining Acquired Inventory. I've defined it as all inventory as of the Closing Date, except the inventory or types (specific inventory may be difficult to predict) of inventory listed in the exhibit. I just think that it is easier to do it this way than to take the reverse

> approach and define Acquired Inventory to include all the inventory listed in an exhibit. You and your attorneys may have your own preferences based in part on how important the subject matter (in this example, the inventory) is to you, and the relative negotiating positions of the parties.

Accounts Receivable

All accounts receivable of the Seller which are outstanding on the Closing Date [except the Retained Receivables disclosed in the attached Exhibit (list Exhibit number)] (the "Acquired Accounts Receivable").

Accounts receivable (sometimes referred to as notes receivable) are monies owed by customers or clients for products sold or services rendered. Depending on the Seller's volume of business, this amount can be substantial. Retained receivables are those that the parties agree will remain with the Seller. In an asset transaction, the Seller may have the incentive to sell the receivables to the Purchaser, figuring that it is easier to collect a bigger chunk of money from the Purchaser at Closing, (even at a discount) rather than collecting it piecemeal from the debtors after the Seller has left the business.

If you are the Purchaser in an asset transaction, you should carefully consider the credit history of the debtors and the age of the receivables when deciding whether to purchase any of them. You should be very wary of purchasing the receivables even if your due diligence indicates that the Seller has been very successful in collecting them in the past. Remember that receivables can be difficult to collect when a new owner takes over.

If you decide to purchase the receivables, do not be eager to overpay for them. Rather, think of yourself as a kind of collection agency. A collection agency would never overpay for receivables, and neither should you. Another strategy if you decide to purchase the Seller's receivables is to negotiate deferred payment terms (pay the purchase price in installments). You can also negotiate an adjustment to the purchase price based on a variety of factors, including your success in collecting the receivables. This way, in case your collection rate is low, you are in a better position to withhold payment. Please refer to Chapter 11 for sample contract language on deferred installment payments, and price adjustment language.

Real Property

All of the [ownership rights of the Seller in the real property disclosed in the attached Exhibit (the "Acquired Real Property"), as well as all] leasehold interests in the real property (the "Leased Real Property") disclosed in the attached Exhibit [list Exhibit number] (the "Acquired Real Property Leases"). The Seller has delivered true and complete

> copies of the all documents evidencing such [ownership and] leasehold interests, including, but not limited to, [deeds of ownership and] the Acquired Real Property Leases.

The most common scenario is where a small business leases (rather than owns) its office space, retail store space, warehouse space, etc., from a third party lessor (landlord). In some cases, the lease will allow the transfer or assignment of the Seller's leasehold interest to the Purchaser, usually with landlord consent. If the lease does not allow such transfer, then the parties can try to negotiate with the lessor to allow the transfer. Failing that, the Purchaser will either have to rent new space, or structure the transaction as a stock sale (if the lease is a very valuable one in terms of location or the financial terms). Note that leases may contain anti-change of control language that restricts the ability to transfer the lease in a stock sale. Assuming that the lease can be transferred, the parties can insert this provision into the APA to cover the transfer. After the Closing, the Purchaser would become the new lessee (tenant) of the property. Sometimes a lessee has an option to purchase leased real property, and if the Seller has this option, then the option should be transferred as well.

Just for your information, I've included some bracketed language that contemplates the sale of real estate actually owned (rather than leased) by the Seller, in which case the parties will need to include in the APA specialized real estate provisions for the sale of the real estate portion of the Acquired Assets, which is beyond the scope of this book.

Fixtures

> All fixtures, leasehold improvements, and other fixed assets owned or leased by the Seller, or located, affixed, installed in or upon the real property owned or leased by the Seller, as more specifically disclosed in the attached Exhibit [insert Exhibit number] (the "Acquired Fixtures").

In addition to the proverbial chandelier installed by the Seller on its leased premises, this category would also include the result of any renovations done to the leased premises (the drywall, cubicles, etc.).

Contracts

> All contracts and agreements [and commitments] entered into by the Seller related to the Business, as more specifically disclosed in the attached Exhibit [list Exhibit number] (the "Acquired Contracts").

Contracts generally would include, for example, distribution agreements, manufacturing agreements, employment and independent contractor agreements, and loan and security agreements. The act of selling (assigning or transferring) a contract is kind of a double-edged sword. When the Seller in an APA assigns a contract, say an exclusive distribution agreement, it is transferring basically two things to the Purchaser: its rights and obligations. It transfers its exclusive right to sell a certain product in a certain geographic territory (for more on distribution agreements, please refer to Chapter 4). However, the Purchaser can't have its cake and eat it too — unless otherwise agreed, the transfer of the distribution agreement will also work to transfer the Seller's obligations to the Purchaser. Such obligations might include the obligation not to sell competing products, and certainly the obligation to pay for any products purchased.

As a Purchaser, the first step as usual is due diligence to determine which contracts you want, as well as whether those contracts allow the Seller to transfer them to you in an asset sale. You can work with the Seller to negotiate with the contract counterparty to allow the transfer in case the contract has restrictive language on assignments.

A Seller's important contracts will be likely be in writing, and therefore easy to identify. If you are the Purchaser, be sure that all of the Seller's important business agreements, understandings, and arrangements are in writing. Verbal agreements are difficult to enforce and "transfer."

Warranties

All written warranties received by the Seller in connection with the purchase of items included in the Assets which have not expired by virtue of their original terms [except as more specifically disclosed in the attached Exhibit (list Exhibit number)] (the "Acquired Warranties").

There may be some overlap between this provision and the above Contracts provision because some of the warranties may be contained in ongoing supply contracts that are being assigned. Other warranties for one-shot purchases like office furniture might be contained in the sales confirmation, packing slips, tags, supplier websites, or even on the sales receipt. You should try to obtain copies of these during due diligence, to help you determine their assignability, as well as any warranty disclaimers and limitations of liability. While the warranty holder may have to comply with certain notification and usage obligations in order to benefit from the warranty, warranties are mostly one-way obligations of the supplier in favor of the warranty holder.

Personal Property Leases

All written contracts pursuant to which the Seller leases from third party lessors equipment and any other personal property, as more specifically disclosed in the attached Exhibit [list Exhibit number] (the "Acquired Personal Property Leases").

There may be some overlap between this provision and the above contract provision, since the lease is a kind of contract. There are two basic kinds of personal property leases. **Operating leases** are true leases in which ownership stays with the lessor; the lessor can depreciate the equipment. The lessee can claim the lease payments as a business expense. Depending on the lease, the lessee might have the option at the end of the lease to return the equipment, or to re-lease or purchase it, but usually at fair market value. Operating leases are typically short-term and used for high-tech equipment like copiers that have a shorter technological life cycle.

A capital or finance lease is a kind of installment purchase contract in which the lessee is able to show the equipment on its balance sheet, and take depreciation. A capital lease typically gives the lessee the option to purchase the equipment for a bargain price (much less than fair market value). Lessees enter into capital leases for a variety of reasons, including cash-flow management and tax reasons.

Intellectual Property

All patents, trademarks, service marks, tradenames, and copyrights (and applications for any of the above), trade secrets, proprietary information, processes, formulas, customer lists, and other intellectual property rights of the Seller, relating to the Business and/or Assets, as well as all licenses to use any patents or other intellectual property rights, as more specifically disclosed in the attached Exhibit [list Exhibit number] (the "Acquired Intellectual Property").

This category includes not just the patents, trademarks, and copyrights, but also pending applications for any of them, plus trade secret type information for which the Seller has not filed any patent or other government registration. The Seller may have both registered trademarks ("®"), and common law trademarks (™). Caveat emptor (buyer beware) for common law trademarks — anybody can put a ™ next to his or her logo. That's not to say that there aren't strong common law trademarks (or weak registered trademarks) out there, just that you should conduct thorough due diligence to help you determine the strength of the trademark. Furthermore, while common law trademark holders do have certain rights, they don't have all the rights which is the exclusive right of registered trademark holders, who have gone full bore through the rigorous trademark registration process with the US Patent and Trademark Office. For example, registered trademark holders can bring an action regarding the trademark in Federal Court, and make a filing with the US Customs Service to stop the import of foreign goods that infringe the trademark. So if you are the Purchaser, be sure to pay accordingly.

Small businesses seldom hold significant copyrights, unless they write software, but in that case they protect much of that property in the form of trade secrets. However, the Seller may have produced some good service manuals and marketing literature that is protected by copyright law.

I've included license agreements with third parties whereby the third party allows the Seller to use third-party patents, etc. This category overlaps somewhat with Contracts (discussed above) because a licence is a kind of contract.

Permits

All permits, government licenses and franchises, zoning variances, and government approvals and authorizations relating to the Business [including, but not limited to, those disclosed in the attached Exhibit (list Exhibit number)] (the "Acquired Permits").

This category includes Federal, state and local government (and quasi-government, think industry association) approvals of all kinds. In the example at the beginning of Part III, the Seller, Cavendish, can't operate its retail food stores without local health department approval. In some cases, Cavendish may have obtained zoning variences to expand its stores beyond the maximum prescribed footprint. For this category, if you decide to list the permits in an Exhibit, consider using the terminology "including, but not limited to" because you will need all the permits to run the business; even one slipping through may jeopardize your ability to run the business. Remember that not all permits are assignable; your due diligence will help you determine which permits are assignable, and which permits lapse upon a sale of the business (forcing you to reapply).

Records

The originals and copies of all records relating to the Assets and Business, including, but not limited to, customer and vendor lists and information, production records, purchase and sale records, bid documents, financial and tax records, other books, records, and files used in or related to the Assets and/or the Business, in any paper, tangible, or electronic format whatsoever.

While the Seller may have no problem furnishing its sales and production records, it might argue that the Purchaser in the asset transaction is not entitled to records related to the selling entity (for example, the corporate minute book and tax returns). But these records are a treasure trove of information that might be useful to the Purchaser as it takes over the business. A fall-back position for the Purchaser might be to get as much of the information as possible in the form of photocopies, but to have the Seller grant access to the original copies of such information for a good chunk of time after the Closing, say several years. You can make the owners personally responsible since most likely, the Seller entity will be liquidated and dissolved right after the Closing.

Prepaid Expenses

All prepaid expenses, security deposits, deposits, and rights to refunds from customers and suppliers relating to the Acquired Assets and Business, except for prepaid taxes and tax deposits.

Prepaid expenses are costs paid for future goods or services that are recorded as assets for accounting purposes, but expensed as the goods or services are received by the company. They include, for example, insurance premiums and rent. In an APA, the right to these prepaid expenses, as well as security deposits, etc., typically are part of the Acquired Assets.

Goodwill

All goodwill, if any, associated with Seller's Assets and Business (the "Acquired Goodwill").

You can be sure that the owners of household brand names have expended a lot of energy and money to build up their brand names. All other things being equal, the goodwill associated with a strong brand name is one reason why large companies with strong household brand names are significantly more than the value of their tangible assets.

But while the goodwill of a small business can also be significant, it is more fragile and far less portable. In the example at the beginning of Part III, Cavendish is a big chain of food stores with a loyal customer following, so it has goodwill that has basically been "institutionalized" and therefore stands a decent chance of surviving the sale. The Purchaser, Consolidated, and its crack team of marketing MBAs will have the infrastructure and financial wherewithal to continue to build the brand.

What if, however, the founders decided to sell the business when it was just a one-store operation on the Lower East Side? Any goodwill generated during the formative years by the Kavinsky brothers (through their merchandising and perhaps their friendly give-and-take with the customers) is very personal to them, and not possible to transfer. If the new owner pays a princely sum for the goodwill, it may find to its chagrin that the goodwill disappears as soon as the Kavinsky brothers leave the scene. Even if the new owner has the ability to "duplicate" the intangible characteristics of the business, it will have overpaid for the goodwill.

Excluded Assets

Excluded Assets mean and include all of Seller's rights to and interests in all of the following: [list Excluded Assets]

In this section, you can list the assets that are specifically excluded from the transaction. The APA Seller and Purchaser are free to negotiate the inclusion or exclusion of any assets. Because the following is a kind of checklist of commonly Excluded Assets, there may be some overlap with the (included) Assets listed above. When you review your APA, be sure that there is no overlap between the Assets to be transferred and the Excluded Assets. That kind of internal inconsistency may lead to a dispute between the parties.

Cash

All cash and cash equivalents of the Seller.

The transfer of cash, in return for presumably cash, is a wash transaction, and therefore excluded.

Certain Contracts

The contracts disclosed in the attached Exhibit [list Exhibit number].

If the parties have a list of contracts, mortgages, auto leases, real estate leases or other agreements that are not being assigned to the Purchaser, then these should be listed in the APA as Excluded Assets.

Corporate Entity Documents/Items

The certificate of incorporation, corporate minute book, seal, stock ledgers, and stock transfer books, as well as the tax and accounting records of the Seller.

These assets belong to the corporate entity and typically are excluded from the APA. If the transaction is structured as an entity transaction (e.g., stock sale), then the Purchaser would be, by virtue of its new ownership interest in the Acquired Company, entitled to have these documents.

Insider Loans

All loans, promissory notes, advances, and accounts representing obligations owing to the Seller by its shareholders, directors, officers, employees, and their affiliates.

The Seller may have its own tax or other reasons for making these loans. Unless there is a compelling reason for the Purchaser to take over these loans, it's best to leave them with the Seller. Even if the payment terms are favorable to the Seller/lender (perhaps to create the impression of an arm's-length transaction), the Purchaser has at least two kinds of risk if it decides to take over these loans. The first is general collection risk. The second is the risk that somebody will challenge and unravel the orginal loan as a questionable inside transaction (violating the duty of loyalty).

Tax Rights

All income tax refunds and credits, if any, and any tax loss carryover of the Seller.

In a plain vanilla asset transaction, a C Corporation recognizes taxable gain on the sale of each asset to the extent the allocated Purchase Price exceeds its tax basis in the asset. Then, each shareholder of the selling corporation recognizes taxable gain on any distribution made by the selling corporation to the shareholder. The Seller can use its losses to absorb some of its asset sale gain and therefore reduce the double-tax impact.

Unliquidated Claims

Unliquidated tort or other claims of the Seller against third parties.

The Seller may have significant claims against third parties for damages or money owned. But, the Purchaser should avoid paying good money (or at least too much money) to purchase assets that are contingent on collection. Court cases can drag on for years, and even if one party wins, it may turn out that after all the appeals, it could take years to collect any judgment.

APA

All rights of the Seller relating to this Agreement.

Some attorneys would argue that this provision is unnecessary because to allow the Seller to assign its rights under the APA to the Purchaser would lead to the preposterous result of the Purchaser becoming both the Seller and the Buyer in the same transaction. But this provision appears quite often in APAs.

10

CORPORATE OBLIGATIONS ASSUMED

OVERVIEW

In a stock transaction, the Purchaser becomes a shareholder of the Acquired Company, and therefore automatically inherits (subject to limited liability of a shareholder) all the known and hidden liabilities of the Acquired Company. In an asset transaction, however, the parties negotiate which liabilities the Purchaser will take over. In the best-case scenario for the Purchaser, it doesn't take over any of the liabilities of the acquired business. This position is reflected in the sample contract provision. Some Purchasers prefer to be more specific, and add a non-exhaustive list ("including, but not limited to … ") of the liabilities that the Purchaser will not be assuming. The most broad of these include any liability arising from or related to the Seller's acts or omissions before the Closing Date ("Seller's Conduct" and "Seller's Default").

SAMPLE CONTRACT EXCERPTS
No Obligations/Liabilities Assumed

[APA version] Except as otherwise provided in this Agreement, the Purchaser is not assuming and shall not be liable for any commitments, debts, liabilities, obligations or responsibilities of, or claims against, the Seller, whether known or unknown, contingent, or absolute (collectively, the "Obligations") [including, but not limited to:]

Seller's Conduct

Any Obligation arising from or relating to the Seller's conduct of the Buiness existing or occuring before the Closing Date.

Seller's Default

Any Obligation (a) entered into after the date of this Agreement in violation of any of covenant contained in this Agreement, or (b) with respect to which the Seller is in default or breach on the Closing Date.

Consult with your attorney to determine the extent you (if you are a Purchaser) may have **successor liability** for certain obligations of the Seller (e.g., employee benefits, environmental, etc.), notwithstanding contract language to the contrary.

Alternative — Certain Obligations Assumed

Except as set forth below, the Purchaser is not assuming and shall not be liable for any commitments, debts, liabilities, obligations or responsibilities of, or claims against, the Seller, whether known or unknown, contingent, or absolute. The Purchaser shall assume only the Obligations as set forth below (Assumed Liabilities). As used in this Agreement, Assumed Liabilities shall mean and include the following, as the same may exist on the Closing Date:

Alternatively, you can negotiate which obligations of the Seller will be assumed by the Purchaser. The sample contract excerpt contemplates that the Purchaser is only assuming certain enumerated obligations of the APA Seller. The sample contract excerpt lists two commonly assumed obligations: the accounts payable of the Seller, and the obligations of the Seller under the contracts to be assigned to the Purchaser at Closing, that is, the Acquired Contracts.

Seller's Accounts Payable

Seller's accounts payable to trade creditors.

Obligations under Assigned Contracts

To the extent legally valid and enforcable in accordance with their respective terms, all obligations and liabilities of the Seller under the Acquired Contracts [contracts assigned or otherwise lawfully transferred to the Purchaser at Closing], except the contracts listed in the attached Exhibit [list Exhibit number].

11

PURCHASE PRICE AND PAYMENT TERMS

OVERVIEW

The **Purchase Price** is the consideration to be paid by the Purchaser to the Seller in an asset transaction and to the selling Stockholders in a stock transaction. In an asset acquisition, the Purchase Price might also consist of the Purchaser's assumption of certain liabilities of the Seller. The **Payment Terms** govern how payment of the Purchase Price will be made, whether cash at Closing, or some combination involving cash, debt (deferred payment), contingent payment (earnouts), and securities, and for asset transactions, perhaps the assumption of certain liabilities of the Seller. In an asset transaction, the parties can agree to an Allocation of the Purchase Price among the assets, with various tax and accounting consequences.

SAMPLE CONTRACT EXCERPTS
Cash at Closing

[APA or SPA version] Subject to the terms and conditions of this Agreement, in consideration of the sale of the Acquired Assets [Acquired Stock], the Purchaser shall pay to the Seller [the selling Stockholders] the aggregate purchase price of [insert dollar amount] (the "Purchase Price") in cash at the Closing.

The most straightforward payment structure is the payment of the full Purchase Price at Closing. In this case, the parties can arrange for payment to be made by company or personal check, but more likely, the seller will require that payment be made by wire transfer.

Alternative — Deferred Payment

[APA or SPA version] Subject to the terms and conditions of this Agreement, in consideration of the sale of the Acquired Assets [Acquired Stock], the Purchaser shall pay to the Seller [the selling Stockholders] the aggregate purchase price of [insert dollar amount] (the "Purchase Price"), based on the following payment terms:

(a) [insert dollar amount] in cash at the Closing;

(b) the balance of [insert dollar amount] in [insert number] installments as set forth below, with each installment evidenced by the Purchaser's promissory note (the "Promissory Note(s)"), in the form set forth in the attached Exhibit [insert Exhibit number.]

[Insert chart showing installment payment amounts and payment dates.]

While full payment at Closing is the best option for the seller, there are any combination of reasons why a Purchaser might want to defer payment of part of the Purchase Price until after the Closing. Deferred payment obligations are usually evidenced by promissory notes. The delivery of the promissory notes should be made a condition to closing.

Financing

The Purchaser might desire to finance the transaction. The seller can provide the financing by allowing the Purchaser to make payment of any balance of the Purchase Price not paid at Closing in installments after the Closing. Any balance due after Closing is evidenced by one or more promissory notes.

Disagreement in the Value of the Business

There's often a gap between the appraised value of the business and the higher amount the seller believes the business is worth. The parties might negotiate an earnout (see discussion on **earnouts** below) so that the Purchaser makes an additional payment later if the earnout goals are achieved.

Security for Indemnity

Deferred payment structures can be used by the Purchaser as a kind of security for the seller's obligations. Promissory notes may contain language allowing the debtor (in this case the Purchaser) to offset any payment due under the promissory note against any debtor claim (for indemnification) against the payee (in this case the seller). The seller can counter that any offset has to be put into escrow (see discussion on **escrow** below) until the claim is resolved, rather than directly offset. Or, as discussed below, the Purchaser can negotiate that a portion of the Purchase Price be put into escrow immediately as security for and in anticipation of indemnification claims. In either case, the seller doesn't get paid until the claims, if any, get resolved.

Alternative (APA) — Cash Plus Assumption of Liabilities

[APA version] Subject to the terms and conditions of this Agreement, in consideration of the sale of the Acquired Assets, the Purchaser shall pay to the Seller the aggregate purchase price of [insert dollar amount] (the "Purchase Price") in cash, and assume the liabilities set forth in attached Exhibit [list Exhibit number] (the "Assumed Liabilities").

This is the same provision as the **Cash at Closing** (APA version), but contemplates a cash Purchase Price amount that is offset by the assumption by the Purchaser of certain specific liabilities of the Seller, such as the obligation to repay a specific loan, pay specific trade payables, etc. Be sure to coordinate this provision with any provision dealing with the non-assumption by the Purchaser of any Seller's obligations (see Chapter 10 for further discussion of this issue).

Allocation of SPA Purchase Price to Individual Selling Stockholders

The Purchase Price to be paid is allocated among the selling Stockholders as follows:

Name of Stockholder	Percent Consideration
[Name]	[20%]
[Name]	[20%]
[Name]	[20%]
[Name]	[20%]
[Name]	[20%]

This provision sets forth how the Purchase Price in a stock transaction will be allocated if there is more than one selling Stockholder. The percentage consideration is based on the percent ownership of the individual sellers. The provision can be adjusted if the Acquired Company is a limited liability company or other entity.

Escrow of Purchase Price

Depending on the risk profile of the Seller (whether the Seller in an APA or the Selling Stockholder in an SPA), the Purchaser might negotiate that some portion of the Purchase Price (for example, up to 15 percent) be put into escrow to help cover any future indemnification claims the Purchaser might have against the seller. The escrowed funds might also be used to pay any Purchase Price Adjustment, if needed. An escrow agreement is an arrangement where a neutral third party such as a bank (the escrow agent), collects and holds the funds in question until disbursement.

Under the agreement, the escrow agent disburses (returns) the funds to the Purchaser only if certain conditions have been satisfied, for example, at the end of a successful indemnification claim against the seller for damages. At the end of the term of the escrow agreement, the escrow agent takes out any fees owed to it, and transfers any remaining balance to the seller. The **term** of the escrow agreement (that is, the length of time the bank holds onto the funds) typically coincides with the length of time the indemnification provisions of the APA or SPA remain in effect (for example, 18 or so months from the Execution Date of the APA or SPA). If you are the Purchaser, make sure that whatever amount you negotiate to put into escrow doesn't become a kind of cap on the liability of the seller or become your exclusive remedy for your claims against the seller.

Expect to use the escrow agent's form of escrow agreement, which contains various and sundry provisions designed mainly to protect the bank. For example, escrow agreements typically provide that the bank is liable only if it is grossly negligent. Also, as a neutral party, an escrow agent never puts itself in a position where it has to decide which party is correct. If any party disputes a disbursement, then the escrow agreement will provide a system whereby it can dispute (and delay or prevent) the disbursement.

Earnouts (APA and SPA)

An earnout is a kind of contingent payment based on the future (that is, post-closing) performance of the the acquired business. An earnout clause in an APA or SPA provides that the Purchase Price will be increased if the acquired business satisfies negotiated financial performance targets during the earnout period (typically a year or two after the Closing). With an earnout, sellers have a vested interest in the future of the company. Earnouts are sometimes used when, after extensive negotiations, the parties are still at loggerheads about the Purchase Price. The seller, predicatably, is all warm and fuzzy about the company, especially its prospects and values the company significantly higher than the Purchaser, who, again predictably, has a much less rosy picture of the company's performance and prospects. Earnouts are theoretically viewed as a "win-win" solution to bridge the gap. But as usual, unclear drafting or unanticipated events can cloud the picture and lead to disputes.

One of the threshold issues regarding earnouts is how to measure post-closing performance. You can measure performance several ways — for example, based on gross sales or net sales. Many sellers prefer to use gross sales as the yardstick because they won't have the ability after the Closing to manage or oversee how the acquired business spends its money. Strategic purchasers may also prefer the gross sales standard because it's just not practical to keep separate books for the acquired business when the whole purpose of the business combination is integration. Purchasers, however, have to be careful if the stockholder managers of the acquired business stay on board to run the acquired business; using gross sales as the earnout standard may give them the incentive to sell, sell, sell, without regard to the customer's credit history.

Earnout Factors

The Purchaser should try to negotiate to exclude from the earnout any predicted post-closing expense reductions to be achieved by the Purchaser — the idea being that the seller shouldn't benefit from any efficiencies introduced by the Purchaser. Most disputes arise from unanticipated events that crop up to throw a wrench into the calculation or the parties' perception of the accuracy, usefulness, or fairness of the measuring methodology. For example, to what extent is any improvement or decline in post-Closing performance due to outside factors like the economy in general or an industry-wide uptick that has nothing to do with management (or even the assets that have been acquired), an unexpected reallocation of financial or operational resources or corporate opportunities, a change in accounting rules, or even market psychology?

The parties need to consider to consider a host of other factors, for example, the impact of intercompany transactions, additional financing requirements of the acquired business, the extent to which the Buyer can compete with the acquired business, and so forth.

Another "unanticipated event" could be that the Purchaser flips the acquired business during the earnout period for a sum significantly higher than the Purchase Price and Earnout sum. The seller might try to cover this scenario by negotiating a provision that has the parties sharing the windfall. The Seller should also negotiate that any breach of the APA or SPA or ancillary documents by the Purchaser (such as the unilateral termination of post-Closing consultant agreements) triggers payment of the earnout.

Hidden Cost

For the Purchaser, agreeing to pay an earnout may seem like a good deal. It pays less now, and if the company does well, then it pays some money later. Throw in some interest and the seller is really happy. And in the best case scenario, maybe the Purchaser flips the acquired business a few years down the road for a sum substantially in excess of the Purchase Price plus Earnout (the seller may not be so happy here, but that's another story). For the Purchaser, it's almost too good to be true. But alas, there's a price to pay for earnouts. The Purchaser in an asset transaction will have to keep the Acquired Assets more or less separate from its existing business in order to calcuate the earnout. While separation is not an issue for new business meant to stand alone from the Purchaser's existing business, this separation prevents the Purchaser from taking immediate advantage of synergy, which for many strategic buyers is a basic reason for entering into the transaction to begin with.

Allocation

One of the main advantages of entering into an asset transaction (versus a stock transaction) is the flexibility to allocate the Purchase Price among the assets purchased. The allocation will determine for tax purposes the Purchaser's basis in each Acquired Asset (and therefore its ability to take tax-saving deductions going forward) and the Seller's gain or loss on the transfer of each Acquired Asset. The IRS will likely recognize any reasonable allocation of the Purchase Price that is negotiated between the Seller and the Purchaser on an arm's-length basis.

IRS Form 8594

With certain limited exceptions, both the Purchaser and the Seller in an asset transaction (where goodwill or going concern value attaches to the acquired business) must file IRS Form 8594 together with their income tax returns to report the asset transaction. Good will or going concern value "attaches" if the Purchase Price paid for the Acquired Assets exceeds the aggregate book value of the assets (other than goodwill or going concern value), or if the Purchaser and Seller (or its owners or employees) enter into a non-compete agreement, or employment or consultant or similar type agreement.

Classes of Assets

Form 8594 requires that the filer categorize each of the Acquired Assets into the following classifications:

- Class I: Cash and general deposit accounts (e.g., savings and checking accounts), other than certificates of deposit held in banks, savings and loan associations, and other depository institutions.

- Class II: Actively traded securities such as US government securities and publicly traded stock, plus certificates of deposit and foreign currency.

- Class III: Assets that the taxpayer marks-to-market at least annually for federal income tax purposes, as well as accounts receivable, and certain debt instruments.

- Class IV: Inventory (that is, property held primarily for sale to customers in the ordinary course of business).

- Class V: Equipment, furniture, fixtures, real estate (land and buildings), vehicles, and all assets other than Class I, II, III, IV, VI, and VII assets.

- Class VI: All so-called "section 197 intangibles" (as defined in the IRS regulations) except goodwill and going concern value, including customer and supplier lists, government licenses, non-compete agreements (entered into in connection with the sale of the business), franchises, trademarks and trade names, books and records, operating systems, designs, know-how, etc.

- Class VII: Goodwill and going concern value.

12

THE CLOSING

OVERVIEW

This chapter sets forth the logistics of the closing of the transaction, including the exchange of consideration (Purchase Price) and title to the assets or stock. The APA or SPA typically has separate sections listing the seller's and the Purchaser's Closing delivery obligations. The sample contract provision below includes a "drop dead" deadline for the Closing to take place. This is just the outside date for the Closing to take place. If it doesn't take place by this date, for example, because one of the parties hasn't fulfilled all of the Closing Conditions (discussed below) then the party not responsible for the delay can terminate the APA or SPA.

SAMPLE CONTRACT EXCERPTS

Closing — Time and Place

[APA or SPA version] The parties shall cause the closing of the transactions contemplated by this Agreement (the "Closing") to take place at the offices of [name], [address], at [time] on [date], or at such other place, time, and date as the parties agree in writing. If the Closing does not take place by [insert drop dead date], then the non-defaulting party will, in addition to all other rights and remedies available at law or in equity, have the right to cancel and terminate this Agreement.

Seller Deliveries at Closing (APA or SPA)

At the Closing, the Seller [selling stockholders] shall deliver to the Purchaser: [list documents discussed below]

The seller's main obligation at Closing is to deliver the documents evidencing the actual transfer of title to the Purchaser in the APA assets or SPA stock. For an asset transaction, this document would be a bill of sale. In a stock transaction, the selling Stockholders would deliver the stock certificates representing the Acquired Stock, accompanied by stock powers. Other documents might include, for example, an escrow agreement or non-compete agreement. And if the Seller insiders plan to continue working for the company after the Closing, then the employment or consultant agreements should be delivered at Closing as well.

Ancillary Documents

(a) a [bill or sale, or insert name of other Ancillary Document] substantially in the form of attached Exhibit [list Exhibit number], fully executed by an authorized officer of the Seller.

The APA or SPA is the primary contract in a sale of business transaction. However, the parties typically enter into **ancillary documents**, which are separate contracts or documents entered into or furnished by the parties to help achieve specific goals related to the sale of the business. These should be executed and/or furnished at the Closing. At a minimum, these include the bill of sale (APA) or stock powers (SPA), but depending on the objectives of the parties, ancillary documents might include the others listed below:

- **Bill of Sale (Used in APA):** A standard short-form document by the Seller confirming the transfer of title to the Purchaser in the Acquired Assets in exchange "for value received" (that is, the Purchase Price).

- **Stock Power (Used in SPA):** Similar to the bill of sale, but used by the selling Stockholders to transfer title to the Purchaser in the Acquired Stock. A stock power is a kind of power of attorney that allows the current registered owner of the stock to transfer ownership to somebody else.

- **Assignment of Patent or Trademark (Used in APA):** A standard short-form document by the Seller confirming the transfer of title to the Purchaser in registered patents or trademarks, or patent or trademark applications. The assignment may be recorded with the US Patent and Trademark Office and serves as notice of the conveyance.

- **Escrow Agreement:** Depending on the risk profile of the seller, the Purchaser might negotiate that some portion of the Purchase Price (for example, up to 15 percent) be put into escrow to help cover any future indemnification claims the Purchaser might have against the seller. The escrowed funds might also be used to pay any Purchase Price adjustment, if needed. An escrow agreement is an arrangement where a neutral third party such as a bank (the escrow agent), collects and holds the funds in question until disbursement.

- **Non-competition Agreement:** After paying a significant sum to purchase a business (and probably a premium over book value), the Purchaser doesn't want to find out after the Closing that the Seller (APA), selling Stockholders (SPA) or any officer, director, or key insider (APA and SPA, as applicable) has set up shop or joined forces with others to compete against it after the Closing. By executing a Non-competition Agreement, the seller promises not to compete against the Purchaser for a fixed period of time and within a fixed geographic territory. Non-competition clauses have to be carefully crafted; they can't be so restrictive as to time, geographic scope, or the scope of restricted activity. See Chapter 1 for a more detailed discussion of non-competition provisions.

  Non-competition agreements also typically contain non-disclosure/confidentiality (NDA) provisions as well as non-solicitation provisions. While these can be made into separate agreements, it's often more convenient to put them all together into one agreement.

- **Non-disclosure Provisions:** One of the key assets being sold in the transaction is the confidential information (trade secrets, customer lists, financial information, etc.), of the Seller or Acquired Company. The Purchaser wants to make sure that the seller and its insiders don't divulge such information to the Purchaser's competitors or use it for themselves after the Closing. By agreeing to the non-disclosure provisions, the seller promises not to disclose or use for itself or anybody else any confidential information about the Acquired Assets or Acquired Company. See Section II, Chapter 6 for a more detailed discussion of the types of provisions typically found in Non-disclosure (Confidentiality) Agreements.

- **Non-solicitation Provisions:** Another concern of the Purchaser is that the seller and its insiders do not interfere with the business after the Closing. Non-solicitation provisions include promises (for a negotiated period of time after the Closing) not to (a) solicit or do businesss with any customers, (b) woo away any employees, consultants or service providers, or (c) interfere with any supplier, license, relationships, etc., that have been transferred to the Purchaser under the APA or SPA.

- **Transition Services:** In some cases, the Purchaser may need to enter into what's called a transition services agreement (TSA) to outsource certain services of the seller until the Purchaser can get it together after the Closing. For example, the Purchaser in an APA might negotiate a TSA to continue to receive certain IT, payroll, or other services from the Seller for a fixed time period after the Closing to help ensure a smooth transition and reduce transition costs. TSA are essentially agreements for the **sale of services**, except in most cases both the service provider and the recipient want the agreement to have a relatively short and finite term. As with all service agreements, the goal is to structure the TSA so that each party's service performance and payment responsibilities are clear cut.

When to Attach Forms of Ancillary Documents

In the above sample contract excerpt, I indicate that the forms of the Ancillary Documents are attached as Exhibits to the APA or SPA. This assumes that the parties have had the time to pre-negotiate the terms of the Ancillary Documents, or that the parties are fine with using whatever standard forms of the Ancillary Documents they can get their hands on. In real life, however, the parties might not have the time luxury of being able to negotiate the Ancillary Documents before entering into the APA or SPA. Furthermore, the parties are unlikely to agree to standard forms without a thorough review. After all, any "standard form" presented by one of the parties is likely to be drafted heavily in favor of that party.

Therefore, the parties often end up agreeing that the Ancillary Document has to be delivered at Closing, but leave the nitty gritty (detailed terms and conditions) to be decided during the time gap between the Execution Date of the APA or SPA and the Closing Date. The parties essentially "agree to agree" on the forms of the Ancillary Documents. So rather than attaching the form of bill of sale, the parties might agree that the bill of sale will be "in form and substance satisfactory to the Purchaser" (gives the Purchaser the most leeway). Or maybe the parties agree that the particular Ancillary Document will be "in form and substance to be mutually agreed" (both parties have to agree) or "in form and substance customary for this transaction." The last standard is somewhat objective, although it leaves open to interpretation exactly what is customary for the type of transaction being entered into.

Officer and Director — Ancillary Documents

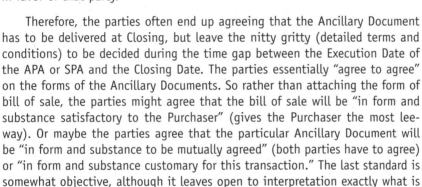

[APA or SPA version] Each officer and director of the Seller [Acquired Company] shall deliver to the Purchaser at or prior to the Closing the following documents, dated the Closing Date:

(a) a resignation [SPA only] substantially in the form of attached Exhibit [list Exhibit number];

(b) a release substantially in the form of attached Exhibit [list Exhibit number];

(c) a non-competition agreement, substantially in the form of attached Exhibit [list Exhibit number]; and

(d) [Note — if applicable to your situation], an employment [consultant] agreement, substantially in the form of attached Exhibit [list Exhibit number].

These are some of the Ancillary Documents that the Purchaser can require from the insiders (e.g., officers, directors, stockholders, etc.) of the APA Seller or SPA Acquired Company.

- **Resignations:** In an SPA the existing officers and directors of the Acquired Company will need to resign so the Purchaser can populate these positions with its own people. In some cases, however, the Purchaser asks some of the Acquired Company's management to stay on board. In an APA, only the assets are being sold and the owners of the selling corporation (Seller) will still own the corporation after the Closing. The officers and directors of the the Seller typically remain on board until liquidation and dissolution.

- **Release:** The Purchaser doesn't want to have to worry about future claims by the insiders. By executing a release, the officer or director will release the Purchaser from any claims (for compensation, tort claims, etc.) it might have, or have otherwise had, against the the Purchaser, as the new owner of the Acquired Assets or Acquired Company.

- **Non-competition Agreement:** The Purchaser wants to make sure that the insiders aren't allowed to compete against it after the Closing. By executing the Non-competition Agreement, the officer or director promises not to compete against the Purchaser (whether by working for or becoming an owner of a competitor) for a fixed period of time and within a fixed geographic territory. Non-competition clauses have to be carefully crafted; they can't be so restrictive as to time, geographic scope or the scope of restricted activity. See Chapter 4 for a more detailed discussion of non-competion provisions. Non-competition agreements also typically contain non-disclosure/confidentiality (NDA) provisions as well as non-solicitation provisions. While these can be made into separate agreements, it's often more convenient to put them all together into one agreement.

- **Employment or Consultant Agreements:** While the Purchaser doesn't want any of the insiders to work for its competitors, it might want to leverage their experience by hiring them to work for it as employees or consultants after the Closing. Financial buyers like private equity firms who don't engage in the day-to-day management of their portfolio companies often employ the owners or managers of the Seller or Acquired Company to continue to run the day-to-day operations of the companies they purchase. Strategic buyers often also retain the services of the insiders, sometimes on a short term (e.g., six months or so) independent contractor basis (without benefits) to help in the transition from old to new management, and sometimes on a longer term employment basis. The Purchaser will need to enter into an employment or consultant agreement with each of these individuals. See Part II for a discussion of service agreements. Due to space constraints this book doesn't contain a detailed discussion of employment agreements.

Closing Checklist

One of the best ways to ensure a smooth Closing is to stay organized. One of the best ways to stay organized is to prepare a checklist of items required for Closing. This job typically falls on one of the attorneys to the transaction. A closing checklist, which is not a legal document, lists the actions or documents (for example, officer certificates, contract consents, government filings and consents, etc.) required to close the transaction. The checklist should briefly state the status of each item, as well as the party responsible for making it happen (for example, Seller's CFO, Purchaser's attorney, etc.). The checklist should be updated on a regular basis, and at least as often as the status of any item changes. One person should be responsible for keeping a master copy of the checklist up-to-date.

Contract Consents

[APA or SPA version] The Seller [selling Stockholders] shall obtain and deliver to the Purchaser at or prior to the Closing all consents required for the execution, delivery, and performance of this Agreement from any party to any contract or understanding to which any or them is a party, or with respect to which any of their respective assets or business is subject.

This closing condition requires the Seller (APA) or selling Stockholder (SPA) to deliver the "consents required for the execution, delivery and performance of this Agreement"; however another commonly used phrase with similar meaning is "consents required for the consummation of the transactions contemplated by this Agreement." For a detailed discussion of contract consents, see Consent of Third Parties to Transaction in Chapter 13.

Government Consents

[APA or SPA version] The Seller [selling Stockholders] shall at or prior to the Closing,

(a) file all applications or notices, and

(b) obtain all consents in each case, required for the execution, delivery, and performance of this Agreement, with or from the appropriate government authorities, courts or other tribunals. The Seller shall at or prior to the Closing deliver to the Purchaser copies of all such filings, notices, and consents.

This provision is often combined with the contract consents provision above, and requires the seller to make all required government-type filings and notices (Subsection [a]) and obtain all required government-type consents to the transaction

(Subsection [b]), and to deliver copies of such documents at the Closing. For a detailed discussion of government consents, see Consent of Government Authorities to Transaction in the chapter on Representation and Warranties of the Seller (Chapter 13).

Legal Opinion

[APA or SPA version] The Seller [Acquired Company] and Stockholders shall deliver to the Purchaser on the Closing Date the opinion of counsel for the Seller [Acquired Company], dated the Closing Date, in form and substance satisfactory to counsel for the Purchaser.

Depending on the size, complexity and type of the transaction, the negotiating leverage between the parties, and the comfort level of the Purchaser in the condition of the Seller (APA) or Acquired Company (SPA), the Purchaser might demand a legal opinion to be delivered at closing. In this case, counsel to the Seller or the Acquired Company would write a letter confirming (a) certain legal characteristics of its client (that it is duly organized, in good standing, etc.), and (b) that the transaction is legally enforceable. While legal opinions may look to the untrained eye like a restatement of many of the seller's representations and warranties, especially the ones that ultimately go to the enforceability of the transaction, seller's counsel will only render opinions as to matters requiring some legal analysis. Counsel will generally avoid giving opinions confirming factual matters directly covered by the representations. The wording of the legal opinion, including any qualifying language, is negotiated among the attorneys.

The legal areas covered in a sale of business legal opinion typically include the topics covered by the following seller's representations and warranties (see Chapter 13): Organization, Power, and Authority to Run Business; Qualification in Foreign Jurisdictions; Authority to Sell; Consent of Government Authorities; No Conflict with Corporate Documents, Contracts or Laws; Enforceability; Capitalization; and Litigation.

In a stock transaction, counsel to the Acquired Company and selling Stockholders might be asked to render its opinion that the offer and sale of the shares are exempted transactions under the Federal Securities laws not requiring any registration under such laws.

Resolutions

The Seller [selling Stockholders] shall deliver to the Purchaser on the Closing Date copies of all resolutions adopted by the Seller's [Acquired Company's] stockholders and board of directors relating to the transactions contemplated by this Agreement, certified by the Secretary of the Seller [Acquired Company] as being in full force and effect on the Closing Date.

This is a fairly standard requirement, that the seller furnish certified copies of the board or shareholder resolutions approving the transaction. Consult with your attorney, as state law may vary on the degree to which shareholder and/or board consent is required depending on the transaction.

Purchaser Deliveries at Closing (APA or SPA)

This section will discuss the Purchaser's general closing deliveries in an asset or stock transaction.

> At the Closing, the Purchaser shall deliver to the Seller [selling Stockholders]: [list items or documents]

Purchase Price

> (a) The Purchase Price pursuant to the terms of Section [list appropriate Purchase Price and Payment Terms section number] of this Agreement;

The Purchaser's main delivery at the Closing is to pay the Purchase Price. This section should also list the delivery of every document by the Purchaser necessary to consummate the transaction. These might include, for example, delivery by the Purchaser of **Ancillary Documents** like an assumption agreement (APA), promissory notes (if the payment of any part of the Purchase Price is being deferred) and security agreements to secure any such deferred payments. Many sellers will require an opinion of the Purchaser's legal counsel to the Purchaser — see **Legal Opinion** above for a discussion of the kinds of things the seller's counsel will look for in the legal opinion (mostly limited to legal matters relating to the ability of the Purchaser to enter into the transaction, as well as the enforceability of the transaction documents).

Ancillary Documents

> (b) [an assumption agreement, promissory note, or insert name of other Ancillary Document] substantially in the form of attached Exhibit [list Exhibit number], fully executed by an authorized officer of the Seller.

Assumption Agreement (Used in APA)

A standard short-form document by the Purchaser confirming the assumption of certain obligations of the Seller (to be used only if the Purchaser is assuming certain obligations).

Promissory Note (Used in APA and SPA)

In some transactions, the Purchaser will be making payment of the Purchase Price in installments, that is, paying a portion on the Closing Date, and the balance in one or more installments after the Closing Date. A promissory note is a short-form (usually) document by the obligor (in this case, the Purchaser) in which it promises to pay a particular amount of money to the obligee (in this case, the seller), plus interest, if applicable. The seller can condition its obligation to transfer title on its receipt of a promissory note from the Purchaser to evidence its obligation to make such payments.

Security Agreement (Used in APA and SPA)

In a simultaneous exchange at Closing, the seller will transfer title in the assets or stock at the same time that full payment is made by the Purchaser. In a deferred payment transaction, however, the seller will part with ownership before the Purchaser makes full payment. This can skew how the parties interact if something goes wrong after the Closing Date.

The Purchaser issues a promissory note or notes to evidence the debt, but if this is by itself, unsecured debt. The seller can, however, secure the Purchaser's obligations under the promissory note (that is, obtaining a security interest from the Purchaser in certain collateral). For example, the Purchaser can deliver a security agreement in which it grants the seller a security interest in the Acquired Assets or Acquired Stock (which the Purchaser owns after the Closing). Remember that if the Purchaser has bank financing, it's very likely that the bank will require the seller to subordinate its security interest to the bank. This means that while the Purchaser's bank may allow the Purchaser to grant the seller a security interest, the seller will have to line up behind the bank if and when it comes time to enforce the security interest. If the Purchaser becomes truly insolvent, there might not be enough in the till for the seller after the bank is through enforcing its rights. Another way for the seller to secure the promissory note is to obtain a personal guarantee from the Purchaser's corporate parent or a deep-pocketed insider.

Given space constraints, this book does not contain a detailed discussion of security agreement provisions.

Resolutions

[APA or SPA version] The Purchaser shall furnish the Seller [selling Stockholder] copies of all resolutions adopted by the Purchaser's stockholders and board of directors relating to the transactions contemplated by this Agreement, certified by the Secretary of the Purchaser as being in full force and effect on the Closing Date.

This is a fairly standard requirement, that the Purchaser furnish certified copies of the board or shareholder resolutions approving the transaction. Consult with your attorney, as state law may vary on the degree to which shareholder and/or board consent is required depending on the transaction.

13

REPRESENTATIONS
AND WARRANTIES
OF THE SELLER

OVERVIEW

If you are the Purchaser of a business (APA or SPA), imagine your dismay if after the Closing Date, a third party initiates an infringement lawsuit against you (the new owner) based on your use of the APA Seller's (or SPA Acquired Company's) trade secrets. Let's say that the Seller in an asset deal did not know about this risk because the third party made no prior attempt to communicate with the Seller (no warning letter, etc.), and that there is no question about the thoroughness in which your attorneys conducted the due diligence. Nevertheless, as the new owner, you'll incur costs to defend the lawsuit, not to mention pay damages if the claim is successful. Putting aside the issue of whether the Seller "should have" known about the risk, what redress might you have against the Seller?

Ask yourself if you would ever buy a business (assets or stock) on an "as is" basis. Probably not, because doing so means that you bear all the risk of the transaction. Think of the Seller's representations and warranties as a way to shift some of the risk back to the Seller. The risk shifting even manifests itself before the Closing — if the Purchaser is able to negotiate a representation from the Seller and then discovers a problem with the business relating to that representation before the Closing, then in many cases, the Purchaser may be in a good position to renegotiate the Purchase Price.

In the above example, while the Seller (in an asset deal, but this analysis also applies to the selling Stockholder in a stock deal) may not have actual knowledge of any infringement, the Seller still is in a better position, *vis-à-vis* the Purchaser, to have known about (or at least to have investigated) potential infringement and other risks impacting its business. If the Seller makes an appropriate representation, the Purchaser will have a claim against the Seller for damages if the Seller's representation turns out to have been false when made, and a possible claim for fraud if the misrepresentation was intentional. Given these consequences, the Seller will go through the list of representations with a fine-toothed comb, weeding out or qualifying representations it's not comfortable making outright (see **How to Qualify Representations** below).

While there is a technical difference between the terms "representations" (i.e., statements of facts) and "warranties" (i.e., statements of fact butressed by an implied obligation to remedy if the statements turn out to be false — think car warranty), they are used interchangeably in contracts.

You also want to be sure that the APA or SPA contains a good indemnity provision (see Chapter 17). While the representations and warranties form the basis for the claim, a good indemnity provision will give your claim more teeth. Remember that an APA or SPA doesn't create a long-term relationship like a distribution agreement or a bank loan agreement. Typically, the parties to an APA or SPA close the transaction, and then go their separate ways (except, for example, to the extent that payment is structured in installments). So it's also important for the representations and warranties to "survive" the Closing Date; this will enable the Purchaser to bring a claim even if it discovers the misrepresentation after the Closing Date.

Terminology Recap

In the sample contract provisions, I refer to the seller in an asset transaction (the individual, corporation, or other entity selling his, her, or its assets) as the "Seller" (capitalized). I refer to the sellers in an entity or stock transaction as the "selling Stockholders" (the term stockholder and shareholder can be used interchangeably). I refer to the corporation or other entity whose stock or ownership interests are being acquired in an entity or stock transaction as the "Acquired Company."

In the detailed discussions of the contract provisions, I sometimes use the shorthand "seller" (not capitalized) when referring to either the Seller (APA) or the selling Stockholders (SPA). Sometimes I use the term "acquired business" when referring to either the Seller (APA) or the Acquired Company (SPA). Finally, sometimes I use the term "Stockholders" to refer to either the selling Stockholders (SPA) or the owners of a corporate Seller (APA).

To the extent that a sample contract provision is used to show both the APA and SPA versions, I usually only use the APA "Seller" in order to reduce clutter, with the SPA "[Acquired Company]" appearing in brackets just the first time it is used in the provision.

How to Qualify Representations

While the Purchaser will want bulletproof representations and warranties from the Seller (or selling Stockholders), if you are the seller, you'll want to water them down a bit. There are several ways to qualify a representation.

- **List the Exceptions:** One way is for the seller to list the exceptions to the representation, either in the Agreement or, if the exceptions are numerous, in an Exhibit. The Purchaser should beware of the practice of some sellers to include a provision that states that disclosures are made generally and not relating to any particular representation or warranty, or to put the same disclosure in exhibits to multiple representations. By doing so, the seller minimizes the risk that it may have missed disclosing something, but the problem for the Purchaser with this approach is that it will never quite be sure exactly what the seller is saying in its disclosures.

- **Knowledge Qualifier:** Another way is for the seller to qualify the degree to which it makes the representation, for example, with the language "to the best of its knowledge." For example, you might revise the wording of the APA "Title to Property" representation (discussed in more detail later in this chapter) as follows: "To the best of the Seller's knowledge and except as set forth in the attached Exhibit, upon the Closing, the Purchaser will have good title to all the Assets of the Seller, free and clear of all liens ... "

  If it turns out that the Assets are the subject of undisclosed liens, then without the "best knowledge" qualifier, the Seller's "no liens" representation would be untrue, and the Purchaser would have a claim. However, by inserting the best knowledge qualifier, the Seller would only liable if it was aware of the liens (or should have been aware of them after making at least a reasonable inquiry). Note that some Sellers will attempt to completely eviscerate the representation by trying to negotiate the qualifier "to its knowledge." In this case the Purchaser would only have a claim if the Seller actually knew about the liens (which is very hard to prove); the Seller would have no obligation at all to investigate the existence of any liens. This goes too far. If you are the Purchaser, you should not let the Seller qualify its representations "to its knowledge."

- **Materiality Qualifier:** Another way for the seller to qualify the degree to which it makes a representation is to add a "materiality" exception. In the APA version of the "Qualification" representation (discussed in more detail later on), the Seller states that it "is qualified to do business and is in good standing ... in every jurisdiction in which ... the conduct of its business requires such qualification." There is very little room for error for the Seller. It's better for the Seller to negotiate the representation that it is qualified and in good standing everywhere "except where the failure to so qualify will not have a **material adverse effect** on its business." So if the Seller is required to but forgets to qualify or maintain its good standing in a state where it conducts only a small amount of business, then the Seller has not breached the representation.

  When negotiating the materiality exception, pay special attention to exactly what is being qualified. For example, let's look at the APA version of the "No Conflicts" representation (discussed in more detail later in this chapter), which states in relevant part — "the performance of this Agreement will not violate any contract to which the Seller is subject." Again, there is very little room for error for the Seller. However, the Seller can build itself a buffer zone by negotiating a materiality exception. It can include any combination of the qualifiers below:

- **"the performance of this Agreement will not materially violate any contract"**: This means that there is a misrepresentation only if the violation is material, even if the contract being breached is small or not important or the impact of such breach on the business is tiny.

- **"the performance of this Agreement will not violate any material contract"**: This means that there is a misrepresentation only if the contract being violated is important to the business, even if the breach is a tiny one with little impact on the business.

- **"the performance of this Agreement will not violate any material provision of any contract"**: This means that there is a misrepresentation only if there is a violation of an important provision of any contract, even if the contract being breached is small or not important or the impact of such breach on the business is tiny.

- **"the performance of this Agreement will not violate any contract except where any such violation will not have a material adverse effect on its business"**: This means that there is a misrepresentation only if the violation has a significant and negative impact on the business.

- **Not a Representation, But Still a Default:** Sometimes, the parties will reach an impasse in the negotiations based on one or two representations. Let's say that the Seller (or selling Stockholders) is steadfast in its insistence that it cannot make a representation about there being no infringement of third-party intellectual property rights, not even with one of the materiality qualifiers discussed above. The seller claims that it simply doesn't know enough about the situation, and refuses to make a representation that it knows might be untrue. Let's say that this issue is extremely important to you (the Purchaser), and you can't compromise by having the seller dilute its representation with a knowledge qualifier.

In this case, in lieu of the seller's representation, maybe the parties can agree that an infringement constitutes the seller's default under the APA or SPA. This compromise achieves your goal as the Purchaser to have the seller bear the risk of infringement. At the same time, it achieves the seller's goal of not being put into a situation where it might make a false statement that may expose it to claims of fraud.

SAMPLE CONTRACT EXCERPTS

Survival of Representations

The representations, warranties, and covenants of the parties contained in this Agreement survive the Closing until the date that is [18 months] from the Closing Date (the "End of Survival Date"). Notwithstanding the above, claims arising under the following sections of this Agreement survive until the indicated dated.

Section number	Corresponding End of Survival Date
Section __ [list section number of the seller's tax representation]	[Insert date]
Section __ [list section number of the seller's environmental representations]	[Insert date]
Section __ [list section number of the seller's employee benefit representations]	[Insert date]
[List other sections]	[Insert date]

In the event that any representation, warranty or covenant becomes the subject of a lawsuit or other proceeding (including any lawsuit or proceeding involving a third party), the End of Survival Date shall be extended until the lawsuit or proceeding (including appeals) has been finally resolved or settled, and actual payment of any judgment or settlement has been paid.

Neither party may make any claim for indemnity under this Agreement after the applicable End of Survival Date. Each party waives any right under any applicable statute of limitations to bring any claim after the applicable End of Survival Date.

Before we get into the bulk of the sample contract representations and warranties, I first want to discuss an important topic — how long the representations and warranties in an APA or SPA survive after the closing.

Contracts like bank loan agreements, employment agreements, and franchise agreements, to name a few, govern long-term relationships. These agreements typically have provisions establishing the term (that is, the length of time the agreement will remain in force absent some kind of termination event like an event of default).

On the other hand, APAs and SPAs are contracts that for the most part, do not contemplate long-term relationships. They typically don't have a term, except to the extent that there is a time gap between the date the Agreement is signed (Execution Date) and the Closing, there are any post-closing obligations like confidentiality, non-compete or transition employment/consultant arrangements, and any of the representations, warranties, or covenants survive the Closing (as discussed below).

Most likely, the entrepreneurial owner is selling the business because he or she wants to retire, cash in, or get out of the business. The seller just wants to move on; it doesn't want to have to "lose sleep" over claims coming out of the woodwork. On the other hand, the Purchaser has a legitimate interest in making sure that the seller backs up what it is selling, even after the Closing.

Purchasers shouldn't assume that the representations and warranties will automatically survive (that is, remain in effect after) the Closing. It's best to explicitly state that they will survive the Closing, and for how long. By the way, most APAs and SPAs put this provision in the indemnity provision because that is the mechanism by which the Purchaser seeks to collect damages from the seller in the event of a misrepresentation. I've decided to include the discussion of survival right here in this section on representations and warranties.

Okay, now that the basic language is in place, the question then is, just how long should the representations and warranties (and the obligation of the seller to indemnify the Purchaser for any breach of representation or warranty) survive the Closing? As usual, the answer is "it depends." From the Purchaser's perspective, the "basic representations" that go to the very core question of the enforceability of the transaction and the ownership of the property being transferred (e.g., Organization, Power, and Authority to Run Business; Authority to Sell; No Conflict with Corporate Documents, Contracts or Laws; Enforceability; Title to Assets; etc.), should last forever. After all, for example, the seller either has the authority to enter into the transaction or it doesn't. The seller doesn't really have a good argument to support shortening the survivor period for these representations. That's cold comfort to the seller, to whom the threat of being sued by the Purchaser probably feels like a Sword of Damocles hanging precariously over its head. The bona fide seller (who is not a con artist) just wants to move on after the Closing.

Survival Time Limits

The parties typically find middle ground and agree to a multi-pronged approach. One example is:

(a) survival forever for the above-mentioned "basic representations";

(b) survival period of 12 to 24 months for the other representations and warranties (for example, no Litigation, accuracy of Financial Statements, etc.). Negotiate the length of time to allow the Purchaser, using reasonable methods, to discover these types of problems during its next audit period.

(c) survival period of up to (or a buffer zone of a couple of months beyond) the applicable statute of limitations for the high risk Tax, Environmental, and Employee Benefits representations.

The sample contract provision could provide another approach — a survivor period of 18 months from the Closing for all the representations and warranties, but longer up to the statute of limitations for the Tax, Employee Benefit, and Environmental representations.

Additional Drafting Information

I include a detailed discussion of the representations and warranties by subject matter category. Any representation discussed below that applies to a corporation can also apply to other artificial legal persons like a limited liability company. The wording of the sample provisions will need to be adjusted for these other entities, but the concepts remain the same.

Keep in mind that APAs and SPAs incorporate a wide variety of drafting styles. Some are short and some are long. Many agreements contain representations that combine, to varying degrees, the representations discussed below. Some agreements even have representations that (incorrectly) contain promises of future action in them. Promises of future action (or inaction) are actually **covenants**, and should be placed in the covenants section of the agreement. As a Purchaser, you may determine after doing a thorough risk management analysis, that you do not need (and as a seller, you may not want to give) every representation discussed below. My subject matter approach will help you to identify and then negotiate whether and to what extent these representations are to be included in your agreement.

Certified Copies of Important Documents

As part of the Purchaser's due diligence, it may want a representation that the seller has furnished to the Purchaser copies of all the important documents relating to the company's business. Include copies of the applicable formation and organizational documents (e.g., Certificate of Incorporation, Bylaws, LLC Operating Agreement, Shareholders Agreement, etc.), corporate administrative documents (e.g., board and shareholder meeting minutes, stock transfer records, etc.), the financial statements, recent tax returns, all contracts (e.g., distribution agreements, leases, etc.), as well as a summary of important understandings not previously reduced to writing (list the name of the counterparty, and a summary of the business arrangement, etc.). Don't forget to include all amendments to any of the above.

If you want that extra measure of comfort you can have the Seller's (APA) or Acquired Company's (SPA) corporate secretary or president certify the copies of the documents as being complete and accurate. Some people actually attach copies of the documents to the APA or SPA as exhibits, but this can be unwieldy and is legally unnecessary.

Subsidiaries

If you are purchasing or selling a company that is large enough or with diverse enough operations to have subsidiaries, then you have to be very careful about how the wording of the APA or SPA impacts the subsidiaries. Subsidiaries are separate legal entities (corporations, limited liability companies, etc.) that are owned by another legal entity. One scenario in the example at the beginning of Part III could be that the Seller Cavendish runs its retail stores through the parent company, Cavendish Markets, Inc., but runs its gift basket business through Cavendish Gift Baskets, Inc., a subsidiary that is wholly-owned (100 percent owned) by the parent company.

Assuming that Cavendish wants to include the gift basket business in the sale, then the parties will have to tweak the transaction and contract language. For example, if the parties structure the transaction as an asset sale, then Consolidated may need to enter into an APA with both Cavendish entities. If, on the other hand, Consolidated purchases the stock of the parent company, then it will automatically become the owner (albeit indirectly) of the stock of the gift basket subsidiary. In either case, the Purchaser should make sure that the representations and warranties (and covenants, closing conditions, etc.), apply to both the parent company and its subsidiaries. It's especially important to have the representations cover the subsidiaries if the parent company is a holding company whose main purpose is to own the shares of the subsidiaries that actually run the business.

Representations Impacting the Parent Company and its Subsidiaries Individually

Just one example is the Organization representation discussed below. It should be tweaked to confirm the due organization, valid existence, and good standing of the parent company and each subsidiary.

Representations Impacting the Parent Company and its Subsidiaries as a Group (i.e., "Taken as a Whole")

In the "Litigation" representation (discussed later in this chapter), for example, the seller will most likely be asked to confirm that there is no litigation pending or threatened against the company or any of its subsidiaries. While a specific litigation might have a huge impact on the subsidiary (to the point of shutting down the subsidiary's business), it may have much less impact when viewed in the context of the entire business (parent company plus subsidiaries). Therefore, the seller should negotiate to qualify the representation that any such litigation will not have a material adverse effect on the parent company and its subsidiaries "taken as a whole."

Financial Statement Representations

You'll also need to tweak the Financial Statements representations because organizations with subsidiaries may prepare consolidated financial statements. "Consolidated" means that financial results of a parent company and its subsidiaries are reported together. Some companies report their financial results on a consolidating basis, which means separately for the parent company and each of its subsidiaries.

Separating a Subsidiary from the Transaction

Remember that share ownership represents a *pro rata* undivided interest in the company. Think of it in terms of how a husband and wife jointly own a house; each person has 50 percent ownership. But it doesn't mean that the husband owns the downstairs and the wife owns the upstairs. Rather each person owns 50 percent of the entire house. Similarly, it's not possible to say that that these shares of stock represent ownership in this set of assets, and those shares of stock represent ownership in that set of assets.

Keeping that in mind, let's say for whatever reason that the parties want to structure the transaction as a stock sale, but agree that the selling Stockholders (who own the parent company, which in turn owns the subsidiary) should keep the subsidiary for themselves. In this case, the stockholders of the parent company might consider transferring ownership of the subsidiary from the parent company to themselves, before the Purchaser acquires ownership of the parent company using an SPA. This is a complicated multi-step transaction, and you should consult with your attorney and tax advisor on the possible tax and other legal ramifications.

Subsidiaries versus Divisions

A division is a business or department within the parent company that typically is not a separate legal entity, but may have many of the trappings of a separate company (its own officers, office space, letterhead, etc.). Be sure to investigate the true legal status of the Seller's "subsidiaries" and "divisions" because businesspeople sometimes use the terms interchangeably.

From a drafting viewpoint, if the division is not a separate legal entity, then any reference to the "Seller" (APA) or "Acquired Company" (SPA) will automatically include the division. If the Seller in an APA is selling only the assets of one or two divisions that are not separate legal entities, the APA should say more than just that "the Purchaser is purchasing the assets of the Seller's ABC Division." Since the assets of ABC Division may overlap with some of the assets of the Seller's other divisions, it's better to clearly define exactly what assets are being acquired, and what liabilities are being assumed.

If the company is large enough to have divisions, the Purchaser can raise the argument that the company should also have the internal resources to prepare separate financial statements for the division. Even if they are unaudited, the financial statements can give the Purchaser a good picture of the adequacy of the division's assets, as well as the extent of its liabilities.

By the way, if you want to purchase just a division of a company (which is not a separate legal entity) or any subset of assets (like inventory or perhaps a brand name or product line), you cannot structure the transaction as a stock purchase. (Unless you first separate the division of assets into a new company, which is beyond the scope of this book.) As discussed above, you cannot say that a certain group of shares in the parent company represents ownership in a particular division or subset of assets.

APA Introductory Language

The Seller represents and warrants to the Purchaser as follows:

This is the basic APA language preceding the individual representations. In an APA, the Seller is the person or entity (corporation, etc.), that owns the assets being sold, although it is possible (though not common) for the Purchaser to negotiate that the individual Stockholders of a selling entity not just provide personal guarantees, but also enter into the APA and make these representations directly. The Seller may attempt to add a blanket qualification to all of its representations by negotiating the addition of the words "to the best of its knowledge" or other qualification language to this introductory clause. Or the parties might negotiate qualification language on a case-by-case basis for the individual representations below (a better approach from the Purchaser's perspective). The Purchaser can be defined to include any subsidiary formed to enter into this transaction.

SPA Introductory Language

The Stockholders [jointly and severally] represent and warrant to the Purchaser as follows:

This is the basic SPA language preceding the individual representations. In an SPA, the seller(s) is/are the owners of the stock/membership interests in the corporation/ limited liability company, etc., that owns the assets. Therefore, the selling Stockholders will be making the representations. Note the bracketed **joint and several** language you can use if there are multiple stockholders. In case of a misrepresentation, joint and several liability will allow the Purchaser to pursue any of the selling Stockholders for 100 percent of the liability regardless of that particular Stockholder's contribution to the misrepresentation. Keep discussion of Joint and Several provisions (please refer to Chapter 25). The selling Stockholders may also negotiate to qualify their representaions (see **How to Qualify Representations** above).

Organization, Power, and Authority to Run Business

[APA version] The Seller:

(a) is a corporation [limited liablity company, etc.] duly organized, validly existing, and in good standing under the laws of the state of its incorporation [formation]; and

(b) has all requisite [corporate] power and authority to own, lease, license, and use its assets and to operate its business.

This representation applies if the Seller in an asset transaction is a corporation or other artificial legal entity. Subsection (a) covers three corporate attributes. **Duly organized** means that the corporation properly filed its certificate of incorporation, and then took all the corporate governance steps (adopted by-laws, issued shares, elected directors and officers, etc.), necessary to transform the corporate "shell" into a "legally functioning" entity. **Validly existing** means that the corporation is still alive, that it hasn't been voluntarily or involuntarily dissolved.

In good standing means that the corporation is up-to-date on all of its annual filings and state franchise tax payments. Note that good standing is a state corporate law concept; being in good standing has nothing to do with whether the Seller is compliant with the income tax laws.

You can also verify some of these corporate attributes during due diligence by ordering a certified copy of the certificate of incorporation and a good standing certificate from the secretary of state of the Seller's state of incorporation. Because these documents are date-stamped when issued, they can only be used to verify the attributes as of that date. That's why it's so important to obtain these representations from the Seller.

The Seller should try to qualify Subsection (b) **Power to Run Business** by adding the bracketed language "corporate"; this will limit the scope of this representation to areas covered by state corporate law (e.g., certificate of incorporation, by-laws, etc.).

On the other hand, the Purchaser will want to take "corporate" out, as this would technically expand the scope of the representation to cover all areas of the law. In this case, the Seller would be confirming that it has all power, consents and approvals (not just under corporate law, but under all regulatory laws — FDA, FCC, you name it) to run the business. If you are the Purchaser of a highly regulated business, then you should also consider adding the representation that "there is no action that is pending or threatened that may result in the revocation, suspension, modification or non-renewal, or sanctions relating to, any consents or approvals necessary to run the business." This will help to ferret out nascent situations before it's too late.

Now why would a Purchaser who is just purchasing the assets care about the due organization, etc., of the selling entity? The answer is that in this and many of the representations listed below, the Seller is confirming that it has the legal capacity to enter into the transaction. For example, if the Seller has been dissolved, then it no longer validly exists. A dead person has no legal capacity to enter into a contract, nor does a "dead" corporation.

[SPA version] The Acquired Company:

(a) is a corporation [limited liablity company, etc.] duly organized, validly existing, and in good standing under the laws of the state of its incorporation [formation]; and

(b) has all requisite [corporate] power and authority to own, lease, license, and use its assets and to operate its business.

In an SPA, the selling Stockholders of the "Acquired Company" make this representation about the Acquired Company to assure the Purchaser that it is purchasing shares of a corporation that has its "house in order," at least from a basic corporate governance standpoint. The Purchaser will also want to verify this information for any subsidiaries owned by the Acquired Company; you will need to revise this and other representations to include any subsidiaries.

Qualification in Foreign Jurisdictions

> [APA or SPA version] The Seller [Acquired Company] is duly qualified to do business and is in good standing as a foreign corporation [limited liability company, etc.] in every jurisdiction in which its ownership, leasing, licensing, or use of its assets or the conduct of its business requires such qualification.

In this Internet age, it's common for even the smallest home-based business to be active around the country. This representation addresses the right of a corporation or other artificial legal entity (APA Seller or SPA Acquired Company) to "do business" in states outside of its state of organization (i.e., foreign jurisdictions). Each state has its own laws about the minimum threshold of activity that constitutes "doing business." If a company passes that threshold, then it typically has to qualify (i.e., register) to do business in that state. But state laws usually don't spell out the exact threshold for "doing business"; rather they list determining factors based on the degree to which the business has contact with the state.

If the acquired business has an office, warehouse or other physical facility in that state, then it almost definitely has to register to do business in that state. At the other end of the spectrum, if the acquired business ships an occassional package to a customer in that state (without ever having to make a sales call or otherwise set foot in that state), then it probably doesn't have to register.

Being in good standing as a foreign corporation means that the company has not only registered to do business in that state, but maintained its registration by being up-to-date with all annual filings and fees. Sellers face a special conundrum with this representation. As discussed above, you can never be absolutely sure whether you are registered in every state you technically need to be. If you are the seller in the transaction, you may want to negotiate a qualification to this representation that the acquired business is duly qualified to do business only in those states "where the failure to so qualify will not have a material adverse effect on the business," or simply to insist that you can't make any representation except to list the states where you know that you are qualified to do business and/or are in good standing.

Authority to Sell

> [APA version] The Seller has:
>
> (a) all requisite [corporate] power and authority to execute, deliver, and perform this Agreement;
>
> (b) duly taken all necessary [corporate] action to authorize the execution, delivery, and performance of this Agreement by the Seller; and
>
> (c) duly [authorized], executed, and delivered this Agreement.

This representation applies to Sellers that are corporations or other artificial entities, and ultimately relates to whether the Seller has fulfilled the basic legal prerequisities required to perform its obligations.

Power to Perform Agreement

Subsection (a) addresses whether the Seller has the authority (e.g., under its certificate of incorporation and other organizational documents) to enter into and perform the APA.

Action to Authorize Agreement

Subsection (b) addresses whether the Seller has taken all actions (e.g., passed board and shareholder resolutions, etc.) necessary to approve the APA. The Seller should try to qualify the representations in (a) and (b) by adding the bracketed language "corporate"; this will limit the scope of the representations to areas covered by state corporate law. Purchasers will want to take "corporate" out, as this would technically expand the scope of the representations to all areas of the law (e.g., regulatory law, tax law, etc.).

Proper Execution of Agreement

Subsection (c) addresses mainly whether the APA has been signed by the right people within the organization. For example, do the Seller's bylaws or the board resolutions require signature by the president or by at least two officers? The worst case but unlikely scenario would be where a rogue employee with the apparent authority to act on behalf of the Seller signs the APA transferring all of the assets. The Purchaser typically bolsters its protection by requiring the signing officers to execute **Incumbancy Certificates**, in which another officer (e.g., the corporate secretary) attests to the authenticity of the signatures of the signing officers. A bootstrap precaution to be sure, but one which together with due diligence and the Seller's representation serves reasonably well to protect the Purchaser.

The Purchaser can negotiate to expand this representation to make the Seller cover not just the "Agreement," but also "all documents to be delivered at the Closing by the Seller under the Agreement." You may have to tweak the language because some of the other closing documents might be signed by persons other than the Seller.

Consent of Third Parties to Transaction

[APA version] Except the consents disclosed in the attached Exhibit [list Exhibit number] (which were duly obtained prior to the execution of this Agreement and remain in full force and effect), no consent of any party to any contract or understanding to which the Seller, or with respect to which any of its assets or business, is subject, is required for the execution, delivery, or performance of this Agreement.

The Seller's contracts (distribution agreements, supply agreements, leases, etc.), are often a valuable part of the assets transferred in an APA. However, most of these contracts have **assignment provisions** that work to restrict their transfer. Some assignment provisions allow assignments to a party that purchases all or substantially all of the assets of the assigning party. This is the easiest situation because all you'll need to do to transfer the contract is to follow the contract's procedure to the letter (e.g., send a formal notice to the contract counterparty). However, other assignment provisions require the consent of the contract counterparty or prohibit transfers alltogether. In this case, the parties have to negotiate with the contract counterparty to allow the transfer. It's best to start this process well in advance of the Closing. You should also pay attention to the assigned contract's other provisions, such as the termination provision. After all, what good is the assignment if the counterparty is permitted to terminate the agreement without cause (at will) immediately after the Closing?

This representation confirms that (a) any such consent has been obtained and remains in effect on the date the APA is signed (you'll need a **Bring Down** — discussed in Chapter 16 to confirm that the consents are still in effect on the Closing Date), and (b) there are no other consents required. In the sample excerpt, I use the term "contract or understanding"; however, words with similar meaning that often appear in this representation include "agreement," "arrangement," "instrument," "lease," and "license."

Sometimes the Purchaser takes the additional step of requiring the Seller to deliver "true and correct copies" of such consents certified by a high level officer of the Seller.

[SPA version] Except the consents disclosed in the attached Exhibit (which were duly obtained prior to the execution of this Agreement and remain in full force and effect), no consent of any party to any contract or understanding to which the Acquired Company (or any of its Stockholders), or with respect to which any of its assets or business, is subject, is required for the execution, delivery, or performance of this Agreement.

This is the analogous representation for an SPA. The language contained in a contract's assignment provision is sometimes unclear regarding the SPA situation where ownership of the entity changes hands. While a typical argument is that a change in entity ownership is not technically an assignment (since the underlying assets (including contracts) of the Acquired Company stay with the Acquired Company), many contracts contain **change in control** provisions that specifically deem a change in entity ownership (100 percent or partial) (or board membership composition) to be an "assignment" requiring consent.

There are two approaches you can take when confronted with unclear assignment provisions. You can cross your fingers and interpret the provision to allow the SPA change of ownership, do nothing and hope for the best. But the better approach is to be a bit more proactive. While you never want to negotiate against yourself, perhaps the company or the company together with the Purchaser can send a courtesy letter to the contract counterparty notifying them of the impending change in ownership. In the letter, you can specifically mention that while you are not required to obtain their consent, you are sending them the letter as a courtesy to them. Fact is, you'll need their consent (from a practical point of view) if you want to start off the new relationship on the right foot.

Consent of Government Authorities to Transaction

[APA or SPA version] Except the consents disclosed in the attached Exhibit [list Exhibit number] (which were duly obtained prior to the execution of this Agreement and remain in full force and effect), no consent of, or filing with, any government authority or any court or other tribunal, is required for the execution, delivery, or performance of this Agreement by the Seller.

This representation is similar to the **Consent of Third Parties** representation discussed above, but confirms that no consents of any government authority or court or other tribunal are required to move forward with the transaction (except the ones that the parties have already obtained and are listed). You'll need to consult with your attorneys on what federal, state, or local government consents, etc., are required based on the structure of the transaction and the nature of the business, for example, notices to or approval of the Federal Trade Commission may be required for acquisition in the media industry. In the sample excerpt, I use the terms "consent of, or filing with"; however, words with similar meaning that often appear in this representation include "approval," "authorization," "certificate," "declaration," "decree," "license," "order," and "permit."

No Conflict with Corporate Documents, Contracts, or Laws

[APA or SPA version] The execution, delivery and performance of this Agreement will not violate or conflict with:

(a) the organizational documents of the Seller [Acquired Company] (including, but not limited to, certificate of incorporation, bylaws, shareholders agreement [or list limited liability company agreement, partnership agreement, etc.] of the Seller, as the case may be);

(b) any contract, agreement, understanding [or commitment]; or

(c) any law, regulation or other rule of any government authority or ruling or other determination of any court or other tribunal, to which the Seller, or with respect to which any of its assets or business, is subject.

This representation confirms that the Agreement won't conflict with (a) any of the APA Seller's (or SPA Acquired Company's) organizational documents, or (b) contracts, or (c) any government law, regulation or ruling. In the sample contract excerpt, I use the terms "violate or conflict with"; however, terms or phrases with similar meaning that often appear in this representation include "contravene," "result in a breach of," and "entitle any party to terminate or call a default." The last phrase is often qualified with the words "with or without the giving of notice or the passage of time or both."

In (c) of the sample contract excerpt, I use the terms "law, regulation, or other rule"; however, words with similar meaning that often appear in this representation include "decree," "order," "regulation," and "statute," and more specifically for court actions, the terms "injunction," "judgment," and "writ."

No Liens Resulting from Transaction

The execution, delivery, and performance of this Agreement will not result in the creation of any lien, encumbrance, or other security interest on the assets or property of the Seller.

Just like it's possible for the execution, delivery, or performance of the APA or SPA to trigger a breach of one of the Seller's (or Acquired Company's) contracts (see **No Conflict** representation above), it's also possible for the APA or SPA to trigger the creation of a third party lien on the assets or stock being sold.

It's best to check the contracts for any provision that imposes a lien in favor of a third party in the event of an assignment or change in control. In the sample contract excerpt, I use the words "lien, encumbrance, or other security interest." As discussed above there are many words that can be used to describe liens. No matter which words you use, make sure that all references to liens in the representations, covenants, closing conditions, etc., are consistently defined.

Keep in mind that the Purchaser's contracts with its lender may contain a provision that automatically grants the lender a security interest in after-acquired property (a provision that gives the lender a security interest in property acquired at a later date), which would include the assets purchased in an APA. This puts the Purchaser in a bind if it needs to finance the transaction because the lender providing the new financing will also want a security interest in the assets.

[SPA version] The execution, delivery, and performance of this Agreement will not result in the creation of any lien, encumbrance, pledge, or other security interest on (a) the assets or property of the Acquired Company or (b) the Stock acquired under this Agreement.

Enforceability

[APA or SPA version] This Agreement is the legal, valid, and binding obligation of the Seller [stockholder], enforceable against the Seller in accordance with its terms.

This representation hinges on the veracity of many of the representations discussed above. For example, if the APA Seller or SPA Acquired Company has not authorized the transaction by board resolution, then the Seller (or selling Stockholders) can't make the **Authority to Sell** representation (discussed above). It follows that it can't make this Enforceability representation either, because proper board authoriztion is one of the elements to the validity and enforceability of a contract.

If you are the seller, you should consider qualifying this representation by adding that "Such enforcement may be subject to applicable bankruptcy or similar laws affecting creditors' rights. Any equitable relief sought may be subject to equitable defenses and the discretion of the court before which any proceeding may be brought."

While as usual, specific language may vary, the idea of this qualification is that when it comes time to enforce the Agreement, the bankruptcy (similar words or phrases include "assignment for the benefit of creditors," "composition or arrangement with creditors," "insolvency," "receivership," "reorganization," and "moratorium") laws impose special rules that may render, or give the bankruptcy court latitude to render the Agreement unenforceable, even though all of the legal prerequisities have been followed.

Capitalization

[SPA version] The authorized capital stock of the Acquired Company consists of [1000] shares of common stock, par value $[1.00] per share (the "Common Stock"), of which [500] shares are outstanding (the "Outstanding Share(s)"). Each Outstanding Share:

(a) is validly authorized and issued, fully paid, and nonassessable;

(b) has not been issued and is not owned or held in violation of any preemptive right of stockholders; and

(c) is owned of record and beneficially by the owners set forth in the attached Exhibit [list Exhibit number], in each case free and clear of all liens, pledges, stockholder agreements, voting trusts, and other security interests.

Except as set forth above, there are no shares of capital stock of the Acquired Company that are authorized, issued, or outstanding.

This representation confirms basic information about the shares of stock being purchased in a an SPA. Please refer to the **Capital Stock Quick Primer** (Chapter 2) for an explanation of terminology used in the sample contract excerpt. Any of the representations in this sample contract excerpt, if untrue, can materially impact the Purchaser's ability to enjoy the ownership rights it bargained for.

Representations (a) and (b) confirm that the shares the Purchaser is acquiring have been authorized and properly issued. For example, shares previously issued to a selling Stockholder in violation of a third party's preemptive rights will call into question the selling Stockholder's ownership interest in the shares it is trying to sell to the Purchaser.

[SPA version] There is no option, warrant, or other security authorized or outstanding:

(d) which is exercisable or exchangable for, or convertible into, capital stock of the Acquired Company; or

(e) which calls for the issuance of capital stock or any other security or instrument, which is convertible into or exchangeable for capital stock of the Acquired Company.

There is no commitment or plan to issue any of the above.

Representation (c), as well as the options and warrants representations [(d) and (e)], help to confirm that there are no undisclosed parties that own stock, or have the right to own stock in the future — either through the enforcement of liens or the exercise of options, warrants, etc. And while the owner of a stock option, warrant, etc., needs to first exercise its rights before it can actually own stock in the company, the options, warrants, etc. represent contingent ownership rights that may work to dilute the Purchaser's ownership interest (financially or the ability to control the company). Basically, the selling Stockholders are confirming that there won't be any third parties (ex-spouses, lenders, business partners, etc.), that climb out of the woodwork after the Closing and assert ownership rights in competition with the Purchaser.

Financial Statements

[APA or SPA version] The Seller [selling Stockholder] has delivered to the Purchaser true and correct copies of the following Financial Statements:

(a) audited balance sheet of the Seller [Acquired Company] as of [insert end date of the most recently completed fiscal year];

(b) unaudited balance sheet of the Seller as of [insert end date of the most recently completed interim period];

(c) audited statements of income, retained earnings, and changes in financial position of the Seller for the year ended [insert end date of the most recently completed fiscal year]; and

(d) unaudited statements of income, retained earnings, and changes in financial position of the Seller for the months ended [insert end date of a most recently completed interim period].

The Purchaser should review the financial statements (which include the balance sheet and the statements of income, retained earnings and changes in finanical position) as part of its comprehensive due diligence of the Seller (APA) or Acquired Company (SPA). Larger companies usually prepare audited financial statements at least annually, and unaudited financial statements quarterly. Let's say that the Seller or Acquired Company has a December 31st fiscal year-end, and that the parties are signing the APA or SPA on May 5th (Execution Date), with a Closing Date of May 31st. If you are the Purchaser, you'll want accurate and complete information about the financial condition of the company covering all time periods through the Closing Date (and beyond if the Purchaser is spreading out payment of the purchase price over time).

Representations (a) and (c) confirm that audited financial statements corresponding to the immediate past fiscal year (ending December 31st) have been delivered to the Purchaser.

Representations (b) and (d) confirm that unaudited financial statements corresponding to the immediate past fiscal quarter (January 1st to March 31st) have been delivered to the Purchaser.

Time Period Covering End of Immediate Past Fiscal Quarter until the Execution Date — The Material Adverse Change representation (discussed below) confirms that there have been no subsequent events (in our example, from April 1st until May 5th) that have materially impacted the business being acquired. In some cases, the parties will agree to a Material Adverse Change provision covering the period after the year-end date of the audited financial statements.

Time Period Covering the Execution Date until the Closing Date: Please refer to the discussion on **Bring Downs** for language you can use to confirm that there have been no subsequent events (in our example, from May 6th until May 31st) that have materially impacted the business (including financial condition) being acquired.

Keep in mind that if you are purchasing the assets of a division of the Seller that is not a separate legal entity, then the financial statements of the Seller (which may not split out financial information about the unincorporated division) may be of limited use to you. You'll need to find other ways to confirm information relating to the financial condition of the division.

The Financial Statements delivered above:

(a) have been prepared in accordance with generally accepted accounting principles consistently applied [throughout the periods involved]; and

(b) fairly present in all material respects, the financial condition of the Seller as of the dates thereof, and the results of operations and changes in financial position of the Seller for the time periods indicated.

I define "Financial Statements" to include the documents listed above. Therefore, I was able to keep this representation brief — confirming generally that the documents conform with **Generally Accepted Accounting Principles (GAAP)** consistently applied (Subsection [a]), and fairly present the "financial condition" of the acquired business (Subsection [b]). Some APAs and SPAs tailor separate Subsection (b) representations for each of the individual types of financial statements.

For example, one representation will confirm that the balance sheet fairly presents the "assets, liabilities, and stockholders' equity" of the company, and another representation will confirm that the income statement fairly presents the "results of operation" of the acquired business.

Of the two parts, Subsection (b) is the provision that gets a fair amount of attention during the negotiations. Subsection (b), which more or less tracks the kind of language that an independent auditor would use to present audited financial statements, is actually pretty tame from the Purchaser's perspective. All it really says is that the financial statements present a fair picture of the acquired business in all material respects; it doesn't ask the seller to represent that the financial statements are "true, complete, and correct" or "accurate and complete." Some aggressive Purchaser-prepared first drafts of APA and SPA will ask for the higher standard, and perhaps even that the acquired business's books and records (upon which the financial statements are prepared) are true, complete, and correct. This is an impossible standard for the acquired business, and it's best to strike the provision or qualify it with "materiality."

Purchasers sometimes mistakenly believe that these representations mean that the Seller or selling Stockholders are confirming that the transaction is a sound financial investment. Yet other Purchasers sometimes take misplaced comfort in the auditing process, thinking mistakenly that somehow the auditor's imprimatur is a stamp of approval of the transaction. Keep in mind that these representations go only to the threshold issue of how the financial statements are prepared, and make no judgment about the quality of the business, except the extent to which bad numbers speak for themselves. As the Purchaser, you'll have to work with your advisors to carefully scrutinize and interpret the financial statements to help you determine whether you should enter into the transaction, and if so, at what price.

If the transaction turns out in hindsight to be a bad deal for you, you can't rely on the Financial Statement representations to sue the Seller or selling Stockholders, unless the financial statements do not, in fact, fairly convey financial information about the acquired business in accordance with GAAP — in other words, that the financial statements contain material inaccuracies or omissions.

No Material Adverse Change

[APA or SPA version] Since [insert end date of the most recently completed fiscal year or insert end date of the most recently completed interim period], there has been no material adverse change in the:

(a) financial condition or results of operations of the Seller [Acquired Company]; or

(b) assets, business, liabilities, operations, or future prospects of the Seller.

Seller knows of no facts or circumstances that may in the future have a material adverse affect on (a) or (b) above.

As discussed in the **Financial Statements** representation, as a Purchaser, you'll want accurate and complete information about the financial condition of the acquired business covering all time periods through the Closing Date (and beyond if you are paying the purchase price in installments). However, there's usually a time gap between the date (or time periods) of the last set of available financial statements (especially audited ones) and the Closing Date. The **No Material Adverse Change (MAC)** representation covers this time gap and helps to confirm that the APA Seller's or SPA Acquired Company's business and financial condition have not deteriorated significantly since the date of the last financial statements.

The last paragraph attempts to capture facts or circumstances known to the Seller that may in future rise to the level of MAC. Sellers will generally avoid giving this representation because, even though it is based on actual knowledge, it doesn't want to risk giving the seller a claim based on a low-level fact or circumstance that matures in hindsight into a MAC. "Future prospects" in Subsection (b) is similarly problematic for sellers because it asks the seller to look hard for anything that might impact the future of the company, even things like competitor activity.

The MAC representation overlaps somewhat with a "Projections" representation discussed above, but is different in several ways. In a "Projections" representation, the seller tries to predict the future, which may be better than, or worse than, the current situation. On the other hand, the MAC representation sets a baseline of historical performance (based on the financial statements) and then confirms (directly or via Bring Down) that the performance of the acquired business hasn't gotten any worse.

The parties will have to negotiate which financial statements to use as the baseline, the most recent audited or unaudited. For the party making the representation, it's better to pick the one that sets the bar lower.

Keep in mind that MAC is a "no-fault" representation. If the performance of the acquired business nosedives then the representation would be untrue whether or not the downturn was caused by the acquired business or by outside forces beyond its control.

If the Seller or Acquired Company has subsidiaries, it can negotiate to qualify (a) and (b) adding "taken as a whole" (see the discussion on Subsidiaries above for a more detailed discussion).

Extraordinary Transactions or Events (Generally)

[APA or SPA version] Since [insert end date of the most recently completed fiscal year or insert end date of the most recently completed interim period], the Seller [Acquired Company]:

(a) has conducted every aspect of its business only in the ordinary course and consistent with past practice;

(b) has not entered into any agreement or other understanding, or accepted any purchase order, that it (or any of the Stockholders) expects will be unprofitable;

(c) has not incurred any [extraordinary] loss or damage, whether or not covered by insurance, adversely affecting its business or financial condition; and

(d) has not authorized, declared or paid any dividend or other distribution with respect to, or redemption or other acquisition of, any of its capital stock.

Some will argue that this is a superfluous belt-and-suspenders type representation already adequately covered by the MAC representation. But a closer look will show that this representation is designed to capture certain events or acts as they happen before they significantly impact the company or rise to the level of being a MAC.

Representation (a) confirms that the acquired business has been conducting its business in the **ordinary course** (think business as usual — no fire sales, no forays into unrelated sideline businesses, etc.) and consistent with past practice (focusing on the manner in which the acquired business conducts even ordinary course business).

Representation (b) confirms that the acquired business hasn't entered into any business that it expects will be **unprofitable**. It may turn out that the business will be profitable, and won't trigger the MAC. But in the meantime, if there's any doubt, the Purchaser will want to know about it.

Representation (c) confirms that there hasn't been any significant property damage or other losses (**extraordinary losses**) even if the loss is covered by insurance.

Dividends and other Payments to Stockholders: Representation (d) confirms that the acquired business hasn't entered into any arrangement to pay any monies to its stockholders. This can be qualified by excepting out payments made in the ordinary course consistent with past practice, if for example, the acquired business makes a dividend payment every year of the same amount. As the Purchaser, you just want to make sure that the acquired business has not commited itself to making any payments to insiders that may weaken its ability to service its outside debt or to pay its expenses.

Other representations include:

- **No Waivers:** that the acquired business hasn't waived any significant rights or claims.

- **No Change in Accounting Methods:** that the acquired business hasn't changed its accounting methods except to the extent required by any change in GAAP.

- **No Insolvency:** If the acquired business has been having significant financial difficulties, then maybe add a representation that there is no pending or threatened, voluntary or involuntary bankruptcy proceeding (similar terms include assignment for the benefit of creditors, composition or arrangement with creditors, insolvency, receivership, reorganization, and moratorium) impacting the acquired business or its assets.

Litigation and Investigations

[APA or SPA version] Except as disclosed in attached Exhibit [insert Exhibit number], no:

(a) lawsuit, litigation, arbitration, mediation, claim, or other proceeding; or

(b) governmental proceeding or other formal or informal investigation;

is pending or threatened against or otherwise affecting the Seller [Acquired Company] or its business or assets.

Except as listed in attached Exhibit [insert Exhibit number], there is no basis (known to the Seller) for the initiation of any of the events set forth in (a) or (b) above.

Litigation or government proceedings like an IRS audit can divert significant resources away from the acquired business's main goal of conducting its business profitably. In this representation, the APA Seller or SPA Selling Stockholders confirm that there is no litigation or government proceedings (Subsections [a] and [b]) or "basis" for those types of proceedings (last paragraph), except the ones listed in an attached Exhibit, regardless of the likely outcome or impact of the litigation or proceedings on the business. There are several ways for the seller to qualify this representation.

Knowledge Qualification

Of course, the seller will want to qualify any representation of "threatened" litigation or government proceedings "to the best of its knowledge." The last paragraph on the "basis" of any proceedings is also subject to knowledge. Sellers also sometimes try to clarify that "basis" is restricted to just facts or circumstances that specifically impact the acquired business, rather than macro-type information like an announced increase in IRS audits of small businesses.

Likely Negative Outcome

The seller can limit the disclosure to only the litigation or proceedings it believes it will lose. It becomes tricky to determine whether a settlement of any litigation would constitute a loss.

If you are the seller of a small business, hopefully you're not going to be the subject of too much litigation, so it's sometimes better to list ALL your litigation in the attached Exhibit, instead of forcing yourself to make the subjective determination of whether you think you will win or lose.

Material Adverse Effect

The seller can also limit disclosure to litigation or proceedings that if determined adversely against it, will have a significant negative impact on the seller and its business. Again, if you are selling a small business with limited litigation, it's best to list

ALL of your litigation in the attached Exhibit, and let the Purchaser attach whatever significance it wants to the information.

Undisclosed Liabilities (Other Than Taxes)

[APA or SPA version] The Seller [Acquired Company] does not have any liabilities or obligations, whether absolute, accrued, contingent or otherwise, except to the extent:

(a) to which full provision has been made on the balance sheet as of [insert end date of the most recently completed fiscal year or interim period] (the "Latest Balance Sheet"); or

(b) incurred after the date of the Latest Balance Sheet in the ordinary course of business and consistent with past practice.

It is important for the Purchaser to recognize that even a "true, complete, and correct" or an "accurate and complete" balance sheet may not necessarily list all the liabilities and obligations of the APA Seller or SPA Acquired Company. This representation confirms the existence of any such "**off balance sheet**" liabilities. These include mainly certain **contingent liabilities/obligations** such as a guarantee by the acquired business of the obligations of another party. Be on the lookout also for standby letters of credit, comfort letters, and basically any document where the acquired business undertakes to back up the obligations of a third party. These represent an area of significant potential liability for the acquired business, even if it may not be on the hook right now.

If the acquired business has any such contingent liabilities, then the seller should list them in an attached Exhibit. Just because a Purchaser in an asset transaction can carefully craft the APA to avoid assuming the liabilties (including contingent liabilities) of the company, it's a good idea to obtain this representation for the sake of due diligence. The representations will help the Purchaser elicit additional information on the strength of the acquired business as well as gauge any potential areas of success or liability. A Purchaser in an entity transaction will be automatically assuming all the liabilities of the Acquired Company, including the contingent liabilities, so it's especially important for the Purchaser to know what these are in advance.

Representation (b) recognizes that the acquired business may have incurred additional contingent liabilites after the date of the latest balance sheet. If the acquired business has incurred any such liablties outside the ordinary course of business or inconsistently with past practice, then the seller should list them in an attached Exhibit. If you are the Purchaser, you should consider tweaking (b) to require the seller to list all contingent liabilities, even ones made in the ordinary course and consistent with past practice. As usual, the Seller will attempt to add a "materiality" qualifier; however, any attempt to qualify the representation to limit disclosure to only liabilities that must be shown in the Financial Statements eviscerates the protection offered by this representation.

Taxes

[APA or SPA version] The Seller [Acquired Company]:

(a) has filed within the required time limits all requisite federal, state, and local tax returns, reports and statements, which are complete and correct in all [material] respects;

(b) has paid within the required time limits all taxes and other governmental charges levied upon, or due and payable by, it or with respect to its business, assets, properties, or income.

(c) has not received any notice from any government authority of any audit or investigation or claim for additional taxes or other governmental charges; and

(d) is not, and its property and assets are not, the subject of any tax audit, investigation, or lien imposed by any government authority.

In representations (a) and (b), the Seller and selling Stockholders confirm that the company has filed all tax returns and made all tax payments on a timely basis. They also confirm in representations (c) and (d) that there isn't any bad tax related news — that the company hasn't received any audit notices and isn't the subject of any tax liens. The seller should list in an attached Exhibit, any bad news, including late tax filings or payments, tax liens and notices, as well as waivers of any statute of limititions (allowing the authorities to keep the investigation going beyond the applicable statute of limitations). In the sample contract excerpt, I use the phrase "federal, state, and local taxes"; however, this representation often includes the following more detailed list of taxes — "employment and payroll taxes," "estimated taxes," "excise taxes," "foreign taxes," "franchise taxes," "fuel taxes," "import duties," "income taxes," "property taxes," "sales taxes," "use taxes," "withholding taxes," etc.

The seller can qualify these representations as follows:

- **Grace Period:** add in (a) and (b) that the acquired business has filed or paid, or "will before the Closing Date" file or pay all required tax returns and tax payments, respectively. Note, however, that from a drafting perspective, adding the action verbs "will file" and "will pay" turns this provision into a covenant. For clarity, it's better to put this type of requirement in the covenant section, and make it a closing condition.

- **Contested Tax Liability:** qualify (a) and (b) that the acquired business has filed all tax returns and made all tax payments, except with respect to matters being contested in good faith by the company, in which case the acquired business should establish on the Balance Sheet a reserve adequate to pay such taxes.

Compliance with Law

[APA or SPA version] The Seller [Acquired Company] is not in breach or violation of any:

(a) organizational documents of the Seller [Acquired Company] (including, but not limited to, certificate of incorporation, bylaws, shareholders agreement or limited liability company agreement of the Seller, as the case may be);

(b) contract, agreement, understanding [or commitment]; or

(c) law, regulation, or other rule of any government authority or ruling or other determination of any court or other tribunal, to which the Seller, or with respect to which any of its assets or business, is subject.

This **Compliance with Law** representation is similar to the **No Conflict with Corporate Documents, Contracts, or Laws** representation with one key difference. The No Conflict representation confirms that the execution, delivery, and performance of the APA or SPA won't cause any problems under any of the company's organizational documents or contracts or applicable laws. This Compliance with Law representation goes beyond that to confirm that the company generally is currently compliant with its organizational documents, contracts, and applicable laws. Sellers should avoid making any representation of historical compliance (i.e., past tense) except as qualified by materiality; there's just no way for the seller to be sure it hasn't been out of compliance at one point or another.

Procedures versus Results: Subsection (c) of this representation goes to whether the acquired business is compliant with laws. In some cases, the law defines compliance as following proper procedure; in other cases, the law will measure compliance based on the result. A basic example of the former is that "employees must wash their hands after using the bathroom." If however, the law measures compliance based on the result, for example, requiring that "employees must not have more than the legally accepted limit of bacteria on their hands," then it's conceivable that the Seller could escape liability by negotiating to qualify this representation by disclosing that it makes its employees wash their hands. Its argument would essentially be, "Look, we clearly disclosed to you that we couldn't guarantee that our employees had hands with compliant levels of bacteria. All we could offer is that we make our employees wash their hands."

Officers and Directors: The Purchaser can negotiate to have the seller expand this representation to confirm that the directors, officers, employees and agents of the acquired business are also compliant with applicable laws, including for example, anti-bribery laws (covering any bribes, kickbacks or other illegal payments or gifts made in return for future business or in consideration of existing business).

General versus Specific: The provision is an example of a Compliance with Laws Generally provision. Purchasers sometimes are able to secure seller representations about compliance with specific sets of law; the above tax representation is just one example. Other examples include environmental laws (see below) and labor and employment laws — it depends on the relative bargaining leverage of the parties and the perceived risk.

Negotiating specific compliance provisions can be tricky; for example, if you are the Seller and have won a hard fought battle to give a narrow environmental representation, you certainly don't want the Purchaser who is precluded from bringing a claim on that rep to turn around and pursue the claim based on a broad general compliance with law provision. To prevent this from happening, Sellers should make sure that any representation regarding compliance with a specific set of laws is the exclusive representation regarding compliance with that set of laws.

The Seller or selling Stockholders can qualify this representation by using any of the **Materiality Qualifications** set forth in the **How to Qualify Representations** sidebar discussed above. For example, the seller can confirm that it is not in violation of any law except where such violation will not have a material adverse effect on its business. By adding this qualification, the seller avoids the need to list minor offenses in a separate Exhibit.

Environmental

[APA or SPA version]

(a) The Seller [Acquired Company] has provided the Purchaser with true and complete copies of the Phase I Environmental Assessment dated [insert date] and all other environmental assessments conducted on the Acquired Real Property (the "Environmental Assessment[s]").

(b) The Seller has provided the Purchaser with a true and complete copy of all permits (the "Environmental Permits") required by any applicable environmental, health, or safety law (the "Environmental Laws") for the operation of the Business on the Acquired Real Property as presently operated, which Environmental Permits are in full force and effect and are listed on the attached Exhibit [insert Exhibit number].

(c) Except as disclosed in attached Exhibit [insert Exhibit number] [or any Environmental Assessment], the Acquired Real Property is [, and has at all times been], in compliance with all Environmental Laws.

(d) Except as disclosed in attached Exhibit [insert Exhibit number] [or any Environmental Assessment]:

  (i) no hazardous or toxic substance or waste that is regulated under any Environmental Law has been generated, stored, transported or released from, in, on, or to the Acquired Real Property;

  (ii) no order, notification or communication from any government or other entity or person with respect to any violation of or liability under any Environmental Law or Environmental Permit, or revoking or threatening to revoke any Environmental Permit, has been received by the Seller;

> (iii) no lawsuit, litigation, arbitration, mediation, claim, governmental or other proceeding, or formal or informal investigation is pending [or threatened] against or otherwise affecting the Seller or its business or assets, which asserts that the Seller has violated any Environmental Law or Environmental Permit; and
>
> (iv) no basis (known to the Seller) exists for the initiation of any of the events set forth in (ii) or (iii) above."

This is an example of a **specific compliance with laws** provision (see the discussion above on **general versus specific compliance with laws** provisions).

Subsection (a) — If your sale of business transaction does not involve a great deal of environmental risk, then there may not be the need for any Phase I or other Environmental Assessment. The only way to really know is to conduct thorough due diligence — see the **Due Diligence** discussion on environmental matters in Chapter 7.

Subsection (b) confirms that the APA Seller or SPA Acquired Company has all Environmental Permits required for its onsite activities. Again, whether you feel you need this representation depends on the type of activity conducted on the property being acquired. Alternatively, the Purchaser could negotiate to obtain the seller's representation that no environmental permits are required for any of its activities.

Subsection (c) confirms that the Seller or Acquired Company is in compliance with environmental laws, specifically, versus all laws in general. Subsection (c) is drafted from the Purchaser's perspective — the Seller may find it impossible to represent that the property "has at all times been" in compliance. The Seller can either delete that part, or negotiate a knowledge qualifier. It can also attempt to negotiate to have its representation cover a limited time period, for example, that the property "is and has during the one year period prior to the Execution Date of this Agreement been in compliance with all Environmental Laws."

Subsection (d) contains basic language confirming the absence of (i) toxic waste events (e.g., spills, etc.), (ii) violation notices or other communications from government agencies like the Environmental Protection Agency (EPA), and (iii) lawsuits and other claims relating to environmental law problems. Sellers can try to dilute some of these by negotiating a variety of materiality, knowledge, and other qualifiers, especially with respect to any "threatened" matters.

Assets

Here is a group of representations regarding the assets of the APA Seller or SPA Acquired Company. The "**Title to Assets**" representation addresses the threshold issue of the extent to which the Seller or Acquired Company actually owns (or leases) its assets (some agreements will say "assets and properties"). The other representations then deal with the non-ownership characteristics of the individual asset categories. For example, in the **Accounts Receivable** representation confirms, among other things, that the receivables are collectible. The **Inventory** representation confirms that the inventory is in good enough condition to be resold in the ordinary course, and so on and so forth.

These types of representations are found in both APAs and SPAs. After all, no matter what format of acquisition you choose, you're still going to want to know all about the underlying assets.

List of Assets

[SPA version] The attached Exhibit [insert Exhibit number] discloses a true and complete list of all:

(a) tangible assets (whether real or personal property or otherwise) owned, leased, or otherwise used;

(b) patents, trademarks, service marks, trade names, and copyrights (and applications for any of the above), and trade secrets, proprietary information, processes, formulas, customer lists and other intellectual property rights owned, licensed, or otherwise used; and

(c) contracts, agreements [and commitments] (the "Acquired Company's Contracts") entered into;

in each case, by the Acquired Company.

This is the SPA version of the representation; in an APA all the Acquired Assets are listed elsewhere in the APA (see Assets to Be Sold in Chapter 9). The Purchaser in a stock transaction is purchasing ownership of the Acquired Company, rather than directly the assets of the Acquired Company. Even so, the Purchaser will still want to know what assets the Acquired Company owns, as well as related information about the cost, book value, and various and sundry financial information about the assets that it can use for tax and financial planning. While I have the seller listing in one exhibit most of the tangible assets (equipment, inventory, etc.), and intangible assets (patents, trademarks, etc.), owned or used by the acquired business, as well as all the contracts entered into by it, you can also list the assets separately in exhibits attached to the corresponding SPA asset-related representations below.

Title to Assets

[APA or SPA version]

(a) Except the assets subject to the Personal Property Leases, Real Estate Leases, and Intellectual Property Licenses and the assets disclosed in attached Exhibit [insert Exhibit number], the Seller [Acquired Company] has good title to all assets (whether real or personal property, tangible or intangible, or otherwise) owned by it or used in its business, free and clear of all liens, encumbrances, and other security interests.

(b) Upon the Closing, the Purchaser will have good and marketable title to the Acquired Assets, free and clear of all liens, encumbrances, and other security interests.

In the APA version, Subsection (a) confirms that the APA Seller actually owns (good title) to all the assets it uses to run its business, free of security interests (what is a security interest? — see sidebar below). Subsection (b) confirms that the Purchaser will obtain good title to the Acquired Assets being sold under the APA free of security interests. The representations in Subsections (a) and (b) go hand in hand. The Seller cannot make the representation contained in (b) unless (a) is true. The word "assets" is not capitalized in Subsection (a) because the Seller is representing that it has good title to all of its property and assets, not just the Assets being sold (except, of course, any leased equipment or real estate or licensed intellectual property).

Note that in an SPA, the selling Stockholders can make the representation in Subsection (a), but not in (b), because the Purchase takes title to the Acquired Stock, not the assets of the Acquired company.

Let's examine why obtaining title that is free of security interests is so important to the transaction. Let's say that before selling its assets to the Purchaser, the Seller grants a security interest to a bank on some or all of its property to secure a loan. If the Seller defaults in any payments, then the bank can enforce the security interest and become the new owner of the property. In the worst case scenario, imagine your surprise when the local sheriff shows up to seize the property you've just purchased because the Seller defaulted in its payments. So if you are the Purchaser, it's very important first to identify any security interests, and then to make sure that the Seller discharges its payment obligations and causes its creditors to release the security interests prior to Closing. The release of any security interests can be made a Closing Condition to the transaction.

If you are the Seller, your main concern is to avoid misrepresentation by making disclosure of all security interests; you can list them as exceptions to this representation in the Agreement or in an Exhibit to the Agreement.

Security Interests

Security interests are property rights of a bank or other creditor in the property of a debtor (in this case the Seller) to secure monies owed to the creditor. In the sample contract provision, I use the words "liens, encumbrances, and other security interests," with the word "other" intended to capture all categories of security interests. Other words commonly used to describe security interests include charges, easements, encumbrances, hypothecations, liens, mortgages, and pledges. Stock can also be subject to security interests in the form of voting trusts and the provisions of a stockholder or shareholder agreement restricting transferability. But no matter which words you use, make sure that all references to security interests in the representations, covenants, closing conditions, etc., are consistently defined.

Title to Assets — Balance Sheet

[APA or SPA version] The Seller [Acquired Company] has good title to all the assets which are either:

(a) reflected on its balance sheet as of [insert end date of the most recently completed fiscal year or interim period] (the "Latest Balance Sheet"); or

(b) acquired after the date thereof; in each case, free and clear of all liens, encumbrances, and other security interests, except:

    (i) the liens, encumbrances and other security interests reflected in the Latest Balance Sheet;

    (ii) as disclosed in the attached Exhibit [insert Exhibit number]; or

    (iii) to the extent that such assets are sold or otherwise disposed of in the ordinary course of business after the date of the Latest Balance Sheet.

This alternate approach confirms the APA Seller's or SPA Acquired Company's title to the assets based on the latest balance sheet. Subsection (a) as well as assets acquired after the date of the latest Balance Sheet (Subsection [b]), in each case free and clean of liens except as disclosed in the balance sheet in an exhibit, or disposed of in the ordinary course.

Sufficiency and Condition of Assets

[APA or SPA version] The assets of the Seller [Acquired Company] (whether real or personal property, tangible or intangible or otherwise) owned, leased, licensed or used by it:

(a) constitute all the assets necessary to its business and operations;

(b) are in good and usable condition (reasonable wear and tear excepted) in the case of tangible assets; and

(c) are uncontested and in good standing in the case of intangible assets.

If you are the Purchaser, you'll not only want to know that the APA Seller or SPA Acquired Company has good title to the Assets, but also that the assets are sufficient and in good condition to run the business.

This representation confirms the sufficiency and condition of the assets to run the business. The Seller or selling Stockholders may want to qualify representation (a) by stating that the assets constitute all the assets necessary to the business "as presently conducted." In an APA sale of a division (or other subset of assets), the Seller may have certain assets it uses for itself and the division that it will not be conveying in the asset sale (for example, a contract to outsource back office functions like payroll and accounting). In this case, the APA or SPA Seller will not be able to make this representation without the appropriate qualification. The Seller might also want to exclude goodwill from representation (c), which is applicable to intangible assets like patents and trademarks.

Sufficiency of Assets in the Sale of a Division

The APA Seller may have certain assets it uses for both itself and the division it is selling. A classic example is insurance — the Seller likely has a policy that covers the entire business, including the division. Other examples might include shared equipment and services, letters of credit that cover the division, and even patents that it is licensing. If the Seller doesn't want to convey these assets, then once the division is severed when it is sold to the Purchaser, the division will no longer have insurance coverage or access to the equipment, the outsourced services, or the patents. These are things you can't take for granted when you purchase (or sell) a division.

This disconnect may impact the degree to which the Seller is able to make the representation that the assets (of the division) are sufficient to run the business (see **Sufficiency and Condition of Assets** representation above).

In this case, the parties can reduce the Purchase Price for the assets, and have the Purchaser make its own arrangements. Or, the Seller can make arrangements to provide these "Transitional Assets/Services," to enable the Purchaser to run the division after the Closing, but before the Purchaser has time to set up its own infrastructure. You'll have to put a value on these Transitional Assets/ Services. If you're the Purchaser, you should negotiate to obtain any Transitional Assets/Services "at cost," the thinking being that the Seller should not profit on this part of the transaction since by not conveying such assets it is putting the Purchaser in the position of not having the full slate of assets "sufficient to run the business." One can imagine all sorts of other legal issues that come up in structuring the provision of Transitional Assets/Services. For example, what happens if there's a problem with the assets or services being provided — who's responsible? For a general discussion of the types of warranty and other issues that may arise, please see Part II.

Inventory

[APA or SPA version] All inventory of the Seller [Acquired Company] is:

(a) new, undamaged, and not obsolete;

(b) merchantable and fits the particular purposes for which the goods are intended, in the case of finished goods; and

(c) usable for the particular purposes for which the materials are intended, in the case of raw materials and work-in-progress.

Inventory is a line item on the balance sheet, and some sellers will object to giving any representation about subject matters already covered by the general representation about the financial statements (see Financial Statements representation above). The seller will argue that the balance sheet is prepared in accordance with GAAP, and what's good enough for GAAP should be good enough for the Purchaser. However, the Purchaser requests this representation to elicit more detailed information not directly stated in the balance sheet, for example, that the inventory of the company is appropriate for resale, or in the case of raw materials, usable to make finished goods that are appropriate for resale.

Inventory is not like land or assembly line equipment because it is constantly changing — new inventory is being introduced to the warehouse as old inventory is being sold off. While the Purchaser in an asset transaction can tailor the definition of Acquired Inventory to exclude unwanted categories of inventory (for example, by SKU), it is not practical to be more specific than that. It can't say, "I want this box of goods, and that box of goods," because it's in everybody's interest that those boxes be sold off by the Closing Date. And in a stock transaction, the Purchaser will automatically "acquire" all the inventory by virtue of its new ownership in the Acquired Company.

In either an APA or SPA, practically speaking, the Purchaser will end up acquiring an interest in the inventory that is in the warehouse on the Closing Date. So in addition to quality, there is the issue of quantity. Therefore, the Purchaser should consider negotiating another representation that inventory levels will at all times fall within a certain percentage range compared to sales volume as measured by the latest financial statements.

The fitness for the "particular purposes" language in Subsections (b) and (c) has far-reaching consequences to the Seller. The APA Seller or SPA Selling Stockholders should consider qualifying Subsections (b) and (c) with warranty disclaimer language from Chapter 4.

Accounts Receivable

[APA or SPA version] All accounts receivable of the Seller [Acquired Company], as reflected on the balance sheet as of [insert end date of the most recently completed fiscal year or interim period] (the "Latest Balance Sheet"), or arising since the date thereof:

(a) have been collected; or

(b) are and will be good and collectible,

in each case on the respective due dates and at the aggregate amounts thereof without any right of deduction or offset.

Like inventory, accounts receivable (sometimes referred to as notes receivable) constantly change — new receivables are born with each sale of goods, while older receivables are (hopefully) paid. A Purchaser is sometimes reluctant to acquire the receivables in an APA, mainly because it ends up paying good money for receivables that may be difficult to collect. But some APA Purchasers take the leap anyway and acquire the receivables. And in a stock transaction, the Purchaser will automatically acquire all the receivables by virtue of its new ownership of the Acquired Company. So it's important for the Purchaser to be comfortable about the status of the receivables.

In this representation, the APA Seller or SPA selling Stockholders confirm the collection or collectibility of the company's accounts receivable without any right of the debtor to offset or deduct any amounts from payment (again, something not necessarily reported on the balance sheet). It is merely a representation on the collection of certain receivables and collectibility of the outstanding receivables; it is not a guarantee of collection. Things like quality claims for goods sold and the creditability of the debtors can impact whether the company ultimately collects its money, and if so how much.

In the sample contract excerpt, I use the phrase "without any right of deduction or offset"; however, terms or phrases with similar meaning that often appear in this representation include "counterclaim," "defense," "deduction," "right of recourse," "return of goods," and "set off."

The seller can add a Knowledge Qualifier (see **How to Qualify Representations**) to representation (b). For example, the seller can separately state that it knows of no facts or circumstances that would lead it to believe that any outstanding receivables will not be collected.

Contracts

[APA or SPA version]

(a) Each Acquired Contract [contract to which the Acquired Company is a party] is the legal, valid, and binding obligation of the Seller [Acquired Company] and each of its counterparties, enforceable against each of them in accordance with its terms.

(b) Neither the Seller nor [to the best of Seller's knowledge] any of its contract counterparties has:

(i) breached or defaulted under any such contract;

(ii) given or received any notice of breach, default or termination of such contract; or

(iii) taken any action or inaction that is inconsistent with such contract remaining in full force and effect.

The main issue for the Purchaser is to make sure that all of the contracts it is acquiring (either directly in an APA or indirectly in a SPA) are in full force and effect, and are not at risk for being terminated.

Representation (a) is similar to the APA/SPA **Enforceability** representation. Whereas the APA/SPA Enforceability representation confirms the legal, valid, and enforceable nature of the APA or SPA, this representation (a) confirms the same characteristics for the contracts being acquired in the transaction. Please refer to the discussion of the APA/SPA Enforceability representation for ways the APA Seller or SPA Selling Stockholder can qualify the representation (i.e., bankruptcy qualification, etc.).

Full Force and Effect: Representation (b) addresses the ongoing nature of the contracts. It confirms that nobody has breached the contracts or given any notice of breach or termination. The catch-all in (iii) confirms that there are no circumstances consistent with the contract about to be terminated or not renewed. For example, many contracts call for automatic renewals unless notice prior to the expiration is given. The Seller can negotiate to add the bracketed Knowledge Qualifier regarding the contract counterparties.

Special Payment Provisions: The Purchaser can negotiate an additional representation that the contracts don't require special payments in the event of breach or termination, for example, liquidated damages, penalty amounts, severance payments, golden parachutes, etc.

Transactions with Affiliates

Many APAs and SPAs contain a seller representation that it doesn't have any contracts or other arrangements with its insiders (e.g., shareholders, officers, directors, etc.), or affiliates (parent company, sister companies, etc.). These might include employment contracts, contracts for the sale of goods and services, license agreements for intellectual property, real estate leases, etc. This information can also be obtained under the Contracts representation (see above); however, including a Transactions with Affiliates representation will force the parties to take a closer look at insider transactions (i.e., non-arm's length), and to see how they impact the post-Closing prospects of the acquired business. For example, if the acquired business licenses key technology from an affiliate that is not being sold, then the Purchaser will be depending on the seller long after the Closing. This is something the Purchaser should be aware of and factor into the negotiations.

Intellectual Property

[APA or SPA version]

(a) The Seller [Acquired Company] has taken all actions necessary to maintain the validity and effectiveness of the Acquired Intellectual Property [intellectual property owned by the Acquired Company].

If you are the Purchaser, you'll want to make sure that there are no problems with the APA Seller's or SPA Acquired Company's intellectual property.

Validity: Representation (a) confirms that the Seller has taken all action to maintain the patent, trademark, etc. This includes administrative paperwork as well as taking action to defend against third-party challenges.

No Infringement by the Acquired Business: Representations (b) and (c) confirm that the intellectual property rights you are acquiring (either directly in an APA or indirectly in an SPA) do not infringe the IP rights of third parties, and that the company hasn't received any notice of infringement. An allegation of infringement ultimately may impact the very validity of the intellectual property (e.g., patents) you are paying good money for. Not to mention the substantial cost and headache of having to defend a patent infringement lawsuit.

No Challenge: Representation (d) confirms that nobody is challenging the validity of your intellectual property rights.

No Infringement by Others: The seller can qualify Representation (e) with the bracketed Knowledge Qualifier since it is not in a position to know for certain whether and to what extent a third party has been infringing its IP rights.

Real Estate

Leased Real Property: The most common scenario is where a small business leases (rather than owns) its office space, retail store space, warehouse space, etc. from a third party lessor (landlord). In this case, the APA Seller or SPA selling Stockholders typically represent(s) that it they doesn't own any real estate, and sometimes represents that the leased property constitutes all the real property used in its business, which is leased under the leases to be transferred to the Seller directly under the APA or indirectly by virtue of the sale of the ownership interest in the acquired business.

Some Purchasers like to have the seller include a litany of representations about the legal status of the leasehold (e.g., relating to enforceability, defaults, zoning violations, etc.). However, leases are contracts, and representations about enforceability and defaults would be covered broadly under the **Contracts** representation. As far as compliance with zoning ordinances, these are covered more broadly under the **Compliance with Laws** representation. If the seller agrees to include specific representations about real property that are already covered more broadly by the other general representations, then it should make sure to indicate that the specific representation is the exclusive representation regarding that topic.

The Purchaser can also negotiate additional representations about the use of the leased premises, for example, that there has been no material interruption in services (gas, electric and other utilities, landlord provided maintenance, cleaning, and other services, etc.).

b)   Except as disclosed in attached Exhibit [insert Exhibit number], no condemnation, eminent domain, or similar proceeding is pending or threatened in connection with the Leased Real Property.

Subsection (b) confirms that there is no condemnation or other proceeding that would effectively preclude the use of the property. The seller typically will negotiate to add a Knowledge Qualifier to "threatened" proceedings.

Owned Real Property: If the transaction involves owned real estate, then you'll need to work with a real estate attorney to confirm the APA Seller's or SPA Acquired Company's fee simple ownership and exclusive possession of the property and improvements, the existence of liens or mortgages, as well as various and sundry other matters (e.g., title reports, title insurance, surveys, plans, building and other permits, tax and assessment matters, certificate of occupancy, freedom of ingress and egress, easements, wetland issues, casualty and other insurance claims — basically any issue that may have an impact on the Purchaser's legal or financial exposure, the value of the property, and the ability of the Purchaser to keep using the property in the same manner that the Seller or Acquired Company has been using it).

The sale of real property either in the content of a sale of a business or on a stand-alone basis is beyond the scope of the book.

Employee Benefit Plans

In these provisions, the APA Seller or SPA selling Stockholders make a series of representations about the acquired business's employee benefit or retirement plans. Consult with your attorney about the level of detail, which depends on what you find in your due diligence (e.g., some plans may be more broken than others), the quantity and size of the plans, your relative bargaining power, and of course the extent to which you'll be assuming or specifically not assuming any of the plans. An APA Purchaser generally can negotiate which benefit plans it will assume, but should consult with its attorney about the extent it legally has no choice but to assume a plan. An SPA Purchaser acquires the legal entity (the Acquired Company) that maintains the plans but should consult with its attorney about the impact of the acquisition on the plans. That the Purchaser does not believe that the acquired business maintains any plans, or a particular category of plan, doesn't mean that the Purchaser can dispense with employee benefit plan representations in its draft of APA or SPA. In order to minimize any post-Closing surprises, the Purchaser should, at a minimum, obtain a representation confirming that the acquired business does not, in fact, have any benefit plans (or a particular type of benefit plan).

[APA or SPA version]

(a) Attached Exhibit [insert Exhibit number] lists all employee benefit plans, programs, and arrangements, whether formal or informal, contributed to, maintained, or sponsored by the Seller [Acquired Company] or any of its affiliates (the "Group Companies"), or with respect to which any of the Group Companies has any obligations, including, but not limited to, qualified and nonqualified plans, defined benefit, defined contribution, and "employee benefit plans" as defined by the Employee Retirement Income Security Act of 1974, as amended ("ERISA") (the "Benefit Plan(s)").

(b) The Seller has provided the Purchaser with true and complete copies of the following documents with respect to each Benefit Plan, (i) the Benefit Plan document, (ii) annual report(s) (e.g., Form 5500) for the previous [insert number of] years, (iii) summary plan descriptions and summaries of material modifications, (iv) trust agreement, (v) actuarial report and data prepared for the previous [insert number of] years and (vi) all notices, orders, filings and other written communications between the Seller or plan administrator and the relevant government authorities, including, but not limited to, the most recent determination letter issued by the Internal Revenue Service with respect to any Benefit Plan intended to be qualified under the Internal Revenue Code.

(c) Except as disclosed in attached Exhibit [insert Exhibit number], the Seller has made all contributions required under all Benefit Plans and has performed all obligations required to be performed under the Benefit Plans.

(d) Except as disclosed in attached Exhibit [insert Exhibit number], no compensation or benefit under any Benefit Plan will become accelerated, accrued, payable, or increased as a result of the execution, delivery, or consummation of the transactions contemplated by this Agreement, including, but not limited to, in connection with any termination of employment undertaken in connection therewith.

(e) Except as disclosed in attached Exhibit [insert Exhibit number], none of the Benefit Plan documents referred to in Subsection (b) above, or in any formal or informal communication to the Seller's employees restricts the Seller from terminating or amending any Benefit Plan.

(f) Except as disclosed in attached Exhibit [insert Exhibit number], each Benefit Plan covers only employees of the Seller (or former employees of the Seller).

List of Benefit Plans: In Subsection (a), the APA Seller or SPA selling Stockholder represents that the attached exhibit is a complete listing of all of the acquired business's employee benefit plans. These would include things like pension plans, employee stock ownership plans, 401(k) plans, nonqualified deferred compensation plans, incentive stock option and nonqualified stock option plans, severance, golden parachutes, and even things like bonuses and vacation plans. Some of these plans are discussed in more detail in the Incentive Compensation section of the Due Diligence part of Chapter 7.

Benefit Plan Documents: In Subsection (b), the seller represents that it has provided the Purchaser with copies of all relevant employee benefit plan documents. These and other documents form the basis of the Purchaser's due diligence.

Employer Contributions: Subsection (c) is a basic version of the seller's representation that it is up-to-date on all monetary contributions to all plans, and that it has performed all obligations with respect to the plans. The seller will usually qualify by adding that it's established adequate reserves in accordance with GAAP in case any of the accrued obligations are underfunded.

No Acceleration: In Subsection (d), the seller confirms that the APA or SPA will not trigger the payment or accrual of any benefit under any employee benefit plan. Depending on how you define Benefit Plan, this would also include severance obligations to the rank and file, as well as golden parachutes for senior management.

No Restriction on Termination or Amendments: Subsection (e) confirms that the acquired business hasn't promised its employees that it won't (or can't) amend or terminate any plan. This is important because the Purchaser wants the maximum flexibility to deal with the plans. Any restrictions may hamper the ability of the Purchaser from taking over the plans, or the seller or Purchaser from terminating the plans. An alternative to this representation is one that confirms that each plan can be terminated without triggering any additional contributions, or resulting in any unfunded liability or acceleration of benefits.

Benefit Plan Covers Employees of Acquired Business Only: Here's one that occassionally shows up in the transaction documents. If any plan covers not just the employees of the acquired business, but also covers the employees of another entity not being sold to the Purchaser, then this makes the sale of business more complicated.

The parties may need to execute a spin-off of assets or some other division of assets. This representation helps to confirm that such a spin-off, etc., won't be necessary.

Compliance with Employee Benefit Laws: The Purchaser often demands a related representation that the acquired business is (and has for some stated prior period been) in compliance with all laws and regulations applicable to the plans, including, generally, ERISA, the Internal Revenue Code, etc., as well as a representation that there are no lawsuits and claims with respect to the plans (except routine employee claims for benefits, and appeals of such claims). While I've not included them because this area is already generally covered by the **Compliance with Laws** and **Litigation** representations, the Purchaser should consult with its attorney on whether it should obtain exclusive representations as they relate to employee benefit plans.

The Purchaser should also consider whether it's necessary to negotiate specific representations confirming the absence of specific forms of employee benefit plan liability, for example, ERISA withdrawl liability or liability to the Pension Benefit Guaranty Corporation for underfunded pension plans.

If qualified plans are being transferred, the Purchaser should consider whether it needs to negotiate a representation that all of the acquired business's plans that are intended to be "qualified" under the Internal Revenue Code are in fact qualified, and have received favorable determination letters from the Internal Revenue Service to that effect. Since the most recent determination letter will likely predate the execution date of the APA or SPA by quite some time, you can also negotiate to obtain the seller's representation that no plan has been amended since the date of the most recent determination letter in a way that jeopardizes the plan's qualified status.

Labor Matters

I've included a series of basic representations for non-unionized small businesses. Refer to **Collective Bargaining Obligations** in Chapter 7 for additional information about this topic. Note that any of the representations below can be qualified by the seller by adding a disclosure exhibit listing exceptions. The seller also typically adds a Knowledge Qualifier to any representation that refers to a threatened event. Note that the Purchaser sometimes negotiates to expand the representations in Subsections (a), (b), and (c) to cover not just the then-current situation, but also to cover some period of time before the execution of the transaction documents.

[APA or SPA version]

(a) The Seller [Acquired Company] is not a party to any collective bargaining agreement. No employee or group of employees of the Seller is represented by any labor union or other employee organization.

(b) The Seller is not the subject of any pending [or threatened] labor union demand for recognition, organization effort, or election activity.

(c) There is no pending [or threatened] labor strike, lockout, or work stoppage or slow-down affecting the Seller. There is no unfair labor practice claim, grievance, or complaint pending [or threatened] against the Seller before the National Labor Relations Board or any Federal, state, or local agency.

(d) The execution and delivery of this Agreement and the consummation of the transactions contemplated hereby will not require any notification to employees or constitute a plant closing or mass layoff under the Worker Adjustment and Retraining Notification Act ("WARN").

Subsection (a) is a simple representation confirming the absense of a collective bargaining agreement. Subsection (b) confirms the absence of union organization activities (e.g., union organizers trying to organize a union at the plant, etc.). Subsection (c) confirms the absence of labor strikes, etc. and unfair labor practice claims. Finally, Subsection (d) confirms that the sale of the business won't trigger any liability under the Worker Adjustment and Retraining Notification Act (WARN), which requires employers to provide 60 days' advance notice of certain "plant closings" and "mass layoffs."

If either the Purchaser or the acquired business is a union shop, then this complicates matters considerably, and each party will want to consult with its attorney regarding its obligations *vis-a-vis* the existing unions, among other issues. The Purchaser will also need to craft additional representations and warranties (and other provisions) regarding the status of the collective bargaining agreements, which is beyond the scope of this book.

No Brokers

[APA or SPA version]

(a) No broker, finder, or other financial consultant has acted on behalf of the Seller [Acquired Company or selling Stockholders] in connection with the transactions contemplated by this Agreement.

(b) There are no claims for broker or finders' fees, commissions, or similar compensation in connection with the transactions contemplated by this Agreement.

Sometimes after a successful closing, a third party appears out of the woodwork claiming to be the broker or finder that put the parties together. It then demands a commission or finder's fee for its efforts, and goes after both the seller and the Purchaser for its compensation.

The seller makes this representation to ensure the Purchaser that the Purchaser won't be on the hook for hidden broker fees or similar compensation. The seller can qualify representation (b) by adding that there are no claims for brokers fees, etc., based on any arrangement or agreement made by or on behalf of the seller. This means that the seller is only willing to vouch that there are no such fees caused by its own actions; it can't vouch that some other party didn't make any arrangements without its knowledge or consent.

Brokers — Alternative

The Seller [selling Stockholders] has entered into an agreement with [name of broker or finder] (the "Broker") pursuant to which it has agreed to be solely responsible to pay the Broker a commission or fee in connection with the transactions contemplated by this Agreement (the "Broker's Commission").

Other than set forth above,

(a) No broker, finder, or other financial consultant has acted on behalf of the Seller [Acquired Company or selling Stockholders] in connection with the transactions contemplated by this Agreement; and

(b) There are no claims for broker or finders' fees, commissions, or similar compensation in connection with the transactions contemplated by this Agreement.

In this alternative, the seller discloses that it has retained a broker or finder for the transaction, but that only the seller (meaning not the Purchaser) is responsible for paying the broker's fee or other compensation.

Full Disclosure

[SPA version] The representations and warranties of the selling Stockholders contained in this Agreement, or any other contracts or agreements entered into, or certificates or other documents furnished in connection with the transactions contemplated by this Agreement [or any statements made or documents furnished in connection with the negotiation of the transactions contemplated by this Agreement] do not contain any untrue statement of a material fact or omit to state a material fact necessary to make such statements, in light of the circumstances in which they were made, not misleading.

This is commonly referred to as the 10b-5 Representation, named after Rule 10b-5 of the Securities and Exchange Act of 1934, which makes it unlawful to make any untrue statements or misleading omissions of material fact (the underlined text in the sample provision basically tracks the language of Rule 10b-5) in connection with the sale of any security, even stock in a privately held small business. Aggressive Purchasers (in SPAs, but also in APAs, plus lenders in loan documents) often try to insert this representation into the agreement as a last line of defense to capture misinformation not otherwise covered by the litany of representations and warranties discussed above.

Sellers in SPAs should keep in mind that even if the agreement does not contain a full disclosure representation, they still may have civil liability under Rule

10b-5 for deliberate misrepresentations and omissions that are reasonably relied on by the Purchaser. While scienter (intent or knowledge of wrongdoing) is an element of 10b-5 civil liability, it's not required to breach the sample contract provision. So in this sense, this representation, which doesn't depend on the seller's state of mind, offers the Purchaser even broader protection because it captures unintentional as well as intentional misinformation. That said, if the misrepresentation or omission is fraudlent, that is, made with scienter, then all bets are off — and depending on the severity of the infraction, it's possible for the Purchaser to shatter any contractually agreed exclusive remedy limitations, liability caps, etc.

The seller should be aware of the following additional issues:

- **Due Diligence:** The bracketed language is Purchaser-drafted language intended to go beyond the representations and warranties and capture even statements made and documents furnished during due diligence. At a minimum, if you are the seller, you should negotiate to eliminate that language; you don't want to spend countless hours parsing and limiting your representations and warranties and disclosure exhibits, only to have the Purchaser get you using the bracketed language.

- **Projections:** If the Seller is furnishing any projections, then it should exclude them from this representation to prevent the Purchaser from using any deviation from the projections as the basis for a claim under this representation.

- **Entire Agreement Provision:** Remember that the full disclosure provision captures not only the written representations and warranties, but also omissions, and if the parties agree to the above-described bracketed language, due diligence information not contained in the representations and warranties. Stuck somewhere in the boilerplate or miscellaneous provisions section of almost all agreements is the rather innocuous looking entire agreement provision (see the CD-ROM), which confirms that the written contract (e.g., the SPA) supercedes all previous (and contemporaneous) writings and verbal conversations, including presumably, the omissions and due diligence information. The law varies depending on the jurisdiction, so consult with your attorney to determine whether such a provision will still work for the seller to knock out the extraneous information in the context of a full disclosure clause (or a Rule 10b-5 civil claim brought by the Purchaser).

- **Non-reliance provisions:** These are seller-inserted provisions in which the Purchaser expressly states that it is not relying on any representations and warranties that are not contained in the SPA (or APA). Like the entire agreement provision, non-reliance clauses would appear to help the seller render inert any due diligence information not specifically incorporated into the agreement or disclosure exhibits. For example, if the SPA or APA contains a non-reliance provision, the seller can argue that the Purchaser can't assert a Rule 10b-5 claim based on any due diligence information disclosed outside of the representations and warranties and disclosure schedules because one of the elements of a Rule 10b-5 claim — detrimental reliance — has been contractually taken out of the equation. Will this argument work?

The law is complex and varies depending on the jurisdiction, so consult with your attorney to determine whether such a provision will still work in the context of a Rule 10b-5 civil claim.

Sandbagging

Sandbagging is the questionable practice where a Purchaser closes the transaction despite unspoken knowledge of the seller's breach (e.g., a misrepresentation), and then makes a claim (e.g., common law, via indemnity, however) based on the breach after the closing. Consult with your attorney because state law may vary regarding the ability of a sandbagging Purchaser to make a post-Closing claim, which may or may not depend on the type of sandbagging provision you put into your agreement.

Keep in mind that smoking gun-type sandbagging cases are the exception, rather than the rule. A more typical case involves a junior level attorney associate or business analyst who "sees" but misunderstands the significance of something subtle while going through boxloads of documents at midnight during due diligence. This makes issues like what constitutes knowledge, proof of knowledge, burden of proof, who knew or should have known, whether the parties should agree in advance to designate persons or officers as people charged with the duty to know or inquire, etc., very complicated, and can turn an already expensive lawsuit into an exorbitant one.

I've included samples of three basic provisions dealing with this issue.

[APA or SPA version]

[Alternative (Actual Knowledge Defence)] — Nothing contained in this Agreement is deemed to limit the right of the Seller [any selling Stockholder] to avail itself of any defense available under applicable law based on the Purchaser's knowledge of the existence of a misrepresentation by the Seller prior to the Closing.

[Alternative (Allows Sandbagging)] — The Seller acknowledges that the Purchaser has entered into this Agreement in express reliance upon the representations and warranties of the Seller. The representations and warranties of the Seller are not affected or deemed waived by reason of (i) any investigation made or failure to investigate by or on behalf of the Purchaser, or (ii) any allegation that the Purchaser (or its attorneys and advisors) knew or should have known that any such representation or warranty is or might be inaccurate or untrue.

[Alternative (Anti-Sandbagging)] — The Purchaser (i) acknowledges that it has had the opportunity to conduct due diligence prior to the Closing, and knows of no breach by the Seller of this Agreement or any document entered into in connection therewith, and (ii) waives any and all rights and remedies against the Seller under this Agreement, or available at law or in equity, arising from the breach of any representation or warranty of the Seller hereunder, but only to the extent [the Seller demonstrates that] the

Purchaser (or its attorneys or advisors) had actual knowledge [knew or should have known] (regardless of whether the Purchaser conducted adequate due diligence) that such representation or warranty is [or might be] inaccurate or untrue.

Actual Knowledge Defense

This first version basically lets the chips fall where they may. The Purchaser acknowledges that the seller may have the defense that the Purchaser knew of the breach but did not bring it up before closing. It leaves to state law to determine who prevails, and the issue of what constitutes knowledge. This is the kind of harmless looking provision that the seller can slip into its counterdraft possibly without invoking any reaction from the Purchaser.

Allows Sandbagging

In this Purchaser-drafted second version, the seller acknowledges that the Purchaser is expressly relying on the representations and warranties of the seller, and accordingly is permitted to bring post-Closing claims regardless of any knowledge of any possible breach before the Closing, and without worrying about proving who should've or could've known or did know something. The provision favors the Purchaser; if there is a problem with the acquired business, the seller has the duty to disclose it, and the Purchaser is relieved of the duty to "read too much into" or second guess what it finds during due diligence.

Anti-sandbagging

In this seller-drafted provision, the Purchaser acknowledges that it's had a chance to conduct due diligence, and waives any right to bring any claim after the closing relating to any breach or misrepresentation it discovers prior to the closing. The bracketed language goes to burden of proof, and knowledge — "actual knowledge," which is better for the Purchaser, versus "knew or should have known," which is better for the seller.

14

REPRESENTATIONS AND WARRANTIES OF THE BUYER

OVERVIEW

The list of the seller's representations and warranties is long, but can be trimmed or expanded depending on the details of the transaction, risk profile of the seller, negotiating leverage of the parties, etc. This is because the Purchaser has a legitimate interest in verifying not just the enforceability of the APA or SPA, but also as much information as possible about the business it is buying. The list of the Purchaser's representations will be much shorter, especially if it will be making full payment of the cash Purchase Price at Closing. The seller's main remaining concern is that the APA or SPA is enforceable. The enforceability of the agreement against the Purchaser hinges on the veracity of these representations. I've included three of the basic representations the Seller should obtain from the Purchaser (in an APA or SPA); Organization, Power, and Authority to Run Business; Authority to Buy; and Enforceability.

Please see the corresponding sections in Chapter 13 for a detailed explanation. Remember that stock-for-stock deals are beyond the scope of this book. In stock-for-stock deals, the Seller is exchanging its assets or stock for stock in the Purchaser. The Seller becomes an investor in the Purchaser and will want extensive representations about the Purchaser.

SAMPLE CONTRACT EXCERPTS

Organization; Power and Authority to Run Business

The Purchaser:

(a) is a corporation [limited liability company, etc.] duly organized, validly existing, and in good standing under the laws of the state of its incorporation [formation]; and

(b) has all requisite [corporate] power and authority to own, lease, license, and use its assets and to operate its business.

Authority to Buy

The Purchaser has:

(a) all requisite [corporate] power and authority to execute, deliver, and perform this Agreement;

(b) duly taken all necessary [corporate] action to authorize the execution, delivery, and performance of this Agreement by the Purchaser; and

(c) duly [authorized], executed, and delivered this Agreement.

Enforceability

This Agreement is the legal, valid, and binding obligation of the Purchaser, enforceable against the Purchaser in accordance with its terms.

Counsel to the selling Stockholders and the Acquired company sometimes requests the following securities law representations from an SPA Purchaser.

Securities Laws

[SPA version] The Purchaser:

(a) is acquiring the Acquired Stock for its own account, and not for the account of others, and for investment and not with a view to the distribution thereof;

(b) understands that it may not sell or otherwise dispose of such shares of stock without registration under, or an exemption from the registration requirements of, the Securities Act of 1933 (the "Securities Act"); and

(c) has access to the kind of financial and other information about the Acquired Company that would be contained in a registration statement filed under the Securities Act.

The federal securities laws were enacted to protect investors (in this case, the Purchaser) by mandating full disclosure of all facts that an investor would find important in making an investment decision, such as the Purchaser's decision to purchase the stock of the Acquired Company in an SPA. The government agency charged with enforcing these laws is the **Securities Exchange Commission (SEC)**. The SEC doesn't vett the quality of the investment; rather it is mainly concerned with the completeness and accuracy of all of the seller's disclosures (for example, representations and warranties, but also verbal statements and electronic ones too) made when marketing and selling the investment.

Does this mean that the seller in the sale of a small business has to register the transaction with the SEC? That depends. Generally, large stock offerings that are deemed "public offerings" (generally speaking, offerings that are made to a large and diverse group of people) need to be registered with the SEC under the **Securities Act of 1933** ("**Securities Act**"), while smaller scale transactions may be exempt from registration. There are a number of exemptions from registration available under the Securities Law. An exemption that is often invoked in small-scale sale of business transactions is the private (or non-public) offering exemption, which exempts from registration "transactions by an issuer not involving any public offering."

While an in-depth discussion of the exemption (Section 4[2]) of the Securities Act or the Safe Harbor rule of Regulation D) is beyond the scope of this book, here are the basic requirements. In order to qualify for this exemption, the seller can't generally solicit the public to sell its stock in the Acquired Company — the offer to sell the stock must be very limited in scope in terms of potential purchasers. Another requirement is that the Purchaser must be a "**sophisticated investor**" — that is, have sufficient business/finance knowledge and experience to have the ability to evaluate the investment, or the Purchaser must be able to bear the investment risk of the transaction.

Furthermore, the Purchaser must have **access to the type of information normally provided in a registration statement or prospectus**. This doesn't necessarily mean that the seller has to prepare a full-blown formal prospectus about the company (like the kind you get in the mail from your stockbroker); but it has to provide the Purchaser with full access to information about the company, whether through due diligence access or otherwise. And the Purchaser has to **agree not to resell, distribute or otherwise dispose of the stock to the public without registration or an exemption**. The Purchaser's representations in (a), (b), and (c) above help to assure the Seller that the Purchaser hasn't done anything to put the transaction afoul of the federal securities laws.

Keep in mind that even if you don't need to register the transaction, all transactions (including yours) are subject to the **anti-fraud provisions** of the securities laws. If you don't make overblown representations and warranties (whether in the SPA, verbally, or electronically in your text messages or emails) about how great an investment in your company is, then you've put yourself in good position to fend off any securities law violation claims. Also, regardless of any exemption you might have under the federal securities laws, you'll need to check applicable **state securities laws** to make sure you don't need to register or file any documents at the state level.

15

AFFIRMATIVE COVENANTS AND NEGATIVE COVENANTS

OVERVIEW

This chapter discusses some of the basic covenants found in APAs and SPAs. Covenants are promises made by either party to act (affirmative covenant) or to not act (negative covenant) a certain way. The seller makes the lion's share of the covenants, mainly to assure the Purchaser that it won't do anything to adversely affect the value of the acquired business prior to the Closing Date. Depending on your transaction, you may need to negotiate a variety of additional deal-point covenants. These may include covenants to take certain steps with respect to existing labor unions or employee benefit plans, or conduct environmental assessments, obtain key-person life insurance, or preserve certain customer or supplier relationships or existing license agreements or other important contracts.

SAMPLE CONTRACT EXCERPTS

[APA or SPA version] The Seller [Acquired Company and the selling Stockholders] covenant with the Purchaser that from the date of this Agreement until the Closing Date:

Access

[APA or SPA version] The Seller shall [selling Stockholder shall use and shall cause the Acquired Company to]:

(a) grant the employees and other representatives of the Purchaser free and full access to the facilities, personnel, books, and records of the Seller;

(b) furnish the Purchaser with such additional information related to the Seller as the Purchaser may from time to time [reasonably] request; and

(c) permit the Purchaser to copy any and all documents and records referenced above.

In covenant (a), the APA Seller or SPA selling Stockholders agree to give the Purchaser's employees and other representatives (can be written to specifically include officers, accountants, attorneys, and agents) access to the acquired business's facilities, personnel, and books and records so that the Purchaser can conduct its due diligence. The seller's main concern is that such access is not disruptive to its business. Therefore, the seller can qualify this covenant by adding that access is only permitted during normal business hours or a compromise time frame, as well as specifically state that the purpose of such access is to allow the Purchaser to complete its review, examination and investigation of the business being acquired. Covenant (b) is a catch-all type provision, where the Seller agrees to give the Purchaser such other information that the Purchaser requests. The Seller can qualify this covenant by adding the bracketed language that such requests be "reasonable."

If the Seller or Acquired Company has subsidiaries, be sure to include the subsidiaries in this covenant.

Consummation of Agreement

[APA or SPA version] The Seller shall use [selling Stockholders shall use and shall cause the Acquired Company to use] its best efforts to take all actions, including, but not limited to, filing all such notices and obtaining all such consents, necessary to consummate the Closing of the transactions contemplated under this Agreement within the time frame contemplated hereunder.

This covenant is a general undertaking of the seller to use its best efforts to fulfill all of its obligations under the agreement so that the Closing can take place. While the failure to fulfill a closing condition allows the Purchaser to terminate the agreement and to not proceed with the Closing, this covenant makes the seller's failure to take requisite action (e.g., obtain consents, etc.), to move toward closing grounds for a breach of contract claim by the Purchaser against the seller for damages.

The background facts of your transaction may require you to negotiate additional detailed covenants. For example, if leased facilities are an important part of the assets, then you'll want to make sure that the seller specifically covenants that it will obtain the landlord's consent prior to the Closing.

This covenant requires the seller to use "best efforts," which could be interpreted to mean "by any means possible, no matter the cost." Therefore, the seller should consider changing the standard to "reasonable best efforts," or better yet "reasonable efforts," which is an easier standard to meet because all it requires is for the seller to apply the amount of effort that a reasonable person would expend under similar circumstances.

Conduct of Business

[APA or SPA version] Seller shall [selling Stockholder shall cause the Acquired Company to]:

(a) conduct its business diligently in the ordinary course of business consistent with past practice;

(b) use its [reasonable] best efforts to preserve its business and the goodwill associated with the business

These covenants are the basic "hold the fort" undertakings to run the seller's or Acquired Company's operations before the Closing in a way that does not impair the value of the business. The Purchaser's goal in negotiating these covenants is to have the seller maintain the business until the Closing so that the Purchaser takes over a business that is as robust and healthy on the Closing Date as it was on the Execution Date of the APA or SPA.

Depending on the risk profile of the APA Seller or SPA Acquired Company, the Purchaser can consider negotiating the following additional, more detailed covenants. Most sellers and selling Stockholders will find these covenants to be too restrictive, so they can try to negotiate qualifiers like the ones discussed at the end of this section. These covenants include:

- **No Misrepresentation/Breach:** the undertaking not to do anything that would result in any representation or warranty not being true, the breach of any covenant or the unfulfillment of any Closing Condition.

- **Maintainance of Goodwill:** the undertaking to not terminate or amend any of its contracts, and to preserve its relationships with its customers, suppliers and others.

- **No New Contracts:** the undertaking to not enter into new contracts, especially long-term contracts.

- **Maintainance of Human Resources:** the undertaking to maintain key employees in place, pay levels and benefit plans.

- **Maintainance of Insurance:** the undertaking to not terminate or amend its insurance policies.

- **No Financial Outlays:** the undertaking to not make payments or enter into financial commitments, for example, pay dividends or make other distributions; lend, borrow, or invest money; incur capital expenses for improvements; incur contingent obligations like entering into guarantees, stand-by letters of credit, and comfort letters.

- **No Giving up of Rights:** the undertaking to not settle lawsuits or waive any rights.

- **No Changes in Corporate Infrastructure:** the undertaking to not amend its certificate of incorporation or other organizational documents; authorize, issue, or repurchase any shares; dissolve, liquidate, purchase, sell or form subsidiaries or divisions; or purchase or sell assets except things like inventory in the ordinary course.

- **Seller Qualifications:** Most sellers will look at the above list and say, "How can I run my business with my hands tied behind my back? And besides, if my business comes to a standstill because of all these restrictions, how can that be in the Purchaser's interests?" The seller can negotiate on a blanket or a covenant-by-covenant basis qualifiers that will allow it to run its business while satisfying the Purchaser's need to minimize risk. These might include materiality qualifiers (see Chapter 13), baskets and thresholds (see discussion in Chapter 17), as well as exceptions for activity undertaken in the ordinary course and consistent with past practice. Another option is to allow the restricted activities with the Purchaser's prior consent, whether in the Purchaser's sole discretion (not a good option for the Seller) or reasonable discretion.

Notice of Changes

[APA or SPA version] The Seller shall [selling Stockholders shall or shall cause the Acquired Company to] promptly notify the Purchaser of any facts or circumstances (or threatened circumstances known to it) that if existing on the Execution Date would have been required to be disclosed in this Agreement or any Exhibit to this Agreement.

The Purchaser is protected somewhat by the Representations and Warranties Closing Condition. That is, if a representation becomes untrue between the Execution Date and Closing Date, the Purchaser will have the right to terminate the Agreement and not close the transaction. This covenant adds another layer of protection by requiring the seller to notify the Purchaser of nascent misrepresentations as soon as they occur.

16

CLOSING CONDITIONS

OVERVIEW

There's often a time gap in an APA or SPA between the Execution Date and the Closing Date. The Execution Date is the day all the parties sign the APA or SPA. The Closing Date is the day the parties fulfill their main obligations under the contract ("Principal Obligations"). For purposes of discussion, the seller's Principal Obligation is to transfer title to the Acquired Assets or Acquired Stock to the Purchaser. The Purchaser's Principal Obligation is to make payment of the Purchase Price. In some cases, the parties will sign and close on the same day. In other cases, the parties will sign the APA or SPA, and then close one, two, or more weeks after the Execution Date in order to obtain all the necessary consents etc., for closing.

By listing the conditions that must be met in order for the transaction to close, the Closing Conditions help to bridge the gap between these two dates. The APA or SPA will list the conditions of each of the Purchaser and the seller to close the transaction. The Closing Conditions address several areas of concern, including any change in the parties' conduct or circumstances (for the worse) that occurs between the Execution Date and the Closing Date, as well as the removal of impediments (obtaining all consents and certificates, putting financing into place, etc.), to the transaction.

Closing Conditions of the Purchaser

Let's say the APA Seller or SPA Acquired Company's financial condition deteriorates prior to the Closing Date, as measured by the criteria set forth in the financial covenants. Or let's say that a key representation becomes untrue during the time gap. Either scenario will make the company a less attractive acquisition at the original Purchase Price. If the APA or SPA doesn't contain any closing conditions, then the reluctant Purchaser will have to proceed with the transaction, or else face a breach of contract claim by the seller. If on the other hand, the APA or SPA provides closing conditions that the Purchaser's performance of the agreement is conditioned on the fulfillment of all the Seller or Acquired Company's covenents, as well as the continued veracity of all of the seller's representations and warranties, then the Purchaser will have the following options.

In the event a Closing Condition is not satisfied, the Purchaser would have the option to terminate the agreement and walk away. At the other end of the spectrum, it could decide for expediency (not recommended), without demanding anything in return, to waive the condition outright and proceed to Closing, or delay the Closing until the condition can be fulfilled. More likely, however, it will use the seller's failure to satisfy the Closing Condition to extract some kind of concession, like a reduction in the Purchase Price. The Purchaser can couple the price reduction with either a waiver of the condition or by postponing the seller's deadline for satisfying the condition until some time after the Closing (that is, make the condition a covenant).

Another issue to be aware of is the fact that there is inconsistency among attorneys in the way they draft the covenants and closing conditions. For example, while it seems logical for the Purchaser to make the seller's delivery of contract consents a condition to closing, the Purchaser sometimes fails to include as a covenant the seller's obligation to go out there and do whatever it needs to do to close the transaction (for example, by obtaining such contract consents). This means that if the seller fails to obtain the consent, the only recourse for the Purchaser is its right to walk away (that is, not close), when what the Purchaser really intended was to reserve itself the right to make a claim for the failure of the seller to fulfill its obligations.

I've decided, for discussion purposes only, to build in some overlap between the covenants and the closing conditions. While the first three conditions (the "Bring Down" of the Representations and Warranties, Compliance with Covenants, and No Legal or Government Action) are frequently included conditions, I've decided also to include the delivery of all consents and ancillary documents as a condition to closing. If you are the Purchaser, be sure that the seller has the obligation (covenant) to obtain these consents and enter into these other documents in other parts of the APA or SPA.

SAMPLE CONTRACT EXCERPTS

The obligations of the Purchaser under this Agreement are subject to the following conditions (the "Closing Conditions"): [list closing conditions]

Representations and Warranties — "Bring Down"

[APA or SPA version] All representations and warranties of the Seller [Acquired Company] or any Stockholder contained in this Agreement [or in any exhibit hereto or in any other document delivered pursuant hereto] shall have been or will be [materially] accurate

(a)   when made; and

(b)   as of the Closing as though such representations and warranties were then made by Seller [Acquired Company] or such Stockholder.

The Purchaser shall have received a certificate dated as of the Closing Date and signed by the chief executive officer of the Seller [Acquired Company] and by each Stockholder certifying the above.

This "bring down" condition is not satisfied if it turns out that any of the seller's representations are untrue when made (condition "a"), or become untrue by the Closing Date (condition "b"). For deals involving installment payments, the representations and warranties of the seller can also be brought down on each date the Purchaser makes a payment of the Purchase Price. Keep in mind that in addition to the right to terminate the agreement (not proceed with the closing), the Purchaser may have a breach of contract or indemnification claim against the seller in the event of a misrepresentation.

This condition is often combined with the **Compliance with Covenants** condition immediately below. I keep them separate because my objective is to present the sample contract provisions organized by subject matter, which allows for a more detailed discussion of each concept.

If you are the seller, you can try to qualify this condition by adding the bracketed "materiality" language. From the Purchaser's perspective, however, this would add "by stealth" a blanket materiality qualifier to individual seller representations that it may have already negotiated for the seller to make "straight up" (that is, without any materiality qualifier). This is especially offensive to the Purchaser if there is a small time gap between the Execution Date and the Closing Date — it makes no sense for the Purchaser (especially a Purchaser that has paid a Purchase Price premium) to extract a straight-up representation from the seller at signing, only to have it qualified by materiality one week later at closing.

On the other hand, the parties may have already negotiated a materiality standard for certain individual representations like "Litigation and Investigations". A significant new lawsuit commenced against the Seller or Acquired Company during the time gap between the Execution Date and the Closing Date would impact the Closing Date veracity of this representation. In this case, however, adding a blanket materiality qualifier to this Closing Condition works to add two layers of materiality to the individual representation. Great for the seller, but ambiguous for the Purchaser from a contract interpretation perspective. Therefore, the Purchaser should try to resist the bracketed "materiality" addition.

Some contract parties compromise to avoid two layers of materiality by including a materiality qualifier for only the representations and warranties made "straight up," but not for the representations and warranties already qualified. Again, any decision to add materiality should be weighed in the context of the amount of time between signing and closing. After all, if the parties sign and close on the same day, then there would be no need for any "bring down."

Please refer to Representations and Warranties of the Seller (Chapter 13) for a more detailed discussion of the representations covered by this condition. One of the most important representations is the **No Material Adverse Change** representation or MAC. The seller represents in the MAC representation that the company's financial performance has not fallen significantly below the baseline of historical performance established by the Seller's or Acquired Company's most recent financial statements. This provision makes a condition to closing that the MAC representation originally made on the Execution Date remains true on the Closing Date.

Officer Closing Certificates

In addition, the Purchaser can also add the condition that the seller provide a signed certificate of an officer of the company (Officer Closing Certificate) attesting to the veracity of the representations and warranties at Closing. Technically, the individual officer signing the certificate may be on the hook if the certificate turns out to be untrue. Therefore, most company officers will take the certificate very seriously and won't sign unless they are sure for themselves that the facts in the certificate are true. Think of the certificate as just another component of the Purchaser's due diligence. The parties can include the form of certificate to the agreement as an exhibit.

Compliance with Covenants

[APA or SPA version] As of the Closing, the Seller [Acquired Company] and Stockholders shall have complied with all covenants and satisfied all conditions required under this Agreement. The Purchaser shall have received a certificate dated as of the Closing Date and signed by the chief executive officer of the Seller [Acquired Company] and by each Stockholder certifying the above.

As drafted, the condition is satisfied if the covenants and conditions are complied with or satisfied by the Closing, even if there is a period of non-compliance that is cured before the Closing Date. The Purchaser can negotiate a less forgiving version of this condition by adding that all covenants and conditions should have been complied with or satisfied "as and when required." By adding this language, the Purchaser will have the right to immediately terminate the agreement as soon as a covenant or condition is breached; it doesn't have to wait until the Closing Date to see whether the seller has cured. Please refer to Affirmative Covenants and Negative Covenants (Chapter 15) for a more detailed discussion of the covenants covered by this condition.

No Legal and Government Action

[APA or SPA version] There shall not have been:

(a) instituted or threatened any litigation or other legal proceeding;

(b) proposed, enacted or promulgated any law, regulation, or other rule of any government authority; or

(c) entered or enforced any ruling or other determination of any court or other tribunal, in any case which

    (i) prohibits, delays, or seeks to prohibit, delay, or otherwise challenge the execution, delivery, and performance of this Agreement; or

    (ii) imposes or seeks to impose monetary or other penalties or damages with respect thereto.

This condition is not satisfied if there is any legal or government action (for example, lawsuit, arbitration, mediation, law, regulation, court ruling, etc.), that challenges the sale of business transaction. If a new law or court ruling prohibits or seeks to challenge the sale of the business, then the Purchaser would have the right to terminate the APA or SPA without penalty.

Contract Consents

[APA or SPA version] The Seller [Selling Stockholder] shall have obtained at or prior to the Closing all consents required for the execution, delivery and performance of this Agreement from any party to any contract or understanding to which any or them is a party, or with respect to which any of their respective assets or business is subject.

This condition is satisfied if all required consents from the APA Seller's or SPA Acquired Company's contract counterparties have been obtained. In the sample contract excerpt, I use the phrase "consents required for the execution, delivery and performance of this Agreement"; however another commonly used phrase with similar meaning is "consents required for the consummation of the transactions contemplated by this Agreement." For a detailed discussion of contract consents, see **Consent of Third Parties to Transaction** in Representations and Warranties of the Seller (Chapter 13).

Government Consents

[APA or SPA version] The Seller [Selling Stockholder] shall have, at or prior to the Closing,

(a) filed all applications or notices, and

(b) obtained all consents in each case

required for the execution, delivery, and performance of this Agreement, with or from the appropriate government authorities, courts, or other tribunals.

This condition is often combined with the **Contract Consents** condition above, and is satisfied if all required government-type filings have been made (condition "a") and all required government-type consents to the transaction have been obtained (condition "b"). For a detailed discussion of government consents, see Consent of Government Authorities to Transaction in Representations and Warranties of the Seller (Chapter 13).

Ancillary Documents

[APA or SPA version] The Seller [selling Stockholders] shall have delivered to the Purchaser at or prior to the Closing all the documents required to be delivered at the Closing by the Seller pursuant to this Agreement.

This condition is satisfied if the seller delivers all the Ancillary Documents referred in the section of the APA or SPA on documents to be delivered at the Closing. Alternatively, the parties can list each and every document to be delivered at closing, such as the bill of sale, officer resignations, the legal opinion, etc.

Financing

[APA or SPA version] The Purchaser shall have received by the Closing Date a loan in the amount of at least US$[insert amount] in immediately available funds from a major financial institution [or list the name of the financial institution] (the "Lender") upon terms and conditions at least as favorable to the Purchaser as those set forth in the attached Exhibit [insert Exhibit number].

One of the seller's main concerns is the Purchaser's financial wherewithal. However, a qualified Purchaser who doesn't have the funds to pay the entire Purchase Price on the Closing Date can make up any shortfall by financing the transaction. For example, it can obtain financing from the seller in the form of deferred payment terms. Or it can seek financing from a third party like a bank. This condition allows the Purchaser to walk away from the deal if it cannot obtain the requisite third-party financing. However, this is a risky closing condition for the seller because the Purchaser is the party that controls whether it is able to obtain the financing, and upon what terms. The seller can mitigate this risk somewhat by negotiating some hard deadlines, for example, for the Purchaser to obtain the commitment letter for the loan by a date in advance of the Closing. If the Purchaser fails to deliver a commitment letter, then the APA or SPA terminates. The seller can always waive any delay if it really wants to close with this Purchaser, and wait for the financing to fall into place.

Other Documents/Actions

[APA or SPA version] The Seller [selling Stockholders] shall have delivered to the Purchaser at or prior to the Closing such certificates and other documents, and taken such other actions, as the Purchaser may reasonably request to enable the Purchaser to verify compliance with these Closing Conditions.

This is a catch-all provision to help the Purchaser verify that all the Closing Conditions have been satisfied.

Additional Closing Conditions to Consider

Minimum Performance

One of the key **Closing Conditions** discussed above is that the seller's representations and warranties (including the No Material Adverse Change representation or MAC) that were originally made on the Execution Date remain true on the Closing Date. The seller represents in the MAC representation that the company's financial performance has not fallen significantly below the baseline of historical performance established by the APA Seller's or SPA Acquired Company's most recent financial statements. The net result is that the Closing Condition is not satisfied if the company's performance falls significantly below this baseline before the Closing, and the Purchaser would have the option to terminate the agreement.

An aggressive Purchaser could take it one step further, and try to negotiate a Closing Condition that the Seller or Acquired Company meet certain minimum performance standards for a set time period before the Closing — for example, by establishing minimum sales and/or profit (income) targets for such period or a minimum net worth target as of the end of such time period. The Purchaser would want to peg these minimum performance standards higher than the baselines established by the MAC.

Title Insurance

If real estate is part of the property being conveyed in an asset sale (or indirectly in a stock sale), then the Purchaser will want some kind of assurance that it will, in fact, have good and marketable title to the parcel after the Closing. While the seller will make its standard Title to Assets representation, that good title will be conveyed (subject to any liens or encroachments listed in an exhibit), the Purchaser should also negotiate the Closing Condition that it receives a commitment for a title insurance policy from a reputable title insurance company.

Title insurance is an insurance policy that guarantees that the person stated in the policy (in this case the Seller or Acquired Company) has title to the parcel of real property in question as well as the right to convey the parcel. Together with a current certified real property survey, the insurance policy works to lessen the Purchaser's risks and potential losses caused by faults in the title resulting from any events that occurred before the Closing.

Appraisal

If real estate is part of the property being conveyed, then another possibility is to condition the Closing on the receipt of an appraisal from a reputable appraiser. If the appraiser determines that the fair market value of the parcel is above a certain dollar amount, then the condition is satisfied, and the Purchaser must proceed to Closing (assuming all the other Closing Conditions are satisfied).

Fairness Opinion

Typically negotiated only in large acquisition transactions (in which each side is represented by investment banks), the Purchaser can condition the Closing on its receipt of a fairness opinion from its investment bank, in which the bank states its objective opinion on the "fairness" of the business transaction to the Purchaser (and its owners) from a financial point of view. Like due diligence and negotiating carefully crafted seller representations and warranties, the fairness opinion is one of many tools that helps the board of directors and the stockholders determine the viability of the transaction.

Hart-Scott-Rodino

This condition requires, if applicable, that the minimum 30 day waiting period under the Hart-Scott-Rodino Antitrust Improvements Act of 1976 shall have expired at or prior to the Closing. Under Hart-Scott, both parties to an APA or SPA need to file a **Premerger Notification** with the Federal Trade Commission and the Department of Justice if certain thresholds based on the value of the transaction and the size of the parties are met. The Premerger Notification contains information about the transaction and the companies involved to enable the governement to determine whether the transaction violates the antitrust laws (basically, whether the transaction has an anti-competitive effect). The parties must wait at least 30 days before closing the transaction, during which time the government may request additional information.

This condition will not apply to most transactions involving small businesses. The current minimum thresholds can be found on the Federal Trade Commission website (www.ftc.gov). Generally speaking, one party must have sales or assets of at least $100 million, and the other party $10 million. And the Purchaser must hold at least $50 million in assets or stock of the Seller or Acquired Company as a result of the transaction (or $200 million regardless of the size of the parties).

Closing Conditions of the Seller

The contract excerpts below contain a representative sampling of the kinds of Closing Conditions that the APA Seller or SPA selling Stockholders can impose on the Purchaser in order for the seller to move forward with the Closing. The sample contract excerpts below are not exhaustive. Depending on the complexity of the transaction, sellers may also need to impose additional Closing Conditions based on the Closing Conditions of the Purchaser.

[APA or SPA version] The obligations of the Seller [selling Stockholders] under this Agreement are subject to the following conditions (the "Closing Conditions"): [list Closing Conditions]

Representations and Warranties

[APA or SPA version] All representations and warranties of the Purchaser contained in this Agreement [or in any exhibit hereto or in any other document delivered pursuant hereto] shall have been or will be [materially] accurate

(a) when made; and

(b) as of the Closing as though such representations and warranties were then made by the Purchaser.

The Seller shall have received a certificate dated as of the Closing Date and signed by the chief executive officer of the Purchaser certifying the above.

The Purchaser should not "knee jerk" counter to add the bracketed "materiality" qualifier because it may trigger the seller to demand the same concession in its corresponding closing condition. Remember that the Purchaser makes far fewer representations than the seller. The Purchaser's representations are also less fraught with risk because they don't relate to the economic condition of the acquired business. On the other hand, many of the seller's reps relate directly to the value of the acquired business. So while the Purchaser might not like to give this condition "flat" (i.e., without the bracketed "materiality" qualifier), it can ill afford to have the seller similarly qualify the corresponding condition.

Compliance with Covenants and No Legal and Government Action

As of the Closing, the the Purchaser shall have complied with all covenants and satisfied all conditions required under this Agreement. The seller shall have received a certificate dated as of the Closing Date and signed by the chief executive officer of the Purchaser certifying the above.

There shall not have been

(a) instituted or threatened any legal proceeding;

(b) proposed, enacted, or promulgated any law, regulation, or other rule of any government authority; or

(c) entered or enforced any ruling or other determination of any court or other tribunal, in any case which

   (i) prohibits, delays, or seeks to prohibit, delay, or otherwise challenge the execution, delivery, and performance of this Agreement; or

   (ii) imposes or seeks to impose monetary or other penalties or damages with respect thereto.

The Seller (APA Seller or SPA selling Stockholders) should add the above condition, which mirrors the Purchaser's Compliance with Covenants condition described above.

17

INDEMNITY

OVERVIEW

If the seller fails to satisfy a closing condition, or it comes to light before the closing that the seller has breached the APA or SPA either by making a misrepresentation or failing to comply with a covenant, the Purchaser has several options.

Termination

It can terminate the agreement, and not close the transaction. While most Purchasers will threaten this outcome, the fact is that depending on how important the condition is, or serious the breach is, a strategic Purchaser that is really interested in the company will likely think twice before exercising this right, especially given the resources it's had to marshal just to get anywhere near the Closing.

Close, but Recover Post-Closing

The Purchaser can allow the closing to take place without renegotiating the Purchase Price or other terms and conditions, but reserve the right to recover its damages after the closing, for example, through the indemnity. Closing without renegotiating with full knowledge of a breach is extremely risky, especially if the APA or SPA contains an **Actual Knowledge Defense** clause (basically a provision that says that if the seller makes a misrepresentation that's discovered later, but the Purchaser knows about the misrepresentation when made but keeps silent, then the seller is off the hook — see **Full Disclosure** representation in Chapter 13. Plus, you have to consider also that any attempted recovery under the indemnity will be subject to the qualifiers contained in the indemnity, things like baskets, caps, etc., (discussed in this chapter).

Renegotiate and Then Close

In many cases, the Buyer waives the breach subject to renegotiated terms and conditions. A key consideration is the severity and nature of the infraction or unsatisfied condition. If it's a breach, is it something that materially negatively impacts the value of the Company? Is it something the seller failed to disclose about an existing condition, and if so, was it on purpose or an honest mistake, or is it something new and significant that occured after signing? If it's an unsatisfied condition, is it something small enough that the parties can close around it? In some cases, the parties can renegotiate the indemnity to specifically cover the infraction, perhaps from the first dollar if the Buyer is concerned about the basket, and to exclude it from the cap. In other cases, for example, a material adverse change that occurs prior to closing, the Buyer may insist on a Purchase Price reduction.

However, the right to terminate does the Purchaser little good when the seller's breach is discovered (or in the case of post-closing covenants like non-competition clauses, etc., occurs) after the Closing, especially since an outright recission of the transaction (where the assets or stock is sold back to the seller) is hard to obtain. In fact, a recission (rescinding or cancelling) by itself may not even be the best solution because of the amount or type of damages suffered by the Purchaser. Or maybe the Purchaser doesn't want to rescind because despite the breach, it still believes that the transaction was a good investment. In most cases, the Purchaser just wants to be made whole.

It can try to make itself whole in one of several basic ways. If the APA or SPA does not contain an indemnification provision, then it needs to sue the seller for damages for "**common law remedies,**" and take its chances in court. Another approach is to negotiate a carefully crafted indemnification provision in the APA or SPA. Keep in mind that even in this case, the parties most likely will engage in some finger-pointing and hard negotiations before the seller relents and agrees to make payment under the indemnity. The Purchaser may even still need to sue the seller to enforce the indemnity. But the advantage of having a well-crafted indemnity is that it makes clear the allocation of risk, including the addition of qualifiers like baskets, thresholds, maximum limits, and survivorship. See the CD-ROM for a detailed discussion of indemnity provisions.

The Purchaser can even negotiate indemnities to allocate risk even where there is no misrepresentation or other breach. For example, the Seller in an APA may have adequately disclosed the existence of environmental problems at its facility, but the Purchaser still wants the Seller to indemnify it for any losses it incurs as a result of the environmental problems. Please refer to the CD-ROM for a detailed discussion of Indemnification provisions, including sample contract language, and ways in which the indemnitor can qualify its indemnities.

Mutual Indemnities

I've talked mainly about how an indemnification provision can help the Purchaser recover damages. But it's certainly also in the seller's interest to have the option to be able to seek indemnification from the Purchaser if the Purchaser breaches. The parties are free to negotiate two-way indemnities, and even reciprocity or symmetry in terms of how the baskets and other qualifiers apply to both parties. Keep in mind, however, that the bulk of the representations and warranties in an APA or SPA are made by the seller. And since the seller makes most, if not all, of the economic representations (regarding, for example, the condition of the assets, etc.), its representations are fraught with far greater risk. The Purchaser will suffer a lot more if the seller makes a misrepresentation, rather than the other way around.

Purchasers (especially in asset transactions) often insist that a certain portion of the Purchase Price be put in **escrow** to cover potential indemnified claims. Remember that in asset deals, the Seller typically liquidates and dissolves after the Closing, so having some funds in escrow, along with perhaps some shareholder guarantees, will help to secure the Seller's indemnification objections.

So while sellers are certainly entitled to request a two-way indemnity, Purchasers should be wary and not be swayed by any argument that reciprocal language applies equally to both sides — the language may be mutual, but the practical reality is that one party will be impacted far more than the other. Just one example — making a $1 million liability cap in an APA mutual sounds "reasonable enough," but actually isn't really fair to the Purchaser, that is making far fewer representations than the Seller. In this case, the Purchaser might want to negotiate a lower cap on the amount of its liability.

SAMPLE CONTRACT EXCERPTS

Since indemnities are used in many types of transactions, including all of the other transactions covered by this book, I've included the sample contract provisions in the Indemnification chapter on the CD-ROM.

Part IV
LOANS

18

TYPES OF
BUSINESS LOANS

OVERVIEW

Small businesses typically have several funding choices. They can request additional capital from the owners. They can seek capital from friends and family. There are many other funding alternatives, such as venture capital, private equity, and taking your company public, all of which are beyond the scope of this book. In the next chapters, I discuss the contract documentation of one of the most meat-and-potatoes ways in which businesses obtain funding — third-party commercial loans from banks or other lenders.

A detailed discussion of the ins and outs of commercial loan documentation can easily fill a multi-volume tome. Instead, I'll focus on the fundamentals. This chapter deals with the basic types of credit facilities available in the marketplace. Chapter 19 contains a discussion of various and sundry commercial loan agreement provisions relating to **loan payment issues** (e.g., repayment of principal and payment of interest, different types of interest rates, prepayment, defaults and events of default, etc.) Chapter 20 deals with **representations and warranties and affirmative, negative, and financial covenants** typically found in commercial loan agreements. Finally, Chapter 21 discusses contract provisions found in **guaranties**; banks often require the owners to personally guarantee the loan obligations of small business borrowers.

In this chapter, I'll discuss the fundametal differences between three common types of commercial business credit facilities — **lines of credit, term loans,** and **revolving loans**.

A detailed look at all the contract provisions found in every type of credit is beyond the scope of this book, and even most legal treatises. Instead, I will focus on "common denominator" provisions that can be found in any type of loan document; for example, provisions on interest rate, prepayment, financial covenants, and the like. I also compare and contrast, highlighting the different approaches, where applicable. Small-business owners are often asked to personally guarantee the obligations of the company. The kinds of obligations that owners are asked to guarantee run the gamut — loan obligations of the company, obligations of the company under an office lease, obligations of the company to make payment under a contract for the sale of goods or services, etc. Therefore, I've included a chapter on guaranties.

Promissory Notes

In addition to the loan agreement, the Lender will probably require you to sign and deliver a promissory note, which is typically a short-form document containing at a minimum, the Borrower's (a.k.a., obligor, issuer, maker, payor or promisor) unconditional written promise to repay the specified sum of money to the Lender (a.k.a. obligee, payee, or promisee) at the specified times (e.g., installment payments of principal and interest, interest only with a balloon principal payment at the end, or some other combination), or on demand, together with provisions relating to the interest rate. However, promissory notes can be quite elaborate, and contain an entire spectrum of provisions (e.g., representations and warranties, covenants, and events of default) that make them look more like full-blown loan agreements.

The basic promissory note, however, almost always starts with the following or similar language: "For value received, the undersigned (the "Payor") promises to pay to the order of [insert name of the Lender] (the "Payee") the principal sum of [insert dollar amount] (the "Note Amount"), together with interest from the date hereof on the unpaid principal balance from time to time outstanding, pursuant to the terms and conditions contained herein." A basic note will then contain provisions setting forth the payment dates (if not a demand note), as well as the interest rate (and the default rate).

Depending on the type of credit facility, the promissory note may or may not contain a list of unfavorable things (e.g., non-payment, deteriorating financial condition, failure to submit financial statements, etc.), that trigger the Lender's right to accelerate the loan and other remedies. In legal parlance, these are called Events of Default (i.e., basically, unfavorable things that have not been cured by the Borrower after notice of default), and Defaults (i.e., "any event, that with notice or passage of time, or both, would constitute an Event of Default," or basically, a nascent Event of Default).

Keep in mind that if your credit is structured as a demand loan, then you will likely be asked to sign a very short form promissory note called a demand note, which if properly drafted (from the Lender's perspective) may not have any language regarding defaults or events of default.

Essentially, a demand note allows the Lender to require repayment of the loan at any time, regardless of your financial condition or whether you've committed "default" type transgressions. So a putative "demand note" that contains default and event of default provisions is ambiguous. In fact, query whether a "demand note" containing default and event of default provisions is really a demand note at all. Consult with your attorney to determine whether any such ambiguity works for or against you, and the extent to which you can legally and ethically harness such ambiguity in your negotiations.

If your Lender requires you to deliver a promissory note, it will most likely include a form to be attached as an exhibit to the loan agreement. Keep in mind that a promissory note is an unconditional promise to pay the specified amount; you shouldn't sign a note until the closing date when you actually receive a corresponding advance of the loan.

LINES OF CREDIT

A line of credit is an undertaking by the Lender to consider advancing short-term loans to the Borrower. As discussed below, the Lender has no obligation to make any advances. Advances are repaid with interest either after a specified period of time (e.g., short-term 90 days) or upon demand.

Lenders usually establish lines of credit with truncated documentation — typically a **line letter**, and a **promissory note**. Lenders don't need the protections afforded by extensive loan documentation (e.g., pages of representations and warranties, etc.), because these are uncommitted credit facilities (i.e., the Lender has no obligation to advance), and in any event payment must be made within a very short time frame, or upon demand.

The line letter is a short form letter that typically begins something like this: "We are pleased to advise you that [name of bank] (the "Lender") agrees to consider in its sole discretion requests from [name of the Borrower] (the "Borrower") from time to time, for short-term loans in the aggregate outstanding amount not to exceed [insert dollar amount], to be used by the Borrower for [describe purpose]."

Lines of credit are usually uncommitted, meaning that the Lender has no obligation to extend credit, even if there is unused credit in the line. Even so, line letters will usually include some conditions to making an advance. For example, a line letter might say "Without derogating from the Lender's right to extend credit hereunder in its sole discretion, any credit extended hereunder is subject to the following: (a) the Lender is satisfied with the Borrower's assets, business, financial condition, and prospects; and (b) the Borrower has maintained and is maintaining a satisfactory relationship with the Lender." In other words, the Lender will still want to know that the Borrower is doing well, but reserves the right not to make an advance for any reason, or for no reason at all.

Lines of credit are short-term, with expiration dates typically of only one year. The Lender can decide of course to renew the line of credit, but it's not automatic. Furthermore and consistent with the discretionary nature of lines of credit, line letters usually give the Lender unilateral cancellation rights (e.g., the right "to cancel at any time any unused portion of the line of credit," including even amounts requested by the Borrower but not yet advanced by the Lender).

Lines of credit are technically not revolving credits, because the Lender has no obligation to advance funds, even if the Borrower has prepaid thus replenishing the available credit limit.

TERM LOANS

A term loan is a single loan or series of loans of specified amount(s), which is typically asset-based and used to fund big-ticket fixed assets like equipment or real estate, or one-off transactions like refinancings. Advances are repaid with interest typically in periodic identical installments, or sometimes with a balloon payment at the end.

The loan amount is commonly a set dollar amount based on the value of the collateral, for example, the orderly liquidation value of equipment, or the appraised fair market value of real estate and improvements. In some cases, the loan amount is based on a percentage of the outstanding debt to a third-party lender.

Lenders establish term loans with extensive documentation, including a **term loan agreement**, a promissory note or notes, and depending on the creditworthiness of the Borrower, security documents such as security agreements and guaranties.

The term loan agreement will contain various and sundry provisions including procedures for advancing loan amounts, payment and acceleration issues, prepayment, and extensive representations, warranties, and covenants. These include some of the representations and warranties and covenants you might find in an asset purchase agreement or stock purchase agreement.

But unlike the sale of a business, a loan transaction contemplates a long term relationship because loans are repaid over time. Therefore, banks have an interest in obtaining more extensive **representations and warranties**, as well as **affirmative** and **negative covenants** controlling what the Borrower can and can't do while the loan is outstanding. The Lender will also impose stringent **financial covenants** (especially for traditional cash flow based loans more so than for asset-based loans), dictating the boundaries of what constitutes acceptable financial condition, for example, minimum debt service coverage, as well as balance sheet maintenance and maximum leverage criteria. These are discussed in Chapter 20 on loan document representations, warranties, and covenants.

Subject, of course, to the terms and conditions of the term loan agreement, including conditions to lending, the Lender is obligated to advance funds under a term loan.

Typically, any advance payment (i.e., prepayment) made by the Borrower is applied to the last installment due. The Borrower may not reborrow any amounts repaid. This makes sense because term loans are used primarily to fund big ticket purchases like equipment (with set dollar purchase prices), rather than to finance the Borrower's fluctuating daily financing requirements. Those are more appropriately funded by revolving loans.

Term loans are typically repaid in periodic installments of principal and interest on fixed payment dates, with the debt retired on a pre-established maturity date. Repayment schedules are pegged to the underlying transaction, with loans to finance short shelf-life equipment having shorter maturities compared to loans to finance real estate.

Term loan agreements have **default** and **event of default** provisions to protect the Lender against the Borrower's failure to make timely payment.

REVOLVING LOANS

A revolving loan or revolver is a medium term (one to three years, sometimes longer) undertaking by the Lender to make multiple loans of fluctuating amounts that in the aggregate do not exceed the available credit, which because amounts repaid in a revolver may be re-borrowed, equals the committed amount (commitment or revolving credit amount) minus any outstanding amounts already borrowed that have yet to be repaid.

Revolvers are used by Borrowers to finance their **working capital requirements/day-to-day operations**, rather than to fund big ticket fixed assets or one-off transactions. Therefore, revolvers are often structured as asset-based loans in which the revolving credit amount is determined using eligible **current asset collateral** like inventory and accounts receivable. Individual advance amounts under the revolver depend on the Borrower's operating needs (subject usually to the Lender requirement that advances be of a minimum specified amount).

Lenders establish revolving loans with extensive documentation, including a **revolving loan agreement**, a promissory note or notes, and depending on the creditworthiness of the Borrower, security documents such as security agreements and guaranties.

Revolving loan agreements contain the same types of provisions that can be found in term loan agreements, but adjusted to incorporate the concepts unique to revolvers, for example, prepayment allowed, amount repaid may be reborrowed, etc. Any differences, to the extent they exist, between term loan and revolving loan provisions are discussed in the following chapters.

Subject to the terms and conditions of the revolving loan agreement, including conditions to lending, the Lender is obligated to advance funds under a revolving loan during the commitment period. Available funds include unused portions of the revolving credit that are replenished by the Borrower's repayment of advances.

Revolving credit facilities typically give the Borrower the right to cancel any unused portion of the revolving credit amount. Once canceled, the amount can't be reinstated without the Lender's approval. Borrowers will exercise the right to cancel if it determines that it doesn't need the entire amount of the commitment, especially since the amount of the commitment fee (see Chapter 19 on Loan Payment Issues for a discussion of commitment and other fees) depends on the amount of the commitment.

Revolving credits typically have one-to three-year terms, which are renewable by the Lender. It's possible also to negotiate an **evergreen revolver**, which automatically renews absent notice of termination by either party.

Amounts repaid under a revolver replenish the revolving credit amount, and become available for reborrowing, subject of course to the expiration of the credit facility.

Revolving loan agreements have **default** and **event of default** provisions to protect the Lender against the Borrower's failure to make timely payment.

Asset-Based Lending

Asset-based lending is a kind of revolving credit or term credit in which the Lender underwrites the loan relying first and foremost on the quality of the Borrower's collateral (generally, by taking a first priority security interest in current assets for revolvers or fixed assets for term loans), rather than on the Borrower's cash flow projections and financial performance, which are the loan criteria focus of so-called traditional bank lending.

Therefore, asset-based lending documents reflect the tendency of asset-based Lenders to focus less on stringent financial covenants than on practical ways to monitor and secure repayment. One of the main tools is a borrowing base formula that the Lender can use to systematically monitor the value of the collateral available to secure the loan versus the actual balance of the loan. The Lender will build a cushion in the borrowing base by lending only up to about 80 percent of the value of the collateral. Lenders also will utilize tools such as collateral reporting procedures, audits and/or establish dedicated collateral accounts, for example, lock box arrangements where the Lender collects the Borrower's receivables in order to repay itself. Historically, unprofitable but collateral-rich businesses (e.g., with lots of tangible fixed or current assets, or even intangible assets like intellectual property) that sometimes didn't qualify for traditional bank loans have been able to obtain asset-based loans.

In addition to the basic lending vehicles discussed in this book, consult with your attorney on the myriad other financing options available in the marketplace. A non-exhaustive list includes:

- **Revolving Loan Followed by a Term Loan:** This is a hybrid facility in which the Lender makes available a revolving credit, and on the expiration of the revolving credit, the Lender makes a term loan to help the Borrower pay its revolver debt. The Lender can structure the term loan so that the Borrower can borrow the entire revolver commitment amount regardless of the amount outstanding on the expiration date, or just the amount outstanding on the revolver on the expiration date. It really makes no difference to the Borrower because it can increase the amount of the term loan by loading up on the revolver just prior to expiration.

- **Senior Stretch Loan:** Also known as an **overadvance loan**, this is a hybrid loan that has characteristics of both asset-based and traditional cashflow-based loans. To maximize the available commitment, Lenders sometimes need to look beyond the receivables, inventory, or fixed assets, for example, lending based on the value of the Borrower's trademarks or other intangible assets.

- **Junior Secured Loan:** These are also called **second lien, term B, or tranche B loans**. While the senior lender typically builds a cushion in the borrowing base by lending only up to about 80 percent of the value of the collateral, the second lien lender takes a junior security position in the collateral, relying on the value of the collateral in excess of the cushion. The Borrower is then able to incrementally borrow more money than it would normally be able to with just the first lender. Fees, interest rates, etc., will be higher for this type of loan because they're riskier for the junior lender (which takes a subordinate position relative to the first or senior lender).

19

LOAN PAYMENT ISSUES

OVERVIEW

In this chapter, I'll discuss some of the basic provisions a small-business borrower should expect to find in a bank-drafted commercial loan agreement regarding the advance and repayment of a loan. Loan agreements tend to be extremely lengthy documents containing myriad provisions designed to give the bank the highest level of protection. So, my goal is to offer an explanation of just the fundamental provisions to help you understand the basic economic issues relating to loans so that you can work with your attorney to negotiate the documents. These include provisions relating to the advance of borrowed funds (a.k.a., loan disbursement), interest rate (whether fixed or floating rate), default interest, payment dates, the basic Lender fees, and prepayment.

Lenders have different styles of drafting these provisions. For example, some Lenders may combine some of these provisions. I've deliberately separated them to facilitate discussion of the distinct concepts involved. In Chapter 20, I'll discuss some of the representations and warranties, as well as affirmative, negative and financial covenants typically found in loan agreements. I've already discussed many of these in the book, so I'll focus on the types of provisions found exclusively in loan documents (e.g., financial covenants for traditional cash-flow-based loans).

SAMPLE CONTRACT EXCERPTS

Advances — Term Loan

(a) Subject to the terms and conditions of this Agreement, the Lender shall make a term loan in the principal amount of [insert dollar amount] (the "Term Loan"). The Lender shall make the Term Loan in a single advance on the Closing Date.

(b) [For purposes of clarification, the Term Loan is a term loan pursuant to which] amounts repaid may not be reborrowed. The Borrower shall execute and deliver a promissory note as evidence of its obligation to repay the Term Loan with interest, in the form attached to this Agreement as Exhibit [insert Exhibit number] (as amended or renewed, the "Promissory Note").

Subsections (a) and (b) are variations of general language establishing the basic conditional obligation of the Lender to make the term loan. Only the principal amount is set forth; the interest rate and obligation of the Borrower to repay the loan and pay interest are set forth in other provisions of the loan agreement (discussed below). This version calls for one Advance to be disbursed on the Closing Date. Many term loans call for multiple advances spread out over a period of time.

The first part of Subsection (b) clarifies that the loan is a term loan, which means that amounts repaid cannot be reborrowed (unlike a revolver). The bracketed language is somewhat redundant, but I include it just to help make the point.

Advances — Revolving Credit Facility

(a) Subject to the terms and conditions of this Agreement, the Lender shall make an unsecured revolving loan facility (the "Revolving Credit Facility") available to the Borrower, pursuant to which the Lender shall make Advances in such amounts as the Borrower may from time to time request during the period from the [Initial] Closing Date until, but not including, the Commitment Termination Date. Notwithstanding the above, the aggregate principal balance of all outstanding Advances at any time shall not exceed the Commitment.

Subsections (a) and (b) (see below) are variations of general language establishing the revolving credit facility and its basic parameters. Subsection (a) contains the basic proposition that the Lender conditionally obligates itself to make Advances (i.e., revolving loans) pursuant to the Borrower's requests from time to time during the commitment period. The commitment period runs from the Initial Closing Date (i.e., the closing date of the first Advance) until the day before what I call the Commitment Termination Date (i.e., the date the Lender's obligation to make loans expires).

The Lender's obligation is subject to the requirement that the requested Advance doesn't cause the aggregate outstanding principal balance of all Advances (including the Advance then being requested) to exceed the amount of the Commitment (i.e., the total committed amount of the revolver), which is related to but different than the situation where the Lender makes an Advance, and the borrowing base dramatically deteriorates some time later. That situation is typically covered by a mandatory prepayment provision (see Prepayments — Mandatory — Revolving Borrowing Base later in this chapter) requiring the Borrower to immediately repay any excess of the outstanding amount of the revolver over the then current borrowing base.

Revolving loan agreements typically also include a provision establishing the procedure, deadlines, and paperwork required for the Borrower to make a request for an Advance. Given space constraints, these are beyond the scope of this book.

> (b) For purposes of clarification, the Revolving Credit Facility is a revolving credit facility pursuant to which and subject to the terms and conditions of this Agreement, the Borrower is permitted from time to time to request Advances, make prepayments and request additional Advances. The Borrower shall execute and deliver a promissory note as evidence of its obligation to repay all Advances with interest, in the form attached to this Agreement as Exhibit [insert Exhibit number] (as amended or renewed, the "Promissory Note"). Any unpaid principal and all accrued but unpaid interest hereunder shall be payable on the Commitment Termination Date.

Subsection (b) starts with language clarifying the characteristics of the revolver (i.e., the Borrower's ability to prepay and re-borrow). Subsection (b) provides that the Borrower's obligation to repay the principal amount of the Advances together with interest will be evidenced by a promissory note. Depending on the Lender and the transaction, the Lender may require a new note for each Advance, or a master note (sometimes called a grid note) to cover all Advances (with the individual Advances and payment history to be recorded in an exhibit to the grid note). Some Lenders dispense with promissory notes altogether, and establish a revolving loan account in which they record the amounts advanced (by debit entry) and repaid (by credit entry) in its records (which are deemed to be correct, but allow the Borrower an opportunity to audit and question the accuracy).

Fixed Interest

> The unpaid principal balance of the Loan [any Advance] accrues interest from the Advance Date to the date repaid at the fixed rate of [insert percent rate] per annum (the "Interest Rate"). Interest will be computed on the basis of a [360] day year [and assessed] for the actual number of days elapsed.

This is a variation of typical loan agreement language establishing a fixed percentage interest rate for the loan. Depending on the jurisdiction and the type of loan, interest can be calculated on the basis of a 360 or 365 day year, with the former being the more expensive for the Borrower (that is, the daily interest rate is higher if you divide the annual rate by a denominator of 360 days versus 365 days). Some loan documents will dispense with the bracketed "[and assessed]" language. Yet another way to say it is that "interest will be computed on the basis of the actual number of days elapsed over a year of [360] days."

Floating Interest — Alternative

The unpaid principal balance of any Advance accrues interest from the Advance Date to the date repaid at a fluctuating rate per annum equal to the Prime Rate in effect from time to time plus [insert percentage rate] (the "Interest Rate"). Each change in the Prime Rate becomes effective on the date such change is announced within the Lender. Interest will be computed on the basis of a [360] day year and assessed for the actual number of days elapsed.

This is a variation of typical loan agreement language establishing a fluctuating or floating interest rate for the loan. The Interest Rate can be pegged to a variety of indexes, including the ones discussed in more detail below, as well as less common ones not discussed in this book (e.g., based on the lower of prime or LIBOR, based on CD rates, etc.). The sample contract provision shows the Interest Rate pegged to the bank's Prime Rate.

Prime Rate

There are two popular versions of prime rate: the bank prime rate and the **Wall Street Journal Prime Rate**.

Historically, loan documents defined the bank prime rate as the "prime commercial lending rate" announced by the bank from time to time. "Prime" implied the "best," meaning the "lowest," rate offered to the bank's most creditworthy corporate customers. Contrast that to the common practice today where bank documents contain provisions that clarify that the bank prime rate is merely a reference rate determined and announced by the bank in its discretion. For example, bank documents will sometimes contain Borrower acknowledgments that "The Lender does not represent the Prime Rate to be the lowest interest rate offered by the Bank," or "The Bank lends at rates both above and below the Prime Rate."

The Wall Street Journal Prime Rate is the prime rate as published in *The Wall Street Journal*. If this index is selected, the bank documents will sometimes allow the Lender to unilaterally select another index in case *The Wall Street Journal* discontinues publishing the rate.

LIBOR

Corporate loans can also be pegged to LIBOR. Shorthand for the London Inter-bank Offered Rate, LIBOR is the fluctuating market interest rate charged by banks to other banks in the London wholesale money market for short-term loans, including those made in Eurodollars (i.e., US dollars deposited in banks outside of the US). LIBOR is calculated every day by the British Bankers' Association at 11:00 a.m., London time, based on interest rate data supplied by a group of big banks for a variety of short-term time periods (e.g., overnight, 30 days, one year, etc.).

LIBOR loan documents typically provide that interest accrues during each defined "Interest Period," which dovetails with the selected LIBOR period. The Interest Period commences on and includes the first day and runs until but excludes the last day of the Interest Period, with the period's accrued interest payable on this last day, which is typically a business day (generally, weekdays excluding bank holidays). Banks typically peg the Interest Period end date to the specified number of months after the first day of the Interest Period, or sometimes by reference to a specific periodic payment date.

LIBOR interest provisions also contain verbiage to adjust the length of the Interest Period if the last day doesn't fall on a business day (some banks don't adjust), if the Interest Period would otherwise mathematically fall on a day that does not have a numerically corresponding day in the immediately preceding Interest Period (e.g., January ends on the 31st, February ends on the 28th or in a leap year on the 29th, March ends on the 31st, April ends on the 30th, etc.), or if the last Interest Period would otherwise end after the Maturity Date.

Default Interest — Fixed Rate Loan

Amounts not paid when due hereunder, whether by scheduled maturity, notified pre-payment, acceleration, or otherwise, accrues default interest up to (but not including) the date of actual payment [after as well as before judgment] at a rate per annum equal to [insert percent rate] (the "Default Interest Rate"). Interest will be computed on the basis of a [360] day year and assessed for the actual number of days elapsed. The Borrower shall pay such overdue amounts, including default interest, upon demand.

Like credit card lenders, it's standard practice for banks to charge their small business or corporate borrowers additional or default interest on overdue amounts, whether principal, interest, or fees. This sample contract provision imposes a fixed rate of default interest, which the Lender will set a few percent higher than the regular Interest Rate. Lenders often include the bracketed "[after as well as before judgment]" or similar language to override any statutorily imposed pre-judgment or post-judgment interest rates that may be lower than the contracturally agreed Default Interest Rate. Obviously, the Lender will want the Borrower to pay overdue amounts immediately, so overdue amounts, including default interest, are payable upon demand.

Default Interest — Floating Rate Loan

Amounts not paid when due hereunder, whether by scheduled maturity, notified pre-payment, acceleration or otherwise, accrues default interest up to (but not including) the date of actual payment [after as well as before judgment] at a rate per annum equal to the Prime Rate in effect from time to time plus [insert percent rate] (the "Default Interest Rate"). Interest will be computed on the basis of a [360] day year and assessed for the actual number of days elapsed. The Borrower shall pay such overdue amounts, including default interest, upon demand.

This is default interest language for **floating prime rate loans**. As drafted, it's pegged to the then current Prime Rate, which in theory could drop precipitously after the default date (bad for the Lender). Some Lenders will revise to incorporate the idea that the Default Interest Rate will be based at a minimum on the Prime Rate announced on the default date. The danger for the Lender here is that the resulting Default Interest Rate could end up higher than the highest rate permitted by law (i.e., usurious), but the Lender will take care of that situation with the safety-valve usury language discussed below.

Usury

Notwithstanding anything in this Agreement to the contrary, the Borrower is not obligated to pay interest to the extent that it exceeds the interest that would be payable at the maximum rate permitted by law (the "Maximum Rate"). Any such excess interest is cancelled automatically. If the Borrower has previously paid any such excess interest payment, the Lender shall, in its discretion, refund to the Borrower any such excess or apply any such excess to the outstanding amount of the Loan.

This is a variation of standard safety-valve anti-usury language, in which the Lender either returns to the Borrower, or applies to the Loan, any amount of previously paid interest to the extent that any portion of it exceeds the interest payable at the maximum rate permitted by law. Some loan documents cast a wide net and clarify that interest payments include any other payments that might be considered interest under applicable law, yet others specifically characterize any nonprincipal payment as an expense, fee, or premium, rather than interest, to the maximum extent permitted by law.

This version gives the Lender maximum discretion on what to do with the excess (some loan documents will clarify that any amount applied to the Loan is deemed a "prepayment" under the loan documents). Some Lenders will spell out how the Lender should treat excess interest payments in case of acceleration or other situations. In some cases, the Borrower is able to negotiate an automatic reduction of noncompliant interest rates to the Maximum Rate, but the Lender may be reluctant unless it's able to negotiate a mechanism to restore the higher rate if and when it becomes non-usurious.

Payments — Term Loan

The Borrower shall

(i) repay principal and pay interest on the Loan in [insert number] equal monthly installments, on the [first, last, 15th, etc.] day of each calendar month [quarter, etc.] commencing on [insert date], and

(ii) repay the remaining principal balance of the Loan, together with accrued interest on [insert the Maturity Date].

Lenders offer a wide range of term loan products reflecting all manner principal repayment and interest payment structures. Examples include periodic payments of principal and interest with or without a balloon payment on the Maturity Date, or periodic payments of interest only with the principal to be paid on or before the Maturity Date (in all cases with no right to re-borrow repaid amounts).

The common denominator for a term loan is that payments adhere to some kind of predetermined periodic installment payment schedule, so that the debt can be retired on the specified Maturity Date. For example, the sample term loan agreement provision calls for the principal and interest to be paid in a predetermined number of equal monthly installments, and one final payment (which might be a large balloon payment depending on the transaction) on the Maturity Date. For LIBOR-based loans, interest is typically paid on the last business day of the specified LIBOR interest period (one month, three months, etc.). Some Lenders like to include a table showing the payment dates, and amount of principal and interest to be repaid and paid, respectively, on those dates.

The principal amount of a revolving credit facility may be prepaid at any time, and then re-borrowed. Interest, however, must be paid periodically. Revolving credit facilities are often structured as asset-based loans, secured by eligible collateral like accounts receivable or inventory. Asset-based Lenders rely on the collateral, rather than on cash-flow projections and the financial covenants of a traditional bank loan. Therefore, asset-based Lenders typically require that a dedicated collateral account like a lock box arrangement be established, from which the Lender pays itself from receivables that are deposited directly into the account.

Prepayments — Optional — Term Loan

The Borrower may prepay the outstanding principal balance of the Loan, in whole, or from time to time in part, together with accrued interest, without the payment of any premium or penalty. The Lender shall apply any such prepayment to the payment of

(i) first, unpaid fees and expenses,

(ii) second, accrued interest, and

(iii) the balance to the outstanding principal of the amount of Loan in the inverse order of maturity.

The Borrower shall

(i) give the Lender at least [insert number] days prior written notice of its election to prepay (including the date and amount of prepayment), and

(ii) make any partial prepayment in the minimum principal amount of [insert dollar amount].

Optional prepayments are by definition allowed in revolvers (and prepaid amounts refresh the Commitment and may be reborrowed). On the other hand, prepayments are permitted in term loans only if explicitly allowed in the term loan agreement (prepaid amounts may not be reborrowed). Many term Lenders do not allow prepayment no matter what. Some Lenders allow prepayment only if you pay a prepayment premium that reimburses it for "breakage costs" (discussed below). Yet other Lenders allow prepayment without the payment of any premium. Before you decide to go with a particular loan with a particular lender, make sure you know the true cost of borrowing the money, including all the exit costs.

The above is a variation of standard Loan Agreement language allowing prepayment of a term loan without having to pay any premium or penalty. Typically, the Lender will first apply the proceeds of prepayment to unpaid fees and then accrued interest. The Lender applies any leftover to the principal amount in the "inverse order of maturity," meaning it credits such amounts first to the final installments of principal. Doing this shortens the maturity of the loan without the hassle of having to modify the repayment schedule. The sample provision calls for the Borrower to give prior notice of its "election" to make prepayment, although many prepayment provisions will require the Borrower to give prior notice of its "intention" to prepay. You should treat both the same — that any such notification triggers your commitment to make prepayment, even if the loan document does not explicitly make the failure to make a pre-notified prepayment a default.

Prepayment Penalties

One way a Lender makes its profit is based on the "spread" or the difference between the interest the Lender earns on money it lends to Borrowers (e.g., small businesses) and the interest the Lender pays to its lenders (i.e., funding sources like commercial paper investors, insurance companies, other banks, etc.).

For example, if your Lender charges you a fixed 8 percent interest rate on your term loan, and pegs it (i.e., based on the same amounts, maturity dates, etc.) to its promise to pay its holders a fixed 6 percent interest rate, then its spread is 2 percent. If you decide to prepay your loan, perhaps to refinance because interest rates have fallen below the 6 percent, this doesn't impact the Lender's existing obligation to the holders. It still has to pay the holders the previously promised 6 percent. So the Lender has to find a way to keep the spread positive. But in a low interest rate environment, it's difficult for the Lender to reinvest, except by charging higher interest rates to less creditworthy borrowers. Some Lenders recover the gap by charging what's called a prepayment premium or fee. This way, it's sure it will be able to pay its funding sources the promised rate of return. If your bank charges a prepayment premium, then you have to include the fee in the calculation of whether it's the right decision to refinance.

Prepayments — Mandatory

Upon the occurrence of [list events] (a "Mandatory Prepayment Event(s)"), the Lender shall no longer have the obligation to make any Advances of the Loan, and the Borrower shall immediately prepay the outstanding principal balance of the Loan, together with all accrued interest and fees.

This is a basic mandatory prepayment provision. It's triggered by any number of identified events (discussed below) that both relieve the Lender of the obligation to make further loans, plus mandate that the Borrower immediately repay the loan with interest. Mandatory Prepayment Events run the gamut, for example, the closing of an anticipated third-party financing, or a sale of the business (assets or stock), merger, or change in control of the Borrower (or its parent company or affiliates). Keep in mind that both a mandatory Prepayment and an **event of default** give the Lender the right to immediate repayment of the loan. Because of this economic overlap between the two concepts, small-business Borrowers could try to negotiate to have certain events be treated as a Mandatory Prepayment Event instead of an Event of Default.

Prepayments — Mandatory — Revolving Borrowing Base

The Borrower shall, without notice or demand, immediately prepay the portion of the Loan to the extent that the outstanding principal balance of all Loan Advances exceeds the Borrowing Base. The Lender shall apply any prepayment received by it to the indebtedness in such order and in such amounts as it determines in its discretion.

Lenders take great care in revolving credit facilities to lend only against eligible collateral, that is, within the **borrowing base**. Despite this care, obviously, it's still possible for the Lender to advance funds, only for the borrowing base to deteriorate later to the point where the outstanding amount of the revolver exceeds the amount of the borrowing base. This is somewhat akin to the "underwater" residential mortgage situation in a falling real estate market where the amount of the mortgage overtakes the value of the home. This is a sample provision found in revolvers requiring prepayment to repay the excess amount.

Commitment Fee — Revolving Credit Facility

During the period the Commitment remains in effect, the Borrower shall pay the Lender a commitment fee (the "Commitment Fee") on the average daily unused portion of the Commitment, the Commitment Fee to be calculated at the rate per annum equal to [insert the rate, typically a fraction of one percent]. The Borrower shall pay the Commitment Fee in arrears on a quarterly basis, commencing on [date] and quarterly thereafter on the [indicate day] of each [calendar quarter], with the final payment due on the date the Commitment terminates.

Hidden and expensive bank fees are a common refrain in consumer complaints about the way banks do business. But a bank charges a **Commitment Fee** in a revolving credit facility to cover not only its administrative costs, but also the very real cost of allocating funds that the Borrower might draw under the revolver. The fee is typically a fraction of one percent of the **average daily unused portion** of the revolving credit amount (Commitment), which can get expensive if the Borrower ends up using only a small portion of the available amount. The average daily unused portion of the Commitment is calculated by subtracting from the Commitment, an amount equal to the average outstanding principal amount of the loan over the course of the designated time period, in this example, calendar quarter. This average amount is obtained by simply adding the principal amount outstanding on each day of the quarter, and then dividing by the number of days in the quarter. The Borrower pays the Commitment Fee in arrears at the end of each quarter until the Commitment terminates.

Facility Fee — Revolving Credit Facility or Term Loan

During the period the Commitment remains in effect, the Borrower shall pay the Lender a facility fee (the "Facility Fee") on the average daily amount of the Commitment (regardless of usage), the Facility Fee to be calculated at the rate per annum equal to [insert the rate, typically a fraction of one percent]. The Borrower shall pay the Facility Fee in arrears on a quarterly basis, commencing on [date] and quarterly thereafter on the [indicate day] of each [calendar quarter], with the final payment due on the date the Commitment terminates.

The sample shows how a bank might draft a provision imposing a Facility Fee in a revolving credit facility (banks also impose these fees for term loans). Banks impose facility fees on the entire amount of the Commitment, and many revolvers will explicitly clarify that this includes both the used and unused portion of the Commitment (i.e., "regardless of usage"). Facility Fees of fixed amounts are also common. In this case, the Lender would require the Borrower to pay a fully earned and non-refundable Facility Fee of a specified dollar amount on each anniversary date of funding (or *pro rata* portion in case the credit facility terminates prior to maturity).

Closing Fee — Revolving Credit Facility or Term Loan

On or prior to the Closing Date, the Borrower shall pay the Lender a fully earned and non-refundable closing fee (the "Closing Fee") equal to [insert dollar amount].

This is an example of a **Closing Fee** provision. Typically, the Closing Fee is a one-time fixed amount paid on the Closing Date of the Loan. A Lender that likes the security of payment by offset might include language authorizing it to deduct payment of the Closing Fee from the amount of the advance on the Closing Date.

Other Fees

The Closing Fee, Facility Fee, and for revolvers, the Commitment Fee are the three main types of fees charged by banks for commercial loans. Depending on your Lender, the type of loan, whether the transaction involves more than one Lender, and of course your bargaining leverage, the bank might charge any number of other fees — things like an acceptance fee, administrative agents fee, application fee, balance shortfall fee, collateral management or monitoring fee, exit fee, funds transfer fee, origination fee, participation fee, prepayment fee, referral fee, service fee, syndication fee, termination fee, unused line fee, and others. Some of these might overlap with each other, or even with the closing, facility, and commitment fees discussed above, but you get the idea. Basically, like a consumer looking for a good home mortgage, small businesses also have to shop around for the best rates and lowest costs.

Let's not forget about legal fees and expenses. Banks typically will insist that the Borrower reimburse it for the cost to prepare, negotiate, and administer the loan documents, as well as the cost to enforce its rights under the loan documents. Depending on your bargaining leverage, there are several things you can try to negotiate to lower the cost. First, try to negotiate that all costs be held to a "**reasonableness**" standard. Try to negotiate a **hard cap** on the expenses, especially the easier to predict document preparation expenses. You can also try to negotiate to pay only for legal fees and expenses of **outside counsel** (not its in-house legal department), and in the event of a dispute or a default, only for such costs incurred if the bank takes **formal legal action** (as opposed to just retaining counsel for advice). And consider negotiating to **claw back** legal fees in case you actually win a default claim initiated against you by the bank.

Defaults and Events of Default — Revolving Credit Facility or Term Loan

Each of the following constitutes an Event of Default:

(a) The Borrower fails to make any payment when due of principal, interest, fees or any other amount due hereunder or under any Promissory Note; or

(b) Any representation or warranty when made or deemed made in any of the Loan Documents [note — defined as the Loan Agreement, Promissory Notes, Guaranty, security agreements and any other documents entered into in connection with the loan] proves to be false or misleading [in any material respect]; or

(c) The Borrower fails to comply with any covenant contained in sections [insert section numbers of no-grace period covenants] of this Loan Agreement; or

(d) The Borrower fails to comply with [any other covenant contained in this Loan Agreement] [any covenant contained in sections [insert section numbers of grace period covenants] of this Loan Agreement], and does not cure that failure within [insert grace period] days after written notice from the Lender; or

(e) The Borrower becomes insolvent or makes an assignment for the benefit of creditors, files a petition in bankruptcy, insolvency, receivership or for other relief under any bankruptcy law or law for the relief of debtors or has any such petition filed against it [which is not discharged within sixty (60) days of the filing thereof], or dissolves, is liquidated, or ceases to do business.

Default/event of default provisions give the Lender the right to terminate its obligation to advance loans (Commitment) and to demand repayment of all outstanding amounts under the loan (i.e., accelerate the loan). The Borrower triggers a default if it (or any Guarantor) fails to make timely payments of principal, interest or fees (Subsection [a]), breaches a representation (Subsection [b]), breaches a covenant (Subsections [c] no grace period and [d] with grace period), becomes insolvent (Subsection [e]), breaches one of its third party credit agreements (i.e., a cross-default, a.k.a., cross-acceleration, Subsection [f]), becomes the subject of a lawsuit or judgment (Subsection [g]), or breaches any of the ancillary Loan Documents (Subsection [i]).

Defaults versus Events of Default

A default by itself usually doesn't give the Lender the right to accelerate the loan, but typically terminates the Borrower's right to receive future advances of the loan (i.e., one of the closing conditions to receiving a loan advance is that the Borrower is not in default).

Most loan agreements require a couple of intermediate steps before a default (sometimes called an incipient event of default) graduates to an event of default, which then entitles the Lender to accelerate the loan. First, the Lender has to give notice to the Borrower of the default. And second, in some cases, the parties negotiate grace periods or cure periods from 0 up to 60 or more days for the Borrower to correct the default. Grace periods vary depending on the gravity of the default and the relationship of the defaulted provision to the Borrower's creditability. So while a bank might be willing to entertain an up to ten-day grace period for interest payments, it might be less willing to grant a grace period for principal payments.

(f) The Borrower [or any Guarantor]:

   (i) fails to make payment of any principal, interest, fees or other amounts owed with respect to any Debt (defined as other than the indebtedness under this Loan Agreement) having an aggregate principal amount of more than [insert dollar amount], beyond any grace period provided with respect thereto (whether by scheduled maturity, mandatory prepayment, acceleration, demand, or otherwise); or

   (ii) fails to perform any term, covenant, or agreement contained in any agreement, document or instrument evidencing or securing any such Debt, beyond any period of grace provided with respect thereto, and the Borrower [or Guarantor] has been notified by the creditor of such default; and the effect of any such failure is to cause, or permit such creditors [or trustees] to cause, any payment of such Debt to become due prior to its due date (whether by mandatory prepayment, acceleration, demand, or otherwise).

Some defaults are by definition not capable of being cured, for example a breach of a representation, which is a statement of fact purported to be true when made. Once a false representation is made, there's really no going back to fix it. The same thing is true for financial covenants since they're based on historical information. You can try to negotiate some grace periods for the affirmative and negative covenants, and Lenders are usually more willing to grant grace periods for some of the affirmative covenants. Those defaults tend to less directly impact the creditability of the Borrower compared to defaults of some of the negative covenants, and in any event are more easily remedied. Please see the next chapter for a discussion of some of the representations, and affirmative, negative, and financial covenants commonly found in loan documents.

Cross Defaults

The default versus event of default distinction is especially important in cross-defaults. Subsection (f) is a pretty moderately worded cross-default provision, designed to trigger a cross-default only when a default under a third-party loan agreement (can be crafted to cover not only third party loan agreements but all Borrower [or Guarantor] obligations to third parties) matures into an event of default as defined by the third-party loan agreement. In other words, a default under a third-party loan agreement doesn't become a cross-default until the requisite third-party agreement notice or grace period has been given or elapsed, respectively.

Aggressive Lenders are more impatient; they'll want a default under a third-party loan agreement to trigger a cross-default under its own loan agreement right away, without the need to give notice and certainly without waiting for the grace period to lapse. In such cases, you'll see a cross-default defined something like "an event that with the giving of notice and/or the elapse/passage of time would constitute an event of default [under the third-party loan document]."

(g) Any of the following takes place:

  (i) a lawsuit, litigation, arbitration, mediation, claim, or other proceeding or governmental proceeding or other formal or informal investigation is filed against the Borrower [or any Guarantor] where the amount claimed is [insert dollar amount] or more;

  (ii) a judgment is entered against the Borrower or any Guarantor; or

  (iii) any government authority takes action that materially adversely affects the Borrower's [or Guarantor's] ability to repay the loan or satisfy its obligations under any of the Loan Documents [note — defined to include the Loan Agreement, Promissory Notes, Guaranty, or any document entered in connection with the loan]."

(h) The Lender fails to have an enforceable first-priority security interest in any property given as security for any Loan; or

(i) A default or an Event of Default occurs under any of the Loan Documents (as defined in that document, subject to applicable notice and cure periods).

Subsection (g) makes certain lawsuits, judgments, and government actions events of default. Subsection (h) is a kind of cross-default provsion, triggered when the Lender loses its first priority security position in any collateral under any security agreement with the Borrower. Subsection (i) is a kind of cross-default provision, but covering only the other Loan Documents entered into with the Lender with respect to the subject loan. The Loan Documents include the Promissory Note, any Guarantee or Security Agreement, and all other documents entered into by the Borrower or related parties in connection with the subject loan. So, for example, if the Guarantor breaches a provision of its Guarantee, then this breach would be captured by Subsection (i) and constitute an event of default under the Loan Agreement, subject to the notice and grace periods, to the extent applicable, contained in the Guaranty. Any grace periods incorporated into any of the other Loan Documents have already been agreed to by the Lender, and it would be disingenuous for the Lender to take them away by negotiating a more aggressive Subsection (i).

Events of Default versus Mandatory Prepayment Events

The Lender might be amenable to reclassifying a default/event of default as a mandatory prepayment event. The bank still has the right to be repaid promptly, but the event doesn't trigger (usually) cross-defaults under your other contracts, and therefore doesn't impact (usually) your credit rating. Note, however, how the "Lender" in our example drafted subsection (f) to treat mandatory prepayment events the same way as traditional defaults and events of default, treating them all as cross-defaults.

Event of Default Remedies — Revolving Credit Facility or Term Loan

Upon the occurrence of an Event of Default, the Lender may, at its option and without notice, exercise any and all of the following rights and remedies (in addition to any other rights and remedies available to it):

(a) declare immediately due and payable all unpaid principal of, together with accrued interest and all other sums payable under, this Loan Agreement or under the Promissory Notes, and all such amounts hereunder or under the Promissory Notes are thereupon immediately due and payable without presentment or other demand, protest, notice of dishonor, or any other notice of any kind, all of which are hereby expressly waived;

(b) terminate the Commitment [Revolving Line of Credit];

(c) refuse to make any Advances hereunder; or

(d) in addition to any other rights provided by law, exercise all of its rights or remedies under the Loan Documents.

This is a very basic provision that sets forth the rights and remedies of the Lender once an event of default occurs. Subsection (a) gives the Lender the right to accelerate the loan and receive payment immediately. Since most loans are evidenced by separate Promissory Notes, the Lender will mention these as well to cover all of its bases.

Subsections (b) and (c) gives the Lender the right to permanently terminate its Commitment to make further loans (typically a revolver, but also term loans that are advanced in separate tranches), or to refuse to make the next or any future advance of the loan (even if the Lender keeps the line open), respectively. Subsection (d) reiterates the parenthetical in the introductory language, and gives the Lender the right to pursue cumulative remedies, basically whatever other rights are available anywhere else (e.g., in the other Loan Documents, by law, etc.). See Chapter 24 for information on **Cumulative versus Exclusive Remedies**. Try as you might, you probably won't be able to negotiate any exclusive remedies with the bank; it's going to want to keep all of its enforcement options open.

If you are providing any collateral to the bank to secure your loan, then this provision will also contain various and sundry provisions allowing the bank to enter your premises, to seize the collateral, etc. These provisions would basically track whatever remedy language is found in your security agreement, pledge agreement, mortgage, or other document evidencing the security agreement. Given space constraints, this book does not contain a detailed discussion of security agreements.

20

REPRESENTATIONS, WARRANTIES, AND COVENANTS

OVERVIEW

A bank or other Lender wants to confirm as much information as possible about the Borrower before it lends any money, much in the same way the buyer in a Sale of Business transaction wants to confirm as much information as possible about the company being acquired. Therefore, the typical Lender will require a Borrower to provide in the Loan Agreement many of the same representations and warranties that are required of sellers in asset purchase and stock purchase agreements.

The actual contract language of many of the representations discussed in this chapter can be found in Chapter 13 (Representations and Warranties of the Seller). Given space constraints, I do not reproduce the representations in this chapter. Rather, I list the names of the representations below so you can refer to Chapter 13 for the actual contract language and a detailed discussion of the particular representation generally, and in this chapter I furnish comments about the representations as they relate to loan transactions specifically. I also discuss some representations that are found exclusively in loan documents. The Borrower's representations must be true on the date made (on the execution date of the loan agreement), and are "brought down" as a closing condition on each day a loan is advanced.

A false representation (i.e., a representation that is false when originally made) is a breach of the Loan Agreement. A representation that is true when made, but later becomes untrue, is not a breach; rather, the representation can't be brought down (and the Borrower fails to satisfy a closing condition). In this case, the Lender has the choice to not advance the loan. Keep in mind that the Lender has the special incentive to obtain as many representations and warranties as possible from the Borrower; the Federal Bankruptcy Code allows the Lender to cite a false representation to counter the Borrower's attempt to discharge (i.e., avoid) the debt if it becomes insolvent.

As the Borrower, you'll want to dilute your representations as much as you can. You can do this by negotiating the same kinds of materiality, knowledge and other qualifers that are available to the seller in a sale of business transaction (see **How to Qualify Representations** in Chapter 13).

CONTRACT CLAUSE DISCUSSION

Organization; Power and Authority to Run Business; and Qualification in Foreign Jurisdictions

The Lender won't lend money to a Borrower that doesn't have its organizational house in order. These representations go to the legal status of the Borrower. The Lender needs to know that the Borrower is a valid legal entity (e.g., corporation, limited liability company, etc.), in good standing (i.e., current with its annual filings and franchise taxes) with the power and authority to run its business, not only in its state of incorporation, but also in any other state where it needs to qualify to do business.

Borrowers with subsidiaries will need to make this representation about the subsidiaries, as well as a representation that they own the stock (or other form of ownership interest) in each subsidiary free and clear of third party security interests, the thinking of the Lender being that if the subsidiaries form part of the basis of the Lender's lending decision, then the Lender needs to be able to control the subsidiaries in case the Borrower defaults. Third-party liens on the stock of the subsidiaries will prevent the Lender from controlling the subsidiaries.

Authority to Enter into the Loan Transaction (i.e., borrow the money and enter into the Loan Agreement, Promissory Note, etc.)

This representation relates to the corporate procedures and board approvals that must be followed or obtained in order to enter into the loan transaction. You may already be familiar with the general resolutions your bank made you sign to open up your corporate bank account; these typically contain general board resolutions regarding borrowings. However, you'll still need to obtain a new board resolution that specifically approves the loan, even if you borrow money from the bank where you deposit your money. It's not uncommon for small business charter documents (e.g., certificate of incorporation, bylaws, etc.) to contain restrictions on borrowing or require shareholder approval (in addition to board approval) before it can incur debt.

Consent of Third Parties to Transaction; Consent of Government Authorities to Transaction; No Conflict with Corporate Documents, Contracts, or Laws

The Lender won't make the loan if it knows that the loan is prohibited (or allowed with detrimental strings attached) by the Borrower's charter documents or contracts, including the Borrower's other credit documents (e.g., outright prohibition or a provision that purports to subordinate the rights of future lenders). Making a prohibited loan would trigger the existing lender's right to accelerate and/or seize collateral, which works to dilute the pool of assets available to the Lender. These representations help the Lender to identify and flesh out these kinds of problem areas, as well as problems any regulatory authority might have with the transaction. Once a problem area is identified, you can work with the Lender to structure some kind of work-around that everybody can live with.

The bank may also ask for the **pari passu representation**, in which the Borrower represents that its debt to the bank ranks "pari passu" or no lower than its obligations to other creditors; this helps to assure the bank that its rights are not subordinate to the rights of the Borrower's other creditors. This is the minimum standard for the bank — ideally, it'll want to jump to the head of the pack by taking a first priority security interest in the collateral it needs to secure the Borrower's entire obligation.

Enforceability

This representation goes to the validity and enforceability (against the Borrower) of the loan agreement, promissory note, and other loan documents (e.g., to the extent applicable to your transaction, any security agreement, guarantee, etc.), which impacts the ability of the Borrower to repay the loan and meet its obligations under the loan documents.

Financial Statements

The Lender always asks for this representation because the financial statements provide a wealth of information about the creditability of the Borrower, including useful information about any assets forming the basis of the bank's lending decision (e.g., existence of prior security interests, etc.). At a minimum, Lenders typically require audited annual financial statements, together with internally prepared interim statements. Lenders are pretty picky about the audit firm — usually they'll ask for a large national or regional accounting firm. If it turns out the financial statements contain an error, then the Lender may have a claim against the accounting firm.

If the Borrower owns subsidiaries, then the Lender may make its lending decision based on the creditability of the Borrower and its subsidiaries, in which case the Lender may require the Borrower to make the representation based on the financial statements of the Borrower and its subsidiaries on either a consolidated basis or consolidating basis. The Lender's approach will impact its ability to make concessions on the **material adverse change** representation (discussed below). If the Lender is lending based on the creditability of the Borrower together with its subsidiaries, then it might be in a better position to agree to consider the impact of a negative event on the Borrower's group of companies taken as a whole, rather than on any individual entity. For example, a $100,000 judgment lien has a far greater impact on one company than it does on a group of same-sized companies taken as a whole.

The strongest possible version of this representation from the Lender's perspective is where the Borrower represents that the financial statements are "true, complete, and correct." Depending on your bargaining leverage, you can negotiate to dilute the representation — by stating instead that the financial statements are "fairly present in all material respects, the financial condition of the Borrower."

No Material Adverse Change

The financial statements paint a financial portrait of the Borrower either "as of" a particular date (in the case of balance sheets) or "for" the specified time period (in the case of income statements). Since financial statements take time to prepare, there's always going to be a time gap between the last day of the immediately completed financial reporting period and the closing date of the loan (and the closing dates of the multiple advances under a revolver). The Lender requires the "no material adverse change" representation to cover this time gap.

Undisclosed Liabilities (Other Than Taxes)

Even the strongest "true, complete, and accurate" financial statement representation won't necessarily account for the existence of all the Borrower's liabilities. This representation confirms the existence of certain contingent liabilities and other off-balance-sheet liabilities, which don't necessarily show up on GAAP-complaint financial statements. Lenders want to know about contingent liabilities because they can represent an area of significant potential liability for the Borrower, even if it may not be on the hook right now. Lenders also want to scrutinize the Borrower's leases — there are significant differences in the way different types of leases are recorded in the financial statements.

Litigation and Investigations

Pending and potential lawsuits and investigations create legal and financial exposure that impacts the Borrower's creditability. At a minimum, banks want to know about lawsuits and other proceedings pending against the Borrower (i.e., where the Borrower is a defendant). Many banks insist on expanded language to cover all proceedings where the Borrower "is a party," which also would include lawsuits where the Borrower is a plaintiff. Practically speaking, defendants almost always try to craft some kind of counterclaim, so all the parties to a lawsuit usually end up playing both offense and defense in the overall case.

In addition, banks want Borrowers to disclose "threatened" lawsuits because these create potential legal and financial exposure. Borrowers can usually negotiate to qualify this part of the representation by disclosing only threatened litigation that is known to the Borrower.

Yet another category includes proceedings "affecting" the Borrower, even if the Borrower is not a direct party to the proceeding, for example, an infringement lawsuit involving a trademark the Borrower is licensing from the defendant. If the defendant can no longer use the trademark as a result of the litigation, then neither can the Borrower, which can impact the Borrower's financial outlook. In most cases, a party asserting trademark infringement will sue not just the licensor, but the known licensees as well.

Some Lenders go beyond threatened and pending lawsuits, and also demand that the Borrower represent that it is complying/has complied with all judgments, injunctions, etc., related to already completed lawsuits.

Compliance with Laws

The Lender needs to confirm that the Borrower is complying with all laws and regulations. Aggressive Lenders will also require that the Borrower represent that it has complied with all laws and regulations for some period of time before execution. Keep in mind that many laws and regulations impose fines and penalties for the failure to comply, which if significant, can quickly add up to negatively impact the Borrower's creditability, and therefore increase the Lender's exposure. Many Lenders also require specific compliance representations relating to Taxes, Environmental, Employee Benefit Plans, and Labor Matters, and others.

The stakes are quite high here. Besides impacting creditability, the Borrower's failure to comply with certain laws like the environmental laws may create independent joint and several liability for the Lender, for example, if the Lender becomes the owner of the Borrower's contaminated property through foreclosure.

List of Assets; Title to Assets; Sufficiency and Condition of Assets

The Lender will require some combination of these representations in order to supplement information about the assets contained in the financial statements. The Lender needs to make sure that the Borrower owns, free of third-party liens, the assets the Lender is using as the basis of its lending decision.

Depending on the type of loan and the business of the Borrower, the Lender may ask for any number of other representations about the Borrower's **Inventory**, **Accounts Receivable**, **Contracts**, **Intellectual Property**, and/or **Real Estate**, among other things. For example, a Lender making an **asset-based loan** (and taking a security interest in the inventory and receivables) will want detailed information about these assets. Think of your home mortgage as an analogy. Your bank lends you money so that you can purchase your house and land. It takes a security interest called a mortgage in these assets to secure your repayment of the home loan. A lot of the hoops you have to jump through to obtain your home loan relate to furnishing the bank with the information it needs about the asset being used to secure the loan — things like the appraisal, title report, title insurance, etc. If the title report reveals a defect, then the bank won't lend you the money until you fix the defect.

Full Disclosure (a.k.a., 10b-5 Representation)

The representation typically tracks the language found in Rule 10b-5 of the Securities and Exchange Act of 1934, which makes it unlawful to make any untrue statements or misleading omissions of material fact in connection with the sale of any security. While the rule deals with the sale of securities, Lenders in loan transactions frequently request this "catch all" because they want Borrowers to vouch for the information contained in all documents furnished during due diligence, whether or not the information is covered by any of the representations and warranties or contained in the financial statements. So if you agree to make this representation, you've essentially agreed to vouch for the accuracy of things like your cash flow statements, *pro forma* statements, inventory reports, accounts receivable aging reports, financial projections and even informal financial analyses — basically whatever you hand over to the Lender during your negotiations.

Covenants

The Lender relies on a variety of tools to limit its exposure in loan transactions. For example, as the Borrower, you'll be asked to furnish a series of representations and warranties (discussed in the sections above) that present a snapshot of your financial condition on the day you sign your loan agreement. However, a loan is a long-term business relationship, and loan documents traditionally contain several other mechanisms to help ensure that you maintain your "loan approval level" of creditability throughout the life of the loan. This includes the time period up through the end of the Lender's obligation to advance loans and your repayment of the outstanding amount of the loan, with accrued interest.

Closing Conditions versus Covenants

One of these mechanisms is the closing condition that the representations and warranties remain true on the day that any advance is made (i.e., the "**bring down**" condition). So in a revolver (or a term loan involving multiple advances), the bank has the option not to make an advance if a representation is no longer true. But this by itself isn't a breach of the loan agreement and won't trigger the bank's right to accelerate the loan, demand immediate repayment of the entire loan plus interest, or seize any collateral in a secured loan.

Representations versus Covenants

To summarize, the representations and warranties are statements of purported facts made by the Borrower to induce the Lender to make the loan, and are brought down (i.e., "refreshed") as a closing condition to all future advances under the Loan Agreement. While the representations and warranties may paint a rosy picture of the your business on the loan advance date, the covenants help to ensure that you stay on the straight and narrow path of maintaining your loan approval level of creditability after the Closing.

In fact, many loan agreement covenants track the concepts contained in the individual representations and warranties. For example, as discussed, you'll need to make a representation about the compliance of your pre-Closing financial statements to GAAP, and usually some statement about their veracity (e.g., ranging from the loose "fairly present" to the strict "true, complete, and accurate"). But the bank also needs you to covenant or promise to deliver up to date GAAP-conforming financial information with the same degree of veracity at regular intervals throughout the life of the loan (i.e., until the loan commitment terminates and all outstanding amounts are paid).

Types of Covenants

These include **affirmative covenants**, which are promises to do certain things, and **negative covenants**, which are promises to refrain from doing certain things, as well as **financial covenants**. Covenants are also included in Chapter 15, but those are less extensive and generally only cover the time period between the execution of the asset purchase or stock purchase agreement and the closing (one exception, for example, being the covenant not to compete, which lasts beyond the closing date). On the other hand, since loan transactions are long-term business relationships, a Lender will likely ask for a far greater number of covenants (including financial covenants, which can be found exclusively in loan agreements).

I like to try to think of the covenants as falling into several broad categories based on purpose. Three of the basic covenants typically found in Sale of Business documents (e.g., asset purchase and stock purchase agreements) focus on **Access to Information**, **Conduct of Business**, and **Notice of Changes**. The Purchaser wants continued access to information during the period between the execution date of the contract and the closing of the sale. It wants the acquired business to continue to operate in a way that either enhances or in any event doesn't dilute the value of what it is purchasing. And it wants to be notified promptly of bad news. Lenders pretty much want the same things. So I find it's helpful to think of the covenants in loan documents as falling in the same broad categories. Again, given the long-term nature of a loan relationship, Borrowers can expect to see a far greater number of covenants within these broad categories.

To compare and contrast these approaches, the Seller in an asset purchase agreement typically makes a pretty general "conduct of business" covenant that it will until the closing "conduct its business diligently in the ordinary course of business consistent with past practice and use its best efforts to preserve its business and the goodwill associated with the business." The agreement usually won't specify exactly how the Seller should do that; it just says that it has to. Most loan agreements, however, include specific (affirmative, negative, and financial) covenants that go into quite a bit of depth and cover areas as diverse as net worth, cash flow, corporate existence, restricted payments, insurance, capital expenditures, investments, and the like.

Access to Information

These include the affirmative covenants relating to financial reporting, books and records, and inspections.

Conduct of Business

I would include in this category the affirmative covenants relating to Maintenance of Corporate Existence, Maintenance of Assets, Maintenance of Business (which is similar to the overall "Conduct of Business" covenant typically found in Sale of Business transactions), Maintenance of Insurance, and Compliance with Laws. Negative covenants in this broad category include covenants restricting certain Debt, Liens, Capital Expenditures, Investments, Mergers, and Sale of Business Transactions, Transactions with Affiliates, as well as Distributions to Shareholders. I'd also lump into this group the financial covenants discussed later in this chapter, which indirectly but decidedly impact the way the Borrower conducts its business.

Notice of Changes

These include any covenant promising to deliver notice of bad news — defaults/events of default, litigation, etc.

Consequences of Breach of Covenant

A breach of covenant is a default of the loan agreement, with similar consequences as the Borrower's non-payment of principal or interest, making a representation that is false when made, and committing a cross default. In most cases, the Lender will have the right (upon default) to cancel its commitment to advance funds, plus the right to accelerate the loan, demand immediate repayment of all outstanding amounts plus interest and/or enforce its security interests, but only when the default turns into an event of default, which occurs when a notified default remains uncured after a specified period of time (e.g., five days, ten days, etc. depending on the infraction, and zero days for some of the financial covenants).

Covenants — How Harsh?

The quantity and severity of the covenants depends on a variety of factors, including the type of loan, amount borrowed, and type of business you own, and of course how creditworthy you are. For example, Lenders will ask for a greater number of stringent covenants in a traditional cash-flow based loan, compared to an asset-based loan where the Lender relies less on covenants than on its practical ability to enforce its security interest in the collateral. And if you're financially weak, then expect your bank to attempt to exert more oversight, for example, require covenants that require you to submit financial reports more frequently, maybe even monthly or weekly, and perhaps even to maintain all of your cash at bank accounts established at the bank (which pulls double duty in allowing the bank to monitor your finances, plus enhances its security position *vis-à-vis* other creditors).

As harsh as the covenants can be sometimes, an ethical and smart lender knows that it has no business actually running your business (e.g., via covenants allowing the Lender to veto you on legitimate business decisions or to approve your personnel). The law imposes harsh penalties on lenders who try to control a borrower. The more it attempts to control how you run your business, the more it risks incurring direct legal liability or undercutting the very legal position *vis-à-vis* other creditors it's worked so hard to protect.

Can Covenants Be Negotiated?

Like all contract provisions, the answer is "Yes, depending on your bargaining leverage." One problem for small business (strong ones as well as weaker ones) is the cost of complying with the covenants. You don't want the cost of complying (including the opportunity cost of the time you otherwise could be devoting to productive activities like sales) to bog you down. An extreme example — while most

Borrowers can understand the need of furnishing audited annual reports, it's overkill for the bank to require you to provide audited monthly reports.

Nor do you want the covenants to overly hamstring the way you do business or restrict your ability to obtain additional financing. Work with your attorney and financial advisor to carefully review the covenants and weed out or pare down "gratuitous" covenants. Your position should be that the covenants should work only to restrict transactions that dilute the Lender's rights or increases its exposure. For example, an overzealous Lender might strong-arm you into making a blanket negative covenant not to incur any new debt for the life of the loan. However, query whether the Lender would be hurt, for example, if you want to refinance some junior debt owed to a third party with new junior debt (lowers the interest rate) or equity (replaces the junior debt with even more junior equity). You can negotiate to carve out such refinancings because they enhance your creditability and therefore reduce the Lender's exposure.

You also want to be sure, to the extent that you've qualified one of your representations, you also try to qualify the corresponding covenant the same way. For example, if you've represented that you're in compliance with all laws (except to the extent that any violation will not have a material adverse effect on your business), the Lender should have no problem with you making the covenant that you will comply with all laws subject to the same bracketed materiality qualifier.

The Lender's attorney will draft the representations and warranties, the closing conditions, and the covenants so that they work together to protect the Lender during all time phases of the loan. This interconnectivity warrants that you work closely with your attorney to make sure that the definitions and other terms used throughout the loan documents are internally consistent. For example, the Loan Agreement and the promissory note may be prepared by different attorneys within the same law firm or bank legal department. Or a super-busy senior attorney who prepares the loan agreement might not have sufficient time to cross-check the work of the junior attorney assigned to prepare the ancillary documents, or the mortgage prepared by a real estate lawyer.

Work with your attorney to negotiate the covenants so that they are internally consistent in your favour. You don't want to spend an inordinate amount of time negotiating a carve-out to a covenant that allows you to take the specified action, only to have the Lender later raise the language contained in another covenant to try to prevent you from taking the same action.

SAMPLE CONTRACT EXCERPTS
Introductory Language (Covenants)

For as long as the Commitment remains in effect or any obligation under this Loan Agreement or any Promissory Note remains outstanding, the Borrower shall comply with the following covenants.

This is typical introductory language to the affirmative, negative and financial covenants. It means that the Borrower must comply with the covenants during the entire life of the loan relationship, that is, for as long as the Lender has any obligation to advance loans (Commitment), and as long as any amounts remain unpaid or obligations remain outstanding under any of the loan documents.

Affirmative Covenants

Here are basic versions of some of the most common affirmative covenants.

Financial Reports

(a) The Borrower shall furnish to the Lender, no later than [45] days after the end of each of the first three (3) quarters of the Borrower's fiscal year, a balance sheet of the Borrower as of the end of such quarter and a statement of income, retained earnings, and changes in financial position for such quarter.

This is a basic version of the Borrower's covenant to prepare and furnish financial statements (Subsection [a] quarterly, and Subsection [b] annually), typically the same categories of financial statements included in the financial statements representation. In addition to the annual (unqualified audited, more on this below) financial statements, and depending on your creditworthiness and other factors, some combination of semi-annual, quarterly, and/or monthly financial statements, the Lender might require you to furnish periodic **financial projections or forecasts**.

The Borrower shall cause such financial statements to:

(i) be in reasonable detail and with all supporting documents, including, but not limited to, all notes and schedules;

(ii) be prepared in accordance with generally accepted accounting principles consistently applied [throughout the periods involved];

(iii) be certified to be in compliance with this section by the chief financial officer of the Borrower; and

(iv) fairly present in all material respects, the financial condition of the Borrower as of the dates thereof, and the results of operations and changes in financial position of the Borrower for the time periods indicated.

Generally Accepted Accounting Principles, or GAAP, allows companies to choose from among various alternative accounting principles (the "first in first out [FIFO]" versus "last in first out [LIFO]" treatment of inventory being the most famous example to non-accountants). Lenders demand consistent application of GAAP principles in preparing the financial reports. They don't want you to be able to mask problem areas simply by switching back and forth between accounting principles.

Item (iv) above calls for a relatively Borrower-friendly "fairly present in all material respects" standard. An aggressive Lender may require that the financial statements be "true, complete, and accurate," which is a far stricter standard.

(b) The Borrower shall furnish to the Lender, no later than [90] days after the end of the Borrower's fiscal year, a balance sheet of the Borrower as of the end of such fiscal year and a statement of income, retained earnings, and changes in financial position for such fiscal year.

The Borrower shall cause such financial statements to:

(i) be in reasonable detail and with all supporting documents, including, but not limited to, all notes and schedules;

(ii) be prepared in accordance with generally accepted accounting principles consistently applied; and

(iii) fairly present in all material respects, the financial condition of the Borrower as of the dates thereof, and the results of operations and changes in financial position of the Borrower for the time periods indicated.

The Borrower shall cause such financial statements to be audited and certified by [insert name of accounting firm] or other independent certified public accountant satisfactory to the Lender, and be accompanied by an unqualified opinion of such accounting firm satisfactory to the Lender.

If you have subsidiaries, the Lender may require either or both **consolidated** and **consolidating financial statements**. Given this level of complexity, be sure the bank leaves you adequate time to prepare and deliver the financial statements. Thirty days after the end of the month is the norm for monthly reports, with 45 days for quarterly, and since audited reports have to be certified by a third-party accounting firm, leave yourself a cushion of at least 90 days to deliver audited financial statements.

Most Lenders add the bracketed requirement that the audited financial statements be "**unqualified**," meaning that the Borrower will be in default if the accounting firm can't deliver an unqualified opinion with respect to the financial statements. Lenders are most concerned if they see the "**going concern**" **qualification**, which means that the accounting firm doesn't believe that the Borrower can survive as a going concern (i.e., a company with the resources to operate indefinitely, or even more simply put, a company not in danger of going bankrupt in the foreseeable future).

In addition to the financial reports, the Lender typically requires Borrower covenants to maintain GAAP-conforming books and records and to grant the Lender access to its facilities, employees, and records (see **Inspections** covenant below), as well as to furnish to the Lender any documents it's required to furnish to its other lenders.

You already know that loans are driven by the Lender's assumptions about your financial condition, which are derived in part from its interpretation of your financial statements. Keep in mind that some of the other covenants discussed below contain concepts that do not necessarily jive with the concepts as reflected in financial statements. For example, banks often insist on a negative covenant restricting all debt (defining debt to include guarantees, sale-leasebacks, etc.), even though these liabilities may be "off balance sheet" obligations or in any event may not be reflected or treated as GAAP debt in your financial statements. You'll probably have no choice but to live with this, but at least you should work with your attorney to identify and understand these issues.

Inspections

(a) The Borrower shall permit the Lender and any duly authorized representatives thereof, upon reasonable notice to the Borrower and at the Borrower's [reasonable] expense and during the Borrower's normal business hours, to:

  (i) examine and make copies and take notes of the Borrower's books and records;

  (ii) visit the Borrower's offices, facilities, and other properties; and

  (iii) discuss the Borrower's business and finances with any responsible officer of the Borrower and the Borrower's independent certified public accountant.

(b) Notwithstanding the above, so long as no Default or Event of Default has occurred and is continuing, the Borrower shall not be required to pay the expenses of more than one (1) visit per fiscal year, or pay more than [insert dollar amount] in the aggregate for all such visits during such fiscal year.

This is a basic version of the Borrower's covenant to allow the Lender access to its facilities, books, and records (make copies, abstracts, or take notes), employees, accountants, and others. Lenders have the limited independent obligation to keep confidential any information obtained from Borrowers and to use such information only for loan servicing purposes. In other words, the Lender can't use information obtained from you to bad mouth you to other lenders, your customers or vendors. Nevertheless, most Borrowers negotiate contract provisions to keep such information confidential.

You may also want to temper the right to inspect by limiting access to designated hours (e.g., your business hours), and perhaps requiring that you and/or your attorney be present during all inspections, audits, interviews, etc. You can also qualify by adding Subsction (b), which caps the number of reimbursable visits that can be made during one year and the aggregate reimbursable amount for all visits made during the year, provided that the Borrower isn't in default.

Maintain Corporate Existence

The Borrower shall preserve and maintain its [and each of its Subsidiaries']:

(a) existence and good standing in its state of incorporation [formation — for LLCs]; and

(b) qualification and good standing in each other jurisdiction [in which the failure to so qualify would reasonably be expected to have a material adverse effect on its financial condition or results of operations, or its assets, business, liabilities, operations, or future prospects].

This is the classic corporate housekeeping covenant where the Borrower promises to preserve its corporate existence, and qualification to do business in other states. The Lender wants you around so that you can repay the loan, so it makes you promise that you won't dissolve the company or merge it out of existence. And if any of your subsidiaries form part of the basis of your loan approval, you'll need to include them in this covenant. You might be able to negotiate some exceptions to the extent that the continued viability of a particular subsidiary doesn't impact the Lender's exposure. Note how I've added standard materiality language (bracketed language) to this covenant.

Mergers and Sale of Business Transactions (a Negative Covenant)

The Borrower shall not enter into any transaction (or series of related transactions) to:

(a) sell, transfer, or dispose of all or substantially all of its assets to any other person;

(b) acquire all or substantially all the assets of any other person;

(c) merge or consolidate itself with or into any other person;

(d) merge or consolidate any other person into itself; or

(e) liquidate, wind up, or dissolve itself (or allow itself to become the subject of an involuntary liquidation, winding up, or dissolution).

[List exceptions, for example] Notwithstanding the above, the Borrower may enter into a transaction with any of its wholly-owned subsidiaries to merge such subsidiary into it or transfer to it the assets of such subsidiary.

I discuss this negative covenant here because it's a close relative of the Maintain Corporate Existence affirmative covenant discussed immediately above. The Lender insists on some form of this covenant because it doesn't want you to disappear or enter into any transaction that detracts from your loan-approval profile, either by entering into one transaction or a series of related transactions. For example, if you decide to sell all of your assets or purchase all the assets of a third party, this would change your profile significantly (in the former, you'd disappear, and in the latter, you'd have an entirely new mix of assets and liabilities).

Exceptions

The sample contract provision is pretty airtight from the Lender's perspective and prohibits pretty much most transactions. But there are a number of exceptions you can try to negotiate, for example, allowing for the merger of a subsidiary into the Borrower (or intra-subsidiary mergers), where the Borrower survives or remains intact after the transaction. If your Lender is making the loan based on the creditability of your companies on a consolidated basis, it may be more inclined to accommodate since moving the pieces around may not affect the overall creditworthiness of the group.

Getting the bank to agree to an exception allowing (i) the merger of a third party into the Borrower, or (ii) the purchase by the Borrower of substantially all the assets of a third party, or (iii) going even further where you're allowed to merge into a third-party successor (where you are not the survivor) is much more difficult because from the bank's perspective it's almost like making a new loan. In (i) and (ii), you survive intact, but the asset and liability mix has been drastically altered. In (iii), you disappear completely into the third party.

> Depending on your credit profile, your Lender might require a broad-based prohibition that not only prohibits the sale of substantially all the assets of the Borrower (which is reasonable — see above), but takes it several amplitudes further to prohibit any sale, including inventory. While most successful businesses don't gratuitously go into "going out of business" mode and liquidate inventory, this kind of restriction is too cumbersome for most Borrowers, who need to be able to sell inventory in the ordinary course and replace old equipment (purchase new, dispose of old) in order to "stay in business." And if factoring (i.e., selling your receivables) is part of your business model, then you'll also need to negotiate an exception if you want to be able to keep doing this.

Maintain Business

The Borrower shall continue to engage primarily in the businesses being conducted on the date of this Loan Agreement, businesses reasonably related or incidental thereto as well as reasonable expansions and extensions of such businesses.

The Borrower promises to continue its existing business and not to enter into new lines of business. You can negotiate an exception allowing you to discontinue unviable lines of business, as long as it doesn't increase the Lender's exposure under the loan. Some Lenders extend this concept and make you promise to continue to perform your important contracts.

Maintain Assets

The Borrower shall, in accordance with customary and prudent business practices:

(a) maintain all of its tangible and intangible assets and property [necessary for its business] in good repair, working order and condition, reasonable wear and tear excepted, other than with respect to assets disposed of in the ordinary course of business; and

(b) from time to time make or cause to be made all needed renewals, replacements, and repairs, including, but not limited to, registrations and renewals of all licenses, trademarks and patents, and other intangible property rights as are reasonably necessary to conduct its business as currently conducted.

The Borrower promises to upkeep its assets, including intangibles like licenses and patents. An exception is made for ordinary wear and tear, the ability to repair and replace, as well as to allow for the sale of assets (e.g., inventory) in the ordinary course of business (which would otherwise be a technical default of this provision). The bracketed language is a kind of qualifier in that it excludes certain assets that are not "necessary" for the business. Without the bracketed language, the failure to replace, say, a broken chair in your office, would be a technical default of this provision. This covenant works together with the **Maintain Insurance** covenant (discussed below) to help ensure that your assets remain viable, so that you can continue to operate your existing business so that you can repay your loan.

Maintain Insurance

(a) The Borrower shall:

(i) keep all of its real and personal property, including, but not limited to, the Collateral, insured against loss or damage by fire, theft, explosion, and all other hazards and risks; and

(ii) maintain liability and other insurance,

in each case in such form, with such insurance companies and in such amounts that are satisfactory to the Lender.

(b) Without limiting the generality of the foregoing, the Borrower shall cause all property policies referred to in Subsection (a) above

(i) to contain a lender's loss payable endorsement that names the Lender as an additional loss payee, and all liability insurance policies referred to in Subsection (a)

(ii) to name the Lender as an additional insured, and for all policies to specify that the insurance company must give at least 30 days' notice to the Lender of any cancellation or modification of the policy.

This covenant is boilerplate in secured loans because the Lender wants to protect the collateral it's using to secure the loan. But you'll usually see some form of this covenant even if the Lender is making an unsecured loan. Any loss (e.g., a slip and fall on your business property, a total loss of an asset, your building going up in flames, etc.), not covered by insurance needs to be covered directly by you. Any money that leaves your coffers or gets diverted from your cash flow to cover the claim or calamity or to replace the asset becomes unavailable to service or secure the loan. This is why the Lender needs you to promise to maintain insurance, often with the additional requirements that the Lender (a) is named an **additional insured** on the policy, as well as **loss payee** with the right to receive payment directly from the insurance company, and (b) be notified in advance of any cancellation or modification of the policy.

Depending on your business, the Lender might specify the amount of the insurance or a particular type of insurance, or give itself the right to pay premiums in case you can't. For example, it might require you to maintain **business interruption insurance** in addition to the standard casualty insurance. Or if you already have **key person insurance**, the Lender might ask you to assign the policy to it so that it can collect the proceeds directly from the insurance company if the specified person dies.

Compliance with Laws

The Borrower shall comply with all:

(a) organizational documents of the Borrower (including, but not limited to, certificate of incorporation, by-laws, shareholders agreement or limited liability company agreement of the Borrower, as the case may be);

(b) contracts, agreements, understandings [or commitments] to which the Borrower, or with respect to which, any of its assets or business is subject; or

(c) laws, regulations, or other rules of any government authority or ruling or other determinations of any court or other tribunal, to which the Borrower, or with respect to which any of its assets or business, is subject.

The failure to comply with laws may result in financial penalties that take away from your ability to repay your loan. Therefore, the Lender needs you to promise to comply with all laws and regulations (subject to, if you can get it, materiality or other qualifying language). This is another core covenant, and tracks the language of the Compliance with Laws representation. Depending on the nature of your business, Lenders may require you to make additional law-specific compliance covenants, for example, the affirmative covenant to file tax returns and pay taxes when due, to comply with environmental laws, labor laws, and ERISA, among others. You can try to qualify this covenant with any of the materiality qualifiers discussed in **How to Qualify Representations** in Chapter 13.

Notice of Changes

The Borrower shall promptly notify the Lender of:

(a) any pending or threatened lawsuit, litigation, arbitration, mediation, claim, or other proceeding, governmental proceeding, or other formal or informal investigation;

(b) any Default or Event of Default under this Loan Agreement, Promissory Note, or any of the Loan Documents;

(c) any default or event of default under any contractual obligation of the Borrower [or Guarantor] with any other person or entity, [which if not cured, would reasonably be expected to have a material adverse effect on its financial condition or results of operations, or its assets, business, liabilities, operations, or future prospects].

In addition to obvious events like litigation and defaults, Lenders may demand prompt notice of other events that may have potentially negative financial consequences, such as the termination of any ERISA employee benefit plan. Defaults include cross defaults (Subsection [c]), i.e., the Borrower's default or event of default under one of its other agreements triggering a default or event of default under the loan agreement, in its strictest variation without even waiting for the cure period under the other agreement to lapse). All of these events may result in liability that diverts cash and assets away from the Borrower's ability to repay the loan. The Borrower can negotiate to include the bracketed materiality qualifier for Subsection (a) ("threatened" lawsuits) with a knowledge qualifier.

Negative Covenants

Here are basic versions of some of the most common negative covenants.

Debt

(a) The Borrower shall not, and the Borrower shall cause its subsidiaries to not, create, incur, assume, permit to exist, or guarantee any Debt, except:

(i) any indebtedness to the Lender;

(ii) Debt existing on the Closing Date, and disclosed in attached Exhibit [insert Exhibit number]; and

(iii) Debt for trade payables in the ordinary course of business.

The sample contract provision shows how a moderately aggressive Lender might draft this covenant; the Borrower promises not to incur any debt except the limited exceptions enumerated in Subsection (a). Debt is defined in Subsection (b) below, which is typically found with the other definitions in the definitions section of the loan agreement.

(b) Debt means all:

(i) indebtedness for borrowed money or the deferred purchase price of property or services, including, but not limited to, reimbursement and other obligations with respect to surety bonds and letters of credit, and obligations under any conditional sale or title retention transactions;

(ii) obligations evidenced by notes, bonds, debentures, or similar instruments;

(iii) obligations under capital leases;

(iv) guaranties, comfort letters, standby letters of credit, swap agreements, interest rate cap or collar agreements, or any other agreement or arrangement entered into to protect any Person [note — defined as any natural person or legal entity] against fluctuations in interest or exchange rates or commodity prices, and any other contingent obligations (except endorsements for collection or deposit in the ordinary course of business).

As discussed above, the Lender typically defines debt very broadly, including not just other bank loans, but also "off balance sheet" items that may not be reflected in your GAAP-prepared financial statements. Subsection (b) contains a variation of broad Lender-drafted definition of debt that includes extended payment terms for the purchase price of goods and services (including the deferred purchase price under title retention/conditional sales transactions [see **Security Interest** covenant below]), letters of credit, and guarantees [e.g., traditional guarantees, standby letters of credit, comfort letters, capital maintenance agreements, etc.].) Subsection (b)(iv) excepts out ordinary course endorsements; otherwise, any time you sign the back of a check, you'd be in technical default of the debt covenant.

Lenders also typically include more arcane items such as factoring (or receivables financing), derivatives (e.g., swaps, etc. — Subsection [b][iv]), and certain ERISA obligations (including the Pension Benefit Guaranty Corporation's right to go after your company for any shortfall in unfunded pension obligations).

Common Exceptions

As the Borrower, you can try to negotiate exceptions, including the basic exception for **trade payables** incurred in the ordinary course (e.g., net 30 day payment terms for the purchase of goods and services — Subsection [a][iii]). Imagine if you had to pay cash up front or COD for everything; your Lender will realize that this is an expensive and impractical way to do business. Therefore, most Lenders will agree to the trade payables exception.

Other commonly negotiated exceptions include existing debt (including the loan from the Lender — subsection [a][i]), refinanced debt that doesn't hurt the Lender (e.g, refinancings that replace junior debt with junior debt or equity, or extends, rather than makes sooner, the maturity date), debt acquired in good faith as part of the acquisition of another company, short-term loans for seasonal inventory purchases, certain loans and guarantees to subsidiaries, among others.

The key is to take a close look at your business to see what your borrowing needs are and will be. For example, if you factor your receivables as a regular part of your business, you'll need to negotiate a carve-out that will allow you to continue doing that. And since factoring can either be structured as secured debt or an off-balance sheet sale of receivables or even a combination of the two, you'll need to work with your attorney to make sure that all the covenants are internally consistent, and allow you to take the contemplated action. You don't want to spend a lot of time negotiating one covenant to allow a specified type of transaction only to find out that another covenant prohibits it in a more roundabout fashion.

Another option is to negotiate a basket that allows you to make additional borrowings of subordinated debt up to the specified amount.

Don't be afraid to ask the bank for a waiver of this or any covenant in case you need one after the agreement is signed. The bank may give you the waiver if you can make the argument that the proposed financing, etc. makes you (and therefore, the bank's position) stronger. There's no need to feel trapped. Lenders may be willing to cut a deal, rather than have you prepay the loan and sever the relationship and move to another bank.

Security Interests

(a) The Borrower shall not, and the Borrower shall cause its subsidiaries to not, create, incur, assume or permit to exist any Security Interests, except:

(i) any Security Interests in favor of the Lender created under this Loan Agreement or any Loan Document [note — defined as the Loan Agreement, Promissory Notes, security agreements and any other documents entered into in connection with the loan];

(ii) Security Interests existing on the Closing Date, and disclosed in attached Exhibit [insert Exhibit number]; and

(iii) Security Interests for taxes, fees, assessments, or other governmental charges or levies, which either are not delinquent or are being contested in good faith by appropriate proceedings and for which the Borrower maintains adequate reserves.

This is the close cousin of the **debt covenant**. Also known as a **negative pledge**, the Borrower promises in Subsection (a) not to incur any security interests going forward (except the negotiated exceptions). See below for a discussion of commonly negotiated exceptions. Security interest is defined in Subsection (c), which is typically found with the other definitions in the definitions section of the Loan Agreement.

(b) The Borrower shall not, and the Borrower shall cause its subsidiaries to not, create, incur, assume, or permit to exist any agreement prohibiting or conditioning the creation or assumption of any Security Interest except pursuant to the Loan Documents.

(c) Security Interest means any assignment, charge, deed of trust, encumbrance, hypothecation, lien, mortgage, pledge, or any priority or other preferential arrangement of any kind, including, but not limited to, any title retention or conditional sale or capital lease or other transaction having substantially the same economic effect, as well as the filing of any financing statement under the Uniform Commercial Code or corresponding law of any jurisdiction.

Subsection (c) defines security interests to include all manner of encumbrances, including liens on tangible and intangible personal property, mortgages on real estate, and pledges on securities, among others.

Lenders also like to restrict encumbrances resulting from non-traditional forms of financing such as **sale-leasebacks**. A sale-leaseback is a kind of financing transaction in which the borrower sells equipment or other assets to a lender that leases it back to the borrower under an operating lease. While the lender doesn't physically control the asset, it's pretty secure because it technically owns the equipment. And by making lease payments over time, the borrower has effectively financed the equipment without incurring a formal lien. These transactions fall under the category of what are sometimes referred to as **title retention transactions** or **conditional sales**, which include any sales transaction where in lieu of a formal security interest, the seller retains title to the goods until payment in full. Most lenders will seek to restrict these transactions.

It's not enough for some Lenders to restrict third-party security interests; some Lenders (see Subsection [b]) also want to restrict the Borrower from entering into any third party agreement that restricts the creation of security interests. This sounds a bit counterintuitive, but the Lender doesn't want there to be any documents out there that restrict the ability of the Borrower to grant its security interest to the Lender, or to grant additional security to the Lender in the future.

Common Exceptions

Commonly negotiated exceptions include your existing liens (including liens granted to your Lender — Subsections [a][i] and [ii]), liens granted as part of your everyday business (e.g., purchase money security interests), certain judgment liens, mechanics liens, liens for unpaid taxes that are being contested in good faith (Subsection [a][iii]), real estate encumbrances (e.g., easements, rights of way, etc.), and liens in favor of other banks, etc. related to the Borrower's deposit accounts held at such institutions (banks typically take a security interest in deposit accounts to secure standard fees for deposit services, etc.).

You may want to negotiate an exception for things like security deposits and your obligations to your lessees or sublessees. Lessees and sublessees have rights; you can't just kick them out on a whim. Think of a landlord trying to evict his or her residential tenant — it's not so easy, even for the most unruly tenants. Or, try to sell a house that has a tenant in it to somebody who wants to move in right away. It's difficult, so in this sense, your property rights have indeed been encumbered. An aggressive Lender may seek to include these in the definition of "lien." Your attorney's job will be to ferret these out, and negotiate to exclude them.

On the flip side, note that some Lenders don't even like it if you are the lessee of **operating leases** of personal property (e.g., photocopiers, etc.). As the lessee of an operating lease, you're not encumbered because you don't even own the property, but depending on your creditability, your bank may not want to risk the lessor taking back the property and depriving you of the ability to operate your business and generate the cash flow necessary to service your debt.

Another option is to negotiate a **basket** that allows you to grant security interests securing debt up to a specified amount (dollar amount or pegged to financial criteria such as net worth).

Another tactic is to negotiate an "**equally and ratably**" provision, which prohibits new security interests in favor of third parties, but only to the extent that an identical lien is not also granted to the Lender. You'll have to consider if this is the best approach for you since you'd have to get the consent of the new creditor and the Lender to the liens granted to the other party, in the form of an **intercreditor agreement**, which can be quite lengthy and expensive (guess who pays the legal fee for preparing one of those).

Investments

(a) The Borrower shall not, and the Borrower shall cause its subsidiaries to not, lend or advance any money, property, credit or other accommodation to any Person [note — defined as a natural person or legal entity], or acquire, purchase, own or otherwise invest in the capital stock (or other ownership interest), or equity, debt or other securities of any Person.

(b) Notwithstanding the above, the Borrower may:

    (i) extend trade credit in the ordinary course of business;

    (ii) purchase readily marketable direct obligations of or obligations guaranteed by the United States or any agency thereof, with maturities of one year or less from the date of purchase;

    (iii) purchase dollar denominated certificates of deposit issued by commercial banks of recognized standing operating in the United States with capital and surplus in excess of [insert dollar amount];

(iv) purchase obligations of state, local or municipal governments or agencies, rated [insert rating, e.g., A] or better by Standard & Poor's Corporation; or

(v) purchase commercial paper maturing not later than [insert number] days after the date of creation, of any US issuer with a net worth of not less than [insert dollar amount] and then currently rated [insert rating, e.g., A-1] or [P-1] or better by Standard & Poor's Corporation or Moody's Investors Service, Inc., respectively.

This covenant prohibits you from making any investment in any other company, including your own subsidiaries. Investments is broadly defined to include equity investments (e.g., purchasing corporate stock, LLC or partnership interests, etc.) and debt investments (e.g., making loans) in any company. The Lender's goal is to prevent you from diverting any money that would otherwise be used to repay the Loan.

Common Exceptions

Subsection (b) lists some of the most commonly negotiated and uncontroversial exceptions, including payment terms you grant to your customers in the ordinary course of business as well as investments in low risk investment grade vehicles like CDs, commercial paper, and Treasury Bills and Notes. You can also carve out an exception for investments in your subsidiaries. As with many of the negative covenants, you can negotiate a **basket** to allow you to make investments up to a specified dollar amount.

Capital Expenses

The Borrower shall not incur Capital Expenditures in an amount greater than [insert dollar amount] in the aggregate in any one Fiscal Year [note — defined as the fiscal year of the Borrower, whatever that is]. The Borrower may rollover up to [insert dollar amount] of unused Capital Expenditure limitations from the prior Fiscal Year into the following Fiscal Year.

This is the sister covenant of the **Investments** covenant discussed above. While the Investments covenant prohibits the Borrower from making equity and debt investments in companies, the Capital Expenses covenant, which is commonly found in private commercial loan transactions, restricts the Borrower from making excess investments "in the business," for example, reinvesting profits to expand manufacturing capacity. As usual, you should assess your business requirements, and negotiate exceptions for any planned expansion. A **basket** or **cap** on these types of expenses, like the one provided in the sample provision, is quite common. You can negotiate a step-up for each year the loan agreement is in effect, or include special exceptions for very large projects that you are contemplating.

Distributions

The Borrower shall not declare, make, set aside any assets or funds for, or pay any dividends or distributions on, purchase, redeem, retire, or otherwise acquire any shares of capital stock of the Borrower [except dividends payable in its own common stock].

[Notwithstanding the above, the Company may declare and pay dividends on its capital stock provided that no Default or Event of Default exists before or after giving effect to such dividends or is created as a result thereof.]

This permutation works to prohibit all distributions to the shareholders or owners of the Borrower (e.g., dividends, redemption or repurchase of stock, basically any disposition of any company assets to any of the owners for any reason), as well as any payments to others such as the subordinated debtholders. From the Lender's perspective, every dollar used to pay the shareholders is one less dollar available to repay the loan. The minimum **working capital** and **net worth** financial covenants (discussed below) also work to restrict these types of payments, but only to the extent that any such payment causes your working capital or net worth to fall below the specified minimum.

Common Exceptions

While the Lender's perspective jives with the legal notion that senior debtholders like the bank rank ahead of equityholders like the shareholders, banks recognize that you also need to give your shareholders (including yourself) a fair share of the profits. One common way around the restriction is to negotiate an exception allowing you to pay dividends in the form of stock [see first bracketed language]; no cash is diverted for this purpose. Common stock is best from the Lender's perspective because unlike preferred stock, common stock comes with no strings attached (remember from Part I that preferred stockholders by definition have certain distribution rights that may interfere with the bank's rights).

Another typically negotiated exception is to craft something similar to the bracketed language that allows dividends to the extent that the Borrower is not in default (or will not be in default as a result of the the dividend). Or maybe allow cash distributions to the extent that the Borrower has net income. The bank is protected since you get to take money out only from your profits.

Related Party Transactions

(a) The Borrower shall not directly or indirectly enter into or permit to exist any agreement, understanding or other transaction with any Affiliate of the Borrower except for

    (i) transactions entered into in the ordinary course of business, and upon fair and reasonable terms that are no less favorable to the Borrower than would be obtained in an arm's length transaction with a non-affiliated Person; or

(ii) salary or compensation arrangements and benefit plans for officers, directors, and other employees of the Borrower entered into or maintained in the ordinary course of business.

(b) "Affiliate" means, with respect to any Person [note — defined as a natural person or legal entity], any Person that owns or controls directly or indirectly such Person, any Person that controls or is controlled by or is under common control with such Person, and each of such Person's stockholders or owners, directors, and officers.

An **affiliate** is any party (e.g., a person or company) that can exercise legal control over or be controlled by another party. Affiliates also include companies under common control by somebody else. Lenders sometimes peg the concept of control to a specified percent ownership or the ability to elect the management. The most basic example is a parent company, its stockholders (upstream) and its wholly-owned (i.e., 100 percent owned) subsidiaries (downstream). Every person or company in that scenario is an affiliate of every other person or company in that scenario. At the other end of the spectrum, it's hard to argue with a straight face that you are an affiliate of Walmart because you own 100 shares of its stock. It becomes less clear somewhere in the middle of the spectrum, although some Lenders will peg "control" at just 5 percent share ownership. Subsection (b) is a typical generic definition of affiliates, usually found in the separate definitions section of the Loan Agreement, but placed here to facilitate discussion of this covenant.

An **affiliate transaction** (also known as a **related party transaction**) is any transaction (e.g., contract, understanding or other relationship for the sale of goods or services, license agreement, or any business transaction) entered into between the company (in this case, the Borrower) and any of its affiliates, including its shareholders or owners. Lenders have a problem with these transactions because these inside transactions may contain non-arm's-length provisions that favor the insider at the expense of the Borrower. Terms that are not so favorable to the Borrower tend to take away potential net worth or cash flow that would otherwise be used to service the debt to the Lender.

Common Exceptions — You'll need to negotitate an exception for existing transactions if you have any, including employment agreements or arrangements (remember, a director or shareholder is considered an "affiliate" by most Lenders — Subsection [a][i]). Another common tactic is to carve out an exception for affiliate transactions that contain fair market terms (Subsection [a][ii]). Try to keep good records of market conditions, so you can prove to the bank that your terms and conditions are arm's length.

Financial Covenants

Financial covenants are unique to lending documents; they are not found in sale of business (asset purchase or stock purchase) agreements.

Lenders use financial covenants in tandem with the **negative covenants** to achieve the main objective — to limit the Borrower's monetary outlays so that there is enough cushion to both run the business and repay the loan. For example, most Loan Agreements have negative covenants that restrict capital expenses and distributions outright (with of course, the negotiated exceptions), and at the same time they also have financial covenants like the minimum working capital covenant (discussed below), that works to restrict capital expenses and distributions but only to the extent that they cause working capital to fall below the specified minimum.

Lenders, especially of cash-flow-based traditional loans, look to the financial condition of the Borrower, as reflected in the pre-Closing financial statements, to make its lending decisions.

Since the loan is an ongoing relationship, however, the Lender will insist that you maintain some baseline level of financial performance throughout the life of the loan. In some cases, the Lender will actually require you to improve your financial condition as time goes on. The financial covenants establish these negotiated baseline levels of performance. I'll discuss just the most common financial covenants. These include mostly balance sheet covenants establishing minimum standards for net worth, working capital, and debt/equity ratios.

Balance sheet covenants include any financial covenant based on information contained in the company's balance sheet. In addition to the net worth, **working capital**, and **debt/equity ratio covenants**, and depending on your creditability and how aggressive your Lender is, it might also request balance sheet covenants relating to how much debt you have compared to your assets or capital, or even covenants mandating a certain level of profits or cash flow (pretty severe). **Coverage covenants** are another type of financial covenant, and quantify how the company is doing based on information contained in the company's income or cash flow statements. See the **Financial Terminology Quick Primer** below for a basic summary of financial statement terminology.

Lending attorneys often think of the financial covenants in terms of landmine tripwires. A Borrower whose financial condition (as measured by a particular financial covenant) significantly deteriorates "trips the wire" (i.e., established by the baseline level of performance), which leads to calamity. In the case of an actual land mine, the calamity is a devastating explosion. In the case of loan, the calamity is a technical default or event of default of the Loan Agreement, even if the Borrower is completely on time with all of its payments.

That being said, most banks want to set the trip wire standards high because they want to be able to catch problems early enough so they can negotiate some kind of solution or workout before your condition deteriorates further towards insolvency. Keep in mind that legally, any 11th hour deal cut by one creditor at the expense of other creditors risks being overturned in bankruptcy by the trustee, so Lenders want to catch and then work with you to fix any problems while the business is still reasonably healthy.

Banks have a certain degree of self-interest to avoid formal action that may force you into bankruptcy because then they'll end up competing with other creditors for your assets. But in a recessionary environment, banks may not be as willing to accommodate if you default, and alternative sources of funding (i.e., refinancing) may be difficult to secure, even for creditworthy companies. Work with your attorney to research and then negotiate reasonably attainable financial covenant standards in your marketplace.

Commercial business loans typically contain **maintenance covenants**, as opposed to **incurrence covenants**, which are more prevalent in public debt offerings. Most financial maintenance covenants require compliance at all times, yet small-business Borrowers (and even most banks) don't have the resources to be constantly monitoring for compliance. Indeed, the very financial reports that are used to measure compliance are required only periodically, and even then not in real time. In other words, in most instances, unless the default is egregious, you'll know about the breach before the Lender. So to avoid any chance of a technical default, work with your attorney if possible to designate the time for which satisfaction of the financial covenants is to be measured.

Here are basic versions of some of the most common financial covenants.

Net Worth (a.k.a., Shareholders' Equity)

The Borrower shall maintain at all times a [Consolidated] Net Worth of not less than [insert dollar amount].

[Alternative] The Borrower shall not permit its [Consolidated] Net Worth as of the end of any fiscal quarter [year] of the Borrower to be less than [insert dollar amount].

Much like you would calculate your personal net worth, a company's **net worth** is the difference between the value of its total assets and total liabilities. For a summary discussion of these concepts, please see the **Financial Terminology Quick Primer** below. Many Lenders tighten the reins and limit net worth to **tangible net worth**, meaning that they don't allow you to include hard-to-measure and illiquid intangibles like goodwill (remember that many small companies don't have transferable goodwill, and that the buyer should not have to pay for something that is likely to dissipate soon after the closing) and trademarks in your calculation of net worth.

Lenders want Borrowers to maintain a minimum specified dollar amount of net worth to ensure that the Borrower always has a cushion of funds in excess of what it needs to repay the loan before any of the owners get their share. The sample provision also includes the subsidiaries of the Borrower on a consolidated basis.

Consider negotiating something similar to the [alternative], which measures the net worth at the end of the reporting period; that is, does not require you to maintain the minimum net worth "at all times." Remember that unless you suffer a catastrophic event, it's difficult for you to tell whether you're maintaining the minimum net worth "at all times" since you prepare your balance sheets only once per quarter and typically deliver them 45 days after the fact.

The bracketed alternative reflects the reality that it's not practical for the bank to check up on you 24/7/365. Typically, given its and your resources, it has no choice but to wait until it receives your quarterly balance sheet to see if you've complied with your financial covenants. Nevertheless, some Lenders may be loath to agree to the less-strict standard because it tolerates non-compliant, mid-period transactions, as long as you clean up your act come balance sheet time.

Financial Terminology Quick Primer

Your accountant and attorney can guide you on balance sheet and income statement matters, but here's a very brief description of some of the terminology you're likely to encounter.

Balance sheets present a summary snapshot of a company's financial condition at the designated point in time (e.g., year-end, half-year-end, quarter-end, or month-end). It shows the company's total assets, total liabilities, and net worth.

Total assets include current assets and long-term assets, and total liabilities include current liabilities and long-term liabilities.

Current assets include cash and certain assets that can be converted to cash in less than one year (e.g., marketable securities, receivables, inventory, etc.).

Current liabilities (a.k.a., current debt or payables) include all money owed and due within one year.

Long-term assets include the company's equipment, real estate and other capital assets (generally, tangible assets that can't be readily converted to cash in the ordinary course of business) to be used more than one year, adjusted for depreciation, if applicable.

Long-term debt includes loans or other obligations with a maturity date of longer than one year. Revolving loans straddle the line between current and long-term debt. Individual revolver advances often look like separate short-term loans (e.g., each is evidenced by a separate promissory notes) with different interest rates. On the other hand, many revolvers don't require repayment within one year.

Net worth (a.k.a., shareholders' equity for corporations, and owners' equity for other legal entities) is the difference between the value of company's total assets and total liabilities.

An **income statement** is a summary of sales, expenses, and net profit for the designated time period (e.g., year, six months, quarter, or month).

> **Net profit,** a.k.a., the bottom line, net income, or net earnings, is the dollar figure obtained by subtracting the company's total expenses from its total or gross revenue (i.e., sales amount). If this number is positive, then the company made a profit during the designated time period (a.k.a., "in the black"). If the number is less than zero, then the company lost money (a.k.a., "in the red").

Working Capital

The Borrower shall at all times maintain Working Capital of not less than [insert dollar amount]. "Working Capital" means the excess of the current assets over the current liabilities of the Borrower.

[Alternative] The Borrower shall not permit its Working Capital as of the end of any fiscal quarter [year] of the Borrower to be less than [insert dollar amount].

Working capital is a kind of liquidity index for the company, and is defined as the difference between the company's (including subsidiairies if measured on a consolidated basis) current assets and current liabilities. Working capital shows the Lender the amount of cash (and liquifiable assets like receivables and inventory) available to the Borrower, and quantifies the Borrower's ability to meet its short term obligations and to weather a bad spell in the business. I've included both the stricter "at all times" and less strict "as of the end of the fiscal quarter [year]" alternatives.

A high working capital requirement essentially sets aside any money otherwise available to expand the business, make capital improvements, make shareholder distributions, etc. This, of course, is the *raison d'être* of the working capital covenant because any cash used for those purposes would no longer be available (or in the case of things like capital assets, not available until you liquidate them outside the ordinary course of business) to repay the Loan.

As usual, you have the freedom of contract to negotiate this provision, including tweaking the definition of current assets and current liabilities for purposes of the working capital definition. For example, revolving loans are a grey area since many borrowers don't repay them within one year. Whether your revolvers are included in your current liabilities may have a substantial impact on working capital, and indirectly on your ability to expand your plant, pay dividends, etc.

The Lender will use the negative covenants in tandem with the financial covenants to achieve its objectives. For example, most Loan Agreements have negative covenants that outright restrict capital expenses and distributions (with negotiated exceptions), at the same time they also have financial covenants like the minimum working capital covenant that works to restrict capital expenses and distributions but only to the extent that they cause working capital to fall below the specified minimum.

Debt/Equity Ratio

The Borrower shall maintain at all times a ratio of [Consolidated] Debt to [Consolidated] Shareholders Equity of not less than [insert ratio].

[Alternative] The Borrower shall not permit, as of the end of any fiscal quarter [year] of the Borrower, the ratio of [Consolidated] Debt over [Consolidated] Shareholders Equity to be less than [insert ratio].

This maintenance (as opposed to incurrence, more on this below) version of the debt/equity covenant requires you to maintain a ratio of total debt to shareholder's equity below the specified threshold at all times. Shareholder's equity is also known as net worth. Lenders want this ratio to be as low as possible; it wants the debt in the numerator to be low compared to the net worth reflected in the denominator. And the Lender can make it just that much tougher for you to comply with this covenant by changing net worth to tangible net worth. Tangible net worth excludes hard to quantify and illiquid intangibles like goodwill. You won't be able to borrow additional funds against your intangibles. I've included both the stricter "at all times" and less strict "as of the end of the fiscal quarter [year]" alternatives.

Unlike the **debt negative covenant** (discussed above), this covenant doesn't outright restrict debt, or certain types of debt. Rather, the **debt/equity ratio financial covenant** allows you to incur additional debt (which is permitted by the debt negative covenant) as long as your net worth increases by the same relative amount. By the same token, since the acceptable level of debt is pegged to a ratio, it's possible for you to breach this covenant down the road if your company suffers poor financial results even if you reduce your total debt.

Maintenance covenants (versus incurrence covenants) are par for the course in commercial business loans and other private loan transactions. If you were to seek money in a public debt offering, then this covenant would be structured as an incurrence covenant, where the Borrower promises not to incur debt only if the new debt causes the total debt to fail the formula. In an incurrence covenant, the level of debt is not "continuously" monitored by formula.

Current Ratio

The Borrower shall maintain at all times a ratio of current assets over current liabilities of not less than [insert ratio].

[Alternative] The Borrower shall not permit, as of the end of any fiscal quarter [year] of the Borrower, the ratio of current assets over current liabilities to be less than [insert ratio].

There are many other ratio covenants besides the debt/equity ratio. Ratios monitor the relative relationship between the figure in the numerator and the figure in the denominator. Therefore, rather than placing a hard cap on any number, the Borrower is in compliance as long as the quotient of the two numbers remains above (or below, depending on the covenant) the specified ratio. I've included both the stricter "at all times" and less strict "as of the end of the fiscal quarter [year]" alternatives.

The **current ratio** (a.k.a., **cash ratio**) covenant is one of the most commonly requested financial covenants, and is closely related to the working capital covenant (discussed above). Both types of covenants work to indirectly restrict the ability of the Borrower to expand its business, make capital improvements, make shareholder distributions, etc. But rather than comparing the difference between the Borrower's current assets and its current liabilities, the current ratio is a fraction with the current assets in the numerator and the current liabilities in the denominator. The Borrower must maintain this ratio above the specified level at all times. If you have a high current ratio, this means that you have the ability to pay your current (i.e., short-term) liabilities. If your ratio is less than one, this means that you are unable to meet your current liabilities.

Some Lenders like the stricter version of the current ratio called the the **quick asset ratio** (a.k.a., acid test). It's the same ratio as the current ratio, but replaces current assets in the numerator with its stripped down version (i.e., just the really liquid assets like cash, marketable securities and good receivables, subtracting out bad receivables and inventory). The acid test, which derives its name from the traditional mining technique of testing the authenticity of gold by submerging the nuggets in acid (gold doesn't corrode in acid), measures the ability of the Borrower to meet its current liabilities without having to sell off its inventory. If you are a retailer, you're likely to have a quick asset ratio that is far lower than your current ratio.

21

GUARANTIES

OVERVIEW

In the loan context, a Guaranty is a separate independent agreement entered into by somebody (Guarantor) to perform the obligations (e.g., pay the debt, perform the covenants, etc.), of the Borrower under the Loan Documents (including the Loan Agreement, Promissory Notes, etc.), in case the Borrower cannot or does not. Because the Guarantor is not on the hook immediately, a guaranty is a contingent obligation, which allows the Guarantor to back up the obligations of the Borrower, without having to drain any cash or resources up front. Depending on the creditability of your business (e.g., a new business with little track record) and your corporate structure (e.g., you start a new subsidiary to start a related but separate business), your bank may require either a guaranty from the Borrower's corporate parent (if any) or a personal guaranty from you (as the owner of the business).

Keep in mind that if you sign a personal guaranty, this means that you are contractually waiving the protection of your **corporate shield** (if your business is a corporation, LLC, etc.), that is, you are allowing the bank to look to your personal assets in case your business cannot or does not meet its obligations. And in most cases, banks draft guaranties to allow them to go after you personally even before they exhaust any remedies against your company, and perhaps in spite of any defenses that your company itself may have (in its capacity as a borrower) to non-payment.

Once the Guarantor performs, it has the right (i.e., **subrogation**) to seek reimbursement from the Borrower. Essentially, the Guarantor becomes a creditor of the Borrower, and succeeds to the rights of the Lender, including the right to enforce any security interests. If you guarantee the obligations of a business of which you are the sole owner, then this isn't too much of an issue. If you are one of several

Guarantors, however, then it becomes quite a bit more tangled. You'll also have to worry about **contribution** issues, where each Guarantor has the right to pursue the other Guarantors for their respective agreed-to portions (based on percentage ownership of the Borrower or by negotiated agreement).

Note that there are alternatives to issuing a Guaranty. Some banks will accept a **comfort letter** from the Borrower's corporate parent, in which the issuer either indicates that it is aware of the loan or promises not to do anything to cause its subsidiary to breach the Loan Documents. Banks are unlikely to accept a comfort letter in lieu of a guaranty unless the Guarantor is very large and creditworthy, or perhaps because the Guarantor is hamstrung, in that it's not permitted by its own credit documents to provide any Guaranties. Many Lenders require negative debt covenants that characterize any kind of credit support, from a full-blown guaranty to a comfort letter, the same way — that is, "can't do it."

Guaranties are just like any other contract, and will have various and sundry boilerplate (see Part V and the CD-ROM), tax and other provisions, not to mention representations and warranties of the the Guarantor. Since these types of provisions are already discussed in other parts of the book, I'll focus on just the several provisions that are unique to Guaranties.

SAMPLE CONTRACT EXCERPTS
The Guaranty

> The Guarantor hereby absolutely, unconditionally, and irrevocably guarantees the full and punctual (i) payment when due of each and every obligation of the Borrower to the Lender under [the Loan Documents], whether at stated maturity, upon acceleration, demand or otherwise, and (ii) performance when due of all other terms, conditions, covenants and other obligations of the Borrower under [the Loan Documents], in each case, whether now owed or hereafter incurred, direct or indirect, absolute or contingent, joint or several, or matured or unmatured (collectively the "Guaranteed Obligations").

This is basic language pursuant to which the Guarantor guarantees the prompt and complete payment of all amounts due under the Loan Documents (e.g., Loan Agreement, Promissory Note(s), etc.) and the prompt and complete performance of all of its convenants and other terms and conditions of such documents. This version limits the Guarantor's exposure to just the Borrower's obligations under the Loan Documents (and its own obligations to comply with the Guaranty).

Your bank, however, might require **blanket language** requiring you to guarantee "all obligations of the Borrower to the Lender," without referring to any specific transaction or loan agreement. This makes it easier for the bank to extend your company new credit (I'm talking about a completely new loan, rather than just another advance under a revolver), without having to worry whether it needs to obtain a new guaranty. If you guarantee the obligations of a business of which you are the sole owner, it may not make a difference. But if you are just a part owner (or a passive owner with no working knowledge of the capital needs of the company), then this kind of blanket guaranty is worrisome because it will cover new facilities whether or not you approve of them.

Keep in mind that even if you are a part owner, and are one of several guarantors, that you can limit your exposure by negotiating a hard dollar-cap or percentage limit (*vis-à-vis* the other guarantors) on your liability.

There are a lot of buzz words in this provision — "absolute," "unconditional," "irrevocable," etc. You'll encounter these and others like "continuing guaranty" in more than one place in a Guaranty, and I'll discuss these concepts below.

Absolute, Unconditional, and Irrevocable Liability of the Guarantor

The obligations of the Guarantor under this Guaranty are absolute, unconditional, irrevocable, and continuing, and except for the indefeasible payment or performance in full of the Guaranteed Obligations, are not affected by any circumstance whatsoever which may constitute a defense available to, or a legal or equitable discharge of, the Borrower (or any guarantor or surety), whether foreseen or unforeseen or similar or dissimilar to any defense or waiver set forth in this Guaranty.

This provision goes into a little more detail regarding the common guaranty buzz words. Put it all together, and the Guarantor's obligations are not affected (meaning not subject to any discharge, impairment, limitation, reduction, or termination) for any reason whatsoever, except, of course, the indefeasible full payment of all of the Guarantied Obligations. Note that this provision refers to the waiver provision discussed below.

A Guaranty is **absolute** or **unconditional** if its effectiveness doesn't depend on any condition (e.g., the Lender's acceptance, etc.). Some attorneys equate absolute and unconditional with the concept of guaranty of payment (discussed below). When you see "absolute and unconditional" language in your guaranty, this basically means that you are fully liable to perform all of your obligations under the guaranty as soon as you sign it.

An **irrevocable** guaranty is one that the Guarantor cannot terminate prematurely; it terminates only when the Guarantied Obligations have been indefeasibly paid in full. A commonly negotiated partial "out" is a provision that allows the Guarantor to terminate the guaranty, but only as to future obligations. You'd still be liable as to the existing debt.

Many Guaranties have a separate provision dealing with the "**continuing guaranty**" concept. I've included a sample below, where I discuss this concept in more detail.

Guaranty of Payment (versus Collection)

The obligations of the Guarantor under this Guaranty constitute a guaranty of payment and not of collection only, without setoff or counterclaim, in US dollars. As such, there is no requirement that the Lender, as a condition of payment by the Guarantor:

(i) proceed against [or exhaust its rights and remedies against] the Borrower, any other guarantor of the Guaranteed Obligations or any other Person [note — defined as any natural person or legal entity], or any security received from any of the above;

(ii) pursue any other remedy whatsoever.

Lenders want to travel the path of least resistence to recovery, and will insist on this provision. They want to be able to collect from the Guarantor immediately, and if they have to sue, they want to be in a position to obtain immediate relief, ideally in the form of a summary judgment (a quick civil litigation procedure used by the judge to decide a case without a trial when there is no dispute as to the material facts of the case; in other words, the Lender prevails as a matter of law).

A **guaranty of payment** means that the Lender can enforce the Guaranty right away; it doesn't have to first take any action (e.g., initiate a lawsuit or other proceeding, or enforce any security interest) against the Borrower, or any other person (e.g., another shareholder, etc.), that may have also guaranteed the loan. The sample provision throws in the bracketed language, which may be a bit superfluous since the Lender doesn't even have to begin any proceeding, much less exhaust its remedies against the Borrower before it can enforce the Guaranty. The provision clarifies that the Lender doesn't have to do anything versus the Borrower or its assets before enforcing the Guaranty.

A **guaranty of collection** requires the Lender to first exhaust its remedies against the Borrower before it can enforce the Guaranty. Therefore, the Lender would have to lawfully repossess all available collateral, sell the collateral and pay itself the debt, initiate a lawsuit against the Borrower for any deficiency, win the lawsuit, enforce the judgment and have the judgment returned unsatisfied (i.e., almost force the Borrower into bankruptcy, etc. — you get the idea), before it can enforce the Guaranty. And it has to go after the Borrower with some gusto, or due diligence, not just go through the motions. A guaranty of collection is better for the Guarantor, if you can get it, because it ties the Lender's hands so that it can't go after your personal assets until it exhausts every avenue of recovery against your company.

Continuing Guaranty

This Guaranty is a continuing inexhaustible guaranty, without limitation as to duration, and may not be revoked, and remains in full force and effect and is binding in accordance with its terms until the indefeasible payment in full of all Guaranteed Obligations.

The Guarantor's payment of any portion of the Guaranteed Obligations does not affect or reduce the Guarantor's liability for any portion of the Guaranteed Obligations that has not been indefeasibly paid in full.

A **continuing guaranty** is one that has indefinite duration, that is, remains in effect until the loan (principal, interest, all fees, etc.) for all advances (including any future advances made under a revolver) have been indefeasibly (i.e., can't be overturned, etc.), paid in full. Some guaranties clarify that the guaranty remains in effect even if under a revolver, the outstanding balance is temporarily zero.

Waivers of Defenses

In theory, Guarantors have a variety of rights to contest payment under the Guaranty (defenses). A Guaranty, however, is a contract, and the parties have the "freedom of contract" to negotiate terms and conditions that alter or even take away some of these rights. Since banks generally have a lot of negotiating leverage, Guaranties tend to be very one-sided in favor of the bank and you end up waiving everything. I've included a selection of commonly requested waivers. There are quite a few, and many Lenders will ask you to waive pretty much all of your defenses. In some cases, they'll overkill by asking you to waive defenses that are not even available to you because they're already incorporated into the buzz-word concepts discussed above.

Note that many Guaranties have a combined provision including either long-form or short-form versions of all the waivers it wants you to give. I've decided to present the waivers topically, to better facilitate discussion of the issues.

Commonly requested waivers include the following:

Waiver of Notices

The Guarantor waives any and all notices, including, but not limited to, notice of (a) acceptance, (b) the (i) creation or incurrence, or (ii) modification, renewal or extention of any of the Guaranteed Obligations, or (iii) default or dishonor.

Notice of Acceptance

Typically, only the Guarantor signs the Guaranty; there's no need for the Lender to countersign. So in theory, there's always the question of whether the Lender knows about and "agrees" to be the beneficiary of the Guaranty. Practically, it's a moot point because nobody really volunteers to give a Guaranty without being asked. But just in case, Subsection (a) asks you to waive your right to receive formal notice from the Lender that it, in fact, accepts your Guaranty. Some Guaranties will supplement by asking you to waive any "proof of reliance by the Lender" upon the Guaranty.

Notice of Incurrence/Modification

Subsection (b) asks you to waive any notice of new advances of the loan, as well as any modification of the terms and conditions of the loan.

Notice of Default

In Subsection (c), the Guarantor waives the right to receive any notice that the Borrower has defaulted on the underlying loan. So in theory, if you grant this waiver, you won't know about the Borrower's failure to make a loan payment until the Lender tries to enforce the Guaranty against you. This may not make much of a practical difference if you are the sole owner and run the day-to-day operations of the Borrower, but it may be an issue if you're a passive investor with minimal contact. No matter your status, try to negotiate the elimination of this waiver; Lenders may appreciate that you want to be notified so that you can help the Borrower dig itself out of the hole without resorting to your Guaranty.

Note that some Guaranties will add the similar **notice of protest** and **demand for payment** waivers to Subsection (c), or add a **waiver of presentment**, meaning that the Lender doesn't have to present (i.e., show) the Guaranty to you in order to enforce it.

Waiver of Guaranty of Collection Rights

The Guarantor waives any requirement that the Lender, as a condition of payment by the Guarantor:

(i) proceed against [or exhaust its rights and remedies against] the Borrower, any other guarantor of the Guaranteed Obligations or any other Person [note — defined as any natural person or legal entity], or any security received from any of the above;

(ii) pursue any other remedy whatsoever.

This waiver is somewhat superfluous if you've agreed to make a **guaranty of payment** (discussed above). The waiver tracks the language in that provision and confirms the Guarantor's waiver of any right to insist that the Lender first proceed or exhaust it remedies against the Borrower, any other guarantor, or any collateral securing the Guaranteed Obligations, before the Lender can enforce the Guaranty.

Waiver of Subrogation and Related Rights

The Guarantor waives any and all rights of contribution, indemnification, recoupment, recourse, reimbursement, and subrogation.

In this provision, the Guarantor waives its significant right to recoup from the Borrower whatever it's paid to the Lender under the Guaranty. Once the Guarantor performs, it has the right (i.e., **subrogation**) to seek reimbursement from the Borrower.

Essentially, the Guarantor becomes a creditor of the Borrower, and steps into the shoes, and succeeds to the rights, of the Lender, including the right to enforce any security interests. The Guarantor also has the right to seek **contribution** from other guarantors for their *pro rata* shares. The other buzz words follow along the same lines.

Lenders started to add this waiver in response to the Deprizio legal case, which subjected creditors to increased risks (of having any payments made to them avoided by a bankruptcy trustee) when they obtained so-called "insider" guaranties (i.e., guaranties from parties like owners who are related to the Borrower). Even though Congress essentially repealed the DePrizio doctrine, Lenders still request this waiver.

The right of subrogation and the other recoupment rights are pretty basic rights. Even though the Lender may argue that your Guaranty is an "independent" obligation, you know that the Lender knows that when you pay under your Guaranty, you're essentially making payment "on behalf of" the Borrower. And since the Lender has been made whole, why shouldn't you be entitled to make yourself whole by recouping from the Borrower? If at all possible, negotiate to keep these rights (that is, to not waive them).

If the Lender allows you to keep your subrogation rights, then expect it to place restrictions on those rights. For example, it may not allow you to exercise your subrogation rights until the all the Guaranteed Obligations have been paid in full. So you won't be able to make a partial payment under your Guaranty, and then immediately go after the Borrower. You'll have to wait until the Lender is paid in full, either by the Borrower, or via your or other Guaranties. This means that if you receive any payment (in regards to the loan; you should get to keep your salary) from the Borrower, you'll need to turn it over to the Lender.

Waiver of Suretyship Defenses

The Guarantor waives any and all defenses based on suretyship.

As discussed above, provided that you (the Guarantor) don't waive your right of subrogation, then you are permitted, after performing your obligations under the Guaranty, to step into the shoes, and succeed to the rights of the Lender, and therefore to recover payment from the Borrower (e.g., via subrogation, reimbursement, etc.). Your right to recover from the Borrower is only as strong as your ability to prevent the Lender from acting or failing to act (either unilaterally or in agreement with the Borrower) in a way that makes it more difficult for you to seek this recovery. A **suretyship defense** is a legal right belonging to the Guarantor that helps to prevent the Lender from impairing your right of recovery. If you are able to successfully raise this defense, then you stand a good chance to be discharged from your Guaranty obligations. If you waive your suretyship defenses (as provided in this sample contract provision), then you're pretty much at the Lender's mercy.

Some basic examples of suretyship defenses include your potential right to be released from your Guaranty obligations if the Lender, without your consent, modifies the underlying loan to increase your exposure (e.g., increases the amount of the Guaranteed Obligations, grants an extension of time for repayment or other accommodation to the Borrower, etc.), impairs the collateral (e.g., reduces the value of any collateral in its possession, fails to create or perfect (or maintain a perfected) security interest, releases the collateral without replacing it, etc.), or fails to take action against the Borrower within the statute of limitations.

Many Lenders will go further, and include Consent provisions, pursuant to which the Guarantor affirmatively consents to any action the Lender takes to modify the Guaranteed Obligations, including extensions of time to make payment, and other accommodations to the Borrower that would normally trigger some kind of surety defense and discharge the Guarantor's obligations under the Guaranty.

Waiver of Borrower Defenses

The Guarantor waives any and all defenses that the Borrower or any other Person [note — defined as any natural person or legal entity] may have with respect to the Guaranteed Obligations or this Guaranty, including, but not limited to:

(a) the illegality, lack of validity or unenforceability of (i) the Guaranteed Obligations, or (ii) any security or any other guarantee for the Guaranteed Obligations,

(b) the lack of perfection of any security for the Guaranteed Obligations;

(c) the discharge, release, or cessation of the liability of the Borrower or any other Person under the Guaranteed Obligations or any security or guaranty therefore arising from any cause whatsoever (other than by reason of the full indefeasible payment and discharge of the Guaranteed Obligations), whether by operation of law or act or omission of the Lender or otherwise.

In addition to its suretyship defenses, the Guarantor can also latch onto any defenses available to the Borrower as the primary obligor (**Borrower Defenses**). In other words, if the Borrower has a defense that will allow it not to pay the loan, then the Guarantor can step into the shoes of the Borrower and assert those defenses in order not to pay under the Guaranty. Most Lenders require that Guarantors waive these Borrower Defenses. If at all possible, negotiate to not waive any Borrower Defenses.

Legal Status of the Loan

By agreeing to Subsection (a), the Guarantor waives any right to raise any defense related to the legal status of the underlying transaction between the Lender and the Borrower (e.g., the Guaranteed Obligations, the loan agreement, etc.). These include a variety of Business Law 101-type issues, for example, the loan is illegal (or contains illegal terms, for example, is usurious), was entered into by mistake or fraudulent inducement, under duress, or any party lacked the legal capacity to enter into the transaction. Other issues include lack of consideration, failure to comply with the statute of frauds (i.e., loan should have been in writing), ultra vires (i.e., borrowing money is beyond the power of the Borrower per its corporate charter, etc.), lack of proper corporate action to authorize the loan transaction (not approved by the board of directors, or signature by an unauthorized officer), or lender liability issues that contaminate the loan, etc.

Invalid Security Interest

There's some overlap between Subsection (b) and the impairment of collateral concept in Waiver of Suretyship Defenses discussed above.

Any Discharge of the Obligations of the Borrower

Subsection (c) is a kind of catch-all provision that captures any cessation of the Borrower's liability. For example, if the Borrower becomes bankrupt, then its liability under the Guaranteed Obligations may be discharged, perhaps only partially, but that still means that the Borrower owes less. You can try to argue that if the Borrower's liability has been reduced, then so should the Lender's under the Guaranty; but good luck making that argument since Lenders require third party guaranties mainly because they are worried about the Borrower going bankrupt. However, you might have more luck negotiating your not being liable for any post-bankruptcy petition charges (which can be significant, e.g., interest, etc. accruing after the bankruptcy petition), that are discharged as to the Borrower.

It might be easier to carve out any contractually agreed settlement of the debt, for example, the partial payment by the Borrower in exchange for the extinguishment of the entire debt (e.g., the Lender says to the Borrower, "Pay me ten cents to the dollar on the debt, and we'll call it even"). If the Lender and the Borrower agree to reduce the Borrower's debt this way, it seems unfair for you to foot the difference (i.e., pay the ninety cents to the dollar that the Borrower doesn't pay).

Reinstatement

This Guaranty continues to be effective if at any time any payment (in whole or in part) of any of the Guaranteed Obligations is rescinded or must otherwise be repaid by the Lender in connection with the insolvency, bankruptcy, or reorganization or similar proceeding as though such payment had not been made.

Normally, the indefeasible (i.e., think "final") payment of any amount by the Borrower discharges the liability of the Borrower under the Loan Agreement and/or Promissory Note, and the liability of the Guarantor under the Guaranty, by that amount. But any payment made by the Borrower to the Lender close to when the Borrower becomes bankrupt may need to be returned to become part of the bankruptcy estate (the pool of the now bankrupt Borrower's remaining assets to be divided up among the creditors). Any such payment is not an indefeasible payment, and this provision protects the Lender by reinstating the Guaranty by the amount returned to the estate. From a legal perspective, it's as though such payments were never made.

Part V
STANDARD CONTRACT CLAUSES

22

BOILERPLATE IN GENERAL

OVERVIEW

Tucked away at the end of many contracts are a bunch of provisions with esoteric sounding names like Force Majeure, Third-Party Beneficiaries, and Successors and Assigns. These are commonly referred to as boilerplate. Many small businesses (and attorneys across the board) eschew a thorough review of boilerplate because they believe that the provisions are inconsequential — "no worries, it's just legalese." And if you work up the nerve to ask for any revisions from the large corporation sitting across the table, you're likely to get the response, "This is our standard boiler-plate. We can't change any of it without our general counsel's permission." Facing a brick wall, many small businesses slink away, taking away the silver lining that it's probably better to be focusing on the "deal points" anyway. This strategy, or rather, non-strategy is fraught with risk.

Like many provisions of a contract, boilerplate works to allocate risk among the parties. Provided you don't violate public policy, you generally have the freedom to negotiate these provisions in a way that suits your needs.

Let's use the Force Majeure provision (discussed in more detail on the CD-ROM included with this book) to illustrate the folly of readily agreeing to any provision put in front of you (or, willy nilly, using any form you find on the Internet). Force Majeure provisions suspend the obligation to perform a contract if performance is impossible or impracticable due to circumstances beyond the reasonable control of the obligor. Force Majeure provisions frequently contain a litany of events that excuse the parties from performance.

A classic example is a natural disaster, like a flood that forces the shutdown of a factory that has a contract to produce goods for you, the customer. Granted, many businesses go through their entire life cycle without ever dealing with a flood. But if you are purchasing goods from a company with its primary manufacturing facility located below sea level next to a 100 year old levee, then it's a good idea for you to negotiate the deletion of "floods" from the list. You might even go one step further and add a provision to clarify that floods are specifically excluded from Force Majeure. If the vendor agrees, then it is agreeing to absorb the risk of floods; in other words, if there's a flood that prevents or impairs its performance, it counts as a breach rather than a no-fault force majeure event.

There are risks associated with even the most innocuous looking boilerplate — for example, the Notice provision discussed on the CD-ROM included with this book. The Notice provision provides the procedures of how the parties must communicate with each other on important matters like breach of contract, termination of contract, delivery of purchase orders, unilateral price changes, etc. Generally, notices have to be in writing, but many contracts still limit communications to old methods like certified mail, fax, personal delivery, or reputable private courier such as FedEx, DHL, or UPS. If you want to text message (not recommended) or email official notices, you've got to negotiate the notice provision to include these other methods; otherwise, you'll give your counterparty ammunition to argue, for example, that the termination notice you sent was not effective to terminate the contract because you didn't send it by one of the required methods.

Given space constraints, a lot of the boilerplate content is included on the CD-ROM that accompanies this book. On the CD-ROM, you will find information on:

- Contract front matter
- Term
- Apportionment of liability
- Force majeure
- Dispute resolution
- Notices
- Waivers
- Entire agreement
- Amendments
- Third-party beneficiaries
- Assignment and delegation
- Successors and assigns
- Taxes
- Indemnification
- Miscellaneous

Keep reading for information on:

- Termination
- Remedies and limitation of liability
- Severability

23

TERMINATION

OVERVIEW

The contract's termination provisions give one or both parties the right to cancel or terminate the agreement in advance of the contract's natural expiration date usually because of an unhappy event — for example, contract breach or the death, bankruptcy, or other intervening event that has caused the other party to default in its obligations or not be in a position to fulfill its obligations.

Some contracts distinguish between **defaults** and **events of default**. If the termination provision has a cure period (a.k.a., grace period), then the event in question (breach, etc.), constitutes a default. If the defaulting party hasn't cured the default within the cure or grace period, then the default turns into an event of default, which entitles the other party to exercise its rights and remedies. If the provision does not have a cure period, then non-compliance is an event of default and the non-defaulting party is entitled to exercise its rights and remedies. Termination is usually just one of these rights. It will also be entitled to exercise a host of remedies, including the right to claim monetary damages, seek equitable relief, and other relief).

Keep in mind as you read this chapter that these provisions often are combined in business contracts. As usual, however, I separate them by subtopic (e.g., termination for breach, termination for bankruptcy, etc.) to facilitate a discussion of the separate concepts. You don't necessarily have to terminate the contract in order to seek remedies. Consult with your attorney on a post-breach strategy best suited to your situation.

SAMPLE CONTRACT EXCERPTS
Termination for Cause (Breach)

Either party may terminate [cancel] this Agreement forthwith by notice to the other party if such other party fails to perform any of its [material] obligations under this Agreement [or any other agreement it is a party to], and such failure is not cured within __ days after notice thereof [or in case of such other agreement(s), the applicable cure period provided for in such agreement(s)].

This provision allows the non-breaching party to cancel the agreement if the other party breaches the agreement and doesn't cure the breach within the specified number of days after notice of the breach.

The non-breaching party first sends a notice of breach to the defaulting/breaching party. The breaching party then has the specified number of days to cure the breach. The specified number of days depends on the negotiating leverage of the parties and the type of breach (typically 14 or so days, but usually significantly less for payment defaults). If the defaulting party still hasn't cured its breach by the end of the specified time period, then the non-breaching party can cancel the agreement immediately by sending another notice.

Follow Procedures to the Letter

The non-breaching party should follow the notification procedures outlined in the provision, as well as comply with the Notice provision of the contract, which establishes procedures to be followed when sending communications under the contract. This will help to quash any attempt by the defaulting party to position your failure to send proper notice as a failure to satisfy a "condition" to cancelling the contract.

Mutual Rights

The sample contract provision calls for each party to have the same rights of cancellation. Depending on the negotiating leverage of the parties, as well as the type of transaction involved, the parties can negotiate different rights for each party, including different cure periods depending on which party is breaching the contract, or different cure periods depending on the type of breach. For example, lenders are very stingy with cure periods for payment defaults by the borrower, but like to give themselves lots of time to cure their own defaults.

Material Breach

A seller in a sale of business transaction can water down its unqualified representations by introducing a materiality qualifier into its indemnification provision. (See the CD-ROM for more details.) Adding a materiality requirement (whether a material breach/material failure to perform any obligation or any breach/failure to perform a material obligation) to a termination provision is another often used back-door way for obligors to water down their obligations. If you agree to add a materiality qualifier to the Termination provision, you will be foregoing the opportunity to call a default until the breach becomes significant. If the only way to move forward is to agree to add the materiality qualifier, be sure to exclude important obligations such as payment obligations or any obligation where time is of the essence.

Cross Default

The sample contract provision includes bracketed language making the breach of "[any other agreement it is a party to]" a breach of the subject agreement. Variations of such language can typically be found in loan agreements and put the borrower in default if the borrower defaults not only on its obligations to its lender counterparty under the loan agreement, but also if it defaults on any another obligation, either owed to the lender or owed to somebody else under some other agreement. Cross Default provisions are useful anytime the contract parties enter into multiple agreements, because they are designed to trigger rights and remedies even if there is a breach of only one of the agreements.

Termination for Cause (Bankruptcy)

Either party may terminate this Agreement effective upon written notice to the other party in the event such other party [This Agreement terminates without notice if either party]

(a) becomes insolvent or makes an assignment for the benefit of creditors;

(b) files a petition in bankruptcy, insolvency, receivership, or for other relief under any bankruptcy law or law for the relief of debtors or has any such petition filed against it [which is not discharged within sixty (60) days of the filing thereof]; or

(c) dissolves, is liquidated, or ceases to do business.

If your contract counterparty becomes bankrupt, it seems reasonable for you to believe that you should have the right to terminate the agreement. After all, you are now dealing with an entity that is no longer viable and won't be able to fulfill its obligations to you.

So most people (including lawyers) don't think twice when they see a termination upon bankruptcy provision, a.k.a., **ipso facto provision** (like the "with notice" and "without notice" sample excerpts presented here). These provisions are typically triggered by a voluntary or involuntary bankruptcy filing, or other act of insolvency like making a written admission of insolvency, an assignment for the benefit of creditors, or a dissolution and liquidation of the company. Yet except in very limited circumstances (which are beyond the scope of this book — e.g., certain intellectual property licensing situations, swap, and other derivative agreements), *ipso facto* provisions are not enforceable once formal bankruptcy proceedings have been initiated.

It helps to think of contract rights as property rights; these property rights become part of the debtor's (i.e., bankrupt party's) estate upon a Chapter 11 bankruptcy filing. Any attempt by a non-bankrupt contract party to terminate the contract is automatically stayed until the bankruptcy proceeding runs its course. So what you have essentially is a kind of "time out," during which the bankruptcy trustee reviews the debtor's executory contracts (i.e., agreements where both parties have important obligations yet to be performed) and decides which contracts to assume, and which contracts to reject. Allowing the non-bankrupt contract party to terminate upon bankruptcy would defeat this purpose.

Despite their unenforceability, *ipso facto* provisions have hung around mainly because of inertia; they were enforceable before the Bankruptcy Code was revamped in 1979. So just keep in mind that just because you see an *ipso facto* provision in your contract doesn't mean that you'll have the right to terminate if your counterparty becomes bankrupt. On the other hand, there's no need to delete them from your contracts because they have some utility — the trustee's rights aren't triggered until bankruptcy proceedings are formally initiated. So it's theoretically possible to invoke the provision to terminate the contract as soon as your counterparty is technically insolvent, but before bankruptcy proceedings have been initiated. This is a messy proposition because once the filing is made, you'll probably have to unravel the termination and face the music in court.

Termination for Cause (Death or Disability)

(a) This Agreement terminates immediately upon the death of [Party B].

(b) [Party A] may terminate this Agreement forthwith with notice to [Party B] if [Party B] is substantially disabled for a period of [thirty (30) consecutive days] [alternative — 180 consecutive or non-consecutive days in any 12 month period]. Substantially disabled means that [Party B] is unable, as a result of any physical, mental, or emotional illness or accident, to adequately perform his [her] obligations under this Agreement.

Termination for death or disability clauses are found in a variety of agreements involving natural person contract parties. Depending on the type of agreement, the death or disability of one of the parties can trigger the right of the other party to terminate the agreement (e.g., employment or consultant agreements), or buy out the decedant's contract or property rights (e.g., buy-sell arrangements in shareholder, partnership, or LLC agreements).

The sample contract provisions presented here are variations of termination for death or disability clauses found in employment or consulting agreements.

Death

Subsection (a) calls for automatic termination if the employee or consultant dies, subject to any other provisions of the agreement providing for death benefits.

Disability

Subsection (b) gives Party A the right to terminate the employee or consultant if he or she is disabled for an extended period of time. Some contracts include the requirement to have a neutral physician verify the disability in writing.

Termination for Cause (Assignment)

Either party may terminate this Agreement forthwith with notice to the other party if such other party assigns any of its rights or delegates any of its obligations under this Agreement in any manner whatsoever, whether such assignment is voluntary or involuntary, or a result of a merger, business combination, or change in control.

This provision gives either party the right to terminate the agreement if the other party attempts to assign its rights or delegate its obligations under the agreement, including as part of any sale of business or change in control. See the CD-ROM for a more detailed discussion of assignment and delegation.

Termination for Convenience

[Party A] may terminate this Agreement at any time without liability by giving [Party B] [sixty (60)] days' prior written notice.

Termination for convenience allows one or both contract parties to terminate the contract for any reason or for no reason at all just by giving notice. It's the business contract equivalent of employment-at-will. To exercise this right, the party terminating the contract must also comply with the Notice provision (see the CD-ROM) of the contract, which establishes procedures to be followed when sending communications under the contract.

While allowing termination for convenience gives the terminating party the flexibility to be able to move on whenever it wants, it also creates a pall of uncertainty over the business relationship. For that reason, it's best not to include this type of provision for traditionally long-term business relationships, especially ones that require you to expend a large amount of resources to ramp up or maintain your contract obligations, for example, sales representation agreements and distribution agreements, or in contracts that require you to make front-loaded payments. Keep in mind for distribution agreements that many states have laws that protect distributors from indiscrimate terminations, and may require special dispensation to terminated distributors (e.g., inventory buy-back, etc.)

Aggressive negotiators will sometimes try to give themselves the right to terminate for convenience even though the contract already includes a termination for cause provision. If your contract only has a termination for cause provision, then in most cases your counterparty would have no right to terminate unless you default and fail to cure the default during the grace period. Including both provisions, at best, creates ambiguity. At worst, it will allow your counterparty to bypass the termination for cause provision and terminate anytime it wants.

24

REMEDIES AND LIMITATION OF LIABILITY

OVERVIEW

It's an unpleasant fact of business life that people breach contracts. They don't always deliver what they promise, or pay what they owe. Most courts nowadays recognize that the remedies for breach (e.g., money damages, equitable or statutory remedies) are cumulative. This doesn't mean that a court will allow a claimant to be made "more than whole." All this means is that absent contract language to the contrary, the non-breaching party is permitted to initially simultaneously pursue all available remedies against the breaching party, even if the alternative theories of recovery are inconsistent. This is the legal equivalent of throwing everything against the wall and seeing what sticks. The typical court will then at some point in the proceedings (usually after the verdict but sometimes before) require the claimant to pick his or her poison, and elect a remedy from among the pool of possible remedies.

However, it is possible to limit by contract the types and amount of damages a contract party is responsible for. So in this section, I'll also discuss how attorneys draft language to help their clients to limit their liability, including liability blind spots to watch out for.

Remedies Quick Primer

Like a physician who prescibes medicinal remedies to make a patient better, courts prescribe legal remedies to make the claimant whole in the event of a contract breach. Courts will look for guidance in the subject contract, so it's important to carefully review your contract's remedies provisions, and seek professional help to negotiate them. There are many types of remedies, and I'll highlight the three main categories of remedies most likely to impact your business. Most businesspeople equate remedies with monetary (or compensatory) damages, but monetary damages are just one subset of remedies. Remedies also include equitable remedies and statutory damages, among other categories.

Monetary Damages

The general goal of money damages is to compensate an aggrieved claimant for damages suffered as a result of a breach of contract. The main type of money damages compensates the non-breaching party for **direct damages** or any out-of-pocket type damages suffered. Basically, you take the value of any partial performance (if any) received and subtract it the market or contract value of the performance promised. The resulting number is the direct damage suffered by the non-breaching party as a result of the contract breach. For example, if you are a manufacturer and your parts supplier fails to deliver the parts you require to make your products, direct damages will compensate you for the incremental cost of going out there and purchasing the parts from a substitute supplier. Of course, you have the duty to mitigate your damages, so you'll have to shop around, but if after reasonable research you find that it costs more to purchase replacement parts, you can claim the difference in the breach of contract claim.

Monetary damages also include the following other subcategories:

- **Consequential Damages:** The non-breaching party may attempt to seek consequential damages to recover indirect damages like lost profits suffered as a result of the breach. If your vendor ships you a bad part that causes you to lose the sale to your customer, the profit you would have made had you been able to ship compliant goods constitutes consequential damages. Consequential damages can also include things like loss of production, opportunity costs, loss of anticipated cost savings, lost business, and lost good will As you can see, consequential damages tend to be a pandora's box, so most obligors try to limit them by contract.

- **Incidental Damages:** The non-breaching party may attempt to seek incidental damages to recover indirect damages, for example, the cost of storing goods that it can't deliver because the buyer breached by missing a payment.

- **Liquidated Damages:** If damages in a transaction will be hard to calculate, the contract parties might decide to specify a dollar figure directly in the contract, which will be deemed compensation to the aggrieved party for breach of contract. A liquidated damages clause injects a certain degree of certainty into the contract. Both parties can breathe a little bit easier — the breaching party has capped its liability (hopefully, see Cumulative and Exclusive Remedies in the sample clauses below), and the non-breaching party has locked in at least an acceptable level of compensation, even if it might turn out to be lower than the actual amount of damages suffered. If the non-breaching party can prove a breach, then it's a simple matter of enforcing the liquidated damages provision.

Equitable Remedies

Sometimes, monetary damages just aren't good enough to compensate the aggrieved party. For example, a leak of secret information protected by a confidentiality agreement can cause untold damage to the owner of the infomation. In such cases, the aggrieved party may apply for equitable remedies by seeking an **injunction** to stop the counterparty from breaching its contract obligations and/or **specific performance** to force the counterparty to perform its contract obligations. They're basically two sides of the same coin — the court orders the breaching party to get its act together and comply!

Statutory Remedies

These are remedies prescribed by statutory law. For example, US trademark law provides statutorily established damages for infringement. For the most part, statutory remedies cannot be diluted by contract.

SAMPLE CONTRACT EXCERPTS

Cumulative Remedies

All rights and remedies provided in this Agreement are cumulative and not exclusive of any other rights or remedies that may be available to the parties, whether provided by law, equity, statute, in any other agreement between the parties, or otherwise.

This is a variation of a standard cumulative remedies provision. It confirms that the remedies provided in the agreement are not exhaustive or exclusive, meaning that the parties are free to pursue any and all other remedies, including remedies available at law, equitable remedies, statutory remedies, remedies provided in other agreements, and otherwise.

While most courts today recognize that remedies are cumulative, absent contrary contract language, it's common practice for lawyers to include a cumulative remedies provision anyway. This is fine as long as the parties actually intend for the remedies to be cumulative, which usually isn't the case if the parties include a liquidated damages clause, a termination fee, or other exclusive remedy provision somewhere else in the contract. A common drafting blind spot is for the parties to enumerate an exclusive remedy provision AND a cumulative remedies provision. This creates an internal inconsistency that may work to eviscerate the "exclusivity" of the exclusive remedy, and therefore make available a host of other remedies even after the aggrieved party takes home its liquidated damages. See below for a work-around to this problem.

Exclusive Remedies

(a) If the Distributor fails to purchase the Minimum Annual Purchase Amount during any Contract Year, the Manufacturer has the right to terminate this Agreement effective the end of the Contract Year ("Termination Right").

(b) All rights and remedies provided in this Agreement are cumulative and not exclusive of any other rights or remedies that may be available to the parties, whether provided by law, equity, statute, in any other agreement between the parties, or otherwise. However, the Termination Right is the Manufacturer's exclusive remedy for the Distributor's failure to purchase the Minimum Annual Purchase Amount during any Contract Year.

Subsection (a) sets forth an example of an exclusive remedy sometimes found in a distribution agreement. Subsection (b) is a modified cumulative remedies provision designed to avoid the internal inconsistency discussed above. While Subsection (a) is typically found elsewhere in the contract, for example, in the section of the agreement dealing with contract breach, or a stand-alone section dealing with minimum purchase requirements, I put Subsections (a) and (b) together to aid in my discussion.

Exclusive Remedy

Subsection (a) specifies termination as the only remedy for the failure to purchase the minimum amounts. Other examples of exclusive remedies include liquidated damages (discussed below), kill fees (i.e., termination fees), nonrefundable deposits, indemnity limitations like liability caps and any kind of fixed or formula-based fee that is paid by any party to give it the right to walk away from or "breach" a contract without fear of triggering additional remedies.

Of special note regarding distribution agreements, many state laws make it very difficult to fire distributors and give terminated distributors the right to sell inventory back to the company that appointed it. In those states, this is a statutory remedy that cannot be opted out of by an exclusive remedy provision like Subsection (a).

Modified Cumulative Remedies

The first sentence sets forth the standard cumulative remedies language discussed above. The second sentence carves out the exception (i.e., the Termmination Right), which applies only if the Distributor fails to purchase the Minimum Annual Purchase Amount. The result is that, on the one hand, the Manufacturer has the right to terminate (and no other remedies) if the Distributor fails to purchase the Minimum Annual Purchase Amount. On the other hand, if the Distributor fails to pay for the goods or commits some other breach, the Manufacturer will have the entire arsenal of remedies (at law, equity, etc.) at its disposal.

Liquidated Damages

(a) The Company may terminate this Agreement for convenience provided that it: (i) gives the Service Provider 45 days prior written notice of such termination; and (ii) pays the Service Provider a termination fee of [insert dollar amount] (the "Termination Fee"). The Termination Fee is intended to be liquidated damages and not a penalty.]

(b) All rights and remedies provided in this Agreement are cumulative and not exclusive of any other rights or remedies that may be available to the parties, whether provided by law, equity, statute, in any other agreement between the parties, or otherwise. [However, the Termination Fee is the Service Provider's exclusive remedy for the Company's termination of this Agreement for convenience.]

Subsection (a) sets forth an example of a simple liquidated damages provision in the context of Termination for Convenience. It specifies the payment of the Termination Fee (a.k.a., "kill fee") as the only remedy available to the Service Provider if the Company terminates for convenience (for purposes of discussion, let's put aside the issue of how easy it would be for the Company to couch its termination as one "for cause" in order to try to avoid paying the Termination Fee). Liquidated damages can be for a fixed amount, or an amount that accrues for each day, week, etc. that the breaching party remains in default. Financial penalties generally are not enforceable; that's why you have to couch the fee as liquidated damages, rather than a penalty.

Subsection (b) is the same **Modified Cumulative Remedies** provision discussed in **Exclusive Remedies** above. We need to have the bracketed language if the parties want the payment of the Termination Fee to be the only remedy for termination for convenience. Of course, if any party commits any other type of breach of the agreement, then the non-breaching party will have the entire arsenal of remedies (at law, equity, etc.), at its disposal.

There are also contracts that go completely in the other direction and specify that "the liquidated damages provided for in Subsection (a) are in addition to, and are not in limitation of, any other rights or remedies that may be available to the parties, whether provided by law, equity, statute, in any other agreement between the parties, or otherwise." However, for the breaching party, making the liquidated damages cumulative (intentionally) seems to defeat the purpose of negotiating a liquidated damages provision in the first place.

Exclusion of Consequential and Incidental Damages

NEITHER PARTY SHALL BE LIABLE TO THE OTHER PARTY FOR ANY INDIRECT, INCIDENTAL, CONSEQUENTIAL, OR SPECIAL DAMAGES SUFFERED BY SUCH OTHER PARTY, INCLUDING, BUT NOT LIMITED TO, LOST REVENUES OR LOST PROFITS, WHETHER ARISING IN CONTRACT, TORT, NEGLIGENCE, STRICT LIABILITY, BREACH OF STATUTORY DUTY, OR OTHERWISE, AND REGARDLESS OF ANY NOTICE OF THE POSSIBILITY OF SUCH DAMAGES.

This is a variation of typical contract language that takes indirect damages such as consequential damages off the table. By excluding such damages, the breaching party will be liable only for direct damages, as well as equitable and other remedies that are not specifically excluded. Note that in addition to lost revenues and lost profits, some contracts will list things like loss of production, opportunity costs, loss of anticipated cost savings, lost business, and lost goodwill.

Liability Cap

Neither party shall have aggregate cumulative liability to the other party arising out of or relating to this Agreement in excess of [insert dollar amount] [__ times the aggregate purchase price payable under this Agreement].

This provision seeks to place a hard monetary cap on each party's liability. Depending on negotiating leverage, or the type of transaction, you can negotiate to cap both parties' liability, or just one of the parties'. The parties can negotiate a fixed dollar amount, or an amount based on a multiple of the purchase price, service fee, or other consideration paid under the contract (which can be based on the aggregate consideration or an individual transaction like a purchase order).

Availability of Equitable Remedies

The parties acknowledge that a breach of this Agreement could not adequately be compensated by monetary damages. Therefore any party shall be entitled, in addition to any other right or remedy available to it, to equitable remedies, and the parties hereby consent to the issuance of such equitable remedies.

This is a belt-and-suspenders type provision that has the parties agreeing in advance to consent to equitable relief (e.g., injunction, specific performance, etc.). Keep in mind that equitable remedies are court-ordered and generally need not be mentioned in the agreement. However, some contracts like confidentiality agreements contain this type of language because the party with the most to lose from a breach (the owner of the secret information) wants the other party to acknowledge in advance that a breach can't be adequately compensated by monetary damages. A court that sees this type of language might be more inclined to grant equitable relief.

25

SEVERABILITY

OVERVIEW

A constant barrage of new statutes, regulations, and case law introduce incremental adjustments and an occasional seismic shift to a constantly changing legal landscape. In order to avoid jeopardizing the enforceability of a contract, the parties must be careful to negotiate contract provisions that not only aggressively serve their respective interests, but do so without overstepping legal limits. Extra care must be taken when negotiating certain types of provisions that have regularly invited the hyperscrutiny of the courts — for example, contract provisions dealing with non-competition, choice of law, limitation of liability, indemnity, liquidated damages, and exclusivity.

In these situations, courts typically look to see if the contract has a **severability provision** (sometimes called a seperability provision), which allows a court to "sever" offending provisions in order to salvage the rest of the contract. Depending on the jurisdiction, the situation, and the contract's severability provision, a court may take one of several approaches on how it deals with an unenforceable provision. Some courts **completely sever** or drop the entire offending provision and enforce the rest of the contract. Other courts apply the so-called **blue pencil approach** to salvage the provision by excising the offending words or phrases without upsetting the integrity of the provision's sentence structure. Yet other courts apply the **rule of reasonableness** to make relatively extensive changes to revise the offending provision so that it falls within legal limits.

Keep in mind that there are certain contracts that are not salvageable no matter what. The most obvious example is a contract to hire a hitman, or perform some other illegal activity. No amount of parsing or revision will save these contracts.

Even when the purpose of the contract is not as outrageous, courts may be reluctant to use any rule to salvage the contract if the overreaching provision is one that forms the basis of the bargain. For example, a court might not bother to reform a broken exclusive distribution agreement if it contains a host of over-the-top anti-competitive provisions that were the essential reason the parties entered into the agreement.

SAMPLE CONTRACT EXCERPTS

I've included three variations of standard severability provisions.

Alternative 1 — Offending Provision Severed

If any provision of this Agreement is unenforceable, the balance of this Agreement remains in full force. If any provision of this Agreement is deemed inapplicable to any party or circumstance, it remains applicable to all other parties and circumstances to the fullest extent of the law.

This language works to salvage the parts of the contract that are enforceable. It severs the unenforceable provision, and to the extent an offending provision is found not to be lawful with respect to one party or a particular situation, it keeps the offending provision alive with respect to all other persons and situations.

I use the word "unenforceable" in the sample excerpt; however, the phrase "invalid, illegal, and unenforceable" often appears in severability provisions.

Alternative 2 — Severable to Extent Determined by Court

If a court of competent jurisdiction finds any provision of this Agreement to be unenforceable, then such provision remains in full force to the extent not held invalid or unenforceable.

This language works to give the court latitude to "rewrite" the offending provision to make it compliant. Consult with your attorney to determine whether the courts with jurisdiction in your transaction apply the blue pencil approach, rule of reasonableness, or some other standard to reform unenforceable provisions.

Alternative 3 — Not Severable

If any provision of this Agreement is unenforceable, then the entire Agreement is no longer in effect and no party has the right to enforce any provision of this Agreement.

Use this one sparingly. If any provision is found to be unenforceable, this language works to void the entire contract, including confidentiality or other provisions you may want to remain in force no matter what.

Alternative Severability Clause for Non-Compete Provisions

In the event a court finds this non-compete provision unenforceable as to geographic scope or duration, then the court has the power to reduce the geographic scope or duration to the extent necessary to render the provision enforceable.

You can add this severability language to temper non-competition provisions that overreach in terms of duration or geographic scope. You should draft the non-compete provision in a way that makes it easy for a court applying the blue pencil approach to simply substitute a different term or geographic territory without adding any other language or impacting the provision grammatically. A simple example would be, "Tom shall not compete against the Company in the State of New Jersey for three (3) years after the termination or expiration of this Contract." If a court finds this provision to be overreaching, it can replace the offensive words with words that make the provision legal again, for example, replace "the State of New Jersey" with "Bergan County, New Jersey" and/or "three years" with "one year."

Remember that the more a court applying the blue pencil approach has to rewrite (for example, move words around, make adjustments for grammar, etc.), the less likely the court will reform the provision. Instead, it may "give up" and determine the entire provision to be unenforceable. Courts applying the rule of reasonableness have more flexibility, but that can be a double-edged sword because an aggressive court could leave its imprimatur on the provision in a way that you didn't anticipate when you negotiated the provision.